On Behalf of Others

On Behalf of Others

The Psychology of Care in a Global World

Edited by

Sarah Scuzzarello
Catarina Kinnvall
Kristen Renwick Monroe

OXFORD
UNIVERSITY PRESS
2009

OXFORD
UNIVERSITY PRESS

Oxford University Press, Inc., publishes works that further
Oxford University's objective of excellence
in research, scholarship, and education.

Oxford   New York
Auckland   Cape Town   Dar es Salaam   Hong Kong   Karachi
Kuala Lumpur   Madrid   Melbourne   Mexico City   Nairobi
New Delhi   Shanghai   Taipei   Toronto

With offices in
Argentina   Austria   Brazil   Chile   Czech Republic   France   Greece
Guatemala   Hungary   Italy   Japan   Poland   Portugal   Singapore
South Korea   Switzerland   Thailand   Turkey   Ukraine   Vietnam

Copyright © 2009 by Oxford University Press, Inc.

Published by Oxford University Press, Inc.
198 Madison Avenue, New York, New York 10016

www.oup.com

Oxford is a registered trademark of Oxford University Press

Library of Congress Cataloging-in-Publication Data
On behalf of others : the psychology of care in a global world / edited by
    Sarah Scuzzarello, Catarina Kinnvall, Kristen Renwick Monroe.
        p.   cm. — (Series in political psychology)
    Includes bibliographical references and index.
    ISBN 978-0-19-538555-7 (alk. paper)
    1. Globalization—Moral and ethical aspects.   I. Scuzzarello, Sarah.
    II. Kinnvall, Catarina.   III. Monroe, Kristen R., 1946–
    JZ1318.O5 2009
    303.48′2—dc22

                                                                2008049588

1 3 5 7 9 8 6 4 2

Printed in the United States of America
on acid-free paper

TABLE OF CONTENTS

ACKNOWLEDGEMENTS

This volume is the first of what we hope will be many successful collaborative efforts between the International Society of Political Psychology's Caucus of Concerned Scholars: Committee on Ethics and Morality and the University of California at Irvine's Interdisciplinary Center for the Scientific Study of Ethics and Morality. It is perhaps especially fitting that the first volume from this collaboration is one dealing with globalization. Much of the motivation behind the ISPP-UCI collaborative efforts was to create a community of scholars throughout the world, united by their desire to further serious scholarship addressing ethical issues. We encourage other scholars to join with us, either by participating in the annual meetings of the Caucus at the ISPP or via a virtual community established and maintained through the UCI Ethics Center's website, located at www.ethicscenter.uci.edu. We hope to provide syllabi, bibliographies and abstracts of papers and books that address ethical issues using the various methodologies of science.

We thank the ISPP and the UCI Ethics Center for their organizational support and encouragement. Bruce Dayton and Radell Roberts of the ISPP, Sandra Cushman of the UCI Ethics Center and Edna Mejia at UCI deserve particular praise for all they do. Adam Martin, Bridgette Portman and William Chiu provided bibliographic assistance. Special thanks go to Bettye Vaughen, who helped create the Vaughen Archives so that material could be shared with other scholars at no cost. Frank Lynch and Bettye Vaughen provided generous financial assistance that was critical in producing this volume and David Easton provided generous funding to support our newly launched Anti-Genocide Initiative, which hopes to provide a three year program focused on scholarly work that increases understanding of the causes of and correctives for genocide. To this end, the Caucus and the UCI Ethics Center are hosting a series of panels on the narratives of genocide and ethnic cleansing, reconciliation and forgiveness at the 2009 and 2010 meetings of the ISPP in Dublin and San Francisco. Interested scholars should contact Kristen R. Monroe (KRMonroe@UCI.Edu) or Catarina Kinnvall (Catarina.Kinnvall@svet.lu.se) for further information.

Catarina Kinnvall and Sarah Scuzzarello would also like to thank the Riksbankens Jubileums Fond and the Crafoord Foundation in Sweden for their generous financial support which has contributed to the establishment of the interdisciplinary Network of Political Psychology at Lund University. In this context we are also grateful for the institutional support offered by Lund University and especially by the Department of Political Science. The Network, established in 2006, has brought together scholars from the Departments of Political Science and the Department of Psychology at Lund University. It has also provided a foundation for joint work with other political science and psychology departments in Europe, the US and Canada. It has proven to be a fruitful and active academic environment and we hope it will further establish and advance political psychology in Europe.

Finally, we wish to thank the superb staff at Oxford University Press, including John Jost and Lori Handelman, for the care they have given our manuscript. As always, a special thanks must go to our families for their personal support and encouragement.

CONTRIBUTORS

C. Fred Alford, Professor of Government, University of Maryland, College Park, Maryland, USA

Daniel Bar-Tal, Professor of Social Psychology, Tel Aviv University, Tel Aviv, Israel

Neil Ferguson, Associate Professor of Political Psychology, Liverpool Hope University, Liverpool, United Kingdom

Christian Fernández, Research fellow, Malmö Institute for Studies of Migration, Diversity and Welfare, Malmö University, Malmö, Sweden

Jakub Gutowski, Ph.D Candidate, Researcher, and Lecturer, University of Finance and Management, Warsaw, Poland

Eran Halperin, Assistant Professor, Interdisciplinary Center Herzliya, Israel

Katarzyna Hamer, Lecturer and Researcher, University of Finance and Management, Institute of Psychology, Polish Academy of Science, Warsaw, Poland

Kai J. Jonas, Assistant Professor, University of Amsterdam, Amsterdam, The Netherlands

Catarina Kinnvall, Associate Professor, Lund University, Lund, Sweden

Robert D. Lowe, Post-doctoral research fellow, Department of Psychology, University of Limerick, Limerick, Ireland

Maria Luisa Martínez, Ph.D. Candidate, Complutense University, Madrid, Spain

Gerd Meyer, Professor Emeritus of Political Science, University of Tuebingen, Tuebingen, Germany

Kristen Renwick Monroe, Professor of Political Science and Philosophy, University of California, Irvine, Irvine, California

Orla Muldoon, Professor, Department of Psychology, University of Limerick, Limerick, Ireland

Paul Nesbitt-Larking, Chair of Political Science, Huron University College, London, Ontario, Canada

Anne Birgitta Pessi (née yeung), Adjunct Professor, Collegium for Advanced Study, Academy Research Fellow, University of Helsinki, Helsinki, Finland

Amiram Raviv, Professor (Emeritus) of Psychology, Tel Aviv University, Tel Aviv, Israel

Nimrod Rosler, Ph.D. Candidate, Hebrew University of Jerusalem, Jerusalem, Israel

Katharina Schmid, Post-doctoral researcher, Department of Experimental Psychology, University of Oxford, Oxford, United Kingdom

Sarah Scuzzarello, Ph.D. Candidate, Lund University, Lund, Sweden

Keren Sharvit, Ph.D., Postdoctoral Research Associate, University of Maryland, College Park, Maryland

Introduction

Catarina Kinnvall, Kristen Renwick Monroe, and Sarah Scuzzarello

A globalized world is for many a world devoid of certainty—of knowing what tomorrow holds. It is also, however, a world full of opportunities and increased possibilities to transcend boundaries and socialized constraints. For many people, though, especially in the West, the world appears progressively more unsafe and violent after the September 11 attacks and the subsequent "war on terror" and invasion of Iraq. In other parts of the world, this perceptual change is not as dramatic, since violence has long permeated political life, informing and constructing relationships and senses of subjectivity, not least in parts of Asia, Africa, and South America. As the main battlefield of the Cold War lay outside the western hemisphere, a belief that one could stay untouched by world events became increasingly pervasive among many in the West. Yet with globalization and the "war on terror," a feeling of perceived danger now appears to be knocking on the door. Increasingly we are witnessing efforts to more clearly delineate boundaries concerning who is an outsiders, who an insiders; who belongs to a certain territory, group, or religious denomination; and who does not. Categories of "us and them," home and away, East and West are constantly being used to defend invisible boundaries and thus create psychological distances between people, nations, and continents. A global world is thus a world open for interpretation, for closing minds or widening perspectives as contradictory forces pull in various directions.

In much current literature (Kaldor, 2006, Gilroy 2005), this new reality has been described in terms of "new wars" and "new nationalisms." If the old wars were mainly concerned with political and ideological systems, territory, or pure economic resources, the new wars are increasingly related to identity and culture. Such wars often base their claim to power on particular iden-tities, be they identity, clan, nation, religion, or language. Similarly, a new kind of nationalism is emerging in the wake of global forces where discourses on security and survival are replacing other nation-states with immigrant others. The enemy no longer lies outside the nation, but threatens the nation-state from within—the enemy in the womb, as it were—and is discursively constructed through nationalism, racism, and xenophobia.

These new kinds of conflict cannot be understood through traditionally constructed theories of contractual violence or just and unjust wars, as they are

1

not about relations between states, but are about conflicts between social actors who share the same geographical space. Local moral worlds are changing through forces beyond local communities, national and global, over which these communities have little or no control. Globalization, albeit not a new phenomenon, hence contains some important changes in expectations and sources of knowledge. Images of war, terrorism, ethnic violence, and religious fundamentalism travel through global media and appear to invade the local worlds of face-to-face relations. Modern nation-states can often be ill equipped to deal with these new circumstances, and individuals gain knowledge through a diverse array of national and global contradictions.

Alongside these changes in expectations, the political and socioeconomic changes brought about by increased globalization are often viewed as a source of moral decadence. Narratives of growing selfishness and a loss of morality and commitment are developing across Western societies. The reasons behind such alleged individualism in the late-modern era are disparate. For some it is godlessness, for others it is capitalism and the market that have corrupted people's sense of morality. For yet others, it has to do with decreasing political consciousness and growing consumerism that have fostered self-seeking individualism and have infected both social relationships in general and the intimate relationships with those closest to us. Violence and criminality, especially when pursued by so-called baby-gangs (groups of under-teenage children, robbing and mugging) are frequently linked to such (perceived) increased selfishness, lack of care-giving, and decline of moral values. The "profound malaise" (Jacques, 2004) hold to be at the heart of Western societies can in itself be conceived of as a form of psychological violence. Such violence can shatter the once-secure moral foundations of society, while failing to endorse potentially positive developments embedded in the socioeconomic and political changes of the late-modern era. These include the development of more democratic and diverse communities, the changes in family lives and personal relationships, and the existence of moral reasoning that informs the way people attempt to balance their own sense of self and the needs of others.

Certainly one can have different opinions about these arguments; indeed, recent research shows that these contentions are not always accurate (see, e.g., Williams 2004). Yet the fact that these perceptions seem to exist (faulty or not) evinces a need to advance contesting ethical ideas that provide new political and moral vocabularies and that allow us to imagine social alternatives. The political psychology of real or imagined violence in a global world calls for new approaches in our efforts to understand collective experience and the shaping of subjectivity. It is difficult, if not impossible, to draw a sharp line between collective and individual experiences of social violence and its consequences. They are intertwined moral processes and emotional conditions, where the former refer to social engagements centered on what is at stake in relationships, while the latter concern the inner world of lived values. Their interaction is created, sustained, and transformed in the sense that violence actualizes this inner world as well as the outer world of contested meanings (Das and Kleinman, 2000). Violence thus can become both a social condition and an individual experience. But violence also includes certain forms of moral condition and is often justified on moral grounds as "they" are perceived as morally faulty while "we" can assume a sense of higher morality.

Resisting violence or acting on behalf of others is as much a moral condition as violence itself. Works on altruism, on reconciliation, or on dialogue are all examples of efforts designed to counter the moral foundations of violence by providing alternative practical, social, or philosophical accounts. In a perceived world of danger, it becomes critical that we attempt to understand the basis of such fears as well as possible ways of overcoming them. This volume is an attempt to do this. The contributions to this volume explore the difficulties and possibilities of caring for others, behaving courageously, becoming committed to other people's narratives, moving beyond cognitive differences and inequalities of power, and finding shared humanity. The individual chapters in this volume thus analyze how care, pro-social behavior, and courage are affected by the psychologically and politically unsettling and powerful late-modern globalization. The authors offer conceptual approaches to the ambiguous relationship between globalization, ethical commitment, and behavior as well as empirical analyses that explore this quandary in specific national contexts. They offer varying interpretations to the question of how we can understand diversity in ways that do not reproduce boundaries between majority and minorities, but rather openly question and challenge such boundaries. Why do some people show courage and intervene on behalf of others? What do people understand as morality and care? Can we talk about universal identification with all human beings? What role do societies' institutional structures play in enabling altruistic, caring behavior? These are the topics that concern us in this volume.

The book is divided into three parts. The first part is predominantly theoretical. In the first chapter of this volume, Paul Nesbitt-Larking explores the relationship between globalization and ethics through the lens of the refrain of Yeats' *Easter 1916*: "a terrible beauty is born." From a critical psychological perspective, he discusses how globalization brings with it a sense of loss and cognitive anxiety, at the same time that new means of mobilization and possibilities of expressing one's own identity develop. Working with the dialectics of risk, on one hand, tied to terror and doubt, and the beauty of the late-modern age, on the other, the chapter analyzes three fields in which the ambiguity of globalization is played out: economy, culture, and politics. Nesbitt-Larking argues that a large-scale economy based on neo-liberal adjustments has created a growing class of contractual, flexible employees who have contributed to a questioning of the traditional role of the nation state. Traditional institutions are increasingly loosing their predominant role in political life and are being replaced by other local and transnational actors, such as local communities and social movements. When the previously secure political and cognitive structures are being shattered, this sense of loss of an individual's or a community's safe haven is countered by the (re)creation of exclusivist and reactionary ethnic, religious, national gated communities that "refuse history, choice, desire, and ultimately hope." How can we conceive of an ethic that promotes hope, inclusion, and action, considering the shattering aspects of globalization? Nesbitt-Larking suggests that we should interpret the insecurities of globalization in terms of doubt and accept the partiality of knowledge. Accepting doubt would enable people to rethink how they perceive difference, diversity, and political action. This reflexivity will lead to choice and deliberation and ultimately to the establishment of an "ethics of beauty" that articulates and promotes discourses of human possibilities and community power.

Christian Fernández (Chap. 2) proposes yet another perspective on how morality should be addressed in the twenty-first century. Fernández unravels how the concept of toleration has developed and changed in the past centuries. He argues that we have witnessed a shift from an old conception of toleration, close to the traditional liberal understanding of the concept that warranted every citizen equal rights, to a new one that tends to be co-terminous with the public recognition of cultural or religious diversity. The latter is in many ways a symptom of the sense of cultural deprivation and existential anxiety that characterizes late-modernity and is usually presented by advocates of multiculturalism. Through a comparison of liberal and multicultural understandings of tolerance, Fernández emphasizes three main points of contention between the two schools. The first includes a shift from a liberal understanding of tolerance to a multicultural one. This can be summarized as a shift from the protection of private and individually chosen beliefs to a protection of collective and socially contingent identities. The second step is tied to a changed understanding of the state from a neutral to an active actor in the recognition of diversity. Finally, Fernández identifies a third shift that encompasses a different understanding of the public sphere. To liberals it is the sphere of universal norms and obligations, while to multicultural theorists, particularity and difference should be warranted within the public sphere. The arguments raised by multicultural theorists address important caveats in liberal theory. Yet, the alternatives provided by multiculturalists have some ambiguities as well. Therefore, in the concluding part of the chapter, Fernández formulates some possible liberal answers to the multicultural critique. He first warns against the multiculturalists' strong emphasis on identity, which tends to be naïve and essentialist and runs the risk of limiting minorities' freedom. He next addresses the issue of state neutrality. Following several multiculturalists, he states that liberalism is not neutral as it builds on a particular conception of the human good. That said, Fernández argues for a public culture devoid of ethnic and religious traits and—in this sense—neutral and liberal.

The relationship between ethics and diversity is further analyzed by Sarah Scuzzarello. In Chapter 3, Scuzzarello provides a first attempt to establish a dialogue between critical multiculturalism and a feminist ethics of care. This involves an approach to multiculturalism that is attentive to the public recognition of minority groups, to their empowerment, and to the unequal distribution of power between minorities and majority society. At the same time, Scuzzarello emphasizes a feminist understanding of ethics that stresses the importance of the values and practices of care encapsulated in an attentive, responsible, competent, and responsive understanding of politics and needs. Through the prism of such an ethics of care, Scuzzarello addresses some basic problems with liberal interpretations of multiculturalism. Relying on an understanding of the autonomous and homogeneous moral subject, liberal authors like Kymlicka and Rex fail to address dilemmas related to inequalities of power and different positionalities of individuals. As an alternative, Scuzzarello set out the contours of a "caring multiculturalism." This understanding of multiculturalism conceives of critical multiculturalism as a good companion, but puts greater emphasis on the conflations between politics and psychology and the ontological interrelatedness of the subject. Departing from an understanding of the self as constituted by immanent differences, a philosophy of multiculturalism informed by an ethics of care will bring about possibilities for dealing with difference and diversity between individuals and social groups, as difference is not seen as threatening and abnormal but as a normal condition of being.

Another way of interpreting care is in terms of courage. Gerd Meyer's and Kai Jonas's chapters provide two different but complementary interpretations of the significance of courage in everyday life. Both authors ask themselves why some people show courage, and how increased feelings of insecurity and fear as well as a growing individualization of politics impact on people's decision to behave courageously. In Chapter 4, Meyer provides an analytical and empirical answer to these questions by developing the concept of *social courage*. The concept is theoretically discussed in relation to other concepts such as moral courage, altruism, and *Zivilcourage* (from the German for "civil courage") and is defined as an action that is bound to a specific situation with an imbalance of power. It is a political action in favor of democratic and humane values, but it also implies the promotion of one's own welfare, contrary to, for example, altruism. Social courage is a nonviolent action that is part of a specific type of social interaction, not a personality trait. To understand the inner dynamic of how social courage unfolds or not, Meyer develops two process models based on the empirical results of 30 topic-guided interviews conducted in Germany. Factors such as political and economic context; social position; emotional closeness to a victim or a problem; gender; personality; personal and social skills and social background are analyzed, discussed, and applied to construct the models. The chapter ends on a critical note. Meyer acknowledges the existence of structural and cognitive obstacles that hinder the development of social courage: people who dare to stand up against oppressive hegemonic structures are not popular, and social courage is a risky virtue, demanding and uncomfortable for the average citizen as well as for those in power. He also recognizes how globalization can have negative effects on socially courageous behavior as people, fearing the dangers and risks of late-modern society, hesitate to care and take responsibility for strangers. But Meyer is keen to stress the social and civic importance of social courage. Therefore, Meyer advocates a stronger public promotion of courageous interventions, as such acts can create a responsible and truly democratic social environment.

A different approach is suggested by Kai Jonas (Chap. 5). Bystanders' morally courageous behavior can be understood if we consider both situational and individual factors that can promote intervention in specific situations. Jonas contends that the interaction of these two sets of factors has been overlooked by the literature on courageous bystander interventions, as it usually fails to consider the importance of non-conscious, automatic factors that trigger intervention in critical situations. In order to overcome this gap, two bodies of literature are brought together: process models of pro-social behavior and self-regulation theories. As individuals need to form a moral standard, a goal, that will induce them to behave courageously, self-regulation theories are particularly suitable to explain how these goals are attained. Drawing on Regulatory Focus Theory, Jonas argues that different goal-attainment strategies—identified as promotion and prevention—predetermine interventions in a critical situation. Jonas applies this analytical framework to two experimental studies: a 3D maze game and a vignette study paradigm. The results show that individuals with a prevention focus react faster in critical situations and that prevention focus predicts indirect bystander behavior. In a real-life setting, Jonas's contribution offers interesting possibilities for further development of existing moral courage training programs. Being instructed and taught from a process-oriented perspective, individuals could potentially show increased levels of pro-social behavior in critical situations.

In the second part of the volume, we turn more explicitly to a number of empirical examples. Fred Alford (Chap. 6) brings together some of the theoretical questions raised in the previous chapters in his discussions of how people reason in regards to morality and care. Alford analyzes thirty interviews with young Americans and tries to trace their reasoning when asked about their perception of themselves as part of a shared humanity. Despite differences in terms of religion, gender, and social background, Alford points to the fact that his informants share a rather coherent understanding of right and wrong and of the conditions of a decent human life. In fact, they disclose a sense of commonality in the fact of being human beings, a position Alford refers to as "metaphysical biology." Alford's informants reveal a belief in a social contract—albeit a minimal one—not because of some form of rationality, as argued by, for example, rational choice theorists. Common humanity grounds his informants' reasoning about morality, not abstract notions of universal morality. In this sense, Alford expresses wariness about the relationship between abstract theories on ethics and moral behavior and people's everyday understanding of morality. He further argues that academics should try to come closer to an everyday understanding of morality, meaning a fuller comprehension of the context in which different narratives on moral behavior are created and how they intersect. Only in the everyday struggle for making sense of ethics in our late-modern world can we find a non-liberal, non-individualistic basis for morality and moral behavior.

Monroe and Martinez also focus on the importance of narratives for moral behavior, doing so via a classroom experiment. Monroe and Martinez describe results from an experimental course program designed to use empathetic involvement with "the other" to help students think deeply about their own attitudes toward people judged to be different, whether these differences are the result of globalization and immigration or from more indigenous differences connected to race, religion, ethnicity, age, disability, sexual preference, etc. The course, taught at the University of California at Irvine, one of the most ethnically diverse campuses in the United States, used a class intervention in contrast with a nominee sample to determine whether a controlled university setting can provide the kind of empathetic involvement philosophers such as Adam Smith have long argued are the basis of ethical action. They used several measures of prejudice, before and after the class intervention, and found that empathetic involvement with "the other" can have an important and significant effect on existing levels of prejudice.

Chapter 8 provides a different understanding of the relationship between ethics, pro-social behavior, and identification with humanity. Here Hamer-Gutowska and Gutowski argue that globalization has opened up the possibility of widening an individual's sense of belonging to broader and perhaps more abstract commonalities, such as Europe or even all humanity. More locally bounded identities, such as identification with one's nation or family, can coexist with broader conceptual understandings of the world as a whole. Relying on the works of Adler and McFarland, the authors demonstrate that broader forms of identification are strongly correlated to emphatic, pro-social behavior. Hamer-Gutowska and Gutowski focus their empirical analysis on Poland. The case is interesting, considering the country's recent transformation from a close, communist, Catholic country to becoming a member of organizations such as the European Union (EU). The authors analyze the extent to which the recent accession to the EU has fostered wider forms of identification among Poles, and ask if in Poland there is a correlation between broad social identities and pro-social behavior. The analysis is based on a questionnaire distributed in Poland in 2005 and proceeds from an adapted version of the "Identification with All Humanity Scale" developed by McFarland and Webb (2003) to measure Monroe's (1996) original development of this concept. Using quantitative analysis, the authors show that the respondents identify themselves more strongly with those who are close to them, such as family or friends. Only few respondents identify with all humanity, and no one spontaneously identifies himself or herself with the EU. In the second part of their empirical analysis, Hamer-Gutowska and Gutowski find a strong correlation between pro-social behavior and identification with all humanity, thus confirming their theoretical argument. Hamer-Gutowska and Gutowski argue for the need to better understand why Poles identify more strongly with their families and what consequences this has for the development of societal pro-social behavior. They conclude by asking what political consequences this may have for the future of Poland and how that would affect future generations' sense of morality and commitment to others' lives.

The complexity of social identity is further analyzed by Anne Birgitta Pessi in Chapter 9. Pessi discusses the role of institutions in promoting altruistic behavior. The chapter is focused on the Finnish church. She emphasizes that altruism can be promoted by teaching, learning, and socializing, and that institutional agents such as churches can play a pivotal role in this process. Here she argues for a departure from an individually based understanding of altruistic behavior in favor of a perspective that recognizes the role of social groups in constructing and maintaining altruistic values. Drawing on the literature on altruism, Pessi discusses how the Finnish church continues to shape values and norms of altruism and care by being an important actor in planning and coordinating welfare activities. She argues that, partly due to the economic depression of the early 1990s, the Finnish church has gained new importance in its response to the vacuum created by the states' budget cuts on welfare. Thus, it has come to be seen as an important actor in confronting the welfare needs of citizens and in maintaining solidarity and cohesion, even in a country like Finland, which is usually depicted as a secular nation. In this way, religious institutions are assuming a renewed political and social importance. Finnish people see the church more as an "agent of altruism," engaged in social work, than as a spiritual actor—the "mouthpiece of God," to use Pessi's terminology. In this sense the church is increasingly being viewed as an important actor in Finnish social life, an actor to be trusted. This takes place despite the evident difficulties that the church faces in late-modernity; i.e., the privatization of religiosity and the majority society's infrequent participation in religious and social activities. Pessi acknowledges that other institutions, such as human rights movements, can be important actors in promoting altruistic behavior. Her contribution presents an important challenge to the sometimes unquestioned political and moral secularism that seems to permeate many discussions on how to teach and foster pro-social, altruistic behavior.

In the third part of the book, we analyze how ethics and morality are shaped by and in turn shape protracted conflicts. Focusing on the prolonged occupation of Israel in the Gaza Strip and the West Bank, the chapter written by Rosler et al. (Chap. 10) discusses the moral dilemmas and the psychological and ethical challenges that prolonged occupation has for an occupying society. The authors argue that prolonged occupations violate universal basic moral principles on the international, societal, and individual level. Occupying societies have to socially, politically, and psychologically come to terms with their contraventions of these norms. In this, they are confronted with difficulties as they have to relate such pressures to their self-image as a morally just society. The authors discuss several socio-psychological mechanisms that are developed by the occupying society in order to cope with those challenges. The occupier thus can develop a set of societal beliefs that provides moral justifications for the occupation that, on one hand, delegitimizes the occupied nation while creating a positive self-image of the occupying group. The development of such societal beliefs, as well as other socio-psychological mechanisms that facilitate people's abilities to cope with moral violations in terms of prolonged occupation shows that even the occupying society suffers high moral and social costs. In the concluding section of the chapter, the authors suggest that the coping mechanisms developed by the Israeli society have accustomed it to mistreating the occupied population. This has diminished its sensitivity to the breaching of moral values, thus seriously impairing the moral principles of the occupying society. To terminate prolonged occupations, it is therefore pivotal to understand and erode the socio-psychological mechanisms that have developed within the institutional structure of the occupying society.

The decline of moral constraints in a society suffering from intrastate conflict and experiences of violence on an everyday basis is further explored by Neil Ferguson (Chap. 11). Here the author focuses on the moral development of Catholics and Protestant youth in Northern Ireland. Previous literature has shown that political violence and intergroup warfare can negatively influence children's moral and cognitive functioning, while adults can experience a regression of their moral and cognitive reasoning. Ferguson acknowledges the importance of ingroup loyalty in accepting partisan decisions that violate moral social standards and that result in processes such as dehumanization of perceived enemies and aggressive actions. The brief of the chapter is to assess whether the partisan solutions associated with ingroup loyalty, as demonstrated by Northern Irish youth, are also employed by Northern Irish adults to a greater extent than their cross-national equivalents. In order to answer his questions, Ferguson conducted an experiment among 133 undergraduate psychology students coming from two Northern Irish and one English university. The participants completed two tests, the Moral Judgment Test and the Political Judgment Test, constructed to measure the capacity to make moral decisions and judgments and to behave accordingly. Ferguson's findings show that the major factor that impacts moral reasoning is not the conflict between Irish Catholics and British Protestants, but the conflict between those who show strong group loyalty and those who seek a culture of coexistence. The former are more prone to support what has been called a "culture of violence" (Darby 1997, 116). Interestingly, the findings of the cross-national comparison between Northern Irish and British students indicate a comparatively normal moral development of the former group. This, the author argues, is probably due to the developing peace process that seems to have reduced the general stresses on moral reasoning. Ferguson's contribution reiterates the observation made by Rosler et al. that social and political violence carry moral and socio-psychological meanings. It also brings attention to the impact of ingroup loyalty for the establishment of a less violent culture in Northern Ireland and to the role of institutional settings in discouraging outgroup hostility.

Lowe, Muldoon and Schmid also focus on the case of Northern Ireland. In their contribution (Chap. 12) the authors problematize the body of literature on social categorization that underlies group conflict. They argue that much of the literature tends to conceive of identities as dichotomous—e.g. Catholic and

Protestant—thus perpetuating social divisions and intragroup hostility. In contrast, they argue for the introduction of multiple dimensions of social categorization for understanding group conflicts. Hence, they examine whether the identifications that become visible in cross-categorization affect outgroup evaluation. Their empirical study, conducted on a sample of 3,000 participants in Northern Ireland and the Border Counties of the Republic of Ireland, shows that while there is a high degree of overlap between religious and national identification in Northern Ireland, a significant minority of people cross-categorize. They endorse an unexpected combination of national and religious identities, such as Catholic-British or Protestant-Irish identity. Schmid and Muldoon thus ask three main questions. Their aim is to explore how expected/unexpected identification affects levels of national group identification, social and political attitudes, and a group's perceived threats. Expected identifiers; i.e., respondents who are categorized as British and Protestant or Irish and Catholic, generally see themselves as more prototypical of their identity group. Hence they evaluate their identities as more positive, regard their identities as more important to their self-concept, and have less favorable attitudes to the religious outgroup. On the contrary, unexpected patterns of identification; i.e., Irish Protestants or British Catholics, generally show less perceived similarity with other group members, as well as less positive evaluations and lower levels of identity importance, and more positive out-group attitudes. The chapter clearly delineates a number of problems with social categorization theory and presents some interesting implications for understanding conflict dynamics and potential conflict resolutions. The authors argue that to disregard the complexity of social identity and the existence of unexpected patterns of identification will run the risk of reinforcing negative intergroup evaluations.

A concluding chapter (Chap. 13) to the volume draws together critical major themes, suggests some questions on which future work might focus, and proposes a relational approach to self and identity. The chapter ends with a call for more collaborative work between scholars and practitioners concerned with the more humane treatment of others in a world in which we can no longer retreat into the safety of our own national, religious, racial, or ethnic group.

REFERENCES

Das, V., and Kleinman, A., 2000. Introduction. In Das, V., Kleinman, A., Ramphele, M., and Reynolds, P. (eds.), *Violence and subjectivity*. New Delhi: Oxford University Press.

Jacques, M., 2004. The death of intimacy. A selfish, market-driven society is eroding our very humanity. *The Guardian*, 18 September 2004.

Kaldor, M., 2006. *New and old wars: Organized violence in a global era.* London: Polity Press.

McFarland, S., and Webb, M. 2003. *Measuring Gemeinschaftsgefuhl: Identification with all humanity.* Paper presented at the International Society of Political Psychology Annual Convention, Lund, Sweden.

Williams, F., 2004. *Rethinking families.* London: Calouste Gulbenkian Foundation.

PART I

Theoretical Approaches to Globalization, Tolerance, Care, and Courage

CHAPTER 1

Terrible Beauty: Globalization, Consciousness, and Ethics

Paul Nesbitt-Larking

Yeats's *Easter 1916* is a masterpiece,[1] the creative act of a poet at the height of his powers. The poem's rhythmic and phonetic structure gives voice to the broad reaches of human experience.[2] On a semantic level, Yeats's words and phrases evoke the excruciating ambivalence of personal and political decisions in a time of bloody upheaval and explosive change.[3] The refrain of the poem, *a terrible beauty is born*, condenses the two faces of fundamental psychic experience in a world of global transformation, then and now. The complexities that emerge in its lines, written by Yeats in the personal and political stresses of revolutionary Ireland almost a hundred years ago, resonate powerfully in the present-day world. Yeats gives voice to the challenges of rapid and uncontrolled change, regarding violence with deep concern and yet grim approval. For him the universal and the diurnal are equally available facets of the same phenomenological experiences. Yeats's treatment of social class and nation reflect his ambivalence. From a romantic and elitist perspective, Yeats regards the common folk as bovine, and the nation as the

---

[1] I very much appreciate the kindness shown by my colleague Dr. Dermot McCarthy, an expert in Irish literature. Dr. McCarthy devoted a substantial meeting with me to a dialogue on Yeats's poetry, and his insights on *Easter 1916* were influential in the shaping of my ideas in this chapter. Despite this, the interpretations offered in the paper are ultimately my own, and I alone am responsible for them.

[2] The full text of *Easter 1916* is widely available, so I have not reproduced it in this chapter.

[3] This chapter is not intended as a detailed contribution to the literature on Yeats's politics. Rather, it adopts the insights of the scholars who regard Yeats's poetry as a heuristic and sensitizing orientation to a complex world, rather than as a lyrical manifesto of set beliefs (Kermode, 1967). The chapter is also grounded in Jonathan Allison's (1996) argument that the complexity and multiplicity of Yeats's poetic vision are a reflection of his own political life, encompassing cultural nationalism, anti-colonialism, worker solidarity, conservative elitism, and flirtations with fascism.

elevated repository of ancient myth, sacrifice and honor. At the same time, he declares that ordinary people can accomplish great things in unusual circumstances and that too powerful an attachment to national pride results in vainglorious heroism and unnecessary bloodshed.

Written in a world grappling with the challenges of modernity (industrial capitalism, class struggle, patriarchy, the nation-state) the core themes and the central tension of Yeats's poem nonetheless serve to open up an exploration into life in our era of late-modern globalization. The dynamic tensions of violent change, the universal in the diurnal, social status, and national identity are the key dialectics of contemporary phenomenologies of the global order. Much has been written about economic, governmental, societal, and cultural aspects of global transformations in the late-modern world, and many of these writings make reference in powerful and important ways to changing identities. A critical psychology reflective of such transformations is only suggested and partially developed, however. This chapter works through some key developments in the current social theory of globalization in order to appreciate consciousness and its ethical consequences in a fragmented and uncertain global existence.

TERROR

Economic Terror

The concept of economic terror resonates in the title of Vivienne Forrester's highly influential essay *The Economic Horror* (1999). While there is nothing new in the transnational spread of capitalism, the shrinkage of time and space has become exponential in the past three decades, and transnational economic relations have become more liquid and more elaborate. Moreover, reflecting Yeats's poem, the global and universal are experienced in direct and tangible ways in the local and everyday. This reality, which Giddens (1992, 22) refers to as the "dialectic of the local and global," has given rise to the popularity of Roland Robertson's neologism of "glocalization" (Bauman, 1999, 120). The very experience of the entire world is always already constitutive of our daily lives. The principal psychological effects have included: a growing sense of vulnerability; a decreasing capacity to locate and hold to account those responsible for economic activity; and a growing fear of unanticipated and large-scale external factors, such as massive and sudden job losses and unexpected changes in the regulatory apparatus leading to deteriorating conditions in and around the workplace, sweeping wage cuts, or cuts in the social wage. In addition to its class-mediated impact, glocalization is simultaneously and powerfully gendered and racialized.

According to Rose's (1999) theory of governance of the self and Beck's (1999) concept of risk in the era of reflexive modernity, the experiences of the current epoch are associated with a deep sense of individuated responsibility. Bauman (1999) suggests that the most appropriate expression of the character of risk in the contemporary world is the German term *unsicherheit*. This word connotes uncertainty, insecurity, and the absence of safety. Unlike danger, *unsicherheit* is not entirely external to the agent or unplanned, and unlike fate, it is to some extent under our control. Economically, physically, intellectually, emotionally, and even spiritually, we can and should plan and compensate for the contingencies of risk in our lives. The riskier life becomes and the more challenging it is to quantify, calibrate, or evade, the greater our anticipated degree of personal anxiety and guilt with respect to coping with the everyday.

The global marketplace has been moving further and further away from traditional conceptions of use value. The largest international markets today are in derivatives. Forrester (1999) tellingly describes the world of derivatives as a kind of parapsychology. She says (1999, 80):

> ...this form of economy no longer invests; it bets.... This speculative economy consists of betting on the variations of business which does not yet exist, and maybe never will. And from there, in relation to those virtual variations, playing around with bets on securities, debts, interest and exchange rates, now skewed of any sense, connected with purely arbitrary projections, approaching the wildest fantasy or prophesies of a parapsychological nature. It consists, above all, in betting on the results of all those bets made on the results of those bets, and so on.

Such speculation might give high rollers the adrenaline rush of an extreme sport. For the majority, the economic impact of such large-scale and uncontrollable speculation is disconcerting. Sennett (1998, 51) refers to the abandonment of highly productive and efficient businesses, with hitherto loyal employees, that are deemed to be incapable of the kind of change and adaptation or hyper-profitability demanded of the new global system.

The largest single economic corollary of the new transnational financial order has been the onset of neo-liberal adjustment policies throughout the West and into the developing world. Most alarmingly, the principles of economic growth and development are now based on minimizing employment. This is the so-called "jobless recovery" of the 1990s. Bourdieu (in Bauman, 1999, 29) refers to the "structural violence" of unemployment. The obsolescence of paid employment was first recognized by the neo-liberal economists of the 1960s and 1970s, who theorized and proselytized the case for the non-accelerating inflation rate of unemployment (NAIRU). Most Western states had adopted the principles of this ideal by the mid-1980s. While in the Keynesian era the accepted level of unemployment was considered to be no more than a little above full employment, under the NAIRU, the ideal unemployment rate was such that there would be enough unemployed people to dampen wage expectations among the employed.

The combined impact of the NAIRU and the decreasing requirements for workers has been to increase rates of unemployment; to increase the ranks of part-time workers, contractual and casual employees; and to reduce the economic value of the minimum wage. Forrester (1999) identifies the injustice of the new economic reality for contemporary employees and job seekers. In an era of large-scale and structural unemployment, in which work as we have known it is effectively dead, "they believe and are encouraged to believe themselves failed masters of their individual destinies...." (Forrester, 1999, 4) The entire socio-economic order remains governed by the obsolete caricatures of lifetime careers and full-time employment opportunities reminiscent of the Fordist era of mass production. Just as Beck (1999, 99) states with respect to *political* institutions in the contemporary West, the empty shells continue to exert an effect even as their agency has been drained out of them. Few are talking to the under-employed and the unemployed about the death of work. Instead, states generate programs of "workfare" or "welfare to work" that compel people to search endlessly for work that does not and will not exist. The failure to find work is highly individualized, and the victims of the jobless society are held responsible for the structural redundancies that created them.

The political economy of *unsicherheit* renders many of the apparatuses of control and persuasion unnecessary. To use a familiar expression of Marx in *The Communist Manifesto*, it is the "icy waters" of negative freedom that exert control over socioeconomic relations. Fear and anxiety are powerful disciplinarians, and they have been successful in keeping people from the *agora* of political life in civil society. As Yeats understood, however, no regime can afford to take its hegemony for granted. Yeats well understood the cultural and spiritual disorientations of a society in question. "All changed, changed utterly," he repeats at the beginning and end of the poem, emphasizing the scope of the impact through his placement of the staccato adverb dramatically at the end of the phonetically soft phrase. In the middle of the poem, Yeats uses the phrase "transformed utterly," thereby accentuating the agency of those who were able to effect such transformation. With Yeats, we recall the beauty of transformation that balances the terror of agentless change; and we return to this theme later.

Cultural Terror

Enlightenment metaphors speak of turning the traditional world upside down, of standing philosophers on their head, or of the view through a *camera obscura.* The underlying assumption is that there is a coherent order that might be inverted. Late-modern metaphors speak instead of implosion, explosion, entropy, shattering, and fragmentation. Salmon Rushdie refers to the modern self as "a shaky edifice we build out of scraps, dogmas, child-hood injuries, newspaper articles, chance remarks, old films, small victories, people hated, people loved" (in Sennett, 1998, 133). In this manner, the self in late-modern society becomes a matter of personal and individual responsi-bility and an open book in which might be written a range of narratives. Giddens refers to these personal choices as "life politics" in which an ever-broadening menu of available influences and choices is available to the self in the ongoing construction of its identity. The individual "must integrate information deriving from a diversity of mediated experiences with local involvements in such a way as to connect future projects with past experiences in a reasonably coherent fashion" (Giddens, 1992, 215). Rosenberg (2002, 336–37) makes similar points and stresses the fact that "people are being asked to actively and self-consciously participate with other people in the definition (and likely reconstruction) of their own and others' identities and in the construction of the rules and values whereby their interaction will be regulated." Given such projects, the late-modern emphasis shifts away from objective structures and representational subjective truths to the realm of social constructionism, contingent meaning and discursive understandings. The cultural reality of the late-modern condition is such that the links between signifiers and things signified are permanently in question, and therefore the most important sites of psychological research are those where meaning is made: discourses, conversations, and cultural interchanges.

The late-modern conception of self carries with it the deep and inescap-able corollary of personal risk management. If we are free to choose our actions, our identities, and our life paths, then we only have ourselves to blame if we make the wrong choices (Bauman, 1999, 146). Beck (1999, 154) refers to this darkly as "the private executive branch":

> This private executive branch, lest anyone be deceived, is in sum precisely the gateway through which the (nightmarish) dreams of the "New Man" can be made a fact, flesh and blood . . . a new nightmare of forming reality in our own image is beginning, this time in everyone's private life and on an explicitly voluntary basis.

Erich Fromm long ago appreciated the consequences of the fear of freedom, and theorized about its consequences in a world of nation-states. In the global context of today, the stakes of freedom are higher, and so the cultural responses to the breakdown of the familiar and the communal have been more dramatic. Bauman (1999, 63) refers to contemporary privatized forms of individuality as modes of "unfreedom." In a telling juxtaposition, he says: "Scared loners without a community will go on searching for a community without fears, and those in charge of the inhospitable public space will go on promising it" (Bauman, 1999, 14). Confronted with mediated images of murder and mayhem, and living in globalized forms of privatized risk, the fortress has become the prison of the gated community or the shopping mall, in which only commodified behavior will be tolerated. In the face of global economic libertarianism and gender liberation, the panicked reaction of religious fundamentalism has taken root from Karachi to Kansas among those who live in fear of their own freedom. Fundamentalists erect their own "gated communities" with the obdurate walls of refusal. They refuse history, choice, desire, dialogue, playfulness, and ultimately hope. "The human landscape of women's liberation and men's defense of their privileges is littered with corpses of broken lives," says Castells (1997, 136), and nowhere does this exhibit itself with grimmer ferocity than in the Bosnian rape camps of the 1990s.

The challenges of cultural choice can exert a stultifying and disabling effect on people. In a global climate of fear and insecurity, there is an overwhelming temptation to close down, to retreat, and to survive. Lerner (1997, 10) says: "Cynicism disempowers and powerlessness corrupts." While acknowledging that conflict and oppression are very real and tangible evils for many people, Lerner (1986, 3) bewails the fact that so many people then seem to disempower themselves even further through the quasi-protective barriers of cynicism and despair. Whether through the escapist routes of television, drugs, or alcohol, or through the adoption of a negative, one-sided view of human nature or history, people are afraid to take the power that they in fact could assume with impunity, if they would only act to assert it. Lerner advocates a "mass psychology of compassion" (1986, 283) toward oneself and significant others. Only through love of oneself can one develop the emotional wherewithal to love others and to actualize one's freedom through a calm sense of entitlement. In this process of mass compassion, social movements and community organizations have a key role to play in nurturing a sense of possibility and entitlement (Lerner, 1986, 291).

Political Terror

The post-communist world has radically called into question the nature of states and nations, and the Westphalian nation-state form itself is increasingly in question. The economic globalization of money, goods, and services, of media and electronic communications, has severely restricted the role of the nation-state in regulating and steering economy and society. Contemporary nation-states are caught in a downward spiral of giving tax breaks to corporations and wealthy individuals. The consequent diminution in revenue further compromises the provisions of the Welfare State, even as it enhances the coercive role of the state. Power operates in the largely stateless domain of transnational interchange, and local and regional states are increasingly vying with national states for power and authority (Castells, 1997, 244). The declining authority of the national state is compensated for to some extent through individual self-governance. The new citizen is oriented toward risk-averse and risk-calculating behavior in economic terms (credentialism, personal flexibility adjusted to the needs of the corporation, the replacement of the "career person" and "company man" with the self-starting individual entrepreneur, who sells services to the highest bidder and builds his own capital) and in cultural terms (a range of personal choices in gender and familial terms, personal health, fitness, style and attractiveness, geographical mobility, and open choice in religious, political, and ideological affiliations). The common theme is the self-governing individual, who neither requires nor desires external authority in order to function effectively.

The privatization of the self finds expression, too, in the traditional domain of politics. The modern institutions of political life, notably the political parties and legislatures, are decreasingly relevant. Bauman (1999, 70) notes that in the privatized state the consistent offers of tax refunds are a matter of getting our "dues" back from the social contract of the nation-state. But deregulation and privatization does not imply the end of regulation or power. On the contrary, deregulation is the transfer of regulatory capacity from states to markets (Bauman, 1999, 74). The citizen as consumer has little power and lacks the capacity to demand what services are provided and how they are provided. Despite the New Public Management rhetoric of responsive public-private partnerships and the proliferation of these hybrids, there is in fact little connection between the needs and desires of citizens and the shape and delivery of public services. Given the impotence of parties and parliaments to influence these organizations and to regulate the community in general, it hardly seems surprising that "politics" as an activity has been draining steadily from the ostensibly political institutions to those that were hitherto "protected by politics in industrial capitalism—the private sector, business, science, towns, everyday life and so on . . ." (Beck, 1999, 99).

Beck (1999, 140) refers to traditional state institutions as "zombie institutions," effectively dead, but unable to lie down. Traditional parties have declined to a point of irrelevance, argue Beck (1999) and Castells (1997), and have been replaced by growing ranks of non-voters and minor parties of principle. Real political life, the vibrant life of decision, power, advantage, and bargaining, takes place beyond these traditional venues and occurs wherever the global has the most impact on the local. Thus, widespread and uncontrolled pollution and climate change give rise to ecological social movements, non-governmental organizations, and Green Parties. The global spread of migration, crime, and drugs gives rise to racist gangs, anti-immigration forces, and ultra-right nationalist parties. The global decline of patriarchy results in an upsurge in fundamentalist religious movements and parties, insisting on having their voices registered in public policy on abortion, homosexuality, women's rights, and other matters. As Beck (1999, 153) says: "Now the microcosm of personal life conduct is suddenly interconnected with the macrocosm of terribly insoluble global problems."

The incapacity of the state to regulate the ebbs and flows of risk in the global arena has the effect of promoting a politics of attack and retaliation. In an era of invisible threats, an identifiable enemy is in fact quite comforting. Bauman (1999, 49) puts it well:

> Threats to safety, real and imputed, have the advantage of being fleshy, visible and tangible; this advantage is topped and reinforced by another—that of the relative facility of confronting them and perhaps even defeating them . . . . no wonder . . . that as a result the popular concerns about safety, nicknamed "law and order," dwarf the popular interest in the productive mechanisms of insecurity and uncertainty and the popular unwillingness to arrest or at least slow down their operation.

Nations exist in the historical imagination of Western subjects to be invoked and invented anew as they are needed. Nationalism remains as the most powerfully rooted and culturally resonant ideology in the late-modern era (Archard, 2000, 159). A pluralistic and civic nationalism is quite feasible, but it is the conservative-romantic form of exclusivist ethnic nationalism that emerges panic-stricken in the era of the decline of the nation-state to rage against the empty and threatening anomie of the global order. As Beck (1999, 62) points out, the boundaries of class, nation, family, and gender role are eroded under reflexive modernization: "Counter-modernization asserts, draws, creates and solidifies all boundaries over again."

The state and the nation are powerfully called into question in Yeats's *Easter 1916* in a way that prefigures the explosion of ethnic nationalist uprisings of the late 20th century. In an evocation of the tension between pragmatic politics and Romantic absolutism, Yeats's final stanza of the poem asks whether the sixteen Irish martyrs needed to die at all. Were the Irish martyrs blinded by their uncompromising love of country? Some analogous sentiments occupy the minds of Israelis and Palestinians as they vacillate between the details of the various peace accords and the uncompromising demands of the combatants. American and British citizens continue to ponder the invasion of Iraq. Was it necessary to remove the regime? Might the objectives have been achieved anyway through less violent modes of intervention?

BEAUTY

Economic Beauty

Written soon after the British authorities had executed sixteen Irish nationalist rebels in 1916, the cadences of *Easter 1916* urge us toward celebration of the spiritual cleansing of heroic bloodshed. Such is the unmistakable effect of the litany of heroic names coupled in a dancing march as the poem comes to an end. At the same time, its sad rhetorical punctuation requires us to stop and ask, "Was it needless death after all?" Yeats's dialectics are condensed into the expression "terrible beauty." The dialectic between these pairs of opposites is evoked through Yeats's naturalistic third stanza, in which he juxtaposes the permanence of stone (symbolizing abiding Irish national consciousness) with the transience of the living stream (a symbol for pragmatic adjustment to changing circumstances). The stone appears to divert the water and compel its flow. However, if we look long enough, the water erodes the very stone that is resisting it. This metaphor of stone and water serves us well as we begin to consider the apparently obdurate compulsion of the global economy. To treat the global economic order as a monolithic and irresistible force is to reify it and to ignore the very real dialectics that the agents whose practices sustain it have set in place. Hirst (2000, 179–182), among others, reminds us that it was a series of voluntary and deliberate state actions that deregulated capital markets and removed exchange controls in the late 1970s and early 1980s. The global economy is then very much an object of state control and policy choice. Moreover, the extent to which markets have been globalized is exaggerated. According to Hirst (2000, 182), the principal indicators demonstrate that economies are more closely tied to the nation-state than is commonly supposed. Ratios of trade to gross domestic product (GDP) among the various nation-states differ little today from their magnitude in the past. Foreign direct investment is highly concentrated, and capital markets are "resolutely domestic." There are few genuine transnational corporations (those with no substantial domestic base), even if there are substantial numbers of multinational corporations that operate from a clear domestic base.

Populist discourse is replete with reified notions of the impact of the global economy. State elites across Western nations have consistently promoted the line that national economies must deregulate, privatize, cut taxes, and limit the welfare state in order to "stay competitive." These ideas have become the nostrums of late-modern political rhetoric. There is little doubt that the policy changes induced by such ideas have exerted serious social and psychological damage, as we saw above. The growing gap between rich and poor, the pervasiveness of unemployment and precarious semi-employ-ment, the unwillingness of leaders and political parties to retake control of national economic levers, the erosion of safety-net provisions and the welfare state have resulted in widespread disillusionment and even despair. The only relief has been in the distractions noted above of whipped-up xeno-phobia and panic campaigns concerning highly dramatic but low-probability events.

So what of beauty? It resides in those sites and practices of resistance that refuse the inevitable. In psychological terms, it incorporates aspects of accommodation and resistance in a range of domains. There is the quiet and grim pragmatism of the Third World worker, confronted with the choice between extreme privation in the rural hinterland or a toxic and oppressive job for a multinational branch plant in the shantytown. We can also consider the First World single mother who must leave her kids unat-tended on a Friday evening for a few hours while she works a minimum-wage shift at the convenience store. In both instances, the attachment of the worker to the business is so brittle and contingent that it makes little sense to construe the contact as safe or assured. Quite to the contrary, the risks are as evident for employers as they are for employees: Those ripped from their families and communities will seek to compensate or at least substitute in some way the organic warmth that has been removed. Oppressed workers, simply put, have a tendency to organize in various ways. If they cannot actually unionize, they may accommodate each other to make life more bearable, irrespective of the benefit to the company. They may not be able to overtly protest, to grieve, or to go on strike, but they can be sullen, uncooperative, strategically and punctiliously co-operative, slow, or delib-erately stupid. They can fantasize, sabotage, borrow, steal, and evade atten-tion. Scott (1990, xiii) says, "poaching, foot-dragging, pilfering, dissimulation, flight. Together, these forms of insubordination might sui-tably be called the infrapolitics of the powerless . . . ." Scott's work on what he refers to as "hidden transcripts" offers an anthropological reading of the myriad ways in which those with few resources survive oppression through the application of their wits and organize in a covert manner for the oppor-tunity to rebel more actively once the conditions are safe. In identifying the hidden transcript, Scott (1990, 120) refers to "unspoken riposte, stifled anger, and bitten tongues created by relations of domination . . . ."

By definition, Scott's acts of subversion are concealed. As he says: "If anonymity often encourages the delivery of an *un*varnished message, the veiling of the message represents the application of varnish" (Scott, 1990, 152). But not all resistance to globalization emanates from the least powerful or the most vulnerable. There is also the vast and growing overt intellectual resistance to globalization evident in the minor parties, social movements, and non-governmental organizations. These social forces bare the actual political choices that underpin economic forces, and they insist on transparency in the crafting of new deals. They take to the streets and make common cause with those who are disadvantaged or disgruntled, in order to retard or even reverse state decisions. They have powerful tools in the new media of spectacle and shock. To the extent that they are able to convey their message through whatever means they have available, they question the legitimacy of those promoting the global economic agenda. To the extent that they keep alive the alternatives to the negative impacts of global capitalism, so they sustain the belief that people can change their own circumstances. Their actions sustain a sense of purposeful agency. Torres (in Castells, 1997, 81) raises the important point that the global economy stands or falls on the basis of trusted and dependable information. Thus, the manipulation of information becomes critical to the sustaining of global competitiveness and profitability. For Torres, "information can be much more powerful than bullets."

Easter 1916 is populated by those Yeats knew personally, with all the beauties and blemishes of everyday people. One (MacDonagh) is "sweet"; another (MacBride) "a lout." Invoking theatrical techniques, Yeats invites us to regard himself and his *dramatis personae* in their diurnal trials from the ironic and detached perspective of role and performance. As Brecht understood, such alienation (*verfremdungseffekt*) is a necessary concomitant of both understanding and action. It is also, of course, a barrier against pain and loss. The dialectical play of self and other, role and person, that occupies Yeats draws us to the defensive strategies that we employ to contend with our existences in the age of globalization. Against the impersonal global reach of corporations and commodities, controlled from metropolitan and affluent centers, stands the familiarity of the local, the vernacular, and the sacred. Confronting the terror of cold spatial domination is the beauty of warm temporal coexistence. Both Castells (1997, 123) and Innis (1971) recognize this dialectical struggle. Technology and information are in play in this dialectic and are never entirely captured. While it is sensible to attend to the huge and devastating human impact of sudden and colossal transfers of liquid capital from Asia or Mexico, we should not overlook the possibilities of "weaving a hyperquilt of women's voices throughout most of the planet" (Castells, 1997, 137).

Cultural Beauty

The emergence of human awareness from early infancy, through which any conception of self and other is made possible, depends upon the acquisition of language, which is "intrinsically public" (Giddens, 1992, 51). There is a powerful sense of openness in the realm of discourse. Such openness is explored in Kristeva's (1986, 89–136) dialectic of the semiotic and the symbolic. While the symbolic is a constant necessity to provide order, coherence, and structure, the semiotic breathes life into the symbolic; affirming, challenging, or refusing its meaning. The semiotic is equivalent to Rose's "stutter" (1999, 20) that interrupts the fluency of the narrative: "digging under its stories, cracking open opinions, reaching regions without memories, destroying the coherence of 'the self'." The very rupturing of the taken-for-granted, the sutured, or the dominant narrative brings into stark awareness the arbitrariness of the sign, and thereby the entire edifice of power.

Such cultural subversion is a sublimely creative act and begins with the simple acts of thinking and speaking. As Forrester (1999, 63) says: "There is no more subversive action than thinking....Thinking is political. And not only political thinking is, far from it. The mere *fact* of thinking is political." Benhabib (in Maclure, 2003, 7) points out that acts of reflection and deliberation lead to critical thinking, and that articulating views in public "imposes a certain reflexivity on individual preferences and opinions." To employ the cultural capacity to redefine one's role is not necessarily to position oneself. Indeed, such reflection and articulation entitle one to disclose anything (or not) and to essentialize oneself (again, or not). To demand the space to define oneself is simply to refuse the definitions and corresponding structured limitations of others' delineation of oneself. Reflecting on the possibilities of queer identities in Hong Kong, Ho and Tsang (2000, 135) speak of the creativity inherent in the "individualized interpretation of a collective name...." In a simultaneously terrifying and exhilarating sense, then, in the late-modern era one's identity is less given and more open than ever before.

To the extent that we open up our own identities and explore the lineaments of their constitution, we sharpen our awareness of the need to recognize and validate difference in others. To reflect in this manner is to risk disrupting, interrogating, and then recombining the pieces of one's own identity. There is, of course, a substratum of coherence in this process, and the degree to which one engages—alone or socially—in acts of deconstruction is variable. Of course, such self-exploration threatens existing identity. But, as Howarth and Stavrakakis (2000, 13) point out: "if dislocations disrupt identities and discourses, they also create a lack at the level of meaning that stimulates new discursive constructions, which attempt to suture the dislocated structure." Renewed identities can be liberating. Patrick (2000, 39) raises to consciousness the cultural masculinism of Rawls's "veil of indifference" that undergirds his conception of distributive justice. She argues that Rawls's concept "presupposes an account of the self in which reason and affectivity are opposed." Lupton (1999, 105–106) opens the door to alternative affectively informed rationalisms, such as those grounded in familiarity and comfort or custom and those based on fatalism. How people contend with risk and opportunity is the consequence of their particular biography as well as their personal idiosyncrasy. Lupton (1999, 122) reminds us of the importance of practical consciousness and of esthetic and hermeneutic judgments formed through the taken-for-granted ideas of acculturation. Monroe (1997) in her critique of rational choice theory offers an alternative in "perspective theory." This theory develops the notion of a broad range of normative, expressive, and social-identity characteristics governing decision-making that go beyond the narrowly conceived logic of rational choice.

Not all action fits within even Monroe and Lupton's generous parameters of plausible motivated behavior, and some of it stretches our interpretation of universally accepted criteria of rationality. Given the potential for boredom and the oppression of strict self-governance, it is not surprising that extreme risk-taking activity becomes attractive in and of itself. The attraction of the bawdy, the extreme, the uncouth and the carnivalesque as vehicles to free oneself from the bonds of the diurnal and the regulated is familiar to all. It is a form of self-actualization. This is the politics of bungee jumping, body piercing, extreme sports, and one's fifteen minutes of fame on reality television.

Against the cultural terror of *unsicherheit*, of risk, Beck (1999, 162–173) posits the beauty of doubt. Between the twin evils of despair and cynicism, both grounded in a disabling sense of determinacy, lies the creative power of doubt. Employing purely phenomenological ideas, Beck regards doubt as a bodily separation out of one's own and others' senses, to "give space and an ear to his own astonishment, his own voice" (Beck, 1999, 164). Refusing to accept anything more than contingent and partial truth, doubt becomes an ally, an agent of our own empowerment. The obsession with caption, with suture, and with the Truth converts doubt into despair of finding the right answer. But a permanent orientation of doubt is a weapon of the weak. To live in radical doubt and a pluralized unwillingness to grant cognitive or affective closure means avoiding the verities and absolutes on which is grounded violence, ethnic hatred, and war. Doubt is "kind and deeply humane" (Beck, 1999, 171); and, in a lyrical moment, Beck describes doubt as "the anti-religious religion of self-limiting modernity" (1999, 171). The dynamics of doubt and the possibilities of agency find reflection in the psychosocial orientations of ethical and critical care as developed by Alford and Scuzzarello in their chapters in this volume. The possibilities of doubt are further echoed in both Scuzzarello's and Fernandez's critiques of multiculturalism in their chapters below. The refusal of doubt is illustrated in the empirical findings of Ferguson in this volume. Based upon his research in

Northern Ireland, Ferguson demonstrates that high levels of identification with a religious denomination correlate substantially with reduced levels of moral competence and a greater propensity to support a "culture of violence."

There is something profoundly liberating about the notion of refusal, of personal and social role-redefinition, and of radical sustained doubt. The will and promise to reconstruct the very real world of oppressive ideological closure and hegemony through the alternative reflexive discourses of stutter and semiotics, through hidden transcripts and through the courage to recognize oneself as having suffered from surplus powerlessness, evoke a powerful feeling of liberation. There are those, of course, who revert to terror and argue that not only does terror trump beauty in many cases, but that the very celebration of *jouissance* and alternative reality construction is insensitive to the agents who have no choice. Criticizing Beck, Lash asks rhetorically "just how 'reflexive' is it possible for a single mother in an urban ghetto to be? Just how much freedom from the 'necessity' of 'structure' and structural poverty does this ghetto mother have to self-construct her own life-narratives?" (Lash in Lupton, 1999, 114–115) Similarly, Smith takes Giddens to task for his statement that "However oppressively the burden of particular circumstances may weigh upon us, we feel ourselves to be free in the sense that we decide upon an action ..,. the actor 'could have done otherwise'..." (Giddens in Smith, 1999, 147). Smith says: "I don't think Giddens would have felt comfortable telling an audience of Iranian workers that 'we feel ourselves to be free' when 'we' is intended to include them ... 'we' who are men do not experience masculine sexualization of women's public life as young women might; we are not Iranian workers, and so on" (Smith, 1999, 152).

The simple correctness of Lash and Smith's claims needs to be registered. It is always hazardous to adopt the voice of the other, and one needs to be cautious in imputing consciousness in others. The point is that *no one* can adequately claim to speak for anyone else beyond a certain level of tentative generality. The question remains whether Beck and Giddens' claims about reflexivity and agentive choice are sufficiently generalizable to be universal. My contention is that they are indeed. Even agents whose life circumstances exhibit the greatest structures of oppression have agentive powers and the capacity to reflect. Lash and Smith are right to compel our attention toward the oppressions and limitations conditioning the lives of "the wretched of the earth." But, of course, this does not mean that the agents remain entirely powerless. Ghetto mothers can fight back against drug dealers and reclaim neighborhoods, and Iranian workers rose up against the Shah and may well do so again against the ayatollahs. There is, in the end, a rather dismissive pessimism in the words of Lash and Smith. The Iranian workers and the ghetto mothers do not need Smith and Lash to defend them, any more than they need Giddens and Beck to define their reflexive and agentive possibilities. What separates these analyses is that Beck and Giddens are aware of this fact and as a consequence exhibit less propensity to restrict the discursive potential of these oppressed people through preemptive closure than do those who would champion them, Lash and Smith. In this regard, Beck and Giddens exhibit an ethics of critical enquiry that consciously promotes the politics of hope.

Political Beauty

Among the greatest dreads associated with the spread of globalization is the notion that the decline of the nation-state has impeded the principal expression of the people's sovereign will. Those who express this concern clearly have a point. Supranational and regional forms of governance have usurped the functions and authority of national states, and both sovereignty and governance capacity are increasingly fragmented. As Hirst (2000, 185) indicates, however, the nation-state remains the critical order of governance in that it controls a territory and it defines citizenship. Essentially, he says that nation-states "donate sovereignty and legitimacy 'upwards' and 'downwards'—to supranational bodies and treaty regimes and to regional governments" (Hirst, 2000, 185). To the extent that Hirst is correct in his analysis of state power, much depends upon how citizens perceive their roles and capacities. If they in fact exhibit a sense of surplus powerlessness vis-à-vis their roles as citizens and the capacity of the national state to act on their behalf, then both the manner in which this is sustained and the potential for it to change need to be explored in psychology.

An important aspect of such research is to investigate the moments when citizens act. Meyer, in this volume, develops the concepts of popular resistance and civil disobedience, and in so doing illustrates how social courage is balanced with fear. Meyer's research brings to mind the following report that appeared in *The New York Times* on December 21, 1989: "The young people started to boo. They jeered the President, who still appeared unaware that trouble was mounting . . . . It was a moment that made Rumanians realize that their all-powerful leader was, in fact, vulnerable" (in Scott, 1990, 204). The will to boo Ceausescu, to stand up and be counted (or in the case of the Soweto teenagers, gunned down), to say "no" or even to absent oneself in passive resistance, should never be underestimated. Castells (1997, 39) says that "communities may be imagined, but not necessarily believed." Any regime or ideologically motivated force can make a claim for authority and influence, but all depends on the extent to which such narratives are incorporated into the hearts and minds of the relevant people. Once they decide to end the oppression that has been visited on them, they are often stunned by the ease with which they can achieve their desired ends. Their small-scale and low-level actions become integrated into an evolving sense of self-respect, dignity, and mass defiance (Scott, 1990, 224). With respect to the velvet revolutions of Eastern Europe, Beck (1999, 100) says:

> There, the citizens' groups—contrary to all the evidence of social science—started from zero with no organization, in a system of surveilled conformity, and yet, lacking even photocopiers or telephones, were able to force the ruling group to retreat and collapse just by assembling on the streets . . . . In a society without consensus, devoid of a legitimating care, it is evident a single gust of wind, caused by the cry for freedom, can bring down the whole house of cards of power.

To the extent that the movements just described are to be successful, they must be grounded in a consciousness of possibility. The fear of risk must be complemented, if not supplanted, with the will to doubt. There needs to be a radical rethinking of boundaries, and an autonomous calibration of "inside and outside," and "us and them." Neighbors come to be regarded as friends, rather than strangers, and foreigners regarded as complementary others, rather than a threat. Lowe, Muldoon and Schmid, later in this volume, report on the importance of those whose social identifications and categorizations transcend familiar either/or categories of "in-group and out-group." The authors report that increased levels of complexity in social identity are related to greater understanding as well as more positive and inclusive attitudes toward others. They remind us that the massive sense of political impotence, the notion that citizens can do little if anything to change their worlds, needs to be overcome by an awareness of the potential of human agency, both individual and collective. There are signs that increasing numbers of people are beginning to live the beauty of their own political agency, and Castells (1997, 351) sees signs of vibrancy in the recreation of local states, the proliferation of democratic and political uses of the micromedia and the worldwide web, as well as among the ranks of the nongovernmental organizations and the social movements.

CONCLUSIONS

The condition of *terror* induces sensations of risk, insecurity, anxiety, and vulnerability. The broadest and most abstract global shifts are mediated into the daily practices of our lives, concretely and bodily. We experience a deeply personal responsibility and guilt over our incapacity to cope. The global economy renders us increasingly vulnerable to layoffs, plant closures, under-employment, and unemployment, as well as to the harsh disciplines of a declining and contingent welfare state. Existing state apparatuses of legitimization and coercion have atrophied to some extent, replaced with the raw market discipline of the dread of failure.

Underpinning the economic horror is a late-modern cultural implosion of the self, increasingly experienced as a shattered, fragmented, and partial entity. We have lost our theoretical, ethical, and aesthetic moorings. Identities are no longer given at birth; they must be constructed, and the task of identity constitution is always precarious and contingent, and often painful. Our private executive branches face daunting challenges in fixing the locus of authority and the constant strains of having to construct and reconstruct self and other. It is little wonder that we have become scared loners, resorting to whatever appear to be simple panaceas. Such psychic orientations fit well with the upsurge in religious and nationalistic funda-mentalisms and the retrenchment of patriarchal orders. These worldviews also help explain the political psychology of gated communities, simplistic law-and-order measures, and the evacuation of large sections of the middle class from the public domain through restrictive balanced-budget legisla-tion. Even for those who do not resort to the extremism of the comforting panaceas of "havens in a heartless world," loose and shifting identity possi-bilities induce in us a sense of paralysis. We do not know the answers to the huge and seemingly intractable challenges of the era. We limit ourselves through the insidious onset of waves of surplus powerlessness and through our willingness to permit others to define us through their recognition or through the withholding of their recognition.

The traditional nation-state form is in decline, along with many modern political organizations and institutions. In the words of Beck, they have become "zombie" organizations and institutions. The real life of politics has been drained from them into the less obviously political domains of private enterprise, the media, civil society, the community, the family, and lifestyle politics. The areas of most active political growth in the current era are the community movements, the nongovernmental organizations, the social movements, and the minor political parties. The most important locus of governmentality is, according to Rose (1990) following Foucault, the soul. Self-government exhibits our capacity to regulate ourselves through our developed volitions.

Corresponding to the terror of late-modern global conditions is an awa-kening of *beauty*. This is premised on the understanding that for every danger there is an opportunity; for every fear an act of defiance; and for every attempt at oppressive closure a liberating overture. In order to grasp opportunity and freedom, it is essential to resist reification (attributing human attributes to mechanisms) and its corollary, hypostatization (attributing mechanistic drives to our human agency). Our agency creates and then destroys all social structures, including states and markets. The nation-state has not become impotent, and it still controls the principal movements of the global economy to the extent that those who come to exert power within it so choose. The capacity of citizens to control and regulate the national state is, therefore, critical and worth the struggle. Even those at the bottom of the socioeconomic order never entirely lack power. The infrapolitics of the powerless is played out in everyday acts of resistance. More organized manifestations of such articulations are evident as forms of protest evolve from the heart and mind to the living room, the shop, the street, the community, and the movement.

To speak of the cultural beauty of resistance is to stress the slow, spiritual, and local power of time against the high-speed, technical, and imperial power of space, and to pay heed to the polyphonous force of the semiotic against the arbitrary rigidities of the symbolic. Our capacities to think and to speak are in themselves subversive activities. Reflexivity leads to choice, deliberation, articulation, and the construction of preferences. Sustained and autonomous doubt is a potent tool in the drive for autonomy. Doubt reflects a refusal to be driven by the closed discourses of agenda and ideology and leaves open the broadest possible engagement with the political needs and preferences of others. Such cultural strengths are grounded in interpretations of the self as a work in progress and as a creative and open potential. Such an orientation is compatible with a confident and demanding citizenship at the core of renewed forms of civil society.

There may seem little hope for an ethics and a politics of doubt in the mindsets of those whose essentialisms and fundamentalisms obdurately refuse politics *qua* dialogical engagement, and of those who cannot see the possibility of a fusion of horizons (Gadamer, 1975). Despair, alienation, retreat, and rage are clear barriers to meaningful participation in the *agora*. What hope is there, then, in an era of the "clash of fundamentalisms"? There are clearly no easy responses to such challenges beyond the continued determination of committed academics, activists, and citizens to promote the advantages of dialogue and engagement and to model the beauty of doubt. It has to be conceded that there are those whose worldviews are unlikely to be open to any overtures from beyond their particular prejudices. Our energies are better directed toward those who retain at least some sense of living in global community. The transformative and healing powers of open encounter with the other are apparent in a range of models and practical experiences, from the applied hermeneutics of Gadamer (1975) to the range of "truth and reconciliation" commissions around the world. Each of us needs deep tolerance and a willingness to suspend judgment in order to glimpse—and to some extent grasp—the worlds of others. Those who adhere to their own fundamental religious "truths" must at the least accept the legitimacy of those who regard all truths as partial or—even more challengingly—regard them as hopelessly ideological or essentialist. For their part, scientific humanists and agnostic skeptics benefit to the extent that they take the transcendental and the mystical seriously and accept religious and other creeds in their fullness for others.

In the end, we return to the inspiring politics of the oppressed, the dispossessed, and those at the margins. Their power in the face of ascribed powerlessness is eloquent testimony to the constructive possibilities of politics, even under the most difficult of circumstances. An ethics of beauty is shared among activists whose principal task is to articulate and promote discourses of human possibility and community power and those whose daily lives engage them, often with little more than applied good sense or common intelligence, in tactics of resistance, evasion, and refusal against the strategic moves of those regimes under which they live. The courage to grasp such power is enhanced to the extent that consciousnesses and cultures of beauty interact through networks of communication, operating at every level from the global to the intimate and personal. To recognize beauty is to stare hard into the eyes of terror and to see behind the reflective steel glare the soft flutterings of insecurity, fear, vulnerability, and possibility.

REFERENCES

Allison, J. (ed.), 1996. *Yeats's political identities: Selected essays.* Ann Arbor: University of Michigan Press.

Archard, D., 2000. Nationalism. In N. O'Sullivan (ed.), *Political theory in transition* (pp. 151–171). London: Routledge.

Bauman, Z., 1999. *In search of politics.* Cambridge: Polity.

Beck, U., 1999. *The reinvention of politics: Rethinking modernity in the global social order.* Cambridge: Polity.

Castells, M., 1997. *The power of identity. Volume II. The information age: Economy, society and culture.* Oxford: Blackwell.

Forrester, V., 1999. *The economic horror.* Cambridge: Polity.

Gadamer, H.-G., 1975. *Truth and method.* New York: Seabury Press.

Giddens, A., 1992. *Modernity and self-identity: Self and society in the late-modern age.* Cambridge: Polity.

Hirst, P., 2000. Globalization, the nation state and political theory. In N. O'Sullivan (ed.), *Political theory in transition* (pp. 172–189). London: Routledge.

Ho, P. S. Y., and Tsang, A. K. T., 2000. Beyond being gay: The proliferation of political identities in colonial Hong Kong. In D. Howarth, A. J. Norval, and Y. Stavrakakis (eds.), *Discourse theory and political analysis: Identities, hegemonies and social change* (pp. 134–150). Manchester: Manchester University Press.

Howarth, D., and Stavrakakis, Y., 2000. Introducing discourse theory and political analysis. In D. Howarth, A. J. Norval, and Y. Stavrakakis (eds.), *Discourse theory and political analysis: Identities, hegemonies and social change* (pp. 1–23). Manchester: Manchester University Press.

Innis, H. A., 1971. *The bias of communication.* Toronto: University of Toronto Press.

Kermode, F., 1967. *The sense of ending: Studies in the theory of fiction.* New York: Oxford University Press

Kristeva, J., 1986. *The Kristeva reader.* (Ed.), T. Moi. New York: Columbia University Press.

Lerner, M., 1986. *Surplus powerlessness: The psychodynamics of everyday life . . . and the psychology of individual and social transformation.* Oakland, Calif.: The Institute for Labor and Mental Health.

Lerner, M., 1997. *The politics of meaning: Restoring hope and possibility in an age of cynicism.* Reading, Mass.: Addison-Wesley.

Lupton, D., 1999. *Risk.* London: Routledge.

Maclure, J., 2003. The politics of recognition at an impasse? Identity politics and democratic citizenship. *Canadian Journal of Political Science* 36:3–21.

Monroe, K. R., 1997. Human nature, identity, and the search for a general theory of politics. In K. R. Monroe (Ed), *Contemporary Empirical Political Theory* (pp. 279–306). Berkeley: University of California Press.

Monroe, K. R. (ed.), 2002. *Political psychology.* Mahwah, N.J.: Lawrence Erlbaum.

Patrick, M., 2000. Identity, diversity, and the politics of recognition. In N. O'Sullivan (ed.), *Political theory in transition* (pp. 33–46). London: Routledge.

Rose, N., 1990. *Governing the soul: The shaping of the private self.* London: Routledge.

Rose, N., 1999. *Powers of freedom: Reframing political thought.* Cambridge: Cambridge University Press.

Rosenberg, S., 2002. Reconstructing political psychology: Current obstacles and new directions. In K.R. Monroe (ed.), *Political Psychology* (pp. 329–365). Mahwah, N.J.: Lawrence Erlbaum.

Scott, J. C., 1990. *Domination and the arts of resistance: Hidden transcripts.* New Haven: Yale University Press.

Sennett, R., 1998. *The corrosion of character: The personal consequences of work in the new capitalism.* New York: W. W. Norton.

Smith, D. E., 1999. *Writing the social: Critique, theory, and investigation.* Toronto: University of Toronto Press.

CHAPTER 2

"Together but Apart, Equal but Different"–On the Claims for Toleration in Multicultural Societies

Christian Fernández

TOLERATION IN QUESTION

We live in a globalized world where cultures continuously cross paths, bump into one another and occasionally clash. As a result, the demands for toleration seem more pressing and omnipresent today than ever before. Everywhere toleration is needed, everywhere it is called for, yet rarely is it really achieved. Just like with human rights and democracy, we are all for it; we only wish we knew how to get more of it. Yet, to the historian, the political philosopher, or anyone familiar with the history of Europe, there is little new about these demands. They have for the last five centuries and with varying degrees of success played a prominent role in the formation of modern societies throughout the West. The modern idea of toleration as we have come to know it first appeared in the sixteenth and seventeenth centuries through well-known thinkers such as Erasmus of Rotterdam, Michel de Montaigne, John Locke, and Pierre Bayle, as a more or less direct response to the religious and political turmoil that swept over Europe during the Reformation and Counter-Reformation. From then on, toleration has been invoked by liberals as a necessary requisite for achieving peaceful coexistence and equal freedom for all citizens, not just the ones who happen to belong to the "right" creed. In this sense, today's claims for toleration of cultural diversity form part of a very familiar project; namely, that of creating liberal states and societies (cf. Barry, 2001).

Yet there is also something unfamiliar about today's claims for toleration. This unfamiliar element first reveals itself in the talk of toleration, which has a new and different ring to it. "Toleration" used to be a matter of granting every citizen a certain amount of freedom through the equal provision of rights. Through these provisions all citizens were to be attached to, and protected from, society in the same way; attached as citizens of the state with rights and duties, and protected as private individuals with personal beliefs and convictions. Today toleration is framed in a different way. It is less a question of equal rights, private freedom, and universality, and more a question of differential rights, public recognition, and particularity. In fact, what used to be conceived of as the solution to cultural diversity in general and religious diversity in particular is now depicted as part of the problem. The new claims for toleration are in large part a plea for protection against a homogenizing liberal culture masquerading as neutral and universal. And they are a defense of the right to be different and detached, not just individually and in private, but collectively and in public (cf. Taylor, 1994).

Arguably, there is something very contemporary about this way of reframing toleration. Along with globalization follows a sense of cultural deprivation and a fear of loss of identity, as well as new means and possibilities of expressing one's authenticity, as Paul Nesbitt-Larking argued in the previous chapter (Chap. 1). The new claims for toleration are in large degree, I think, an expression of such sentiments. On the following pages I will explore this relative shift from what we might call "old" to "new" toleration as it is expressed and motivated in academic discourse. My aim is, not to explain why and when this shift came about, but rather to flesh out its main elements and discuss some of its moral implications. Hence, my approach is that of the political theorist, not the historian or the sociologist.[1]

The argument advances in three steps. In the first section I give a brief and general definition of toleration and discuss some of the difficulties associated with the concept. In the second section, the relative shift from the "old" liberal toleration to the "new" multiculturalist toleration is portrayed through a comparison of what I take to be the main points of controversy. The first point is a shift from the focus on beliefs to the focus on identities; the second is a shift from the norm of neutrality to the norm of recognition; and the third is a shift from toleration through universal rights and provisions to particular rights and provisions. The third and last section is a critical reassessment of the multiculturalist critique and its implications for a liberal theory of toleration. The conclusion of this reassessment is that, although there are important lessons for liberals to learn from the multiculturalist critique, there are reasons to be skeptical of the proposed alternatives.

---

[1] Another approach to the concept and analysis of toleration is applied in Chapter 7 of this volume. In that chapter, Kristen R. Monroe and Maria L. Martinez study the "fostering" of "tolerance" as an individual virtue or trait, while my chapter deals with toleration on a collective, societal level where the role of the state is central to the degree of toleration in society.

Thus, without abandoning the liberal approach, the chapter ends with a brief suggestion of how liberal toleration may evolve in order to better respond to the conditions and needs of contemporary multicultural societies.

THE CONCEPT OF TOLERATION

Toleration is a peculiar value. (I know, it is an unoriginal way to open an argument, but bear with me.) Most of the "big" values in political philosophy are important because they correspond to ideals or ends that we intuitively find valuable in their own right. Take freedom, equality, or justice, for example. We pursue freedom because we believe people are happiest when they are free. We demand equality because we believe all people have the same moral worth. And we want justice because we believe people should get what they deserve and what is fair; and so forth. Toleration, however, is different. Let me try to explain why.

Reasons to Object

In common parlance, the word *tolerant* is frequently used as a synonym for *open-minded* or *liberal*. Very often the word is defined negatively by reference to its opposites—narrow-minded, prejudiced, bigoted—which are easier to pin down than the meaning of the concept itself. In philosophy, the concept of toleration is associated with the acceptance of the right of others to hold beliefs and convictions that depart from one's own, especially when there is no certain, objective way of telling right from wrong or good from bad. In liberal political philosophy, toleration is the fundamental principle that guarantees freedom of opinion and action to every individual member of society. Anyone who takes the concept of toleration seriously, however, will object to so simple and unambiguous a picture. Toleration often requires sacrifices and self-imposed duties, not just a generally sympathetic attitude to pluralism. It is not an attitude or outlook that we naturally possess, and it does not give us any personal gratification. On the contrary, it is more appropriate to think of it as a form of self-restraint, for it requires us to refrain from doing or saying things we intuitively think are right and true, and that we consequently feel we are entitled to impose on others. Bernard Williams puts it nicely:

> If we are asking people to be tolerant... [t]hey will indeed have to lose something, their desire to suppress or drive out the rival belief; but they will also keep something, their commitment to their own beliefs, which is what gave them that desire in the first place. There is a tension here between one's own commitments and the acceptance that other people may have other and perhaps quite distasteful commitments. This is the tension that is typical of toleration, and the tension which makes it so difficult (Williams, 1999: 66-67).

The element of self-imposed restraint can be traced to the very word *toleration*, stemming from the Latin *tolerantia* for endurance and *tolero* for "endure" or "put up with." It is perhaps more clearly exposed than elsewhere in the Stoic conception of toleration. To philosophers such as Marcus Aurelius and Cicero, toleration was a highly esteemed virtue, characterized by self-restraint, moderation, and individual autonomy. It was thought of as an ability to control one's emotions and to resist negative and un-reflected judgment, and as an attitude that required a considerable amount of character and self-discipline, since it was bound to be in frequent conflict with the more private interests of the individual (Fiala, 2003, 151–154). Although less pronounced—or rather differently pronounced—today than two millennia ago, self-restraint remains a crucial element of the concept of toleration. It urges us to accept beliefs and actions in spite of our having reasons to object. This *reason to object* is thus a necessary condition of toleration (see Cohen, 2004, 68–69; McKinnon, 2006, 18; Short, 2005, 280). Without it we would not speak of "toleration," but of "affirmation" or "indifference" (Cohen, 2004, 71–74; Forst, 2004, 315). For instance, it would not make any sense for me to say that I tolerate the homeless as long as they do not sleep on my lawn, or that I tolerate South American immigrants because I like their food and music. The first statement is based on indifference and the second on affirmation, and as long as this is the case I can have no reasons to object and cannot act either tolerantly or intolerantly. If, however, the homeless were to camp on my lawn, I would have a reason to object, and suddenly I would be presented with the choice of tolerating or rejecting my new guests.It is not enough for me to have reasons to object in order to act tolerantly, however; I must also have the ability to do so. It would make no sense to say that I tolerate bad weather or economic recessions, because it is not within my power to do anything about them. Only when it is within my power to object can there be a really free choice not to object, and only when there is such a free choice can my self-restraint be defined as an act of toleration. Consequently, toleration requires three things: a reason to object, the power to object, and a free choice not to object (cf. Shorten, 2005, 280; McKinnon, 2006, chap. 2).

Reasons to Tolerate

The reason to object immediately raises a second question: *Why not* object? Why should we tolerate beliefs or behaviors if we feel we would be better off without them? Directly related to these questions is another characteristic of toleration; namely, *overriding reasons*. If toleration means that I accept beliefs and behaviors although I find them objectionable and although I have the ability to object, there must be some overriding reason that motivates my tolerance. Otherwise I am just acting irrationally (cf. McKinnon, 2006, chap. 2). Toleration for toleration's sake has no value; it is a means to other ends, and without such ends it makes no sense.

> Toleration is what I call a normatively dependent concept, which, in order to have a certain content (and specifiable limits) is in need of further normative resources that are not dependent in the same sense. Tolerance is thus, contrary to a common view, not a value itself but rather an attitude called for by other values or principles (Forst, 2004, 314).

Although I think Rainer Forst may be overstating the point in arguing that tolerance is not a value, this "normative dependence" tells us something that is crucially important: Toleration is valued not so much for what it *is* as for what it *does* for other, overriding reasons. For what reasons, then, is toleration so precious? The simplest way to answer this question is to say that toleration is a necessary attitude or virtue of the citizenry and the state, because societies consist of people with mutually incompatible beliefs, commitments, and lifestyles. If we want peace, stability, and freedom to prevail, we must have a way of accommodating this diversity—hence the need for toleration. It is sometimes thought that this is a lesson learned quite late in history, in early modernity during the Protestant Reformation and the Counter-Reformation, and liberals often claim special ownership and authorship of the idea. Such conceptions require a very narrow understanding of the concept, however (cf. Nederman, 1994; Bejczy, 1997). Some ancient and medieval empires—the Roman, the Byzantine, the Arabic in Spain, the Ottoman, et cetera—periodically excelled in the practice of toleration *vis-à-vis* ethnic and religious minorities, not because they did not have the power to repress or convert them, but simply because it was thought of as a more effective and righteous way to achieve peace and stability (Nederman, 1994; Walzer, 1997, 14–17; Briggs, 2004). For example, the well-known system of Ottoman rule through *millets* (religious communities) endowed conquered colonies with a considerable amount of freedom in exchange for obedience to the rulers and non-interference with neighboring colonies. Thus, despite the differences between modern and pre-modern regimes and theories of toleration, both are distinguished by a desire to accommodate rather than eradicate diversity. All theories of toleration take the acceptance of such diversity or pluralism as their common point of departure.

But if the defense of pluralism is a point of convergence for advocates of toleration, the more specific reasons for this defense are not. There are many points of divergence and disagreement, one of them being on what grounds pluralism should be justified—pragmatism (Locke), skepticism (Montaigne, Bayle, and Descartes), value pluralism (Mill and Raz), or reasonableness (Rawls). For our purposes, however, another point of divergence is more important; namely, the roots of pluralism and its implications for the defense of toleration. In relation to this, one question is whether the causes of pluralism should be sought on the level of the *individual* or the *collective*. In the first case, pluralism is conceived of as the result of differences in beliefs and behaviors of individuals, each with her or his own conception of how a good, virtuous, and meaningful life should be lived. This is the typically modern and liberal defense of pluralism, which is historically associated with the quest for religious freedom and individual rights (cf. Grell and Scribner, 1996; Zagorin, 2003). Accordingly, this defense of pluralism is a defense of individual freedom, for only in a society that respects and offers diversity can people make the choices they really wish to make. In the second case, on the other hand, pluralism is conceived of as stemming from cultural differences of identity and belonging between collectives of people. This is typically how pluralism was conceived of and defended in the old empires. But it is also how it has been conceived of and defended in the modern international system of states and to some extent—as we shall see in the next section—in contemporary multicultural societies (cf. Nederman, 1994; Walzer, 1997). Accordingly, this defense builds on the notion of groups and communities' being—in relative terms—internally homogeneous and coherent, and externally different. These cultural differences between groups and communities are of sufficient moral significance to preclude evaluation and judgment on any supposedly inter-collective moral grounds, and must therefore be respected. In its most principled version, this defense of pluralism is a defense of cultural autonomy, for only in a society that accepts and protects a multitude of cultures can people freely maintain a sense of belonging and independence (see Raz, 1998).

Another, related question regarding the causes of pluralism is whether societal diversity should be conceived of as the result of beliefs and behaviors that are more or less voluntarily *chosen,* or as the result of beliefs and behaviors that are not the result of reflection, but rather *inherited.* In the first case, *pluralism* refers to the variety of lifestyles and commitments that people more or less rationally choose to have, in which case it is relatively easy to hold them responsible for the choices they have made. In the second case, pluralism is the result of a variety of customs and traditions that people view as defining traits of who they are: in which case it is much harder to hold them responsible for actions or behaviors motivated by such traditions (see Galeotti , 2002, 78–80; Parekh, 2000, chaps. 3–5). Any theory of toleration must take these differences into account. According to a common saying, the question of toleration and intolerance does not concern people as such, only the actions and behaviors of people. But many of our actions and behaviors are not consciously and deliberately chosen. They are inherited and socially internalized patterns of behavior that tell us something about who we are as persons. In such cases, toleration or rejection of a person's behavior implies in a sense toleration or rejection of the person herself or himself.

In reality, the distinctions made above are not mutually exclusive. The causes of pluralism are both individual and collective; both chosen and inherited. Very few advocates of toleration, if any at all, would deny this. In theory, however, we cannot have it both ways; we have to choose. How we choose to conceptualize and defend pluralism is therefore crucial to how we formulate a theory of toleration.

Toleration and Power

The question of power cannot help but be raised in a discussion on toleration. If toleration is defined as withheld rejection by someone who has the power to reject, it can easily be seen that toleration often has to do with the asymmetrical relation between a powerful tolerator and a weak tolerated one. For this reason, many a philosopher has been skeptical of toleration. Even though the act of toleration is well intended, it is bound to reflect the overall distribution of power between the parties involved. Thus, Goethe once wrote (cited in Forst, 2004, 316): "Tolerance should be a temporary attitude only: it must lead to recognition. To tolerate means to insult." According to this view, toleration is always conditional; it is accompanied by explicit or implicit expectations that are supposed to be met in exchange for acceptance, which means that toleration always implies some degree of dependence and subordination.

I think there is a large portion of truth in skeptical objections like the above. Toleration is no different from other political principles in that it always contains aspects of power. But what does this actually imply? Perhaps toleration is not the ideal solution to social diversity and conflict, but sometimes it is the only solution. In places such as Northern Ireland and Israel and the Palestinian territories, mutual toleration and peaceful coexistence would be no small achievement (see chaps. 9–11). Power is always part of the picture, but it can be so in many different ways, and we need to separate the ways that are reasonably acceptable from the ones that are not. One way of doing this is by the fairly common distinction between toleration as *permission* and toleration as *respect*. Toleration as permission corresponds well with the skeptical remarks above. According to this conception, toleration is typically the relationship between a superior majority and an inferior, dissenting, or "different" minority. The majority gives a qualified permission to the minority to live according to its beliefs and convictions as long as the members of the minority respect the superiority of the majority, and as long as they keep their "deviance" within private limits and do not expose it publicly or claim equal political and social status on behalf of it (Forst, 2004, 315–316; Habermas, 2003). The old Jewish saying "Jewish at home, German in the street" captures this conception well. Toleration as permission, then, is comparable to a favor that can be withdrawn at any moment and therefore has to be earned continuously by the party who depends on it. Clearly, this is what toleration has been like throughout most of history. This is not to say, however, that toleration as permission is solely motivated by pragmatism as a means of upholding peaceful coexistence; it is also morally motivated by the belief that it is wrong to force others to give up their beliefs and convictions (Forst, 2004, 315–316; Braude and Lewis, 1982; Briggs, 2004; Menocal, 2002).

The second conception, on the other hand, is toleration as respect. As opposed to the former conception, this one seeks to overcome the asymmetries in power between the majority and the minority by mutual respect and equality in status (Forst, 2004, 316; Habermas, 2003). Typically, toleration as respect is not just a temporary attitude or favor, but an unconditional principle granted through individual and/or collective rights. It builds on norms that all parties supposedly can accept and does not favor any of them over the others. Obviously, this is what most modern advocates have in mind when they defend toleration. Still, it must be asked whether this is a possible, realistic conception at all. Can toleration be sufficiently unconditional to produce equal and mutual respect? No matter how tolerant the society, will not the culture of the majority be dominant and conceived of as normal due to its numerical superiority, and will not the culture of the minority be conceived of as different and deviant due to its numerical inferiority? Even in a modern and duly constitutional and democratic society, some asymmetries of power and status appear to be inevitable, as Walzer suggests:

> [M]inority groups are unequal by virtue of their numbers and will be democratically overruled on most matters of public culture. The majority tolerates cultural difference in the same way that the government tolerates opposition—by establishing a regime of civil rights and civil liberties and an independent judiciary to guarantee its effectiveness. (Walzer, 1997, 55)

This asymmetry of power is, generally speaking, what motivates the claims for new means of toleration. In order to better understand it, we need to leave the purely conceptual discussion aside and turn to theory.

THEORIES OF TOLERATION

How should a state or any other kind of polity promote toleration as respect? This is where contemporary mainstream liberals and multicultur-alists part company. The standard liberal answer to the above question builds on the well-known distinction between the public and the private spheres. This distinction is crucial, for it tells liberals what one needs to be tolerant about and what not. The public sphere is the sphere of political authority, of laws and of obligations. From the liberal point of view it represents the minimal and necessary interests that we as citizens all have in common—e.g., peace, order and justice—regardless of how numerous and pervasive our differences may be in other respects. As members of such a public we are all (formally) equal. The private sphere, on the other hand, is the sphere of freedom. In it, we are free to live life as we see fit, to join the associations and communities of our choice, and to worship the god(s) of our faiths. Here we are all different and authentic individuals, autonomous and free from public restraints. A tolerant liberal society is a society that draws the boundaries of the private sphere of freedom generously and subsequently tolerates all the "deviant" behaviors that take place in that sphere.

The public sphere, however, has little need for toleration since it is not a sphere of diversity but of uniformity. An intolerant society draws the boundaries of the public widely so that church, religion, sexuality, and so forth, become matters of concern to the state. A tolerant liberal society draws them narrowly so as to make these things matters for the private individual to decide. Regardless of how the boundaries are drawn, however, the liberal public is always a sphere of uniformity, defined as it were by the goods and provisions of which we as citizens have an equal need. To the mainstream liberal, then, toleration as respect basically requires three things: (1) a *generous* interpretation of what issues belong to the private sphere, (2) a strong sense of *respect* for the public/private divide, and (3) *equal treatment* of all citizens in public matters.

This liberal theory of toleration is not enough to promote toleration as respect, multiculturalists argue. Although there are considerable variations in the formulation of a multiculturalist standpoint, I believe that the major thrust of the argument can be summarized along the lines of three relative and interdependent shifts: (1) from beliefs to identities, (2) from neutrality to recognition, and (3) from universality to particularity. Let us deal with each of them in turn.

From Beliefs to Identities

The first step in the transformation of toleration is a critique of liberal individualism. Essentially, this is a critique of the liberal inclination to view human diversity as constituted by differences between individuals, and not as constituted by differences between groups and sub-communities living within the same society. I am calling this step a shift in focus from the protection of private and individually chosen *beliefs* to the protection of collective and socially contingent *identities*. In the first case, toleration is needed for the sake of individual privacy. In the second case, toleration is needed for the sake of cultural pluralism. In order to understand this shift, we need to address the ontological assumptions that underpin it. Let me elaborate.

The liberal understanding of the division between private freedom and public authority implies two predispositions or tendencies in the liberal conception of the self. Firstly, it implies an element of *atomism*, in the sense that the individual is (implicitly) conceived of as an autonomous agent with a set of pre-political interests and beliefs. The origins and formation of those individual beliefs are of little or at least of secondary interest to liberalism. Rather, it is with the ability and opportunity of every person to without restraints hold such beliefs and to live accordingly that liberalism is concerned (Held, 1989, chap. 7). As a result, the liberal individual is understood in terms of the beliefs and interests he or she seeks to realize, and not in terms of where and why he or she adopted those beliefs and interests in the first place. It is therefore normatively assumed that community is a secondary and instrumental structure—not a moral entity in its own right—the purpose of which is to protect and promote individual liberty as much as possible (see Gauthier, 1986, 330–332). The freedom of conscience, which was more central than any other freedom to the early defenders of liberal toleration, is a case in point. To John Locke and many of the liberal philosophers who would come after him, religion was a question of personal conviction and faith; a belief coming from "within" that could not and should not be controlled or influenced from the "outside." In *A Letter Concerning Toleration* it is striking how much emphasis Locke puts on the affirmation of this argument, which leads him to the (liberal) conclusion that religion and church are affiliations of voluntary choice and not of birth and descent:

> All the life and power of true religion consists in the inward and full persuasion of the mind; and faith is not faith without believing [...] A church then I take to be a voluntary society of men, joining themselves together of their own accord, in order to the public worshipping of God, in such a manner as they judge acceptable to him, and effectual to the salvation of their souls. I say it is a free and voluntary society. Nobody is born a member of any church; otherwise the religion of parents would descend unto children, by the same right of inheritance as their temporal estates (Locke, 2003, 219; 220; cf. Creppell, 2003, 115–116).

Secondly, the public/private division also implies a *dualism* in the liberal conception of the self. In a language that once again can be traced as far back as Locke, the liberal individual is on one hand a bundle of beliefs, sentiments, emotions, and convictions that together define how and to what ends she will use her freedom. On the other hand, she or he is a rational agent, capable of leaving private beliefs and desires aside whenever she or he enters the secular public sphere (Creppell, 2003, 93–94). The logic of our behavior and actions in one sphere does not, and must not, spill over to the other, since this would compromise both individual freedom and public unity. And so the boundary between these two aspects of the self was crucial to Locke and still is to liberals today. It places toleration, not on a ground of mere abstract principles, but on the psychological ground of an essentially modern and divided self (Creppell, 2003, 117).

The atomistic and dualistic conception of the self is primarily a normative ideal in liberal theory, not an empirical stipulation, at least not in modern liberalism (cf. Rawls, 1985). Nevertheless, multiculturalists argue, it presupposes certain ontological assumptions that tend to obscure the collective and social embeddedness of the self. These assumptions constitute the main object of criticism to multiculturalists just like it was for communitarians in the late 1970s and early 1980s (see among others McIntyre, 1981; Sandel, 1982; 1984; Walzer, 1983; Taylor, 1985). First, multiculturalists argue, our beliefs and convictions—among them religion—are not private and personal matters, as liberals tend to assume. Notwithstanding the freedoms of religion, association, and expression, and the separation of state and church, people do not choose their affiliations and communities. They are born into them and socialized by their cultures and common values. Even if we assume a secluded sphere of private freedom, it is wrong to assume a sphere devoid of sociocultural structures and sub-communities that group people and configure their choices and beliefs. The private sphere is not a sphere of complete individual diversity, as liberals tend to assume, but a sphere constituted by a diversity of groups and sub-communities, minorities and majorities, who collectively seek expression and approval for the beliefs they have in common and define who they are. The ability of people to move between and switch communities is obviously greater in modern globalized societies than it was or is in traditional ones (cf. Walzer, 1990), but the need for communal belonging is not. The basic problem with liberal atomism, then, is an overly optimistic conception of individual autonomy and a failure to recognize the extent to which individual freedom hinges on cultural inclusion and identification (see Parekh, 2000, chap. 3; and Kymlicka, 1995, chap. 5). As Will Kymlicka argues in his own culture-oriented version of liberalism, the "availability of meaningful options" that are central to the liberal conception of freedom "depends on access to a societal culture, and on understanding the history and language of that culture" (Kymlicka, 1995, 83). Without access to such a culture, the opportunity for free and meaningful choice is severely restrained (Kymlicka, 1995, 84–88).

Somewhat related to the above is the *dualism* in the liberal conception of the self. The division of the self into compartmentalized units may be warranted by Locke's boundary drawing between what is private and what is public, but it gives a false conception of human nature and identity, multiculturalists claim. The neat distinction between a private self of subjective beliefs and passions, and a public self of objective rationality, is a grave misconception that obscures the interconnections and linkages between the two. Who I am in private affects how I behave and act in public, and vice versa. It is this clear-cut division between private culture and public rationality in liberal theory that Kymlicka tries to overcome through the introduction of the concept of "societal culture," which essentially constitutes the connection or, better yet, the structure that encompasses both of them (Kymlicka, 1995, 76-78). Accordingly, multiculturalists prefer to talk about *identity* rather than *beliefs* and *interests*. Identities are deeply rooted and pervasive; they define who we are and they transgress the fine line between private and public. They are not entirely private, subjective, and personal, as liberals take beliefs to be, nor are they entirely public, objective, and rational, as liberals take common interests to be. Most important, they can hardly be conceived of as chosen, but rather are socially constituted and internalized.

What, then, does the liberal (mis)conception of the self imply about the liberal theory of toleration? According to multiculturalism, it implies a blindness and inability to address discrimination and inequalities that are collective, implicit, and socially structured. In focusing on the level of the individual, liberals see society as made up of a diversity of individual beliefs and convictions, each of which is equal—that is to say, equally different. What liberals fail to see, then, is that these differences are not equally and symmetrically distributed. Some differences are shared by a powerful majority that is perceived as normal and culturally neutral—maleness, whiteness, straightness, Christian— whereas other differences are shared by a marginalized minority that subsequently is perceived as deviant and culturally biased—femaleness, blackness, gayness, Muslim (Galeotti, 2002, 57; 60). Confining these differences to the private sphere does nothing to alter the asymmetries in toleration and the uneven distribution of respect between such groups. Hence, the kind of toleration that is called for needs to do more than the liberal protection of private freedom.

From Neutrality to Recognition

The second step in the transformation of toleration builds on the first. It amounts to a shift in the way toleration is promoted and in the view of how it should be practiced by the state. If protecting the sanctity of the private sphere and individual freedom is not enough, as multiculturalists maintain, then the state must be more active in the promotion of certain groups who still suffer from a lack of toleration due to the color of their skin, their religious beliefs, their sex, and so forth. I am calling this step a shift from passive *neutrality* to active *recognition*. Instead of using toleration as an argument for "cultural abstinence" on behalf of the state, multiculturalism uses it as an argument for cultural involvement and support. In order to fully understand this objection, however, we need to understand why and how neutrality is important to liberalism.

So far I have argued that the place of toleration in liberal theory is to assure the sanctity of the private sphere so that people can choose freely how to live their lives. To early liberals, such as Locke, this was quite enough for a defense of individual freedom and peaceful co-existence. It does not do away with the inequalities in social status and political influence between different groups of society, but it puts a stop to the religious persecution of religious minorities. Modern liberals, however, aim for more. They have to, if toleration as respect is what we aim for. Hence, apart from having the same right to be left alone, citizens should also have a right to equal treatment in the public sphere. In dealing with public institutions, no citizen should be discriminated or favored over another, regardless of being part of some minority culture. In order for this to be the case, the liberal state needs to be *neutral*. Exactly what state "neutrality" means is a widely debated question among liberals, but generally speaking it means that the liberal state is a state that does not favor any particular conception of what a good and meaningful life is as long as those conceptions do not challenge the very foundation of the liberal order—e.g. rule by law, democracy, individual freedom. The liberal state is a just state defined by the ambition to treat all members of society evenhandedly, but it does not take responsibility for the personal moral development of its citizens. The separation of state and church—which means that the state has no influence over the "spiritual well-being" of the people—is one important expression of this principle of neutrality.

More specifically, the principle of state neutrality implies two similar things. Firstly, it implies a principle of action which is commonly referred to as "benign neglect." Benign neglect denotes a deliberately *assumed* indifference toward all the private differences that are tolerated in the private sphere. It means that public officials will look beyond, even be blind to, behaviors and beliefs that clash with their own and those of the majority culture, as long as these behaviors and beliefs have no bearing on public matters. Hence, benign neglect is not tantamount to special consideration or preferential treatment of minorities; it is the presumed abstinence of differential consideration and treatment of any kind, positive or negative. Traditionally, the principle of benign neglect was advocated with respect to the separation of state and church, in which case it meant looking beyond the differing practices and symbols of, say, Catholics, Lutherans, and Calvinists. Today it is obviously advocated in matters of ethnicity, sexual orientation, and skin color, too. According to this principle, then, "state neutrality" means that the public sphere should be a space equally accessible and available to everyone; a place where no particular group of citizens is able to *feel* less included than any other. Obviously, no liberal would argue that this is actually the case in any absolute sense of the word, but as an ideal and strategy, this is what the public sphere needs to be like. The culture of the public sphere must therefore be "sterile," not only with respect to the influence of religion and church, but with respect to other implicit norms such as patriarchy, heterosexuality, and whiteness (cf. Walzer, 1994, and 1997, epilogue). A liberal public culture, then, must consist of norms that are acceptable and equally favorable to everyone. This argument undergirds the well-known distinction among contemporary liberals between *ethnic* nations, where public culture builds on a homogeneous package of shared language, religion, traditions, and heritage, and *civic* nations, where public culture is secular and devoid of ethnic markers of identity (cf. Kohn, 1944; see also Smith, 1986). A liberal public culture is thus grounded in a civic conception of the nation, and it builds on a widespread acceptance of and loyalty to a set of political norms that are integral to any just and democratic society and that consequently relate equally to all ethnic and religious groups (see Habermas, 1992; 2001; Tamir, 1993; Miller, 1995; Ignatieff, 1993).

The multicultural critique of liberalism can be boiled down, I think, to two objections regarding the alleged neutrality of the state. One of them is *direct*, being explicitly aimed at liberal theory, and the other is *indirect*, being more concerned with the liberal conception of what a nation-state is than with liberalism as such. According to the first critique, the so-called neutrality of liberalism is false. Just like other ideologies, it originates from a particular historical and cultural context, within which it has been molded and shaped. It does not speak to humanity in its entirety, as liberals want to believe, and it is not equally applicable across all cultural borders (Parekh, 2000, 109). Liberalism does not offer a "possible meeting ground for all cultures, but is the political expression of one range of cultures, and quite incompatible with other ranges," as Charles Taylor argues (1994, 62). Of what, then, does this cultural contingency consist? One familiar element is of course that it represents an essentially *Western* (European) experience of the state and society. It bears the imprint of ideals and values that are constitutive of Western civilization, such as individualism, human rationality, autonomy, self-reliance, and self-development; whereas it puts less emphasis on other ideals and values that are central to other civilizations, such as family, honor, solidarity, contentment, and humility (cf. Parekh, 2000, 338–339). Liberalism is also essentially Western in the sense that it is marked by the religious conflicts that took place during its inception. The consequences of this pedigree can hardly be overestimated, for it has given liberalism the propensity to interpret all cultural conflicts as conflicts of world-views (i.e., religions) and all claims for toleration as claims for the right to choose and practice those world-views freely and privately. Today, however, the claims for toleration have less to do with freedom of conscience and peaceful coexistence, and more to do with inequalities and discrimination stemming from differences in sex, skin color, or ethnicity; differences that cannot be stuffed away and contained in the private sphere as if they were invisible in public (Galeotti, 2002, 57; 64; and 65–67).

The second, indirect, critique is not aimed at liberalism *per se*, as mentioned above, but at the "nation-building element" of the modern state, and liberalism's inability to develop a proper way of dealing with this fact. According to this objection, it does not matter whether or not liberal theory in itself is neutral, as argued by liberals. The liberal state cannot be neutral as long as it has to be realized within the setting of a nation-state, since the nation-state—as idea as much as phenomenon—is from the very beginning *one nation's* state with an inbuilt predisposition to pursue and preserve ethnic homogeneity. It is therefore incompatible with any liberal notion of neutrality toward ethnic or other cultural differences (see Kymlicka, 1989; 1995; and Raz, 1986; 1998). The more ethnic diversity increases, the more hollow and futile will the principles of benign neglect and civic nationhood prove to be (Kymlicka, 1995, 49). Admittedly, the ethno-cultural component is more pervasive in some countries than others, as the liberal distinction between ethnic and civic nations suggests, but it is always present as a standard of normality with respect to official language, religious festivities, core curriculum in education, requirements for acquiring citizenship, and so forth (Parekh, 2000, 184 ff.; Raz, 1998). Even in traditional immigrant countries that are assumed to be multiethnic and multireligious in their very essence, state neutrality is in fact a distant ideal that remains far from being realized. Consequently, even in the United States with its supposedly post-ethnic, secular, civic conception of the nation, the dominant position of Anglo-Saxon Protestants, "WASPs," as the nation-bearing group above others remains firmly in place unchallenged (Castles and Davidson, 2000, 161; Bader, 1997, 774–777).

To sum up, the problem with the liberal notion of state neutrality, from the perspective of multiculturalism, is that it does not do enough to promote equal and mutual respect between all citizens. The presumed neutrality of the liberal state works as a coverup for a public culture that represents the interests, norms, and lifestyles of a dominant majority. The passivity of the state that goes hand-in-hand with this neutrality amounts to nothing more than a tacit, factual acceptance of the uneven distribution of social status and power between members of the majority and members of the minorities. In such a system equal and mutual respect can only come after the assimilation of minorities into the majority culture is completed. Without such assimilation, multiculturalists argue, toleration is only granted as long as the minorities keep their cultural deviance private and unexposed—i.e., toleration as permission. Instead, what multiculturalists propose in the place of neutrality is *recognition*. If the liberal state tends to block out differences from the public realm by force of a majoritarian culture portrayed as neutral, what is needed is overt public recognition of those differences as equally valid and legitimate. Hence, recognition is more than anything else a *symbolic* measure aimed at the public exposure and endorsement of cultures and identities that previously had to be hidden. And it is a measure that necessarily involves the state, for only by such symbolic acknowledgement by the authorities can the subordinate cultures and identities gain the dignity and self-esteem they need in order to be equally included, without being assimilated, in society. Anna Galeotti illustrates this point nicely:

> If the government declares that homosexuals can be admitted into the army, or that Islamic symbols can be admitted in public schools, what is gained by the direct beneficiaries of such decisions is more than the literal freedom involved. The public visibility of differences that has resulted symbolically represents the legitimization of their presence in public. In its turn, the legitimization of their presence in public signifies their inclusion in the public sphere on the same footing as those whose practices and behavior are "normal." This inclusion then implies the acceptance of the corresponding identity and, hence, the acceptance of those who are marked by such identities. (Galeotti, 2002, 100–101)

This turn in the practice of toleration from a "politics of neutrality" to a "politics of recognition" is based on the conviction, discussed in the previous section, that what matters most for toleration as respect is the ability to express one's identity, not the ability to pursue one's private beliefs. It seeks to dig out and give recognition to the authentic collective identity of each group. Equal inclusion means equal respect and recognition of the differences of identity that make me into me and you into you (Taylor, 1994, 31–33; 64–65).

From Universality to Particularity

The third and last step in the transformation of toleration follows from the previous two and has to do with the practice and organization of toleration. In practice, if not in theory, toleration is always a question of keeping people both apart and together in the best possible equilibrium. People must be kept apart because they have beliefs, convictions, and identities that are incompatible and conflict with one another. But they are also inescapably drawn together, for they are members of a society that makes them mutually dependent and vulnerable to one another. The question of toleration is to determine how these two facts of life should be balanced against one another. The liberal answer builds on the dichotomy between the private and the public sphere, which respond to the need for separation and integration respectively. The public sphere corresponds with the needs or qualities that we as citizens all have in common, which makes it a sphere of uniformity; that is, a sphere of norms and ideals, and more concretely laws, provisions, and obligations that are *universal*. This universalism presupposes firstly that citizens are attached or potentially attached to the public sphere in much the same way—regardless of how different they may be as private individuals—as discussed in the first step of the transformation. Secondly, it presupposes that the state is neutral with respect to all cultural differences that are politically irrelevant, as discussed in the second step of the transformation. If, however, the first and second preconditions of liberal toleration should be discarded because they are false or misguided, as multiculturalists maintain, the principle of universality must be discarded as well. This in turn means that the basic equation of toleration, "together and apart," has to be solved in a new way.

The multiculturalist solution is grounded in the opposing principle of *particularity*. If the problem with liberal universalism is a false conception of the similarity in human needs, the correction of that misconception must be greater sensitivity to difference and particularity. Different groups have different needs and value different things. Consequently, equal respect should not be understood as synonymous with equal rights, provisions, and goods. Rather, equal respect should mean endorsement and protection of different rights for different groups, for only then can toleration become something more than conditional permission. More specifically, the emphasis on particularity implies two norms that go against the mainstream liberal legacy of toleration. The first is *differentiation* and the second is *state activism*.

Differentiation implies a rupture with the liberal idea of a uniform citizenship. It means that public policy should not (primarily) be based on the needs and interests of the citizenry as a cohesive entity—since the notion of such common needs and interests is a chimera—but on subdivisions or groups of society. It means that public officials must conceive of and relate to the citizenry, not equally and with an assumed blindness to cultural differences, but differentially and with great sensitivity and flexibility. Quite often, advocates of multiculturalism justify such differentiation with the analogy of distributive justice as in the re-allocation of money through progressive taxation (see Turner, 1997). Just like the state practices differential treatment with respect to socioeconomic class, it should do so with respect to religious affiliation and ethnic origin. Some groups are under-privileged in terms of income, others in terms of public recognition, and it must be the responsibility of the state to rectify both types of injustice—at least if one believes in distributive justice (cf. Fraser, 1997; Philips, 1999). Typically and more concretely, this argument leads the way for a general justification of affirmative actions *vis-à-vis* groups that over long periods of time have been discriminated against and therefore deserve compensation, such as African and Native Americans in the United States and Canada.

Thus far, however, there is no fundamental conflict over differential treatment. Most egalitarian liberals support affirmative action in cases such as the above—although as a retroactive and individual compensation for unevenly distributed opportunities—and they see it as a temporary means to the more permanent ends of inclusion and integration. The multicultural claims for differential treatment do not stop here, however. A public policy based on differentiality does not only imply compensating the weak, marginalized, and stigmatized; it also implies protecting and seeking recognition of the differences that matter the most to such groups. Indeed, if the subtle subordination and gradual assimilation of minorities is the problem, then the protection of differences must be the prime objective of toleration. Typically, such differential policy is implemented through the establishment of group rights that serve to protect "endangered minority cultures" that are threatened by assimilation into majority culture. In some cases such groups are exempted from legislation that is binding to the rest of society—for example, the exemption from the obligation to wear a motorcycle helmet (Sikhs) or to respect the Christian tradition to refrain from commerce on Sundays. In other cases minority groups are granted special rights and provisions that serve to protect important elements of their culture—such as linguistic and educational rights. In cases such as these, especially the latter, differential treatment becomes controversial because it is incompatible with the liberal norm of universality .

The second norm is a logical consequence of the first. The urge to differentiate between ethnic and religious groups in society is a direct plea for *state activism*. It is not enough for the state, as the liberal would argue, to even-handedly stimulate the formation of voluntary ethnic associations and a vibrant civil society. The state must also take an active part in singling out, empowering, and protecting cultural minorities. In many countries throughout the West, such activism has increased over the last decades. In the United States, for example, the now dominant "ethno-racial pentagon," as Hollinger calls it, consists of the following five groups defined on the basis of skin color and descent: Euro-Americans, Asian-Americans, African-Americans, Hispanics, and Indigenous people (Hollinger, 2000, 23). In a growing number of policy areas the pentagon is used to categorize citizens, thus enabling a host of differential treatment policies initiated and monitored by public authorities (Hollinger, 2000, chap. 2). Hence, classifications such as the pentagon offer a necessary instrument for states that actively seek to empower minority and powerless groups, multiculturalists argue, by using the very traits for which those groups were discriminated against as points of resistance and public recognition.

To sum up, the move from universality to particularity in the practice and organization of toleration marks a simultaneous move away from the public–private distinction, which is so central to liberalism. If the personal characteristics that liberalism defines as private—skin color, ethnicity, and religion—form the basis for public policy, the boundary between the private and the public sphere begins to erode. And, if citizenship is divided into cultural subgroups with special exemptions, rights, and freedoms, the very characteristic that distinguishes the public from the private sphere—uniformity—disappears. For these reasons, the "politics of difference" advocated by multiculturalists (cf. Young, 1990) is highly controversial from a liberal point of view. Nevertheless, it is a logical result of the shift from beliefs to identities and from neutrality to recognition. The resulting multicultural solution to being "together and apart" is a different model of toleration. It substitutes the division between private individuals and public citizens for an alternative division between different groups of citizens constituted on the basis of cultural identities that perforate the "old" boundary between public and private—African-Americans, female Americans, homosexual Americans, and so forth.

REASSESSING LIBERAL TOLERATION

In conclusion I want to return to the distinction between toleration as permission and toleration as equal respect. As stated in the first section, the dichotomy provides an instrument of evaluation that helps us distinguish between "good" and "bad" forms of toleration. Equal respect means not only acceptance, but *equal* acceptance of all tolerable forms of behavior, ideas, lifestyles, and beliefs, regardless of how many or how few, how common or how unusual the members and the practices of the group may be. This is what both liberals and multiculturalists have in mind when they speak of multicultural toleration. The question is, does the liberal theory of toleration do enough to promote this ideal? The multiculturalist answer to this question is "no," as we have seen, and I think there are important lessons for liberals to learn from that critique. What multiculturalists like Taylor, Kymlicka, Parekh, and others have managed to do is point out blind spots in liberal theory that affect how we think about and practice toleration. What they have not managed to do, however, is to present coherent and consistent alternatives to the theories they criticize. In these last pages I will therefore address some of the assumptions behind the multiculturalist critique and make some suggestions regarding what liberals should make of them.

Which Identities Matter?

The individualism for which liberalism has received so much criticism by Marxists, communitarians, feminists, and now multiculturalists can be divided into two different elements that one needs to discuss separately. The first is the *ontological aspect* of this individualism. Clearly, the multicultural claim that individual beliefs, interests, and commitments develop through (involuntary) socialization in cultural environments replete with norms and values, is true. Inasmuch as this is the case, it may seem more accurate to talk about toleration of collectively shared identities than of individually chosen beliefs. It is quite unclear, however, what this should imply for a theory of toleration. People have many identities that matter in defining their beliefs, passions, and interests as individuals. Moreover, these identities are not stable and constant over time; some of them are strengthened by external circumstances and events, others fade away, and new ones appear. Depending on the context and situation some identity becomes more relevant than the others, and depending on the identity, some communal attachment becomes stronger than the others. For this reason, framing the identity of a black Jewish single mother born in Ethiopia and living in London, for example, is no simple thing. There is no objective and singular way of classifying who this person really is and which group of citizens she really belongs to. Still, it seems undeniable that this is what a toleration based on identity must do. In order to tolerate people for what they *really* are, we must group them together under different labels that explain how they are similar to one another and how they are different from other groups. Thus, in order to defend toleration based on a politics of identity, we must assume that the element that defines who a person really is, her *self*, is a collectively shared identity that needs to be dug out and recognized in public. The problem with the conception of the self, which multiculturalists are forced to accept because of their striving for group recognition, is a strikingly naïve, unsubtle, and essentialist notion of identity (cf. Appiah, 1994, 155–156; Hollinger, 1999, 122; Benhabib, 2002, 61–64). The consequence of this conception and the politics of recognition that go with it is a model of toleration that tends to lock individuals into groups that are defined on the basis of superficial characteristics such as skin color and descent; group identities that the members in question may not have had chosen themselves if given the opportunity. The danger with this emphasis on identity, then, is that it runs the risk of limiting the freedom of people, or more precisely persons, to choose their own commitments by blocking out alternative identities that may matter as much or more to them. Admittedly, Kymlicka argues that such "internal restrictions" must not be permitted, but when the very existence of group autonomy granted by the state hinges on the persuasiveness of cultural authenticity and difference, it is quite easy to see just how strong the incitements to forge and reproduce such authenticity and difference must be. Viewed from this perspective, it is uncertain what liberal toleration stands to gain from a more identity-oriented conception of toleration. In fact, it can be argued that the liberal individualist conception of the self—which represents a guiding ideal of individual freedom and diversity rather than a theory of the constitution of personal identity—is defensible simply because it makes no over-simplifying and essentializing assumptions about identity. As such it provides better conditions for toleration of difference, not just between but within groups.

The second aspect of liberal individualism is individualism as a level of analysis. In this respect, it seems to me that the charge against it by multiculturalists is more relevant and convincing. The (classical) liberal tendency to see societal diversity as a result of differences in personal beliefs, aspirations, and lifestyles is a result of such individualism, which has little to do with the conception of the self and much more to do with where and how one looks at society. In focusing on the individual, it is difficult to see injustices and inequalities that are structural and collective in origin. Egalitarian liberalism has over the years to some extent accommodated the critique by Marxists and feminists of structural injustices associated with class and gender. Culture as ethnicity and religion, however, is more difficult for liberals since it is conceived of as more subjective and (partly) chosen identity than social class and sex, in which case it falls into the category "personal and private" as opposed to "collective and public." As indicated in the previous section, however, I do not think that this has to be the case for a liberal theory of toleration. Just like egalitarian liberals support progressive taxation to rectify some of the unjust rewards of the free market, they have come to support affirmative action with respect to, not only women, but ethnic minorities as well. It must be kept in mind, though, that the liberal justification of such measures is quite different from the multiculturalist's. To the egalitarian liberal, affirmative action is justified as a temporary means to compensate for historical and structural injustices, and as a means of leveling the playing field with the aim of granting equal opportunities and respect—or at least something close to it—to everybody. Hence, the aim is individual empowerment and integration and not, as in the case of multiculturalism, differentiation and protection of group autonomy.

Neutrality of What?

My second observation has to do with the liberal conception of state neutrality. There is something alarmingly important about the multicultural critique of liberal neutrality, because if true it is very serious. The production and reproduction of an allegedly neutral, egalitarian public culture that in fact serves only the interests of a dominant class of the majority is not compatible with any theory of liberal toleration. Part of this problem, however, has to do with the concept of *state neutrality*, the meaning of which is far from evident. It seems to me that mainstream liberalism is clinging to a concept or ideal that is vague, contested, and to some extent also futile, because it causes a degree of confusion that exceeds the merits it brings. In order to make this point, I need to distinguish between two kinds of neutrality, just like I did with respect to individualism above. The first of these is neutrality with respect to the kind of moral or value diversity with which liberals traditionally have been occupied (see Rawls, 1993). In this respect, I think critics such as Parekh and Taylor are right on target. Liberalism is not neutral. Just like other theories of political philosophy it builds on a particular conception of the human good with ensuing interpretations—freedom, autonomy, equality, human dignity, self-development, et cetera—which have priority over other, nonetheless esteemed, ideals and goods—e.g., solidarity, loyalty, contentment, selflessness (Galston, 1991; Parekh, 2000, 338–339). Liberal individualism is also a culture, and just like other cultures it is molded and reproduced by the institutions of the liberal state, as Charles Taylor correctly points out: "the free individual who affirms himself as such already has an obligation to complete, restore, or sustain the society within which this identity is possible" (Taylor, 1985, 209). And so, just like some liberal critics of neutralism have argued before (see among others Barry, 1973; Galston, 1991; and Macedo, 1990), I believe that recognizing this ethical basis or inclination of liberalism, which is not only procedural but also substantive, would give a more accurate, clear, and convincing picture of what liberalism is and what it is not. It would also (hopefully) do away with the delusion that liberalism is transcendental and equally natural in all environments. Finally, I think it might help rectify one of the great weaknesses of liberal toleration: the inability to draw a clear boundary between toleration and indifference. The neutral state that can only intervene when direct physical or emotional harm can be proven often works as a *carte blanche* for politicians and bureaucrats to evade responsibility and commitment by claiming to be tolerant. A non-neutral state that openly recognizes a set of values and a conception of the human good is less likely, *ceteris paribus*, to conflate toleration with indifference. Such guidance, with respect not only to the means of greater toleration but also to the necessary *limits* of toleration, is crucial in a multicultural society.

Does this mean that the liberal state cannot be neutral? Obviously, in terms of moral diversity, this is what the above conception of liberalism means. I do not think, however, that this implies that we also have to abandon the idea of neutrality with respect to the secular and civic state, as Kymlicka and others suggest. To strive for a public culture devoid of ethnic and religious traits is not tantamount to ignorance or insensitivity to the historical discrimination of minorities, nor is it tantamount to denying that most, if not all, nation-states have one majoritarian identity that has been more influential than others in defining the content and scope of public culture. It is probably true that most modern liberals have been naïve and perhaps deliberately ignorant of the ethno-cultural component of the modern nation-state. But this ethno-cultural component is a fact of historical development, not an inherent condition of liberal theory. The answer may very well be more and not less liberalism. The argument that Kymlicka and other multiculturalists are trying make is mainly circumstantial, as a lawyer would call it. And the proposed solution with ethnically segmented citizenships through differential rights strikes me as both exaggerated and counterproductive, at least if applied as a permanent model and not as temporary means. What it all comes down to, I think, is whether or not the numerical superiority of the majority should be conceived as a source of power asymmetries so great that toleration as equal respect becomes impossible. The way the multiculturalist argument is framed this seems to be the general conception. Admittedly, it would be foolish to deny that members of the majority tend to dominate political and economical resources in multicultural societies, if for no other reason than for the simple fact that there are more of them than of the minorities. Does this mean that toleration through the universalistic and uniform liberal citizenship can never lead to completely equal respect? Possibly. But, if so, what will? Trying to compensate minorities for their numerical inferiority through particularistic, protectionist, and "tailor-made" citizenships is not likely to do the job. The potential groups that may come in question for such differential and protective rights are not natural and objective in any meaningful sense of the word, as I argued in the previous section. They have to be deliberately constituted and evoked—"invented"— in order to be real and politically relevant. The role of the state in the constitution of such groups is crucial and must therefore be handled with great care and moderation. In most cases, I would rather have a liberal state that actively promotes integration of all through a vibrant civil society and a social welfare system dedicated to creating equal opportunities, than a multicultural state that tries to meet the changing needs of changing groups through differential rights and ethno-cultural enclavization.

REFERENCES

Appiah, A. K., 1994. Identity, authenticity, survival: Multicultural societies and social reproduction. In A. Gutman (ed.), *Multiculturalism: Examining the politics of recognition*. Princeton: Princeton University Press.

Bader, V., 1997. The cultural conditions of transnational citizenship: On the interpretation of political and ethnic cultures. *Political Theory* 25(6): 771–813.

Barry, B., 2001. *Culture and equality*. Cambridge: Polity Press.

Barry, B., 1973. *The Liberal theory of justice*. Oxford: Clarendon Press.

Bejczy, I., 1997. Tolerantia: a medieval concept. *Journal of the History of Ideas* 58(3): 365–384.

Benhabib, S., 2002. *The claims of culture: Equality and diversity in the global era*. Princeton: Princeton University Press.

Braude, B., and Bernard L. (eds.), 1982. *Christians and Jews in the Ottoman empire: The functioning of a plural society*, vol. 1. New York: Holmes and Meier.

Briggs, X. de Souza., 2004. Civilization in color: The multicultural city in three millennia. *City and Community* 3(4): 311–342.

Castles, S., and Alastair D., 2000. *Citizenship and migration: Globalization and the politics of belonging*. Hampshire and New York: Palgrave.

Cohen, A. J., 2004. What toleration is. *Ethics* 115: 68–95.

Creppell, I., 2003. *Toleration and identity: Foundations in early modern thought*. New York and London: Routledge.

Fiala, A., 2003. Stoic tolerance. *Res Publica* 9: 149–168.

Forst, R., 2004. The limits of toleration. *Constellations* 11(3): 312–325.

Fraser, N., 1997. *Justice interruptus: Critical reflections on the "postsocialist" condition*. New York: Routledge.

Galeotti, A. E., 2002. *Toleration as recognition*. Cambridge: Cambridge University Press.

Galston, W., 1991. *Liberal purposes: Goods, virtues, and duties in the liberal state*. Cambridge: Cambridge University Press.

Gauthier, D., 1986. *Morals by agreement*. Oxford: Oxford University Press.

Grell, O. P., and Scribner B. (eds.), 1996. *Tolerance and intolerance in the European Reformation*. Cambridge: Cambridge University Press.

Habermas, J., 2003. *Religious tolerance—the pacemaker for cultural rights. Philosophy* 79: 5–18.

Habermas, J., 2001. The postnational condition and the future of democracy. In M. Pensky (ed.), *Jürgen Habermas: The postnational constellation: Political essays.* Cambridge, Mass.: MIT Press.

Habermas, J., 1992. Citizenship and national identity: Some reflections on the future of Europe. *Praxis International* 12(1): 1–19.

Held, D., 1989. *Political theory and the modern state.* Cambridge: Polity Press.

Hollinger, D., 2000. *Postethnic America: Beyond multiculturalism.* New York: Basic Books.

Hollinger, D., 1999. Authority, solidarity and the political economy of identity: The case of the United States. *Diacritics* 29(4): 116–127.

Ignatieff, M., 1993. *Blood and belonging: Journeys into the new nationalism.* London: Vintage.

Kohn, H., 1944. *The idea of nationalism: A study of its origins and background.* New York: Macmillan.

Kymlicka, W., 1995. *Multicultural citizenship.* Oxford: Oxford University Press.

Locke, J., 2003[1689]. A letter concerning toleration. In I. Shapiro (ed.), *Two treatises of government and a letter concerning toleration. John Locke.* New Haven and London: Yale University Press.

Macedo, S., 1990. *Liberal virtues: Citizenship, virtue and community.* Oxford: Oxford University Press.

MacIntyre, A., 1981. *After virtue: A study in moral theory.* London: Duckworth.

McKinnon, C., 2006. *Toleration: A critical introduction.* London and New York: Routledge.

Menocal, M. R., 2002. *The ornament of the world: How Muslims, Jews, and Christians created a culture of tolerance in medieval Spain.* Boston, New York and London: Little, Brown and Company.

Miller, D., 1995. *On nationality.* Oxford: Oxford University Press.

Nederman, C. J., 1994. Tolerance and community: A medieval communal functionalist argument for religious toleration. *The Journal of Politics* 56(4): 901–918.

Parekh, B., 2000. *Rethinking multiculturalism: Cultural diversity and political theory.* Cambridge, Mass.: Harvard University Press.

Parekh, B., 1993. The cultural particularity of liberal democracy. In D. Held (ed.), *Prospects for democracy: North, south, east, west.* Cambridge: Polity Press.

Phillips, A., 1999. *Which equalities matter?* Cambridge: Polity Press.

Rawls, J., 1993. *Political liberalism.* New York: Columbia University Press.

Rawls, J., 1985. Justice as fairness: Political not metaphysical. *Philosophy and Public Affairs* 14 (Summer): 223–239.

Raz, J., 1998. Multiculturalism. *Ratio Juris* 11(3): 193–205.

Raz, J., 1986. *The morality of freedom.* Oxford: Oxford University Press.

Sandel, M., 1982. *Liberalism and the limits of justice.* Cambridge: Cambridge University Press.

Sandel, M., 1984. The procedural republic and the unencumbered self. *Political Theory* 12(1): 81–96.

Shorten, A., 2005. Toleration and cultural controversies. *Res Publica* 11: 275–299.

Smith, A., 1986. *The ethnic origins of nations.* Oxford: Basil Blackwell.

Tamir, Y., 1993. *Liberal nationalism.* Princeton: Princeton University Press.

Taylor, C., 1994. The politics of recognition. In A. Gutman (ed.), *Multiculturalism: Examining the politics of recognition.* Princeton: Princeton University Press.

Taylor, C., 1985. Atomism. *Philosophical Papers* 2. Cambridge: Cambridge University Press.

Turner, B. S., 1997. Citizenship studies: A general theory. *Citizenship Studies* 1(1): 5–18.

Walzer, M., 1997. *On toleration.* New Haven and London: Yale University Press.

Walzer, M., 1994. Comment. In A Gutman (ed.), *Multiculturalism: Examining the politics of recognition.* Princeton: Princeton University Press.

Walzer, M., 1990. The communitarian critique of liberalism. *Political Theory* 18(1): 6–23.

Walzer, M., 1983. *Spheres of justice: A defense of pluralism and equality.* New York: Basic Books.

Williams, B., 1999. Tolerating the intolerable. In S. Mendus (ed.), *The politics of toleration: Tolerance and intolerance in modern life.* Edinburg: Edinburg University Press.

Zagorin, P., 2003. *How the idea of religious toleration came to the West.* Princeton and Oxford: Princeton University Press.

Young, I. M., 1990. *Justice and the politics of difference.* Princeton: Princeton University Press.

CHAPTER 3

Multiculturalism and Caring Ethics

Sarah Scuzzarello

From the 1970s and onwards the growth of temporary and permanent movements has become more globalized, diversified, gendered, and more accelerated.[1] This has put Western nation-states in a new, challenging situation as they are all trying to find a way of coming to terms with the challenges associated with the arrival and settlement of culturally, religiously, and ethnically different migrants. The years following the tragedies of September 11th, 2001, up to the riots in France in the autumn of 2005 have exacerbated the debates on migration, multiculturalism, and integration. Questions of whether Westerners and immigrants can live side by side have often been brought to the public fore, and several scholars talk today of a crisis of multiculturalism. Yet the debate on the "clash of civilizations" dates more than ten years back, with Samuel Huntington (1996) being its most famous representative. Alongside this debate, we have witnessed the emergence of intellectual and political movements led by ethnic, religious and cultural groups that argue for recognition of the legitimacy of their diversity.[2] Migrants have thus started mobilizing politically and are becoming increasingly active actors in the political sphere. Their demand for recognition goes further than a mere plea for toleration, however—the latter being problematic as it maintains stereotypes that mark the other as

[1] I would like to thank Tariq Modood, Catarina Kinnvall, and Paul Statham for their insightful and encouraging comments on earlier drafts of this chapter. I would also like to thank the Department of Sociology at Bristol University for the opportunity to work in a stimulating environment in the spring of 2007 while writing this chapter.
[2] Of course there are other groups making similar claims, such as feminists, gay/lesbian/ bisexual/transgendered groups, etc.; I do not want to minimize their importance in the contemporary political arena. Given, however, that the main focus of this chapter is on ethnic and cultural differences, I will not discuss those other groups' claims to equal rights.

deviant, as someone that the majority society should tolerate.[3] Rather, they ask for the acceptance, respect, and even public affirmation of their differences (Parekh, 2000). The question of how to deal with these claims has given birth to a plethora of public national policies that varies depending on a country's institutional settings and national identity (Koopmans et al., 2005). Within Western European academia in the past few decades, the debate on multiculturalism has been highly dynamic. Different authors have of course been informed by different philosophical approaches. Scholars like Will Kymlicka (1995) and John Rex ([1986], 1996) have promoted a liberal theory of multiculturalism. In their work, researchers such as Iris Young (1990), Bhikhu Parekh (2000), and Tariq Modood (2005; 2007) have criticized and reformulated those liberal responses to diversity. These authors have presented different arguments for the respect and recognition of difference free from the implicit assumption of superiority and inferiority of groups that characterizes liberal understandings of multiculturalism.

Along with the growing claims that the majority societies should recognize the legitimacy of certain group differences, there has been from the 1980s onwards a substantial development of what is today known as *care ethics*, which emerged as a critique of the dominant moral theories. In contrast with the dominant views that prize values such as independence, autonomy, rationality, and rights, an ethics of care emphasizes that human beings are ontologically interrelated to and dependent on each other, and we should therefore value those relations and the emotions related to them, such as empathy and shared concern (Held, 2006; Porter, 2006). An ethics of care has developed during the last twenty years into a moral theory that sees caring not only as a value but also as a political practice that goes beyond the face-to-face interaction such as the relationship between mother and children, and that it should concern "institutions, societies, even global levels of thinking" (Tronto, 1993, 145). As correctly argued by Elisabeth Porter, however, "there is minimal application of these themes to those political issues of international relations, where the care of distant humans is paramount" (2006, 98–99). I believe the same criticism can be addressed when it comes to the analysis of how Western European states have come to terms with the diversity brought about by growing migration flows. Feminist theorists working with caring ethics have mainly worked with the racialization of care work and on the establishment of new slave–master relations (Williams, 2002). With few exceptions, theorists of

---

[3] See Christian Fernández' contribution in this volume for a more accurate critique of the concept of toleration.

an ethics of care have not explicitly dealt with issues of ethnic, cultural, or religious diversity, and migrant integration policies.[4]

The scope of this chapter is therefore to initiate a discussion about how we can understand difference, and how we can come to terms with it from the perspective of an ethics of care. A critical and caring understanding of multiculturalism differs from the liberal and the communitarian approaches. It is different from a liberal understanding of multiculturalism because it questions the liberal principle of equality as based on the idea of original sameness (Sevenhuijsen, 1998, 40–54) and its understanding of human autonomy. A philosophy of multiculturalism informed by an ethics of care will also question the idea of group and culture as the basis for identity, something common to both the communitarian and the liberal under-standing of multiculturalism. In arguing for a critical and caring multicultur-alism I am not arguing that multiculturalism, in its more critical[5] forms (e.g., Young, 1990; Parekh, 2000; Modood, 2005; 2007), and an ethics of care propose completely different views of diversity and inclusion. Rather, I share Sevenhuijsen's idea that an ethics of care can be seen as a companion to critical multiculturalism. This does not imply, however, that an ethics of care should merely be conceived of as an "add-on" to critical multicultur-alism. An ethics of care has its own moral vocabulary that challenges the theoretical and normative boundaries that shape the context within which we interpret the life we live and thus excludes other understandings of morality (Tronto, 1993). This approach to ethics also provides useful insights into how relations of power and political processes are conflated with psy-chological processes, a process that is not always at the center of critical multiculturalism. Given its foundations in a feminist understanding of

---

[4]Fiona Williams has addressed the issue of difference and care and argues that we should move towards an "inclusive diversity" (2002), but she does not develop this clearly, nor does she provide an empirical analysis of the understanding of "inclusive diversity." Some authors, for instance Selma Sevenhuijsen (1998; 2003), would say that Iris Young has contributed to the development of the ethics of care. While it is clear that Iris Young was sympathetic to this approach to ethics (see Young, 1994), I would not agree that she has directly been involved in developing the ethics of care. From my understanding, her focus lies in the importance of empowerment and democracy, not on how to develop a caring understanding of democracy.

[5]I am not using the concept "critical" here to suggest that all these scholars situate their analysis in the tradition of critical theory as it has been developed by the Frankfurt school. I use the word "critical" in a less theory-loaded way to describe an approach to multiculturalism that is critical of certain aspects of liberal philosophy and that has a theoretical emancipatory ambition.

morality, an ethics of care adopts an intersectional understanding of power; i.e., it is attentive to the different positionalities of the gendered and racialized subject in different social relations and contexts.

I argue that a development of a feminist understanding of multiculturalism should not only be concerned with the crucial issues of gendered constructions of collectivities (Yuval-Davis, 1997) and with power relations within and between groups (Brah, 1996), but it should also see the caring practices and values as central to their politics and policies. By "care" I refer to a concrete political activity guided by a moral and theoretical framework that sees responsibilities as the very basis for our existence as relational and moral beings (Sevenhuijsen, 2000). As Fiona Robinson argues, an ethics of care will allow the analytical scrutiny of the contextual relations within global politics (1999). In the case of multicultural politics, an ethics of care, similarly to an "ethics of beauty" advocated by Nesbitt-Larking (in this volume), will open up the way for an approach that is more attentive to and respectful of the needs of migrant minorities, an approach that allows for an understanding of diversity that acknowledges power inequalities, and finally, an approach that emphasizes a model of moral obligations and responsibility; i.e., care that includes strangers. In fact, as Joan Tronto maintains, "the practice of care describes the qualities necessary for democratic citizens to live together well in a pluralistic society, and ... only in a just, pluralist, democratic society can care flourish" (1993, 161–162).

In the following argument I will present the main characteristics of an ethics of care. I will argue that a liberal understanding of multiculturalism, as presented by Will Kymlicka and John Rex, is inadequate to deal with diversity, as it reproduces a flawed idea of the subject and her or his relations with others. Furthermore, I will stress the importance of reformulating certain ideas of critical multiculturalism in order for them to be more attentive to the context that determines the conditions of their relevance.

AN ETHICS OF CARE

In this section I present the growing body of literature in moral philosophy that has challenged the traditional focus on the autonomous, rational agent of morality and on justice as the primary value of ethics and society. This approach stems from a feminist understanding of ethics that emphasizes a relational ontology, breaking the dichotomy between autonomy and dependence. The main tenet of this approach to feminist ethics is that people are in a relationship of interdependence, need each other to lead a good life, and, as

Selma Sevenhuijsen argues, "they can only exist as individuals through and via *caring relationships* with others" (2003, 183, emphasis added).[6]

The debate on an ethics of care has its origins in the work of Carol Gilligan, a developmental psychologist. In her book *In a Different Voice* (1982), Gilligan challenged a model of moral development put forward by Lawrence Kohlberg that seemed to suggest that girls progress more slowly than boys in reaching moral maturity. Gilligan and her co-workers argued that Kohlberg's model was valid only for measuring the development of one aspect of moral orientation, which focuses on the ethics of justice and rights. She maintained that there was another, feminine, way of interpreting moral judgments, a way that was more responsible and concerned with actual relationships between persons. She then concluded that women's morality does not develop more slowly, but rather that their interpretation of morality is different—but equal to men's. According to Gilligan, a more comprehensive understanding of ethics should encompass the feminine ethics of care and the masculine ethics of justice. Gilligan's findings have been heavily criticized for essentializing gender differences and have been questioned on empirical grounds (Held, 2006; Robinson, 1999; Tronto, 1993). Her work has been crucial, however, as it has embarked on an alternative, feminist perspective to moral problems, thus questioning moral values and practices that were presented as givens.

Authors such as Joan Tronto (1993), Selma Sevenhuijsen (1998), Fiona Robinson (1999), and Virginia Held (2006) have contributed to a move away from the debate on essentialist notions of gender differences to an exploration of how an ethics of care can influence institutional practices and our understandings of politics, democracy, and citizenship. Tronto is quite explicit in this sense as she advocates an understanding of care as a value *and* a practice. In her book *Moral Boundaries: A Political Argument for an Ethic of Care* (1993) she notes how, in its original formulation, an ethics of care did not really challenge Kohlberg's theory, as care was kept in its traditional place; i.e., the private, feminine sphere. If care is thought of as an aspect of private life, as the antithesis of justice traditionally connected to the masculine public sphere, it will be associated with household activities and thus will be greatly undervalued in most societies. From this perspective, care will always be an additional item to already-existing moral categories. If we are to take an ethics of care seriously, we need to begin by broadening our moral

---

[6]It is important to stress here that even if the ethics of care is important within the field of feminist ethics, it would be incorrect to maintain that all feminists wholeheartedly embrace this interpretation of ethics. See Robinson (1999, 11–12) for a discussion on this issue.

understanding of what caring for others means. We need to change the public value associated with care and thus restructure social and political institutions to include the values and the practices of care (see also Held, 2006; Hutchings, 2000; Sevenhuijsen, 1998). Thus an ethics of care provides a strong criticism of the private/public divide. This divide has traditionally positioned (rational and independent) political decision-making and deliberation in the public sphere, while nurture and care have been relegated to the private sphere, outside the realm of political and social participation. Feminists have argued that this distinction is flawed because it depoliticizes highly political issues, such as family relationships, and retains structures of power that position women and care receivers outside the public realm (e.g., Young, 1990). According to Tronto (1993), the public/private divide shapes how a society's morality and its interpretation of the good life are defined, and excludes an understanding of morality that values qualities and perspectives traditionally tied to the private sphere, such as, for instance, care.

According to Tronto (1993, 105–108; 127–137; 1998), an ethics of care is characterized by four analytically separated, but interconnected, phases, each with a corresponding value or virtue. *Caring about* involves becoming aware of and paying attention to the need for caring. The corresponding value is *attentiveness. Caring for* is the phase when someone assumes the responsibility to meet the identified need, *responsibility* being the value that counts here. *Taking care of* or *care giving* entails the direct meeting of the needs for care, the performance of a necessary caring task. *Competence* is the moral dimension of this. Finally, *care receiving* is the fourth phase of the politics of care and involves the moral element of *responsiveness*. These four phases of care do not denote a one-way flow from the care-giver to the care-taker. A person's position as care-giver or care-taker shifts in time and space. This does not only take place when our physical abilities are for some reasons limited by, e.g., age or illness. For instance, an immigrant can find herself in the position of receiving care when she is the beneficiary of specific policies aimed at preventing racial discrimination in the labor market. She provides (unacknowledged) care to the (more powerful) majority society, however, if she works within the health care or in the service sector.

Two of the values mentioned above need further clarification. First, I will look closer at the relation between care and responsibility. A work that might involve caring for someone can be carried out without a sense of responsibility for the cared-for. By paying taxes, the majority society takes care of immigrants and indirectly funds public integration policies. A committee that sets up a national antidiscrimination board or launches a law aimed at protecting immigrant rights takes, in a sense, care of immigrants. This type of care is not direct, but "detached" (Tronto, 1993, 144) and supports the opportunity of the most privileged to ignore certain adversities that they do not face.[7] In every modern society, it is impossible to always provide direct care to all those we might feel responsible for or who need care. Tronto rightly warns us, however, that detached care can lead some people to become deluded about how and who we are helping, for what reasons, and for how long. So, when non-Western migrants are in the position of care-takers, they become doubly targets of the process of othering. They are cognitively positioned as "others" to the majority society, *and*, as they are dependent on somebody else's care, they are alienated and devalued as dependent "others" to the rest of society, which is instead constructed as efficient and independent, an argument I develop in the next section. This can give support to discriminating views that see migrants as the undeser-ving recipients of care since they are not doing enough to integrate, to find a job, or to learn the majority's language. Furthermore, it can legitimize the majority's lack of responsibility for rooting out prejudice and discrimination because they themselves do not believe they are being prejudiced.

The second value I wish to clarify is responsiveness. It does not mean to put ourselves in the position of those who need care. Instead it means that we consider the other's position as she expresses it (Tronto, 1993, 136). Young's notion of "asymmetrical reciprocity" can help us to better understand this value (1997, 38–59). She argues that the idea that one should put oneself in the position of those who are less privileged is flawed, as it obscures the social positions of the parts, thus neglecting their different positions in the distributions of power. Furthermore, one's attempt to put oneself in the situation of the other often carries projections and fantasies about the other and their situation, something that is also ignored in the idea of reversing perspectives. Instead we should retain an asymmetrical understanding of reciprocity through a communicative interaction that acknowledges the specificity of positions of the parts involved and their unique life histories and psychological constitution.

Even though there are several ways of theorizing about an ethics of care, I agree with Virginia Held (2006) that we can distinguish some major features that virtually all proponents of an ethics of care discuss. In the following sections, I will unravel some of those features and contrast them with different understandings of multiculturalism.

---

[7] Tronto calls this form of privilege "privileged irresponsibility" (1993, 121).

RELATIONAL MORAL ONTOLOGY AND AUTONOMY

The dominant approaches to modern political philosophy, influenced by liberalism, interpret the person as a rational, self-interested, autonomous agent. Thomas Hobbes gives us quite a clear formulation of this state of the person: "Let us consider men ... as if but even now sprung out of earth, and suddenly, like mushrooms, come to full maturity, without all kind of engagement to each other" (in Benhabib, [1987]1992, 156). As stressed by several feminist scholars (e.g., Fraser, 1989), this vision of men is an ultimate picture of autonomy. The denial of being born of women frees the male self from the most basic bond of dependence (Benhabib [1987], 1992). He is born freely, out of earth, and is therefore self-sufficient from birth. As Held writes, this conception fosters an illusion that society is composed of independent individuals who can freely choose to associate with others who are always their equals (2006, 14).

An ethics of care provides a constructive critical perspective on the norm of independency and autonomy. In contrast to idea of the self expressed by liberal theories, an ethics of care is guided by a relational moral ontology, whose core concepts are relationality and interdependence (Sevenhuijsen, 2003, 183). It directly criticizes the assumption of the moral self as independent and autonomous, and understands the self as existing through a series of networks of relationship with others (Robinson, 2006, 13). We may of course perceive ourselves as autonomous, but this is only possible because of our relationships of interdependence. As Fiona Williams stresses, a paid worker's independence is actually achieved through systems of support by those who care for that person's children, house, cooking, etc. (2002, 507). The guiding line of an ethics of care is therefore that people need each other in order to live a good life and that they can only exist as allegedly independent individuals through caring relationships with others (Sevenhuijsen, 2003, 183). A relational understanding of the self entails people developing a sense of who they are because there are others who recognize and confirm their individual characteristics. Individuals do not remain fixed and unchanged throughout their interaction with others, but rather they derive their identity from the dynamic processes that are human relations (cp. Emirbayer, 1997).

The liberal idea that autonomy is the ultimate goal of human beings is reflected in Will Kymlicka's work on multiculturalism. In his *Multicultural Citizenship* (1995, 85–93), he argues that culture is necessary for a person's development as a human being. This is because it defines and structures one's world and helps in making moral judgments and reach human autonomy. On the other hand, culture gives a person a sense of identity and belonging and contributes to the construction of stable communities and to human well-being. The former is beneficial, according to Kymlicka, as it will lay the groundwork for a "good life"; i.e., a life that all human beings have an interest in living and where people can freely and autonomously choose the ends they think are worth pursuing. A good life should be lived from within; i.e., free from conventions and social pressures. When it comes to multi-cultural societies, Kymlicka draws a sharp distinction between national minorities, immigrants, and refugees and thinks that the cultural claims of those groups have different moral weights (1995, 95–101; 167–170). Since immigrants have voluntarily[8] decided to uproot themselves and to come to a liberal country, it is legitimate to compel their respect for liberal principles, argues Kymlicka. Immigrants can claim "polyethnic rights"; e.g., the right not to be discriminated against and the right to maintain their language; but they cannot claim right to self-government and cultural autonomy.

Looked at from the prism of an ethics of care, Kymlicka's theory on multiculturalism is problematic. In arguing that individual autonomy and self identity are tied to memberships in one's societal culture[9], he links the process of identity construction to a narrow set of meanings that disregards an individual's location and position in a society and ignores the multiple and processual ontology of a person's sense of self. Self identity is not only based upon a sense of belonging to an "intergenerational community," but is

---

[8]The argument that immigrants have *voluntarily* chosen to uproot themselves from their culture and to move is highly problematic, both theoretically and empirically. It makes little sense to argue that once I leave my home country I automatically leave most of my culture behind. Moreover, as argued by Parekh (2000, 103), if culture is so crucial for achieving autonomy and liberty, it is difficult to understand why a person would voluntarily choose to leave it. Empirically, Kymlicka's assumption is overstated. Even if war, famine, or economic difficulties may drive people to move voluntarily, there is no indication that this decision is taken lightly. Rather, the conception of *home* (country) becomes crucial for immigrants. Several scholars (Dupuis and Thorns, 1998; Bauman, 2001; Kinnvall, 2004) stress the role of the category of *home* as a bearer of security in that it links the material environment with an emotional set of meanings that is associated with physical and cognitive permanence and continuity; i.e., home is a secure base on which identities are constructed (Dupuis and Thorns, 1998, 28–31).

[9]*Culture, nation, people,* and *societal culture* are used interchangeably by Kymlicka (Parekh, 2000, 101), and they refer to "an intergenerational community, more or less institutionally complete, occupying a given territory or homeland, sharing a distinct language and history" (Kymlicka, 1995, 18). "It provides meaningful ways of life across the full range of human activity" (1995, 76).

constructed at the intersection of different personal self-narratives and is influenced by an individual's position in the distribution of power. As far as autonomy is concerned, it is exercised within social relations that make certain individuals more independent than others, not by abstractly independent persons (Held, 2006, 84).

Secondly, Kymlicka's proposition that one should live a good life from within presupposes, as Bhikhu Parekh points out (2000, 106), a distinction between inside and outside that separates oneself from others. Kymlicka thus relies, without openly acknowledging it, upon a culturally loaded understanding of morality conceived of as something to be experienced and developed inwardly. This separation of the self from others is underpinned by a conception of the self as a homogeneous moral subject that is inherently different from others. This division between self and other, however, is highly gendered and racialized and defines "the other" by what she or he lacks compared to the moral subject: autonomy, independence, the phallus (Benhabib [1987]1992, 279). An ethics of care moves away from this conception of the self and stresses, as pointed out previously, a relational ontology and a conception of the subject as fragmented and multiple, capable of experiencing the other within the self (Sevenhuijsen, 1998, 60; cf. Kristeva, 1991). This brings us close to a Levinasian understanding of morality (in Bauman, 1993), where the moral subject should be capable of being *for* the other; i.e., take unconditional responsibility for her, and not only of being *with* the other; i.e., physically close but ontologically separated.

Thirdly, Kymlicka's suggestion that "voluntary" immigrants have the weakest claim to cultural protection and that they should merely accept the legitimacy of state enforcement of liberal principles (1995, 170; 176–181) is problematic since this logic ends up stressing the a-normality and the inefficiency of immigrants in the recipient society. It follows that the only way for immigrants to become part of the recipient society is to undergo a process of socialization through integration in order to learn "how we—the majority—do things," a process that tends to become a reflection of power and exclusion (Scuzzarello, 2008). This has been criticized by authors like Uma Narayan, who warns us of "paternalistic care" that is reminiscent of the sort of care found in colonial discourse that construed the colonized "other" as "in need of the paternalistic guidance and rule of their superiors" (in Robinson, 2006, 14).

Finally, Kymlicka fails to understand the power of the context within which moral theories are formulated and thus reproduces ideas that function as boundaries to exclude some ideas of morality, such as feminist morality, from consideration. Joan Tronto (1993, 6–11) identifies three such moral boundaries: the boundary between morality and politics, the "moral point of view" boundary, and the public/private boundary. I find that Kymlicka's approach implicitly maintains the second boundary, which requires that moral judgments be made from a standpoint of distant, detached, and autonomous actors. Even if he acknowledges that "the state unavoidably promotes certain cultural identities, and thereby disadvantages others" (1995, 108), his standpoint describes a morality that views those who are most successful and adept in society, those who adopt basic liberal principles, as the most moral individuals. It thus preserves the privileges of the powerful ones and delegitimizes other understandings of morality and other ways of pursuing a good life (cp. Parekh, 2000). This is particularly clear in his distinction between the rights of immigrants and those of the recipient society. Furthermore, he ignores differences in terms of gender, age, and sexuality that position members of a specific group differently and thus obscures oppression as a systematic, structural process. I will deal with this question in the next section.

SOCIAL RELATIONS AMONG EQUALS? DEPENDENCY AND POWER

Several attempts to bring multiculturalism and liberalism together reproduce the idea of contractual equality (Kymlicka 1995; Rex [1986] 1996). John Rex expresses this quite clearly when he describes the ideal multicultural society as one where all individuals are equally incorporated and have equality before the law; where they have the same rights to exercise political power in the public sphere through the vote or by other means ([1986] 1996, 18–19). The idea that places equality and sameness as pivotal principles of ethics and of the constitution of a political system may seem an attractive ally to feminist ethics—at first sight. As pointed out by several feminists, however, the problems associated with the norm of equality reside principally in its underlying assumption of sameness; i.e., that all human subjects are identical to each other, that there exists a uniform human subject that can serve as a starting point for normative reasoning (Sevenhuijsen 1998, 42). This falsely gender-neutral language allows, as Okin stressed in 1989, most theories to ignore the highly political issue of gender and permits the reproduction of societal norms based on masculinity and men's needs.

Furthermore, this understanding of ethics ignores oppressive and exploitative social and economic structures and cultural norms that can prevent individuals from exercising political power (Robinson 1999, 64). This critique could be directed to authors such as Charles Taylor. In his essay *The Politics of Recognition* (1994) he argues for the recognition of the equal values and worth of other cultures. While I am sympathetic to this, his understanding of "cultural group" implies the (faulty) existence of homogeneous social groups whose members have similar social aspirations. One may thus legitimately ask who is included in the "we" that constitute a community. Yuval-Davis (1997) argues that one should be aware that women have historically been excluded from the public process of community formation. Women are instead expected to carry a "burden of representation" (1997, 45), as they are constructed as the symbolic and biological bearers and reproducer of the collectivity's identity and honor while being traditionally excluded from the public political realm. Furthermore, to argue that a community has collective goals is problematic, as it assumes what Iris Young has called "equality in access and voice"; i.e., that every individual has an equal possibility to choose a good life, to express her opinion (in Sevenhuijsen 1998, 65). This is not the case at all times. Single community representatives, not always democratically nominated, can be considered by, for example, public institutions as the true bearers of a community's voice, and their demands are therefore seen as the whole community's demand. This can in its turn conceal the needs of other members of the same community; for instance, women (Kinnvall and Nesbitt-Larking, forthcoming). This problem is overcome by an ethics of care as it works with a multifaceted, intersectional understanding of power (Sevenhuijsen 1998, 66). People's access to power often depends on the specific situation at hand. While one can be discriminated against along one axis of power, gender for instance, one can assume a more powerful position in regards to another axis; e.g., ethnicity. This has been one of the key criticisms that black feminists and post-colonial feminists have raised against Western feminists' idea of universal sisterhood (hooks 1981; Collins, 1991; Mohanty, 1993). When it comes to the construction and maintenance of social and cognitive boundaries between majority and minorities, an ethics of care opens up for critical reflection on why patterns of community-making serve to undermine the ability of moral agents to identify and understand others as concrete others; i.e., people with concrete history and identity (Robinson, 1999, 47, cf. Benhabib [1986], 1992). Positioning the needy ones as deviant from the normal, the autonomous self then becomes a cognitive process that secures the latter's sense of the self as not-needy and independent (Tronto, 1993, 145).

Several theorists of an ethics of care criticize the premise that social relations consist of exchanges among equals and the related assumption that these relations are voluntary. As Iris Young argues, many relations are between unequals, where one party is dependent on the other for some or all of her welfare (1994, 40). This of course poses a challenge to an ethics of care, since, if we fail to recognize the relations of power involved in care, we will fail to recognize that caring relations can lead to forms of paternalist oppression (Tronto, 1993; Sevenhuijsen, 1998; Held, 2006). Instead, we must recognize that social relations often occur among un-equals and that they are likely to be filled with contradictions and conflict. Therefore it is crucial that the one who is able to access power more easily is attentive to this and willing to use her or his power in a positive manner, acknowledging the interdependence of human beings—and consequently her or his own dependence on others.

The relational ontology typical of an ethics of care breaks down the dichotomy between autonomy and dependence that characterizes the current understanding of politics that positions autonomy and independence on higher moral rungs than dependence. This dichotomy fails to recognize the difference between dependency in the sense of *mutual dependence* for the achievement of a good life, and *unwanted dependency* that maintains an unequal distribution of power and constructs dependent people as unfit (Williams, 2002). An important contribution of an ethics of care has been to question the paradigm that links moral agency and full citizenship to independency (Young, 1990, 55). The idea of a just society informed by an ethics of care would accord participation in decision-making to those who are dependent on public institutions, as, for instance, is the case for many immigrants. They would not be relegated to the margins of the public sphere in particular interest groups. I am *not* arguing against the mobilization of oppressed groups in order to challenge discriminatory social structures and practices. I want, however, to point out as a problem the tendency to favor the establishment of particular interest groups, such as immigrant groups within trade unions or political parties, and the ways that those potentially powerful groups are used by the majority to legitimize their privileged irresponsibility.[10]

Several practices of multiculturalism are unable to achieve their emancipating and empowering goals because they fail to see the difference between mutual and unwanted dependency, and instead tend to prize the splendid independence and self-sufficiency of the traditional liberal ideal of the subject. In Sweden, for instance, national integration politics tend to elevate paid work as the overarching principle through which immigrants' economic and social segregation will be eradicated. According to the Minister of Integration; Nyamko Sabuni,

---

[10] For a study on immigrant organization in Swedish trade unions, see Mulinari and Needgaard (2003).

the most important undertaking for successful integration is to open up for increased possibilities for economic self-maintenance and empowerment through policies that facilitate employment and encourage the establishment of private enterprises (*Integration och mångfald*, 2006).

While paid work is important, this statement defines a norm by which economically autonomous immigrants are considered positively, as non-dependent. This construction of normality defines in turn who is deviant: in this case, unemployed immigrants who are dependent on social benefits. The mechanisms of this are of course filtered through existing structures of sexism and racism. Stereotyped assumptions about immigrants tend to be reproduced even in certain theories of multiculturalism whose explicit scope is to make immigrants integrate in the recipient society (e.g., Kymlicka, 1995). Implicitly, these philosophies stress immigrants' cultural diversity as something inherently diverse from the "normality" of the majority society. They are kept in the position of "strangers"; i.e., people who come in contact with the majority society but are not organically connected through ties of kinship and locality to it (Simmel, 1950, 404). Immigrants enrich the recipient society through their cultural differences. At the same time they are alienated and excluded so that the majority's cognitive boundaries are confirmed (Perrone, 2001, 50–53). Thus, multiculturalist policies informed by this theoretical understanding of cultural differences indirectly embrace an excluding understanding of difference that maintains processes of boundary-maintaining that secure a sense of the self as intrinsically diverse from the migrant stranger (Scuzzarello, 2008).

Iris Young's work provides an illustration here. In a study on policies for pregnant addicts, Iris Young, following Foucault, argues that people who do not conform to a certain model that defines social membership—where the proper, law-abiding individual is not needy—are punished because they are needy, dependent, unable, or unwilling to work (1994). Holding independence as a norm amounts to defining dependent people as second-class citizens. Thus, she argues,

> Because punishing the pregnant addict does next to nothing to prevent the birth of babies harmed by the chronic use of drugs of their mothers, punishment seems only to have the function of *marking the women as deviant*, publicly *reaffirming their exclusion* from the class of upstanding citizens (1994, 39, emphasis added).

An ethics of care allows for a different basis of moral responsibility as it shifts the focus from a model of contractual equality to a hierarchical model of social relations. The privileged and the more powerful would in fact refrain from taking advantage of the less powerful and would instead care for the needy and be concerned for their equality and rights (cp. Porter, 2006). Therefore I disagree with Fernández (this volume) that the answer to a more equal society is "more and not less liberalism." While I am sympathetic to his critical analysis of liberalism, I find—for reasons presented in this chapter— the ontology and the normative underpinnings of liberalism incomplete and, in some cases, flawed. By criticizing the individualistic, atomistic ontology of liberal political theory, the care perspective sees the persons as "concrete" rather than "generalized," to use the wordings of Benhabib ([1987],1992). Where the latter indicates an understanding of every individual as a rational being entitled to the same rights and duties we would want to ascribe to ourselves, the standpoint of the "concrete" person requires us to view everyone as an individual, with a concrete history and identity (Benhabib, 158–159). Thus our relation to other persons is characterized by equity and complementary reciprocity, rather than formal equality and reciprocity that govern the standpoint of the generalized other. Most importantly, this approach allows us to consider differences as complementing rather than excluding one another. This is particularly relevant when it comes to the analysis of multicultural societies where claims upon the recipient society are clustered around the rights to diversity.

CONTEXTUAL UNDERSTANDING OF OPPRESSION, DIVERSITY, AND NEEDS INTERPRETATION

One of the guiding thoughts in care ethics is to go beyond the mere normative stances of political philosophy and to formulate constructive proposals for restructuring the democratic practices in ways that recognize the giving and receiving of care as a central aspect of human existence. This is achieved through the combination of normative and empirical analysis where the examination of "the actual, concrete conditions within moral relations that can and do occur, and seeking to understand to nature of those moral relations" (Robinson, 1999, 29). In other words, an ethics of care focuses on the social, economic, and political contexts in which particular claims for justice, needs, and rights arise. An ethics of care does not seek to set out universal principles. Rather it is a practical, principled morality that refers to specific contexts, specific relations—not only of intimacy but of power— among concrete individuals. This does not make an ethics of care relativistic, as the values and relations it seeks to analyze are relative to a context, but can apply to more situations (Sevenhuijsen, 1998). The attention to particular examples of relations of power has been criticized by several scholars. For instance Alison Jaggar argues that the focus on specific situations prevents us from criticizing the social institutions that structure it (in Robinson, 1999, 103). Her criticism is in many ways legitimate, as several theorists of care have failed to broaden their analysis to include both the micro- and the macro-levels of analysis. I agree with Fiona Robinson, however, when she states that:

> Close attention to the specificities of moral situations need not obscure perception of the larger social context in which they are embedded if the process of understanding, knowing and caring for a person who is different from you involves an understanding that difference is actually constructed through relationships which are not personal but social, and which are often characterized by both power and privilege (1999, 103).

Analytically, this means that the development of a philosophy of multiculturalism that is grounded on an ethics of care must take seriously the relationship between practice and philosophy. The relationship between the practices and philosophy of multiculturalism is highly debated, however. While some authors argue that a stronger commitment to multiculturalism would help overcome the present state of polarization (Modood, 2007), others are more critical of it and tend to throw the baby of multiculturalism out with the bathwater because, in their opinion, it has failed to achieve what it promised (see Banting and Kymlicka, 2006, for a review of critiques of multiculturalism). A theory of multiculturalism informed by an ethics of care, thus attentive to contextual specificities, would adopt a position that does not only examine practices of multiculturalism in a critical manner, as many authors already do. It would also consider the reformulation of the philosophy of multiculturalism in ways that address the difficulties and flaws of contemporary practices of multiculturalism. We might consider reformulating a critical approach to multiculturalism, morally and politically, in such a way that it becomes more attentive to the specific institutional contexts in which the multicultural policies are set up, and responsive to the needs defined by groups whose members share a common sense of belonging and a specific political claim. This requests an open discussion of what Nancy Fraser has called "the politics of need interpretation" (1989). Taking for granted the definition of the needs conceals the fact that the interpretation of people's needs is a political stake, and in the context of multicultural societies and minorities' claims, it is *the* political stake.

An ethics of care has been criticized for being affected by parochialism and for defining the needs of others in paternalistic manner (Tronto, 1993). A care ethics that is seriously concerned with attentiveness, responsibility, competency, and responsiveness, however, would recognize the crucial importance of establishing a dialogue between care-givers and care-takers in a way that exposes the asymmetric positions of every actor. The approach that I am arguing for is in many ways sympathetic to Iris Young's ideas on group representation and the politics of difference (1990). As Sevenhuijsen argues, however (1998, 146), Young's theory does not completely acknowledge the fragmented nature of the self, and it can encourage thinking that members of a group have a clearly defined identity, that they live in only one world at a time (Calhoun, 1995). Arguing for a narrative approach to moral subjectivity, an ethics of care focuses instead on the concrete subject's stories about his or her needs to live well and her fragmented sense of the self (Sevenhuijsen, 1998).

It is important to stress here that I am not arguing against the ultimate scope of multiculturalism of groups' and individuals' right to equal dignity and respect. Rather, I am criticizing the philosophy of multiculturalism for indirectly maintaining the moral boundary between morality and politics (Tronto, 1993, pp. 6–9). Instead of consistently seeing morality and politics as a set of congruent and intertwined ideas, several contemporary theories of multiculturalism tend to focus too strongly on the moral principles that should inform the political world. Some of them in fact fail to describe how those principles should inform political reality (Taylor, 1994), while others at times underestimate how politics are influenced by philosophy, and vice versa (Parekh, 2006).

When we try to apply a conception of ethics characteristic of an ethics of care to issues of diversity and multiculturalism, we need to address especially one of the shortcomings of this approach: its focus on caring professions and on face-to-face relations; and its typical national perspective. Joan Tronto argues that the practices and values of care should be placed at the center of our political and moral universe (1993, 154), an appeal that Iris Young restated in 1994 when she argued that the values of an ethics of care "can and should go beyond face-to-face personal relations, to the interconnections of strangers in the public world of social policy and its implementation" (1994, 41). Despite Tronto's and Young's call for a broader understanding of who should be the target of caring practices, in 2006, the political scientist Elizabeth Porter noted that most of the examples used by feminist scholars advocating an ethics of care still tended to focus on the political aspects of the caring professions such as child care, elderly care, disability, and health—all of which involve face-to-face relations. When it comes to the field of migration, feminist theorists working with caring ethics have mainly analyzed the racialization of care work and the establishment of new slave–master relations (Williams 2002). Authors like Williams argue that the feminization of migration meets the need of professionally employed women workers who increasingly employ immigrant women as private nannies or cleaners. On the other hand, immigrant women also meet the needs of the public sector, which is increasingly hiring them in low-rung employment as low-paid workers in private institutions (Lewis, 2000). No doubt, issues such as the racialization of care and the invisibility of informal care are of extreme political and sociological importance, but I agree with Fiona Robinson (1999; 2006) and Elizabeth Porter (2006) that an ethics of care can and should *also* have a broader understanding of what the practices of care should apply to. It is from this perspective that I argue that an ethics of care can and should apply to integration politics and can contribute to developing a different understanding of multiculturalism.

WHERE DO WE GO FROM HERE—A CARING MULTICULTURALISM

Liberal understandings of multiculturalism, as well as several practices of multiculturalism, tend to reproduce an understanding of the moral subject as independent and autonomous. The needy ones are constructed as opposites to this view of the subject, and they are positioned on the lower rungs of the distribution of power. Even the more critical perspectives on multiculturalism tend to overlook and at times reproduce the boundaries that define a society's understanding of morality. In particular, the boundaries between public and private and the boundary between politics and morality are maintained. In this chapter I have argued that we need to reconsider the values and practices of care in order to formulate an understanding of multiculturalism that does not only aim at warranting groups and individuals the right to equal dignity and respect. In fact, following the principles of an ethics of care, we need to be attentive to specific sociopolitical processes of group formation and to relations of power within and between groups. This would be possible only if we broke down the boundary between morality and politics and revised the philosophy of critical multiculturalism so that it can address the flaws and difficulties of the practices of multiculturalism. Thus, from an analytical point of view, a caring multiculturalism would be attentive to the specific contexts in which relations of power develop, and would attempt to answer questions of who is claiming rights to public recognition. Who is defining the boundaries of inclusion and exclusion of a specific group? How can we reformulate the concepts of moral subject/ member of a group/citizen so that the dependent and vulnerable ones are not seen as deviant from what has traditionally been defined as the normal citizen?

An ethics of care does not provide a straightforward solution to the stereotyping and othering of immigrants that are embedded in the process of securitization of the self. I rather see it as a challenging attempt to redefine the boundaries of our moral and political understanding of multiculturalism to include the point of view of those positioned as dependent in the realm of moral political debate. In this sense we need to move away from an understanding of equality based on a falsely gender- and race-neutral idea of sameness (as advocated by, for instance, Kymlicka). Thus an ethics of care works as a critical companion to the philosophy of multiculturalism as put forward by, for example, Young (1990), as it departs from the assumption that the self is interdependent and acknowledges the inequalities of power in influencing the public sphere. An ethics of care, furthermore, allows us to see the other, not as inherently different from the self (because she is needy and dependent), but as part of the self, and it forces us to think concretely about people's real needs and to question what we ultimately value in the public sphere.

REFERENCES

Banting, K., and Kymlicka, W. (eds.)., 2006. *Multiculturalism and the welfare state. Recognition and redistribution in contemporary democracies.* Oxford: Oxford University Press.

Bauman, Z., 1993. *Postmodern ethics.* Oxford: Blackwell.

Benhabib, S., [1987]1992. The generalised and the concrete other. In *Situating the self. Gender, community and postmodernism in contemporary ethics.* Cambridge: Polity Press.

Brah, A., 1996. *Cartographies of diaspora. Contesting identities.* London and New York: Routledge.

Brubaker, R., 2005. *Ethnicity without groups.* Harvard University Press.

Carlbom, A., 2003. *The imagined versus the real other. Multiculturalism and the representation of Muslims in Sweden.* Monographs in Social Anthropology. Lund, Sweden: Lund University.

Calhoun, C., 1995. *Critical social theory.* Oxford: Blackwell.

Dupuis, A., and Thorns, D., 1998. Home, home ownership, and the search for ontological security. *Sociological Review* 46(1): 24–48.

Emirbayer, M., 1997. Manifesto for a relational sociology. *The American Journal of Sociology* 103(2): 281–317.

Fraser, N., 1989. *Unruly practices: Power, discourse, and gender in contemporary social theory.* Cambridge: Polity.

Gilligan, C., 1982. *In a different voice. Psychological theory and women's development.* Cambridge: Harvard University Press.

Held, V., 2006. *The ethics of care. Personal, political and global.* Oxford: Oxford University Press.

Hill Collins, P., 1991. *Black feminist thought: Knowledge, consciousness and the politics of empowerment.* Boston: Unwin Hyman.

hooks, b., 1981. *Ain't I a woman: Black women and feminism*. Boston: South End Press.

Huntington, S., 1996. *The clash of civilizations and the remaking of the world order*. London: Free Press.

Hutchings, K., 2000. Towards a feminist international ethics. *Review of international studies* 26:111–130.

Integration och mångfald., 2006. www.regeringen.se/sb/d/2279. Document retrieved 14 March 2007.

Kinnvall, C., 2004. Globalization and religious nationalism: Self, identity, and the search for ontological security. *Political Psychology* 25(5): 741–767.

Koopmans, R., Statham, P.; Giugni, M.; and Passy, F., 2005. *Contested citizenship. Immigration and cultural diversity in Europe*. Minneapolis: University of Minnesota Press.

Kristeva, J., 1991. *Strangers to ourselves*. New York: Columbia University Press.

Kymlicka, W., 1995. *Multicultural citizenship. A liberal theory of minority rights*. Oxford: Oxford University Press.

Lewis, G., 2000. *"Race," gender and social welfare*. Cambridge: Polity Press.

Modood T., 2006. British Muslims and the politics of multiculturalism. In A. Triandafyllidou, T. Modood, Tariq and R. Zapata-Barrero (eds.), 2006. *Multiculturalism, Muslims and citizenship. A European approach*. London and New York: Routledge.

Modood, T., 2005. *Multicultural politics: Racism, ethnicity, and Muslims in Britain*. University of Minnesota Press.

Modood, T., 2007. *Multiculturalism*. Cambridge: Polity Press.

Mohanty, C. T., 1993. Under Western eyes: Feminist scholarship and colonial discourses. In P. Williams and L. Chrisman, (eds.),1996. *Colonial discourse and post-colonial theory. A reader*. New York: Harvester Wheatsheaf.

Kinnvall, C., and Nesbitt-Larking, P. Forthcoming. *The political psychology of globalization: Migration, minority rights and the Muslim diaspora*.

Okin, S., 1989. *Justice, gender, and the family*. Basic books.

Parekh, B., 2000. *Rethinking multiculturalism. Cultural diversity and political theory*. Houndmills: Macmillan Press.

Parekh, B., 2006. Europe, liberalism, and the "Muslim question." In A. Triandafyllidou, T. Modood, Tariq and R. Zapata-Barrero (eds.), 2006. *Multiculturalism, Muslims and citizenship. A European approach*. London and New York: Routledge.

Perrone, L., 2005. *Da straniero a clandestino. Lo straniero nel pensiero sociologico occidentale* (From stranger to clandestine. The stranger in Western sociological theory). Naples, Italy: Liguori.

Porter, E., 2006. Can politics practice compassion? *Hypatia* 21(4): 97–123.

Rex, J., [1986] 1996. *Ethnic minorities in the modern state. Working papers in the theory of multiculturalism and political integration*. Basingstoke: Macmillan.

Robinson, F., 1999. *Globalizing care. Ethics, feminist theory and international relations*. Oxford: Westview Press.

Robinson, F., 2006. Care, gender and global social justice: Rethinking "ethical globalization." *Journal of Global Ethics* 2(1): 5–25.

Scuzzarello, S., 2008. National security vs. moral responsibility. An analysis of integration programs in Malmö, Sweden. *Social Politics* 15(1): 5–31.

Sevenhuijsen, S., 1998. *Citizenship and the ethics of care. Feminist considerations on justice, morality and politics*. London and New York: Routledge.

Sevenhuijsen, S., 2000. Caring the third way: The relation between obligation, responsibility and care in Third Way discourse. *Critical Social Policy* 20(1): 5–37.

Sevenhuijsen, S., 2003. South African social welfare policy: An analysis using the ethics of care. *Critical Social Policy* 23(3): 299–321.

Simmel, G., 1950. "The stranger." In *The sociology of Georg Simmel*. Translated, edited and with an introduction of Kurt H. Wolff. New York: Macmillan.

Taylor, C., 1994. The politics of recognition. In A. Gutman (ed.), 1994. *Multiculturalism: Examining the politics of recognition*. Princeton: Princeton University Press.

Tronto, J., 1993. *Moral boundaries. A political argument for an ethic of care*. London and New York: Routledge.

Tronto, J., 1998. An ethic of care. *Generations*. 22(3): 15–20.

Williams, F., 2002. The presence of feminism in the future of welfare. *Economy and Society* 31(4): 502–519.

Young, I., 1990. *Justice and the politics of difference*. Princeton: Princeton University Press.

Young, I., 1994. Punishment, treatment, empowerment: Three approaches to policy for pregnant addicts. *Feminist Studies* 20(1): 32–57.

Young, I., 1997. *Intersecting voices. Dilemmas of gender, political philosophy and policy*. Princeton: Princeton University Press.

Yuval-Davis, N., 1997. *Gender and nation*. London: Sage.

CHAPTER 4

Taking Risks for Others: Social Courage as a Public Virtue

Gerd Meyer

Insecurity created by the challenges of globalization and international terrorism touches virtually everybody. Violent regional and international conflicts and an endangered natural environment create helplessness rather than readiness to intervene. Feelings of insecurity are strengthened by increasing violence in schools and on the streets, and by racism and intolerance against people of a different color or culture. Political alienation and indifference result from a lack of trust in politicians, parties, and their ability to solve pressing social problems. If we look at social courage on the level of individuals and small groups or organizations, as social and political psychology normally do, we have to start from this wider perspective on global and societal contexts in order to better understand the *conditions for taking risks and showing social responsibility in modern globalized societies*.

SOCIAL COURAGE AS A PUBLIC VIRTUE IN A GLOBALIZED WORLD

Nesbitt-Larking in this volume explores in more depth the "phenomenologies of power in an era of uncertainty, the *subjectivities of risk and security*, doubt and certainty, trust and betrayal, efficacy and powerlessness, and identity and dislocation." We notice not only growing general feelings of insecurity, but also a lack of normative orientation, caused by the questioning of traditions and basic values. These feelings have many sources: social insecurity and strong competition on the job market; a growing demand for, as well as a lack of belief in, (more) social justice; demands of "flexibility" that make it difficult to plan and master life, hence preoccupation with "private" and material interests; as well as little inclination to take responsibility for collective, public, and global affairs. Following Beck (1999) Nesbitt-Larking observes the emergence of the "self-governing individual" preoccupied with "personal risk management." In the workplace, people adapt and keep quiet, many being afraid to lose their job (in Germany between the years, 2000 and, 2007, 60 to 70 percent said so). So, understandably enough, most people focus on themselves or their small "life worlds." They do not want to take risks and responsibility beyond their immediate concern, beyond their family, friends, or (at best) the local community, much less (if at all) for people whom they do not know, for abstract ideas of general or global welfare. Morale and values become individualized and ego-centered, and the postmodern attitude of "anything goes" gains ground.

On the other hand, it is obvious that parts of the population notice the dangers and consequences of inactivity, of giving way to violence and intolerant ideologies. There are *countermovements*, discourses and parts of elites that aim to strengthen public morale and democratic norms in both domestic and international politics. Political and educational efforts to foster a tolerant and concerned civil society, and widespread non-nationalist patriotism, both defending humane and democratic values, encourage collective responsibility and risk-taking for people and the world beyond narrowly defined circles. The threats of terrorism and a growing consciousness of global interdependence seem to enhance the readiness, at least of minorities, to defend a democratic society's core values and to look for more social justice for the underprivileged. More and more citizens notice that society disintegrates, and that it is enlightened self-interest rather than abstract moralizing when we ask for more social responsibility in everyday life, at the grass-roots level as well as from those in power. A growing number of courageous nongovernmental organizations and opposition groups criticize and mobilize for alternate ways of human development. Nesbitt-Larking in this volume draws our attention to concealed forms of subordination and passive resistance in contrast to open protest (or, as we may add, to public acts of social courage), to "hidden transcripts of doubt" and the growing potential not only for discontent, but for "human agency, both individual and collective" that may finally lead to systemic changes. One may debate whether Beck's and Nesbitt-Larking's relative optimism about the hidden power of the powerless and the potential of "self-organization" (Beck) will become effective in the near future.

In the last two decades, German democracy has been severely challenged by open xenophobia, violence, and a growing number of right extremists who have committed hundreds of crimes. In thoughtful, persuasive, and encouraging addresses, politicians, police officers, teachers, and journalists have appealed to concerned citizens to demonstrate social courage. Indeed, social courage in everyday life is in much demand: to intervene, to speak out in public, to swim against the current, to stand up for others as well as for ourselves, even if we are in the minority or subordinate, and even if some risks are involved. Not only in Germany are we confronted with demands to take responsibility, to act and not to look away where injustice happens: on the job, on the bus, in schools and churches, in political parties, in the community, or at the political arena at large. Many of these situations are not spectacular; often they do not involve violence and do not require heroic action, but "only" a little more concern and courage. But why is it so difficult to act with courage in conflicts where important values or someone's integrity are being violated? Why do some people show social courage, but others do not?

THE CONCEPT OF SOCIAL COURAGE

What is meant by social courage? Social courage is a specific form of courageous action–not just for myself (e.g., a bungee jump), but towards others and in public. What are typical situations, patterns of behavior, and motives of someone acting with social courage?

Social courage is a type of social action in *specific situations,* which are characterized by the following features:

- an event that violates the psycho-physical integrity and/or values and interests essential to a person or group;
- a conflict with others resulting from this violation;
- pressure to act, but also room for alternative action,
- an observing and/or participating public (i.e., more than two people are present),
- a real or perceived imbalance of power; e.g., the actor is in a minority/majority situation in a group, or in a position of subordination in a hierarchy, being dominated or dependent, which is often combined with a strong pressure to comply or to conform;
- risks; i.e., the success of actions with social courage is uncertain, disadvantages are likely and have to be accepted by the actor.

Social courage is a specific type of social action which takes place in specific situations (as defined above),

- in different social contexts and related publics,
- when a person or a group voluntarily stands up for the legitimate, primarily non-material interests and/or the integrity or welfare primarily of other persons, but also of herself or himself,
- following humane and democratic principles.

What predominantly distinguishes social courage from general forms of pro-social behavior (like helping, altruism, and solidarity) or from courage in general, is the *specific character of the situations* where it is in demand: there is a conflict, an imbalance of power, risks, or possible disadvantages, and interactions are public. Social courage is not limited to acute or single situations ("emergencies") that unexpectedly require immediate action. Often, but not always, there is a "perpetrator" and a "victim." It may also include situations in which dissatisfaction and pressure to act increase over time; e.g., on the job, in institutions, or in the community. If someone wants to act courageously in these situations, he or she usually waits for "the right moment and the right place" to articulate himself or herself, alone or supported by others.

Modes of Action

In most but not in all cases, social courage is displayed by individuals. Groups can also show social courage, however, mostly related to public affairs. Social courage is part of a specific type of social interaction, not a personality trait. It does not imply a permanent pattern of behavior. Acting with social courage can be spontaneous or carefully planned; it can be determined in a more rational, emotional, or intuitive way. In many situations, fear and other intrapersonal thresholds have to be overcome. In most cases, people acting with social courage do so independently of their chances for success or external rewards. Or, in the perspective of an observer, social courage does not necessarily require reckless or heroic action or even blind sacrifice.

As a rule, social courage means *nonviolent action*. Yet, as an exception, there may be cases of self-defense or emergency situations where in order to safeguard higher-ranking values; e.g., the physical integrity of a person, immediate intervention using force is necessary and legitimate as a last resort; i.e., if no alternative or help from outside are available. Much more political in character is another type of nonviolent public action: *civil disobedience*. It can be regarded as a form of collective social courage. But civil disobedience also differs from and "transcends" social courage in three major respects: (1) it usually aims at a larger public and wants to attract attention for some bad or dangerous state of public affairs that needs to be changed via policy and public conscience; (2) it has to be nonviolent, but it breaks rules and laws on behalf of overriding, legitimate values, goals, and interests; (3) actors are prepared to meet opposition and have to be ready to accept sanctions, including being taken to court. (Gugel, 1996) Civil disobedience is a form of resistance that involves the state much more than most acts of social courage.

We distinguish between three types of acting with social courage:

- To *intervene* in favor of others, in most cases in unexpected situations, in which one has to decide quickly what to do and to act spontaneously.

- To *stand up* for important values and ideals, for other people's rights or legitimate interests, often without acute pressure to act, especially in organized contexts; e.g., at work or in institutions.
- To *defend primarily oneself* (but in some cases also others), to stand by one's convictions, to withstand, to resist, to say "no." In many cases, this means to defend oneself, maybe also a group, or one's personal integrity, against unreasonable demands, injustice, harassment and aggression.

MOTIVATION AND JUSTIFICATION

Acting with social courage means standing up voluntarily, noticeably, and actively *for humane and democratic values, as well as for the rights and/or legitimate interests* of individuals or groups. Consequently, "courageous" advocacy of xenophobia, authoritarianism, and right-wing extremism, for hate, war, or violence to solve social conflicts, should not be regarded as social courage. One may question the normative option implied in this definition. If one prefers a value-free definition, any acts of social courage for any goal against the existing will of any majority would be included in the notion. It would comprise, for example, the courage of an extremist who wants to substitute an authoritarian order for a democratic one; or the courage of prejudiced and intolerant citizens who consider all Muslims to be potential or real terrorists who should leave the country. However, as a concerned researcher, I follow the normatively oriented concept of social courage (*Zivilcourage*) prevailing in German-speaking countries (and elsewhere in Europe). Hence I am not interested in doing research on courageous, but non-democratic behavior.

If one acts with social courage, then one voluntarily and publicly takes responsibility for others, but also for oneself. Altruistic care for others, *moral principles (e.g., social justice) and humanistic values (e.g., personal dignity)* are certainly a strong positive motive for social courage, and usually prevail in acts of social courage. But they are not required *by definition* as the *only* motivation and justification. Social courage implies the promotion of the welfare primarily of others, but also more or less for oneself or for a group. The rights and legitimate interests of those acting with social courage may be included. Social courage should be inclusive and universal, but in reality it is often restricted to one's own group or organization, yet without the will to discriminate or suppress others. In addition, altruism, solidarity, and general welfare–so-called values of "self-transcendence"–usually go with some "self-interest" to keep one's moral self-concept or a good conscience, or to follow the ideas of a group. Hence, there is always some personal satisfaction in helping (and avoiding the costs of non-helping), but there is *no dominance* of interests of "self-enhancement" (e.g., material benefits, professional advancement, power, support of voters, prestige, publicity).

Social courage is principally motivated by *non-materialist motives*, values, and interests. *Legitimate interests* are legally and morally justified goals. In a democracy this means actions that are "good and just" according to generally accepted norms and principles, in particular basic values and human rights in constitutions or in United Nations charters, ethical norms, and unwritten rules based on an overwhelming consensus in society. So, financial interests (e.g., money/income, goods, services), to pursue particularistic goals beyond democratic procedures, or activities that are unfair and do harm to others, are excluded from this *normative concept* of social courage. As it is not always easy to determine the limits between democratic or nondemocratic actions, legitimate and illegitimate interests, judgment will remain controversial in some cases, both in politics and in science.

Social courage is a concept that is so far *rarely used in English*. Instead, some authors (e.g., Staub, 2003, 2005, 2006) speak of *moral courage* or *psychological courage* (cf. Putman, 1997). The concept of social courage is similar to Staub's understanding of "moral courage," which he defined as the "courage to express important values in words and actions, even in the face of opposition, potential disapproval, ostracism, or a violent response"; and if there is no physical intervention, "it often requires only what may be called 'psychological courage'." According to Staub, it is "moral courage" only if the motivating "beliefs and values (including affective reactions like empathy) involve promoting human welfare" (Staub, 20, 2005). I agree with this general normative restriction, but acts of social courage are not *necessarily or primarily* driven by *moral* values and beliefs. Staub's definition also does not include legitimate interests whose advocacy is a major element of social courage in labor relations and politics. The term *moral* courage also tends to individualize and personalize, and neglects the weight of social determinants such as situational factors and institutional and systemic contexts. In contrast to moral courage, the concept of social courage is bound to specific situations (as defined above). As *social* interaction in smaller or larger publics, it is also more *explicitly* linked to its structural contexts and understood as part of a responsible civil society. The term *moral courage* also tends to depoliticize social courage as a form of public action that often has political relevance and a background well beyond the ethics of individuals. Yet the two notions are close enough to be reconciled in future discussions.

In German-speaking countries, the term *Zivilcourage* (*civil* courage) is predominant both in the public and in research. In Germany, however, the term *Zivilcourage* is mostly related to perpetrator–victim, emergency, or violent situations, or to bullying/mobbing, often with a strong political connotation. (e.g., Jonas and Brandstätter, 20, 2004; Heuer, 20, 2002; Singer, 2003; Meyer et al., 2004). I have also used the term in earlier writings (Meyer and Hermann, 1999; Meyer, 2004). I now, however, prefer the term *social courage* (*sozialer Mut*). It basically means the same thing, but covers, and may be more directly associated with, "normal" situations and conflicts in everyday life and society at large. Hence I use the concept of social courage instead of civil or moral courage in this chapter. (It may also be more easily understood in an international context.) Finally, if we want to stress the rights and duties of people as citizens, we may even speak of *civic* courage, similar to the Dutch *burgermoed* (van der Zee). So, we may choose different adjectives for this type of courageous public action depending on what we want to stress: the general social, the civil (also nonmilitary), the civic, or the moral character of action in different situations and sociocultural contexts.

To sum up, social courage is *an empirical, theoretical and normative concept.* Although referring here mostly to Germany, I am convinced (and supported by international discussions) that both the concept and the analytical approach can be fruitfully applied at least to most "Western-type" democratic societies. It is an open question, however, to what extent social courage is a *culturally bound* concept; e.g., the limits between the private and the public sphere, of legitimate intervention, may be drawn in quite different ways in different cultures: legally, morally, or habitually. In many Asian countries, for example, people avoid by all means "losing face" (or making others lose face) through open conflict. Last but not least, conditions are very different *in authoritarian systems* where repression is strong, and where to show social courage means to take serious risks–in extreme cases, also to jeopardize one's life and that of others.

EMPIRICAL FINDINGS: WHAT FOSTERS, WHAT HINDERS SOCIAL COURAGE?

In the English-speaking countries, little empirical research has so far been done on social courage (or what is meant by it here). The only exceptions are two special forms of social courage: whistleblowing (e.g., Alford, 2001) and the kind of heroic courage that it took to rescue Jews from Nazi persecution all over Europe, starting in 1933 (e.g., Oliner and Oliner, 1988; Fogelman, 1995; Monroe, 2006; and in Germany: Benz, 2003; Benz and Deutschkron, 2002; Kosmala, 2004; Kosmala and Schoppmann, 2004). Heuer (2002), in his excellent qualitative study of former German Democratic Republic citizens, used *habitus* as the main concept of explanation. John F. Kennedy's famous

Profiles in Courage (1955) deals with courage in politics, not in everyday life. There has, however, been extensive research on all forms of pro-social behavior for many years, in particular on altruism, helping, and solidarity (for overviews see, e.g., Batson, 1991, 1994, 1998; Bierhoff, 2000, 2002; Eagly and Crowley 1886; Staub, 1993, 2003). We not only draw substantial benefit from this research, but also from some related works in social psychology (for overviews, see Jonas and Brandstätter, 2004; as a synthesis of interdisciplinary research on civil/social courage, Meyer, 2004). More recently, several empirical studies on *Zivilcourage* have been conducted in Germany, focusing on young people; on problems of violence, bullying, and xenophobia; or on factors supporting social courage as proven by trainings and seminars (e.g., Jonas and Brandstätter, 2004; Labuhn, 2004; Labuhn, Wagner, Dick, and Christ, 2004; Oswald, Frey, Greitemeyer, and Fischer, 2007; Zitzmann, 2004).

The Design of the Pilot Study

In our pilot study on young adults in Germany (Meyer and Hermann, 1999), we wanted to examine the conditions and dynamics of social courage (*Zivilcourage*) in everyday life. The key questions were: Why do certain people show social courage while others, in similar situations, do not? What fosters and what inhibits social courage? What does someone think and feel, how does he or she interact with others, and how is a decision to act (or not) reached? Which experiences, which motives and values cause people to show social courage? Are there specific differences in someone's behavior depending on the social context and the type of public? As a heuristic basis for further studies, we wanted to find out more about the experiences, the inner dynamic of how social courage unfolds (or not), and the major factors shaping this type of public action.

In 1997 we asked 30 apprentices to participate–young people who in the German system were at the stage of getting a professional education, both at the workplace and in a professional school. They were between 18 and 23 years of age; they divided equally by gender; they belonged to various professions (workers in small and large companies and banks, doctor's receptionists, or manual workers from different trades); and they came from a large variety of social backgrounds. They all lived in two neighboring cities in Southwest Germany with 70,000 and 100,000 inhabitants respectively. In our qualitative study, we used topic-guide interviews of 60 to 90 minutes' duration, posing 20 key questions. We then developed a scheme of categories for interpretation, based on a combination of "grounded theory" (Glaser and Strauss, 1998) and qualitative content analysis (Mayring, 1983, 1996). In the light of later research, the findings of our qualitative pilot study still appear to be relevant, and many of them were confirmed later on in quantitative empirical studies.

We asked the respondents one week before the interviews to remember one or more social situations in which somebody had been threatened or discriminated against, or where there had been an open conflict, and where they thought "I should do something" or "I had better leave it alone," *and* where some courage was needed to say or do something to improve the situation. We did not use the term *Zivilcourage* (civil courage) in order to avoid any biased associations or moral demands. We were interested in the participants' "stories," of course not being able to verify what they had really done.

As a result, we got accounts of 41 real-life situations as recalled by our respondents, which showed different degrees of involvement, ranging from passivity to very courageous action. Six situations took place at the workplace, nine at school, eleven in the street, four on the bus, six in or close to a discotheque, five in a more private setting. Ten said they did not interfere. We classified actions according to our typology: seventeen intervened (type 1), twelve stood up mainly for others or certain values (type 2), ten defended themselves or others (type 3); in three cases we found a mixture of type 2 and 3 actions. We first painted a short portrait of each respondent and his or her story. We then looked for major factors of more or less courageous action in each of these stories, brought them into a systematic order, analyzed their interrelationship in general, and in four instances did in-depth case studies. Finally, we modeled three complex patterns of the inner dynamic of how people reacted in situations where social courage was in demand.

In our study, we mainly took *a situational approach*; i.e., we regarded the factors that result from the actual situation as more important than personality factors that we considered as a potential or predisposition that is more or less activated in a situation. So personality features function analytically as independent variables that partly explain the more or less courageous behavior of respondents. This is why in both models (see below) the situational factors received a prominent role in the decision-making process, or as major independent variables for the explanation of the results of (non-)courageous action. Situational and personality factors interact in an intricate way: situations evoke reactions that are strongly influenced by personal dispositions (values, personality traits, and biographical experience in particular); certain persons are more attracted by certain types of other persons and/or get more easily "drawn into" certain types of situations, and hence have more opportunities to show social courage—or not.

Here, I will first report the most important factors that hinder or foster social courage as we found them in our pilot study in at least a quarter of the cases and that were described in some detail. (Obviously, further quantitative measurements were either not possible or did not make much sense with very small numbers.) Then I will fit these factors into two updated models that are based on research on social/civil/moral courage and similar types of behavior.

Political, Economic and Social Contexts

Social courage can only be understood by looking into the specific political, institutional, social, and cultural contexts of interaction. The democratic character of the political system and its institutions, freedom of opinion, the rule of law, supportive moral norms, and a climate of tolerance in the national political culture fostered through education, the media, and social practice, are basic conditions for making sure that social courage is not an existential risk. In our study, we found, supported by many observers of the situation in the workplace nearly all over Germany, that the difficult situation on the job market and the insecurity in terms of how courageous behavior will be sanctioned at school and at work were the most important obstacles to showing social courage and risky solidarity. We talked to young people looking for their first job; but many others in Germany are also afraid of losing their jobs and social status if they speak up–and therefore keep quiet. Closely related, but also a historical legacy of German political culture, are pressures to conform and relationships of authority that are still effective in hierarchical institutions and in business. As an important general factor, we also noticed culturally, legally, and individually defined boundaries between the private and the public sphere as a major obstacle to courageous action even when the physical or psychic integrity of a person was threatened.

The specific social contexts are structural frameworks (i.e., power hierarchies, formal and informal rules and roles, elites, corporate patterns), in which we then find a specific situational constellation formed by particular persons and their interactions. Action is primarily determined by the participants' *subjective perception* of this social context, particularly by the room for action, legal provisions, hierarchies, the chances to exert some influence, and the internal "climate" of a company or at school. In interactions, the way bosses or elites use their power or how they are expected to, plays a major role. In our study, room for courageous action at the workplace was rated much lower, sometimes zero, than in schools. There we found a large spectrum ranging from strong support by teachers and principals to a complete lack of solidarity, last but not least, by peers in the classroom.

Social Position and Role

A person who perceives his or her position and role in a group or institution to be secure is more willing to voice his or her opinion or to speak up for others. Recognition by the peer group as a result of one's performance or personal qualities, a high status, and a feeling of superiority are important factors that foster social courage. Social courage is even more promoted if there is active support by others, or if one's status can be improved by such an action. Inversely, respondents were rarely willing to demonstrate social courage if they perceived their status to be weak or insecure, or if they were afraid of disadvantages (e.g., conflicts with colleagues, sanctions, exclusion from the group, or even losing their job). Formal and informal roles can also have positive effects. For example, the "official" role as a class spokesman provides a feeling of security, of legitimacy when intervening. To be an informal "leader" or "counselor" in a group made some respondents more inclined to stand up for others.

Our respondents displayed many types of *conformity*; i.e., the inclination to adapt attitudes and behavior to societal norms or group standards, also demanding that others comply with them. Depending on the social place, however, we observed significant variation in the willingness to conform, up to open rejection of courageous non-conformity. The willingness to display (non-)conformity in institutional contexts, in schools and in private companies for instance, is closely linked with fear of disadvantages. Our respondents' main motive for conformist behavior was the desire to belong to and to be accepted by their reference group(s), their peer groups for example. They tended to conform if they were afraid of being marginalized in the group because of nonconformist behavior; e.g., by standing up for others or principles that are "unpopular."

Situational Factors

Many factors that we found in our study have also been observed in research on helping, altruism, and conflict management. A crucial factor for showing social courage is to pay attention and to show concern for what happens to others, to feel at least partly responsible, and the readiness to act accordingly. Then the behavior of spectators or bystanders has a strong impact on whether somebody intervenes and shows social courage or not: on one hand, there may be diffusion of responsibility, pluralistic ignorance, or the fear of disgracing oneself; while on the other hand there may be support ("active bystanders"), solidarity in the group, or help from outside. A high degree of personal autonomy is favorable for social courage, but decisions are often the result of a shaky balance between autonomy and dependence on others' reactions. To understand this dynamic, two factors deserve some attention: characteristics of the addressees, and violence.

Social or emotional closeness to a (group of) victim(s) or to a problem seems to be more important than the (non-)reaction of bystanders. By closeness we mean a close specific or general emotional and/or social bond with the person in need of support: e.g., one knows him/her personally, or there is a feeling of belonging together and/or solidarity as a member of the same group, based on ethnicity, color, religion, or nationality, or similar experiences. In our study, all respondents said they would intervene (and did so in many cases) if someone from their own group they felt close or committed to was threatened or in distress. This included friends, a clique, or their own family. One person said: "If my family is concerned or my friend, I do need to help. In general, however, I'm convinced that everyone is responsible for himself." To most respondents, taking a risk for persons you feel close to appeared to be "natural" and went "without saying." For young males in particular, there seemed to be a kind of "code of honor" to intervene for their "buddies." Therefore, the "laws" of diffusion of responsibility and pluralistic ignorance need to be differentiated according to the specifics of situations, addressees, and group norms, and the degree of exclusivity of caring for others. In general, the willingness to take responsibility and intervene in favor of others increases with the subjective *closeness to the problem or conflict*.

The number of *violent situations* that were reported to us (and judging by many studies and statistics) allow for the conclusion that, by now, violence seems to be a fact of everyday life for most young people in Germany (and elsewhere). It involves personal violence as a result of jostling, fighting, and sexual harassment, or "just" intimidation by threats. Generally speaking, violence is a major obstacle for courageous intervention. Not surprisingly, the inhibiting threshold is higher the severer the actual or threatened violence is. Violence, however, is no obstacle, if one's own *friends* are concerned. If those are affected, then, among male respondents in particular, not even the degree of violence plays a role. Female youth regularly stood up for female friends, if they were sexually harassed or violently attacked. In these situations, they usually tried to solve the conflict through verbal intervention, often with considerable success. In contrast, courageous intervention became less likely if *strangers* became victims of violence by strangers. In this case neither the perpetrator nor the victim was known. As a result, it was difficult to judge how the conflict would develop and to calculate whether one faced the danger of injuring oneself. These situations occur primarily in the public sphere, in which anonymity is predominant. Here, few of our respondents said that they felt responsible for others.

Especially *women* reported that they met situations where they had to defend themselves against harassment or even violence, threatened or real, by men. The majority of women interviewed stated that, for sure, they would defend themselves against violence. Yet this was not always the case. In particular, personal closeness seemed to inhibit the respondents from defending themselves: Attacks by their own boyfriend or friends caused surprise and a lack of understanding among the women affected. They were rarely able to view these "friends" as perpetrators, however, especially if they expected their protection.

Personality Factors

In our study, we found that, besides the predominant situational and contextual factors, the combination of personal capabilities, attitudes, and motives, as well as the kind of socialization and biographical experiences a person had, were of major importance as independent variables to explain why some people take a risk and act with social courage and why others do not (Nunner-Winkler, 2002, Singer, 2003; Oswald; Frey; Greitemeyer; and Fischer, 2007). When social courage is shown, perceptions, attitudes, and emotions are probably more closely interlinked than in most other types of pro-social action, and they strongly affect each other–yet in which way is still an open question. The following list of capabilities or features of personality are, without a clear ranking order, also indicative of what type of efforts might foster social courage in education, on the job, and in the public arena of civil society and politics.

Personal, Social and Cognitive Skills and Capabilities

Especially conducive to social courage are the following personal, social, and cognitive capabilities and skills that function as individual resources or as a potential that can be activated in a given situation, if a person is willing and able to do so:

- Self-confidence, felt inside and proved in interactions; a positive self-image, a sense of competence, efficacy, "ego strength"; belief in your decisions ("to do the right thing").
- The ability to take quick, decisive action; to have a repertoire of adequate reactions or strategies, particularly in situations of threat, risk, and disadvantages.
- Moral beliefs and values (e.g., in justice, equality, tolerance, freedom); moral sensitivity and indignation; caring, feeling responsible for others, concern for the general welfare.
- Personal autonomy in groups and institutions, the ability to act in a nonconformist way.
- Empathy, compassion, sympathy, a personal closeness to the problem or conflict; and the ability to put oneself in someone else's shoes (see it from their perspective).
- The adequate assessment of risks, advantages, and disadvantages; and what you are ready to accept, both as "costs" of helping or non-helping; to let reason prevail.

- The ability for reflection and self-awareness, including your own anxiety ("angst"); the ability to admit fears, to keep control, and to avoid asking too much of yourself or others.
- The ability to respond to conflicts in an appropriate and flexible manner; e.g., to assess a situation and one's own competence adequately; the ability to calm down or to mediate; to know (and maybe having exercised) adequate strategies (e.g., of de-escalation).
- Communicative competence, the capability to articulate clearly and argue convincingly.
- Knowledge and awareness of rights, duties, rules, and operating procedures.

Motivation and Value Orientations: Social Courage as Moral Action?

Pro-social attitudes; altruism; democratic and humane value orientations; rational reasons and solidarity in the pursuit of legitimate interests; a sense of justice–all these orientations served as a main source of motivation and readiness to act with social courage in our pilot study also. Motivations can be *conscious or unconscious*. Consciousness, or the ability to verbalize motives, is not a prerequisite, but may support intra- and interpersonally, acting with social courage. But three *conditions* have to be met so that these dispositions can become effective as a main force in social courage as *moral* action:

1. Values and principles have to be internalized so that they are an integral part of a person's *moral self-concept*; part of his or her personal identity or integrity has to be kept intact so that he or she will not allowed it to be violated without considerable psychic costs.

2. Moral beliefs and attitudes usually need *moral feelings* to make people act (Montada, 1993). These can be: rage, indignation, or anger about the violation of central values and/or a person's integrity; compassion, empathy, concern; blame of others or shame, as well as blame of oneself; identification with actions and actors that are "morally right"; the pangs of conscience, to preserve one's own identity. We also observed a "negative" moral and emotional motive: to avoid the costs of non-helping, feelings of guilt and shame.

3. A *"caring" morality* that underlies the readiness to take *responsibility* for others, and also for oneself, a commitment that can be either emotional or rational in character. Caring is stronger if a person is seen as the victim of a culprit; moral responsibility is however refused, if he or she herself or himself is perceived to be responsible for his or her situation.

It is then an *empirical* question in which way and to what degree people's social courage is *actually* determined by moral motives, or whether these are used only *ex-post-facto* described as "good," socially desirable reasons to explain their actions (Oser and Althoff, 1992; Heuer, 2002). In general, in our study, *gender differences* in moral motivations tended to play only a minor role. However, at some points, we did observe significant contrasts. *Post-facto*, men referred to common moral values, whereas women hinted of moral feelings and connected them with a certain person. For young men the membership in a "clique" was more important than for women, who tended to stress the role of good bilateral relations. For young men the fear of losing their position within a reference group, as well as professional and material disadvantages, proved to be stronger obstacles than for young women. We have to leave open whether we met here two gender-specific types of ethics; i.e., a more so-called "masculine" one of justice and a more "feminine" ethics of care. (Cf. the general debate with Gilligan, 1982; Kämmerer and Speck, 1992; Nunner-Winkler, 1991; for further discussion on gender specific aspects of social courage, Grimm, 2007; on helping behavior in general, Eagly and Crowley, 1986.)

If positive action should be taken, it is obvious that its advantages have to outweigh the disadvantages, no matter how they are defined by the actor(s). It is a characteristic of social courage that those who demonstrate it, consciously or not, are willing to accept some short- or long-term disadvantages. In general, particularly if people stand up for others in organized contexts when they do not have to act spontaneously, those acting (or intending to act) with social courage weighed up advantages and disadvantages. There are many possible disadvantages: loss of time, other plans have to be postponed, other persons neglected; endangering yourself, getting hurt, at least all kinds of inconveniences. In our pilot study, we found that fear or anxiety strongly inhibits social courage, but fear alone does not prevent it. (It is not true that in all cases fear has to be overcome by courageous actors: some said they did not feel any fear; that it was "natural" to act this way; that "it went without saying" that they would do thus and so.) You cannot expect thankfulness, recognition, or career advancement; often the contrary happens. You may lose support in your reference group, or even become an outsider. On the other hand, there may be advantages such as being able "to express compassion, to demonstrate knowledge and enjoy personal competence, to follow your conscience and be proud that you stick to your principles, receive recognition, to show solidarity, to put an end to an emergency and to be a model for others" (Bierhoff, 2004, 64).

Social Background, Socialization, and Biographical Experiences

None of the "classical" *social background* variables seemed to play an important role in determining whether a person shows some social courage or not:

neither age, sex, or neighborhood, nor class or status variables like education, income, profession or public prestige did so. The effects of specific political or religious beliefs and organizational affiliations are not clear. But there are quite obvious effects of socialization in the family and at school, and in terms of the way in which biographical experiences are dealt with. In our study, we focused on relationships with actual persons, with parents, teachers, and superiors (on the job).

The willingness and ability to defend oneself against injustice or to stand up for others were strengthened if young people developed trust in at least one parent and were taken seriously in the *family*. It was also important that they could voice their opinion, or were able to settle conflicts openly. Social courage was also strengthened if children or young people were allowed to act with independence and responsibility of their own, and if they were encouraged to stand up for themselves–or, as one young woman put it: "My mother taught me that you always speak up if you do not like something ... that one does not put up with everything. You have no back-bone, if you say yes to everything and if you always do what others want." Someone who has learnt to act with social courage at home or among peers does not, however, automatically act the same way in hierarchically struc-tured contexts such as the school or in a company. Here, the distribution of power and one's own position, potential disadvantages, and chances of success are rather carefully assessed before acting with social courage.

Young people developed only limited self-confidence in their actions if criticism and *conflicts* in the family were suppressed or if parents educated their children to avoid conflicts. In this case, their present pattern was to avoid or withdraw from such a situation. Some parents were authoritarian and provided their children with strict guidelines of proper moral conduct. If young people accept these norms, then they may show social courage out of a moral obligation, driven by a strong super-ego, but not because of an auton-omous morale. They also tend to comply with the orders of authorities and to act conformingly to group majorities. An authoritarian education also influ-ences how one intervenes: Someone who has been socialized to perceive herself or himself as powerless tends to act in a power-oriented way; i.e., to intervene in an authoritarian manner for instance (giving orders, shouting), or will soon call upon higher authorities. In general, whatever the educa-tional background, subordination to personal authorities or strong social conventions inhibits or even prevents nonconformism and social courage.

In our study, we also found that the way *biographical experiences*, positive or negative ones, are "digested" is an important factor in the readiness to care for others by showing social courage. Above all, we have to look at experi-ences with discrimination, violence, and lack of solidarity. If such an experience is admitted and reflected upon, it may result in an attitude like "everybody has to care for himself; don't expect any help or risk-taking from others." Alternatively, a woman who showed courageous solidarity said: "Yes, I thought back to my childhood, I would also have been glad if I had some support." The willingness to stand up for others tends to be reduced if a person does not want to be confronted again with the role as a victim and/or a situation where he or she had no support when badly needed. Somebody is more prone to act if he or she experienced his or her strength after dealing with an awkward situation successfully on his or her own.

TWO MODELS OF ACTING WITH SOCIAL COURAGE: THE PROCESS OF DECISION-MAKING AND FACTORS FOSTERING SOCIAL COURAGE

Two models serve as heuristic tools to give, in a very concentrated form, an idea of the complexity of this type of public action. The process model (Diagram 1) reconstructs how *decisions* for courageous action are made. The factor model (Diagram 2) takes a systematic look at the *determinants* that influence behavior in conflict situations where social courage is asked for. It combines factors that we found in our study with variables positively tested in later, mostly experimental studies (Oswald, Frey, Greitemeyer, and Fischer, 2007). Many of them are also known from research on helping, altruism, and conflict management: e.g., the perception of the situation, the place, the contents of conflict, the course of interactions, and the social context. So, by analogy and transfer, they too may serve to generate hypotheses and research designs (cf. Bierhoff, 2004).

HOW TO FOSTER SOCIAL COURAGE IN EVERYDAY LIFE

Social courage is asked for in all spheres of social life as well as in dealing with the state and power elites. Its "place" is in both the private and the public realm. Social courage is a public virtue, demanding and uncomfortable for the average citizen as well as for those in power. We therefore have to ask first: *Does a society actually want social courage*, both at the top, among and towards elites, and at the grass-roots level of citizens? Based on our findings, we have our doubts with regards to some aspects of German society where we were alarmed by the lack of social concern and responsibility; e.g., on the job or in the streets. Nonconformists, people who contradict and stand up for "a right cause" (not grousers, fundamentalists, or extremists), are not

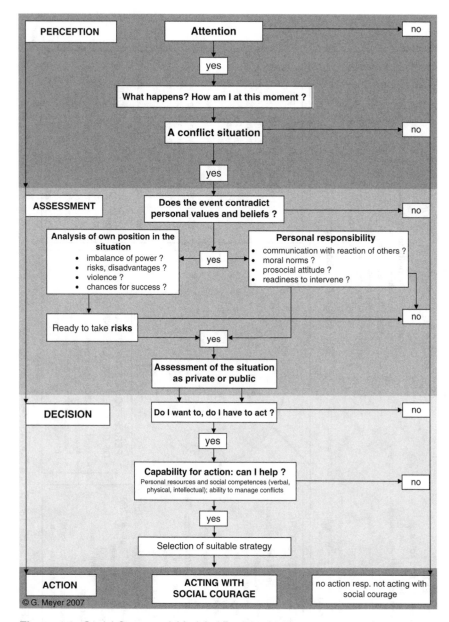

Figure 4.1   Social Courage—A Model of Decision-Making

necessarily popular or rewarded by their bosses, and they are less likely to make a career.

Social courage is an important characteristic of socially responsible citizens, of a vigilant and "caring" (Staub, 2006) civil society. Social/civil/civic

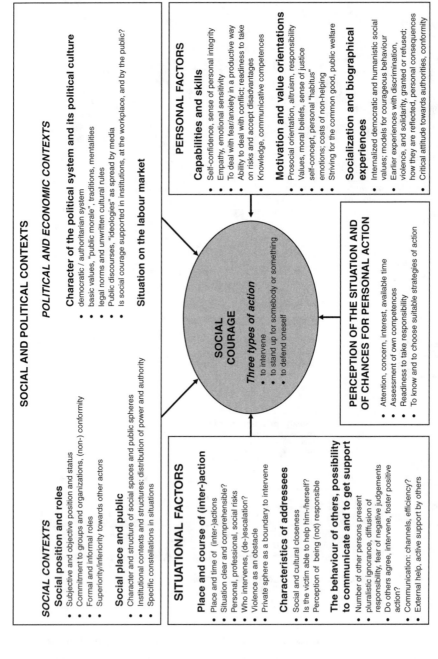

SOCIAL AND POLITICAL CONTEXTS

SOCIAL CONTEXTS

Social position and roles

- Subjective and objective position and status
- Commitment to groups and organizations, (non-) conformity
- Formal and informal roles
- Superiority/inferiority towards other actors

Social place and public

- Character and structure of social spaces and public spheres
- Institutional contexts and structures; distribution of power and authority
- Specific constellations in situations

POLITICAL AND ECONOMIC CONTEXTS

Character of the political system and its political culture

- democratic / authoritarian system
- basic values, "public morale", traditions, mentalities
- legal norms and unwritten cultural rules
- Public discourses, "ideologies" as spread by media
- Is social courage supported in institutions, at the workplace, and by the public?

Situation on the labour market

PERSONAL FACTORS

Capabilities and skills

- Self-confidence, sense of personal integrity
- Empathy, emotional sensitivity
- To deal with fear/anxiety in a productive way
- Ability to deal with conflict; readiness to take on risks and accept disadvantages
- Knowledge, communicative competences

Motivation and value orientations

- Prosocial orientation, altruism, responsibility
- Values, moral beliefs, sense of justice
- self-concept, personal "habitus"
- emotions; costs of non-helping
- Striving for the common good, public welfare

Socialization and biographical experiences

- Internalized democratic and humanistic social values; models for courageous behaviour
- Earlier experiences with discrimination, violence, and solidarity, granted or refused: how they are reflected, personal consequences
- Critical attitude towards authorities, conformity

SOCIAL COURAGE

Three types of action

- to intervene
- to stand up for somebody or something
- to defend oneself

SITUATIONAL FACTORS

Place and course of (inter-)action

- Place and time of (inter-)actions
- Situation clear and comprehensible?
- Personal, professional, social risks
- Who intervenes, (de-)escalation?
- Violence as an obstacle
- Private sphere as a boundary to intervene

Characteristics of addressees

- Social and cultural closeness
- Is the victim able to help him-/herself?
- Perception of being (not) responsible

The behaviour of others, possibility to communicate and to get support

- Number of other persons present
- pluralistic ignorance, diffusion of responsibility, fear of negative judgements
- Do others agree, intervene, foster positive action?
- Communication: channels, efficiency?
- External help, active support by others

PERCEPTION OF THE SITUATION AND OF CHANCES FOR PERSONAL ACTION

- Attention, concern, interest, available time
- Assessment of own competences
- Readiness to take responsibility
- To know and to choose suitable strategies of action

Figure 4.2 What Fosters, What Hinders Social Courage?–A Factor Model

courage is a *key element of a democratic political culture,* of democracy understood as a way of life and a principle of social organization, not just as rules
for the state and political decision-making. But the more we get into public
affairs, at least courage, if not social courage is needed by those who utter
public criticism of the powerful, by dissidents and minorities. (In politics, often
no clear distinction is made between courage in general and social/civil
courage in the specific sense as defined above.) Social courage becomes an
even riskier virtue for whistleblowers, investigative journalists who dare to
reveal public scandals, or for active politicians who disagree with the majority
of their own party or parliamentary group. So we need to change structures,
norms and behavior that create feelings of powerlessness and fear.

If a society truly wants to promote social courage in key sectors, it has to
appreciate and publicly support courageous intervention in favor of others.
It has to create an atmosphere fostering "top-down" and "bottom-up" social
courage at home, in school, and at the workplace, as well as in public
administration and in national and international politics. The author
initiated a handbook (Meyer et al., 2004) that combines scientific analyses,
examples of how social courage is practically supported by activities of civil
society and the state in Germany, as well as tested designs and teaching
materials for seminars and training in civic education, both for young people
and adults (see also Zitzmann, 2004; Jonas, Boos, and Brandstätter, 2007).

Thus, research in this field has theoretical and practical relevance for the
growth, vitality, and stability of any democratic political culture. Scuzzarello
in this volume argues for an *"ethics of care"* not just in personal relations, but
as a political practice that comprises the care for institutions, societies, and
even on a global level for "distant humans." For her, *caring* means to take
"responsibilities" for "concrete others," not in a paternalistic way, but based
on the principles of "equity and complementary reciprocity," particularly in
multicultural settings. A "culture of recognition" and productive conflict-
management, a supportive public and personal morality would help a lot to
prevent discrimination against or even punishment of those who show social
responsibility by social courage. Shown, proven, successful social courage is
probably the most efficient way to encourage people to do the same.

REFERENCES

Alford, C. Fred., 2001. *Whistleblowers. Broken lives and organizational power.* Ithaca
    and London: Cornell University Press.
Batson, C.D., 1991. *The altruism question: Toward a social-psychological answer.*
    Hillsdale, New York: Erlbaum.

Batson, C.D., 1994. Why act for the public good? Four answers. *Personality and Social Psychology Bulletin* 20:603–610.

Batson, C.D., 1998. Altruism and pro-social behavior. In: Gilbert, D.T., and Fiske, S.T. (eds.), *The handbook of social psychology*. New York: McGraw-Hill (pp. 282–316).

Beck, U., 1999. *The reinvention of politics. Rethinking modernity in the global social order*. Cambridge: Polity.

Benz, W. (Hrsg./ed.), 2003. *Überleben im Dritten Reich. Juden im Untergrund und ihre Helfer*. (Surviving in the Third Reich. Underground Jews and their helpers). Munich: Verlag C.H. Beck.

Benz, W., and Deutschkron, I.(Hrsg./eds.), 2002. *Stille Helden: Zeugnisse von Zivilcourage im Dritten Reich* (Silent heroes: Examples of civil courage in the Third Reich). Frankfurt/Main: Kulturstiftung der Deutschen Bank.

Bierhoff, H., 2000. *Sozialpsychologie. Ein Lehrbuch*. 5. Aufl. (Social Psychology. A textbook. 5th ed., esp. pp. 73–101). Stuttgart/Berlin/Köln: W. Kohlhammer.

Bierhoff, H., 2002. *Prosocial Behavior*. Hove: Psychology Press

Bierhoff, H., 2004. Handlungsmodelle für die Analyse von Zivilcourage (Models of action for the analysis of civil courage). In Meyer, G.; Dovermann, U.; Frech, S.; and Gugel, G. (Hrsg./eds.), 2004. *Zivilcourage lernen–Analysen, Modelle, Arbeitshilfen* (Learning Civil Courage: scientific analyses, models of social practice, seminar designs and teaching materials), (pp. 60–68).

Eagly, A. H., and Crowley, M., 1986. Gender and helping behavior: A meta-analytic review of the social psychological literature. *Psychological Bulletin* 100:283–308.

Fogelman, E., 1995. *"Wir waren keine Helden." Lebensretter im Angesicht des Holocaust. Motive, Geschichten, Hintergründe* ("We were no heroes." Life rescuers facing the Holocaust. Motives, stories, backgrounds). Frankfurt/Main, New York: Campus Verlag.

Frankenberger, R.; Frech, S.; and Grimm, D. (Hrsg./eds.). *Politische Psychologie und politische Bildung. Für Gerd Meyer zum 65. Geburtstag* (Political Psychology and civic education. Festschrift for Gerd Meyer). Schwalbach/Taunus: Wochenschau Verlag.

Gilligan, C., 1982. *In a different voice: Psychological theory and women's development*. Cambridge Mass: Harvard University Press.

Glaser, B.G., and Strauss, A.L., 1998. *Grounded theory: Strategien qualitativer Forschung* (Grounded theory: Strategies of qualitative research). Bern/Göttingen: Huber.

Grimm, D., 2007. Mut zu umfassender Veränderung! Ein feministischer Zugang zu Zivilcourage (Courage for comprehensive change! A feminist approach to civil courage). In: Frankenberger, R.; Frech, S.; and Grimm, D. (Hrsg./eds.), *Politische Psychologie und politische Bildung. Festschrift für Gerd Meyer* (Political psychology and civic education. Festschrift for Gerd Meyer), (pp. 139–166). Schwalbach/Taunus: Wochenschau Verlag.

Gugel, G., 1996. *Wir werden nicht weichen. Erfahrungen mit Gewaltfreiheit. Eine praxisorientierte Einführung* (We will not give way. Experiences with non-violence. An introduction to nonviolent practice), hrsg. vom/ed. by Verein für Friedenspädagogik Tübingen e.V. (Institute of Peace Education), Tübingen.

Heuer, W., 2002. *Couragiertes Handeln* (Acting with courage). Lüneburg: Verlag zu Klampen.

Jonas, K. J., and Brandstätter, V., 2004. Zivilcourage. Definition, Befunde, Maßnahmen (Civil courage. Definition, findings, activities). *Zeitschrift für Sozialpsychologie,* 35(4): 185–200.

Jonas, K. J.; Boos, M.; and Brandstätter, V., 2007. *Zivilcourage trainieren! Theorie und Praxis* (Trainings for civil courage! Theory and practice). Göttingen: Hogrefe Verlag GmbH and Co. KG.

Kämmerer, A., and Speck, A. (Hrsg./eds.), 1999. Geschlecht und Moral (Gender and morale). In: *Heidelberger Frauenstudien* [Heidelberg Women's Studies], edited by Frauenbeauftragtenn der Universität Heidelberg, Bd. 6, Heidelberg.

Kennedy, J. F., 1955. *Profiles in courage.* New York: Harper and Bros.

Kosmala, B., 2004. Zivilcourage in extremer Situation: Retterinnen und Retter von Juden im Dritten Reich (1941–1945) (Civil courage in an extreme situation: rescuers of Jews in the Third Reich). In Meyer, G.; Dovermann, U.; Frech, S.; and Gugel, G. (Hrsg./eds.), *Zivilcourage lernen–Analysen, Modelle, Arbeitshilfen* (Learning civil courage: Scientific analyses, models of social practice, seminar designs and teaching materials). Bonn: Bundeszentrale für politische Bildung.

Kosmala, B., and Schoppmann, C. (Hrsg./eds.), 2002. Überleben im Untergrund: Hilfe und Rettung für Juden in Deutschland, 1941–1945 (Surviving in the underground: Help and rescue for Jews in Germany, 1941–1945). In: *Solidarität und Hilfe für Juden während der NS-Zeit* (Solidarity and help for Jews during the Nazi regime). Berlin: Bd. 5.

Labuhn, Andju S., 2004. *Zivilcourage. Inhalte, Determinanten und ein erster empirischer Zugang* (Civil courage. Contents, determinants and a first empirical approach), Frankfurt am Main: Verlag für Polizeiwissenschaft.

Labuhn, A.S.; Wagner, U.; van Dick, R.; and Christ, O., 2002. Determinanten zivilcouragierten Verhaltens: Ergebnisse einer Fragebogenstudie. (Determinants of civil courage: results of a study based on a questionnaire). *Zeitschrift für Sozialpsychologie* 35:93–103.

Mayring, P., 1983. *Qualitative Inhaltsanalyse: Grundlagen und Techniken* (Qualitative content analysis: Principles and techniques). Weinheim: Beltz.

Mayring, P., 1996. *Einführung in die qualitative Sozialforschung: eine Anleitung zu qualitativem Denken* (Introduction to qualitative social research: teaching qualitative thinking). Weinheim: Psychologie-Verlags-Union.

Meyer, G., 2004. *Lebendige Demokratie: Zivilcourage und Mut im Alltag. Forschungsergebnisse und Praxisperspektiven* (Living democracy: Civil courage and courage in everyday life. Research findings and practical perspectives). Baden-Baden: Nomos Verlag. (2nd. ed. 2007) (A table of contents in English is available under: www.uni-tuebingen.de/ifp/meyer.htm)

Meyer, G., 2004. Civil courage in social conflicts. Paper presented at the 27th Annual Scientific Meeting of the International Society of Political Psychology, Lund/Sweden, July, 2004.

Meyer, G., 2005. Social courage, moral values and political culture–Conceptual and functional aspects. Paper presented at the 28th Annual Scientific Meeting of the International Society of Political Psychology, Toronto, Canada, July 2–6, 2005.

Meyer, G., 2006. Choosing concepts: "social" rather than "moral" courage. Paper presented at the 29th Annual Meeting of the International Society of Political Psychology, Barcelona, Spain, July 10–16, 2006.

Meyer, G.; Dovermann, U.; Frech, S.; and Gugel, G. (Hrsg./eds.), 2004. *Zivilcourage lernen–Analysen, Modelle, Arbeitshilfen* (Learning civil courage: scientific analyses, models of social practice, seminar designs and teaching materials) Bonn: Bundeszentrale für politische Bildung. (A table of contents in English is available under http://www.uni-tuebingen.de/pol/meyer.htm or www.uni-tuebingen.de/ifp/meyer.htm; the full text in German under: bpb.de or: www.friedenspaedagogik.de/themen/zc_lernen/zc_in.htm; also book orders.)

Meyer, G.; and Hermann, A., 1999. "... *normalerweise hätt' da schon jemand eingreifen müssen. Zivilcourage im Alltag von BerufsschuelerInnen. Eine Pilotstudie* ("... normally somebody should have intervened." Civil courage in everyday life of students in professional training. A pilot study). Schwalbach/Ts: Wochenschau.

Monroe, K., 1996. *The heart of altruism. Perceptions of a common humanity.* Princeton: Princeton University Press.

Monroe, K., 2006. The hand of compassion: Portraits of moral choice during the Holocaust. Princeton: Princeton University Press.

Montada, L., 1993. Moralische Gefühle (Moral feelings). In: Edelstein, W. (Hrsg./ed.). *Moral und Person* (Morale and person), (pp. 259–277). Frankfurt am Main: Suhrkamp.

Nunner-Winkler, G.(Hrsg./ed.), 1991. *Weibliche Moral. Die Kontroverse um eine geschlechtsspezifische Ethik* (The morale of women. The controversy over gender-specific ethics). Frankfurt/New York: Campus.

Nunner-Winkler, G., 2002. Zivilcourage als Persönlichkeitsdisposition–Bedingungen der individuellen Entwicklung. In: *Zivilcourage und demokratische Kultur* (Civil courage as a predisposition of personality–conditions for its development with individuals. In: *Civil courage and democratic culture*), (pp. 77–105). Hrsg. v. Ernst Feil, Münster.

Nunner-Winkler, G., and Edelstein, W., 1993. Einleitung (Introduction). In *Moral und Person* (Morale and person), (pp. 7–30). Frankfurt am Main: Suhrkamp (cf. 37.)

Oliner, S. P., and Oliner, P.M., 1988. *The Altruistic personality. Rescuers of Jews in Nazi Europe.* New York: The Free Press.

Oser, F., and Althof, W., 1992. *Moralische Selbstbestimmung. Modelle der Entwicklung und Erziehung im Wertbereich* (Moral self-determination. Models of development and education for values). Stuttgart: Klett-Cotta.

Oswald, S.; Frey, D.; Greitemeyer, T.; and Fischer, P., 2007. Erarbeitung eines Prozessmodells für Zivilcourage (Development of a process model for civil courage). In Frankenberger, R.; Frech, S. and Grimm, D. (Hrsg./eds.), *Politische Psychologie und politische Bildung. Für Gerd Meyer* (Political psychology and civic education. Festschrift for Gerd Meyer), (pp.114–138). Schwalbach/ Taunus: Wochenschau Verlag.

Putman, D., 1997. Psychological courage. In *Philosophy, psychiatry and psychology* 4(1): 1–11.

Singer, K., 2003. *Zivilcourage wagen* 3. Auflage. (Daring to show civil courage. 3rd ed.). München/Zürich: Ernst Reinhart.

Staub, E., 1989. *The roots of evil: The origins of genocide and other group violence*. New York: Cambridge University Press.

Staub, E., 1993. The psychology of bystanders, perpetrators and heroic helpers. *International Journal of Intercultural Relations* 17:315–341.

Staub, E., 1999. The roots of evil: Personality, social conditions, culture and basic human needs. *Personality and Social Psychology Review* 3:179–192.

Staub, E., 2003. *The psychology of good and evil: Why children, adults and groups help and harm others*. New York: Cambridge University Press.

Staub, E., 2005. The roots of goodness: The fulfillment of basic human needs and the development of caring, helping and nonaggression, inclusive caring, moral courage, active bystandership, and altruism born of suffering. In: Carlo, G., and Edwards, C. (eds.), *Moral motivation through the life span*. Nebraska Symposium on Motivation, Lincoln, Nebraska.

Staub, E., 2006. *A brighter future: Raising caring, nonviolent, morally courageous children*. New York: Oxford University Press.

Zitzmann, C., 2004. *"Alltagshelden"–Aktiv gegen Gewalt und Mobbing–für mehr Zivilcourage* ("Everyday heroes"–Active against violence and mobbing–for more civil courage). Schwalbach/Ts.: Wochenschau Verlag.

CHAPTER 5

Self-Regulation of Courageous Bystander Interventions

Kai J. Jonas

Imagine that you analyze the following situation: "A perpetrator threatens a victim in an urban side-street. It is a clear dispute and the victim is inferior to the perpetrator. Some passersby ignore the situation; others watch it to find out what is happening; and a third group immediately acts upon the situation. Think of one person who pulls the victim away from the perpetrator, or of another person who animates other passersby to grab hold of the perpetrator." If we focus on the intervention behavior shown in this situation, some intervened early, others later, and above and beyond, some people did not do anything. One individual has shown individual intervention behavior, whereas another has demonstrated bystander activation behavior. The first type of action can also be described as direct intervention, the latter as more indirect intervention. Is the individual showing the latter type of indirect, bystander intervention behavior less courageous than the first one? Was that person wrong not to intervene directly to the benefit of the victim, or was the indirect behavior on display just another form of courageous intervention and driven by a different perception of situational or individual constraints? Of course, critical situations where courageous intervention behavior is needed are not homogenous in their characteristics; thus, intervention can take many forms.

Our focus in this analysis points to processes underlying all cases of bystander intervention behavior independent of their context. Therefore, our approach here is not to demonstrate that we deal with the context, but *how*, process-wise, we deal with any given context. From a sociological or philosophical point of view (as outlined in the chapters by Nesbitt-Larking and Fernández [this volume]), this approach to situational influences may seem quite limited. It suffices for a micro-level analysis usually done in social psychology, however. This is not to say that macro-level changes do not influence bystander intervention behavior; in fact, they do, but the psychological challenges of the past may have been as demanding as the ones we face today. Multicultural societies may be as complex to deal with today as was the single stranger who only showed up once in a lifetime in an isolated village. Since we cannot determine the extent to which psychological demands differ between past and present, we exclude important macro-level influences (such as rapid global, economic, and societal change) in order to discuss some very basic psychological processes active in bystander intervention contexts.

It should also be pointed out that these situational factors, their controlled processing, and related conscious cognitive processes may only account for half of the actor's reasoning, or, in statistical terms, for half of the variance actions. There are additional individual factors, also interacting with the situation, which determine how individuals reach their goals to intervene and help threatened others. Modern motivational theorizing, so-called self-regulation theories (for recent overviews, see Fitzsimmons and Bargh, 2004; and Higgins and Spiegel, 2004), can add to this analysis. The advantage of such a motivated-cognition perspective with a focus on automatic effects is the integration of underlying processes in the analysis of the antecedents and determinants of human behavior (or ignorance as a crucial type of non-behavior) in these situations. This chapter is organized around the integration of self-regulation theories into the research on courageous bystander interventions. First, we will define the topic of investigation. Then, using existing frameworks of controlled, conscious determinants, we will point to stages in these process models where self-regulation theories should be integrated to further uncover relevant mechanisms of perception and behavior, and will refer to research that provides initial results. In the summary, we will suggest further developments to integrate the body of existing research with this hardly noticed theorizing in the field of pro-social behavior.

THE TOPIC UNDER INVESTIGATION: ZIVILCOURAGE

The situation described initially would be considered in the German-speaking countries as a rather prototypical situation in which *Zivilcourage* would be necessary. In these countries, the term *Zivilcourage* is a standard expression and denotes courageous behavior shown by an individual in public to the benefit of a threatened or endangered third person or group (Jonas, Boos, and Brandstätter, 2007a; Jonas and Brandstätter, 2004; Nunner-Winkler, 2002, 2007). Thus, it describes a triadic relationship between an actor, victim, and perpetrator. Still, victims do not have to be physically present; they can be defended or protected vicariously. Perpetrators do not have to be physically present either; for example, in the case of institutionalized discrimination.

In all cases, the attitude and the related behavior are motivated by universal values and human rights and not by mere benefits on a group membership level. Clearly, this value background is ethnocentric and potentially limited to Western societies. This is not surprising, since the concept of *Zivilcourage* was formulated against this cultural background and has been subject to a good century of development in application, scholarly discourse, and societal debate (this is not to say that other, non-Western societies could not, or have not yet, come up with similar concepts). Still, we have to question the contingent universalism of the "universal" values. Conceptually, we are close to the grounds of the tolerance debate that is addressed by Fernández (in this volume)—how much derivation can we accept, while still maintaining our own set of values? Is there an integration of values possible; can we determine consensual overlap? As a side note, this has already turned out to be a difficult task in applied contexts. Hence, when teaching *Zivilcourage* to (mostly) male Muslim teenagers in German schools, conveying these "universal" human rights values has proved challenging.

Coming back to the conceptual clarification of *Zivilcourage* we embarked on earlier, we want to point to a difference compared to helping behavior. Acting in a *Zivilcourage* manner might entail negative social or physical outcomes for the actor, as it can be more closely associated with negative consequences than helping behavior (Fischer et al., 2004). Furthermore, actors may find themselves in a double bind, since they have to break a rule or a law to guard another value, rule, or law that they consider being of greater importance in the specific situation—for example unharmed physical or psychological existence is deemed more important than a privacy norm salient in a society, a norm that would actually prevent an intervention. Facing the challenge to translate such a term into other languages such as English, one can go down different paths. The term *morally courageous intervention* stresses that the reasoning for the courageous intervention is driven by moral values (Staub, 1993, 2003, 2005, 2006). Indeed, research on altruism and helping behavior has theoretically derived and empirically validated several motives and individual differences that can serve as a source of individual reasons to courageously intervene (Bierhoff and Rohmann, 2004; Nunner-Winkler, 2002, 2007; and see the chapter by Fred Alford in this volume). The other path is to frame the translation of the expression more in terms of *social courage*, as suggested by Meyer (Meyer, 2004; this volume), to account for its social embedding and to reduce its value-laden character. Surely, given other languages and cultures, other translations and conceptual adaptations are necessary, and the issue of translation should not be regarded as the core problem. More important than the mere international naming, and especially relevant to cross-cultural approaches, conceptual validations are necessary in order to apply the concept to other cultures and, subsequently, to compare intervention data and evaluation results. These efforts have not yet been undertaken, nor has the cross-cultural debate on whether we can use other value backgrounds as foundations for *Zivilcourage*, or not.

For the time being, we will use the term *moral courage* throughout this chapter since it conceptually contains a desired end state, defined by the underlying abstract moral standard that is being ensured and protected when we talk of courageous bystander interventions in critical situations as described above.

CONTROLLED AND CONSCIOUS PROCESSES IN MORAL COURAGE BEHAVIOR

Research on moral courage, given its close kinship to, but also distinctness from, to helping behavior (which is usually dyadic and does not entail threats and negative consequences for the actor) has mainly drawn on previous findings, determinants, and process models of pro-social behavior (for an overview, see Jonas and Brandstätter, 2004). The process models in particular (e.g., Latané and Darley, 1970; Schwartz and Howard, 1981) still provide crucial frameworks in the theorizing and within the applied context of moral courage training (see also Meyer for an expansion of these process models in this volume). The original and widely used models describe steps that lead to the exertion of pro-social behavior or not. For each step towards the final performance of pro-social behavior, one can describe an obstacle that prevents this step from being successfully taken and subsequently the behavior to be performed. One can distinguish between the following five steps:

1. perceiving the situation,
2. judging the situation as critical; i.e., perceiving the need, the threat etc.,
3. feeling responsible to act in regards to the perceived situation,
4. deciding how to intervene or how to help,
5. performing the actual behavior.

These are the steps that one has to move through, or abort consciously on the way to intervention behavior. All of the steps are necessary to finally perform the behavior: some may be dealt with rather automatically, and others may receive a lot of conscious control, depending on the individual and the specific situation. Yet, this path is not guaranteed, since obstacles can be described for each of these steps. For step 1, distraction is the crucial negative condition. If the perceiver is too busy to recognize the situation, he or she will not recognize the (potential victim in need) and thus, will take none of the further steps. Secondly, pluralistic ignorance puts an end to the path at step 2: given other bystanders, if none of them acts upon the critical situation, the perceiver may judge the context as non-critical, too, and this aborts further steps. Again multiple bystanders, by diffusing responsibility, reduce the chance of intervention at the level of step 3. Following the individual reasoning that another person could perform the necessary behavior, none of the potential helpers does anything at all. For step 4, a perceived lack of competence forms the exit criterion in this case: the perceiver may have recognized the situation, judged it as critical, and felt responsible to act upon it, but subjectively felt the lack of adequate competence to do so. At the fifth and final step, all the previous steps have successfully been taken, and none of the obstacles tied to the steps before has led to an abandonment of the path to action, but social blocking may put an end to the behavior now, before it could be exerted. *Social blocking* may entail a fear of contact with the person in need, or the fear of being judged for one's behavior, or just the fact that one would possibly stand out from the masses for a moment and be identifiable with the performed behavior. Thus, these path models describe both steps towards pro-social behavior and obstacles that lead to the termination of the pro-social pathway. Later we will integrate possible self-regulatory mechanisms into these controlled process models. The process models described above hardly address the initial reasoning why one would intervene or help and position this question in the demand characteristics of the situation (i.e., perceiving the critical situation). Conscious reasoning in regards to why one intervenes to the benefit of another individual or group in the context of moral courage is often tied to simple "one just does" arguments. At least this confirms the anecdotal evidence we received in many moral courage training sessions—the author developed such a training program ("Göttingen Zivilcourage-Impulstraining" [Göttingen Moral Courage Impulse Training]; Boos et al., 2007; Jonas et al., 2002) and is continuously involved in its implementation—and in interviews with individuals who had previously shown this morally courageous intervention behavior. Apart from Germany and Switzerland, no intercultural research in the context of moral courage training programs has been undertaken, but we dare to suspect that most of the reasoning would be similar elsewhere in the world. For the moment, research by Scheele and Kapp (2002) who argue for a gender-specific (following Carol Gilligan's (1982) argument of a "male" justice and a "female" care ethic) development of moral reasoning relevant for morally courageous behavior and arguments, as they are reported in the chapter "The Psychology of Natural Law and Care" by Fred Alford in this volume, have to act as the indicator for this approach. Also based on anecdotal evidence from the training programs undertaken by the author is the finding that interventions are positively sanctioned by common group membership of the intervening bystander and the victim, or by overlearned behavior that can be tied to group relations (e.g., mothers are much more likely to help children in general). Research on group memberships and helping has found similar results (Laner, Benin, and Ventrone, 2001; Levine, Prosser, Evans, and Reicher, 2005; Levine and Thompson, 2004). Thus it is quite likely that in the context of moral courage intervention, similar processes are active. Of course, negative attitudes towards specific groups, in the sense of prejudice, can prevent moral courage. Labuhn, Wagner, van Dick, and Christ (2004) have provided evidence for this. In their vignette study, prejudice against foreigners impedes interventions to their benefit. This list of determinants could most likely be prolonged endlessly, integrating findings such as class differences or gender in general.

Yet, all these findings pertain mostly to structural determinants or to the conscious question within the individual of whether morally courageous behavior is being shown or not, and thus point to influences that we have sought to exclude for the moment (as discussed in the beginning of the chapter). These studies do not, however, take into account automatic cognitive-motivational process analyses that focus on the processes active in each human being. Furthermore, these variables cannot fully explain our perceptual and behavioral differences outlined in the beginning of the chapter. We believe that is it necessary to be able to answer the initial perceptual/behavior differentiation question by analyzing the underlying automatic processes that potentially lead to the early or late perception and the various forms of intervention behavior. To do so, we draw on the mentioned self-regulation theories and integrate them with theorizing about courageous intervention behavior. Self-regulation theories in general focus on the automatic processes of goal attainment. The very content of the attained goal or standard is not important, actually denoting an advantage above thematically bound motivation theories (e.g., Deci and Ryan, 2002). Goals are defined as desired end-states (Austin and Vancouver, 1996) that direct human behavior. In our current context, such individual goals could be rather abstract level goals; for example, the ensuring of human rights or tolerance values, or rather specific goals such as to protect a certain group of discriminated-against victims whenever such an instance arises. Goals can be activated and attained consciously, but also unconsciously (Bargh, 1990; Bargh, Gollwitzer, Lee-Chai, Barndollar, and Trötschel, 2001). The latter case describes the initiation of goal-attainment processes by means of situational stimuli that are not consciously processed. Of crucial interest from the perspective of a self-regulation approach to morally courageous behavior is the non-conscious goal attainment process. Are goals framed, for example, as an ideal or an "ought"; how are cues perceived that serve as means to attain the goals; are they pursued in terms of approach or avoidance behavior; what are the relevant criteria to determine (un)successful goal attainment; and what are affective consequences to theses outcomes? We will turn to these specific aspects later in detail.

Above and beyond the theoretical impetus, we should use this knowledge and reflect upon how we can optimize a person–situation fit in the sense that the type of intervention behavior shown in a critical situation fits both the necessities of the situation and the traits and states of the intervening individual. This is especially desirable since recently developed training programs (for an overview, see Jonas, Boos, and Brandstätter, 2007b) aim to increase morally courageous behavior within the general public. It is rooted in the nature of training programs that they have to make some sort of process assumption, and this could be used as a starting ground to analyze automatic elements of moral courage behavior processes. To enhance morally courageous behavior in training programs, different forms of behavior are being conveyed, yet mostly under a situation–behavior fit. The perspective by which this behavior (and its fit) is being construed differs between the training programs. For example, the *Göttingen Zivilcourage-Impulstraining* (Göttingen Moral Courage Impulse Training) developed by Jonas and colleagues (Boos et al., 2007; Jonas et al., 2002) uses the process model developed by Latané and Darley (1970)—described before—and a severity dimension to determine appropriate interventions in the last two steps. Thus, the assumed process to moral courage interventions first follows the process model of pro-social behavior. This is followed by a situational evaluation in order to determine the appropriate behavior. Clearly, this defines a controlled process. As another example, the training *Kleine Schritte statt Heldentaten* (Small Steps Instead of Hero's Deeds) developed by Brandstätter (Brandstätter, 2007) uses a severity dimension as well and adds an implementation intention technique (Gollwitzer, 1999) to characterize the perception/action pathway. The use of implementation intentions is of interest here, since they form an automatic process. Taken together, moral courage behavior, as conveyed in the training programs, draws on automatic and controlled elements. Yet, implementation intentions need to be formed beforehand to be operative. Individuals need to form a goal. In the case of moral courage behavior, this is most likely to be a rather chronic goal or even a standard. This is quite likely to happen, since morally courageous behavior is strongly driven not only by attitudes but also by moral convictions and standards, as we stated above.

SELF-REGULATORY PROCESSES WITHIN MORAL COURAGE
INTERVENTIONS

In the initially described situation, both individuals who intervened have followed a goal—for example, to ensure and restore universal unharmed living conditions—but have used different means to attain this goal. One has watched the situation closely; the other has acted upon it immediately. One has used direct individual intervention behavior, less concerned with associated costs; the other has implemented indirect bystander activation behavior, a type of behavior that allows for individual cost control.

Thus, a theoretical background is necessary that allows us to distinguish between different perceptual routes and pathways to attain goals relevant in moral courage situations. Perception of crucial situations can be shaped by implementation intentions (Gollwitzer, 1999; Brandstätter and Frank, 2002). Implementation intentions are overlearned "if:then" rules, which tie an external cue (for example, a threatening person or a dark street) to predetermined perceptual or behavioral responses (for example to be more vigilant or to act directly upon this cue). This behavior is exerted without the conscious control of the individual and is a product of the perception of the cue (*if* element) and the subsequent activation of the linked behavior (*then* element). This form of self-regulation has proven to be a successful means of fostering courageous bystander interventions (Brandstätter, 2007). Locating implementation intentions (the automatic component) in the helping behavior path models (the description at the controlled level), we see how they impact at an early stage of perceiving critical situations and leading to immediate behavior, without the actor's wasting time and cognitive effort by ruminating on possible forms of interventions. Furthermore, behavior exerted on the basis of implementation intentions is less prone to obstacles such as diffusion of responsibility.

Developing the argument regarding goals further, we see that individuals can have very different goals when intervening in such a moral courage situation. As we noted before, some of the goals can be rather abstract (e.g., ensuring human rights) and thus cannot lead to immediate intervention behavior. In this case, subsequent, functionally related goals at a more specific level have to be automatically activated. This is likely to happen, as the findings of the goals systems theory (Kruglanski et al., 2002) suggest. Goals systems theory describes general functional and inhibitory goal–means relations, based on an associative representation assumption. In the case that rather specific goals have been activated, some individuals may focus on the quick separation of perpetrator and victim, again neglecting individual costs. Others, being aware of these costs, may deem it primarily appropriate to activate other bystanders or authorities. To determine systematic goal-driven differences in intervention behavior, we make use of regulatory focus theory (Higgins, 1997, 1998). Regulatory focus theory distinguishes between two main types of goals that result in fundamental differences in self-regulation. Accomplishment and growth (nurturance needs) characterize the so-called promotion focus, whereas safety and protection (security needs) are specific to the so-called prevention focus. The self-regulation, or in other words the goal attainment process, differs in various aspects in both foci. Success and failure in a promotion focus are experienced as gains and non-gains. Typical affects associated with success and failure are cheerfulness and dejection, respectively. On the behavioral level, eagerness means and approach behavior fit a promotion focus. In contrast, prevention focus serves the need for security and is associated with goals that can be described as duties, oughts, or obligations. Goal attainment criteria (i.e., success and failure) are experienced as non-losses and losses in a prevention focus. In this focus, affects associated with success and failure are quiescence and agitation, respectively. Goal attainment means assuring that vigilance and avoidance behavior fit a prevention focus. It has to be noted that the strength of the promotion orientation and prevention orientation vary independently of each other. Therefore, both self-regulatory strategies can be high or low simultaneously, given situational and individual variation. There is evidence that there is no perceptual defense for undesirable stimuli; instead an automatic vigilance can found that is expressed in consistently longer response latencies for undesirable stimuli compared to desirable stimuli (Pratto and John, 1991). The authors used a color-naming paradigm in which colors of desirable and undesirable traits had to be voiced as fast as possible. Latencies were consistently longer for color-naming of undesirable traits compared to desirable traits. If perceptual defense kicked in, briefer latencies for color-naming of undesirable traits would become evident, yet if negative stimuli grabbed attention because they needed an individual to immediately attend to them, longer latencies would result. One can map these findings on situations with negative cues (i.e., a threat to the well-being of the individual) and suspect an automatic vigilance effect instead of a perceptual defense. In terms of the presentation of a mere negative stimulus, one could expect a latency effect, too. Furthermore, these situations are especially critical to individuals high in prevention focus, since they are preoccupied with preventing losses (Sassenberg and Hansen, 2006). The authors can show in their studies that participants in a prevention focus show more anger and agitation after being subjected to social discrimination, because experiencing social discrimination is similar to experiencing failure. Adding to the basic finding, the pattern of results was more pronounced when social discrimination was based on losses compared to being based on non-gains (i.e., when the ingroup was evaluated more negatively vs. less positively compared to the outgroup). Promotion focus did not have any predictive value in these studies, which is likely to be due to the focus on gains, which should not be applicable in a social discrimination context.

If one applies this theorizing and empirical evidence to typical moral courage situations, then it becomes evident that moral courage situations have characteristics that make them especially salient for implementation intentions, automatic vigilance, and self-regulatory processes. Derived from the definition of moral courage, as a courageous, public behavior to the benefit of a threatened individual or group and based on universal values (for a summary, see Jonas and Brandstätter, 2004), it is possible to determine cues that should be particularly relevant for prevention regulatory strategies. We have outlined above what makes moral courage situations specific. To recapitulate, first of all there is a triadic relationship of perpetrator, victim, and intervening third party. The perpetrator is a threat both to the victim and potentially to the intervener. Thus, the perpetrator can be seen as a typical source of negative outcomes to which a promotion-oriented person is not sensitive, but to which a prevention-oriented person is. Secondly, the situational context in which this triadic behavior is rooted in is highly ambiguous in its impact on the outcome (i.e., how the threat situation is resolved, or how it is escalating). Again, this presumably poses a highly relevant cue for prevention-oriented, but not for promotion-oriented individuals. Both situational characteristics should lead to self-protective types of intervention behavior to reduce the potential of negative outcome for the prevention-oriented individual. In the context of morally courageous behavior, this could be bystander activation behavior, because the intervener still intervenes (and thus attains his/her intervention goal) but reduces possible costs of this behavior by approaching non-threatening individuals in the situation. Yet, if the intervening individual can reduce the outcome ambiguity by any means—for example, via previous knowledge about the usual situational script and its outcome—other types of intervention behavior are individually possible. The strength of the self-regulatory approach also lies in the fact that goal attainment strategies can be described above and beyond typical sociodemographic variables, such as gender or class. In theory, virtually all combinations are possible, and thus, the approach is not limited to a specific subgroup of individuals. Yet, one can—based on the regulatory fit approach—describe further characteristics that make a specific regulatory style more likely to be shown. This person–situation or individual–group fit has been shown for example in the case of prevention focus and low status groups. There is a perceived fit in this case, since the prevention focus individual with its monitoring to prevent negative outcomes reflects this regulatory style in low-power group membership—given that members of low-power groups are also monitoring their environments for threats and possible negative effects (Sassenberg, Jonas, Shah, and Brazy, 2007).

Taken together, the impact of automatic vigilance and regulatory focus strategies seems an important factor to address in the context of moral courage, since interventions are goal-driven types of behavior. We found evidence for our theorizing in two studies. Using a game paradigm, we tested whether a critical situation in a 3D maze game is perceived more quickly, using response time measures as the main dependent variable in a within subjects design, by prevention focus–oriented individuals (Jonas, 2007a). The results show that automatic vigilance (i.e., lower response latencies in the critical situation) is pronounced for prevention focus but not for promotion focus. The second study, using a vignette paradigm, tested whether prevention focus is a predictor for indirect, bystander activation behavior. This effect was found, and it was further moderated by situational familiarity. Situational familiarity, assessed as one's own experience, interacted significantly with prevention focus and led to more direct intervention behavior (Jonas, 2007b).

To report these results in more detail, Jonas (2007a) found initial evidence that automatic vigilance effects that are pronounced for given negative social information are determined by regulatory foci. Prevention focus led to faster responses in such a situation, whereas promotion focus had, as hypothesized, no effect. We count this as initial evidence that self-regulatory strategies play a determining role in pro-social goal attainment processes, especially regarding the detection of critical situations for attaining a goal. Like the implementation intentions mentioned earlier, these effects pertain to early steps in the controlled level path models of pro-social behavior.

On the contrary, the effect to be summarized now is more focused on the later two steps of the model; namely, the selection of adequate behavior and its enactment. In other words, we sought to explore the behavioral consequences related to the regulatory foci. In a questionnaire study, participants initially filled out a regulatory focus questionnaire. After having read a vignette describing an urban assault situation, they indicated behavioral intentions and supplied sociodemographic information. The vignette contained a short text in which a grave assault situation was described. It portrayed a perpetrator assaulting a weaker victim in an inner-city side street, with other bystanders being present. After having read the vignette, participants were asked to imagine themselves in this very situation as a bystander and, having done that, they were asked to indicate on rating scales what kind of intervention behavior they would intend to exert. The option not to intervene was purposely left out to force the variance into the intervention behavior items. Half of the items described direct interventions behavior that would entail personal intervention, either by acting against the perpetrator directly, or by withdrawing the victim from the assault scene. The other half of the items referred to rather indirect intervention behavior and contained behavioral options that would leave the individual out of the situation; for example, watching the situation closely to deliver a proper witness report to the police or trying to activate others to intervene directly. Bringing the results of this study together (Jonas, 2007b), it can be argued that a prevention focus leads to an increase in indirect bystander activation. This effect appears as hypothesized. This general pattern is influenced by previous individual experiences with similar situations as used in the vignette. For bystander indirect activation, the effect of prevention was only found for the participants with no experience. On the contrary, individual direct intervention, for which there was no main effect of prevention, can be predicted by a prevention focus if the individual has had previous experience with such a critical situation. As expected we did not find any effect of promotion focus on the intervention behavior. The individual familiarity predictor shows a pattern of effects that is counterintuitive for the moment. In general, prevention focus predicts behaviors that reduce uncertainty and do not lead to unwanted negative side effects. Thus, it is rather implausible that a prevention focus can lead to individual intervention behavior in cases when there is no given situational familiarity: these individuals just want to protect themselves. Yet this seems not to be the case for individuals with previous experiences: individual intervention in moral courage situations still clearly affects the potential for hardly predictable negative outcomes and unwanted side effects. We interpret this interaction result as an extension of the scope of avoidance of negative outcomes to the victim in the situation. In other words, individuals with a prevention focus, but with no previous experience, show behavior (i.e., indirect bystander activation) that reduces or avoids losses mostly for themselves, whereas previous experiences lead to behavior that reduces or avoids losses on a broader, interpersonal basis that can also include threatened others (i.e., the activation of direct intervention behavior). One could rephrase this experience-based effect as a capacity for perspective-taking, too. An individual familiar with the threatening potential of such situations "knows" that certain types of behavior are more peremptory and "effective" to prevent further harm for the victim than others, even if the latter are safer for the helper than direct individual interventions. Interestingly, as one might suspect, gender did not have any moderating effect at all in this research.

Regarding critical aspects in the latter set of the data, one could criticize the fact that the moderating effect of familiarity is based on a quasi-experimental variable. Yet the distribution of previous experiences is quite balanced, given a general student population, and also quite telling about their social reality. Of course, and there is anecdotal evidence coming from moral courage training, members of groups coming from very stable and nonviolent social backgrounds may lack this familiarity knowledge and thus would not show the interaction effects. Yet, if we take this laboratory study, as one should, as merely a process-explaining example, other socio-demographically determined content familiarity based on other social backgrounds and respective applicable contexts should lead to the same effects.

Furthermore, the question determining our quasi-experimental factor does not allow us to distinguish between different types of previous experiences our participants had; for example, as a witness or as a victim. Still, in both cases there is presumably a clear and very vivid memory of what went wrong in the situation and which behaviors would have been desirable, both from the perspective of a victim or as a witness. A second critical aspect is the ecological validity of the reported experimental data gained in laboratory settings. This is a structural disadvantage of experimental psychological sciences in general, but the 3D maze used by Jonas (2007a) is, given the usual limitations of the field, a rather valid approach. Participants act out vigilance behavior in a game they are immersed in. From the perspective of other disciplines this may be judged as an improvement to be neglected, yet one may not overlook the sole possibility to track down basic psychological processes in laboratory settings. The beauty of the field of moral courage lies in the fact that these findings can be immediately turned into elements of intervention programs and then be evaluated in ecologically valid contexts.

GENERAL DISCUSSION

In this chapter, we have argued for an integration of automatic and controlled processes in the field of courageous intervention behavior. So-called self-regulatory processes, such as implementation intentions, or regulatory focus theory, can be neatly tied to the existing and empirically well-researched process models of helping behavior. The aim and currently the partial results of such integration is the gain in knowledge of how intervention processes are perceived and acted out, with and without automatic and controlled elements of behavior. Clearly, this denotes the start of a story, since the field of self-regulation theorizing offers a larger set of approaches than dealt with in this chapter. To name a few, one could analyze means–end relations in moral courage contexts from a goal systems perspective (Kruglanski et al., 2002); another option is to integrate Kuhl's state- and action-orientation whereas, according to Kuhl (1994), state-oriented individuals are less effective than action-oriented individuals in down-regulating such threats to the self that are typical for moral courage situations.

Taken the research presented here, the results of the use of implementation intentions within the training of Brandstätter (2007) and the effects found by Jonas (2007a, 2007b) can be counted as evidence for the impact of self-regulatory strategies on a special form of courageous intervention behavior. Implementation intentions form the pathway for predetermined interventions given a critical cue. In general, critical situations are perceived and reacted upon faster by individuals in a chronic prevention focus. Concerning intervention behavior selection, promotion focus does not predict any type of behavior, yet prevention focus predicts indirect, bystander activation behavior. Individual experience moderates this effect in the sense that, given previous experience with such a critical situation, prevention focus predicts direct, individual intervention, whereas no previous experience in conjunction with a prevention focus still predicts indirect intervention. These results shed light on the underlying automatic processes of moral courage intervention and help us gain a deeper understanding of the self-regulation at work in such a situation.

Given a rather chronic fit of moral courage situations and prevention focus, since the situation is in essence threatening, one has to determine whether there is actually promotion-type goal pursuit in such a situation. This might be the case for very specific target populations; e.g., victims of social discrimination with a social movement background, politically extreme left-wing youth (*Antifa* in the German context), "streetwise" persons, with a lot of experience with such situations, or individuals with a martial arts or self-defense background. In any case, identifying such groups of individuals could be used as indicators for improved training content or the specific tailoring of training interventions for specific populations.

To sum up, a deeper understanding of implementation intentions, automatic vigilance effects, and the fit of self-regulatory strategies and intervention behavior could be used and implemented in existing moral courage training programs. Being instructed based on these and future findings, individuals could potentially show increased levels of helpful behavior in critical situations.

We commenced the chapter by introducing *Zivilcourage* as a rather culturally bound, German concept, and thus one may object to the intercultural generalizability of the effects found under these auspices. On the contrary, we do not expect any cultural limitations for the effects found, at least in

Western, industrialized societies, since the concept of *Zivilcourage* was never mentioned in the operationalization of this research. In fact the situations such is the 3D maze and the vignette spoke for themselves and were not framed for the participants in a *Zivilcourage* context. Urban assault, hate crimes, bullying, mobbing, and domestic violence are abundant types of threats one can encounter almost everywhere. The strength of the self-regulatory processes unveiled here is rooted in this universal applicability. Thus, the term *Zivilcourage*, or its respective translations or conceptualizations in other cultures, should serve only as a vehicle either to consciously motivate citizens to engage in such behavior or to give a catchy name to intervention programming. In doing so, one can distinguish "*Zivilcourage*" as a culturally defined practice, as a type of social learning, from underlying universal values that actually drive the individual behavior (see the chapter on natural law and care by Fred Alford in this volume) or from group memberships that make interventions to the benefit of ingroup members more likely (Laner, Benin, and Ventrone, 2001; Levine, Prosser, Evans, and Reicher, 2005; Levine and Thompson, 2004) and from the automatic processes that tell us more about the "how" courageous intervention behavior is being exerted. In other words, a split of the underlying automatic processes from a culturally coined practice could actually help to further spread the behavior without the conceptual limitations induced by certain terminology.

REFERENCES

Austin, J. T., and Vancouver, J. B., 1996. Goal constructs in psychology: Structure, process and content. *Psychological Bulletin* 120:338–375.

Bargh, J. A.; Gollwitzer, P. M.; Lee-Chai, A.; Barndollar, K.; and Trötschel, R., 2001. The automated will: Non-conscious activation and pursuit of behavioral goals. *Journal of Personality and Social Psychology* 81:1014–1027.

Bargh, J. A., 1990. Auto-motives: Preconscious determinants of social interaction. In: Higgins, E. T., and Sorrentino, E. M. (eds.), *Handbook of Motivation and Cognition: Foundations of Social Behavior* (vol. 2). New York: Guilford.

Bierhoff, H. W., and Rohmann, E., 2004. Altruistic personality in the context of the empathy-altruism hypothesis. *European Journal of Personality* 18:351–356.

Boos, M.; Jonas, K. J.; Backes, S.; Büttner, N.; Ehrenthal, J.; Schütt, M.; and Prasse, A., 2007. Göttinger Zivilcourage-Impulstraining (Göttinger Moral Courage Impulse Training). In Jonas, K. J., Boos, M., and Brandstätter, V. (eds.), *Zivilcourage trainieren! Theorie und Praxis* (Training moral courage: Theory and practice). Göttingen: Hogrefe.

Brandstätter, V., 2007. Kleine Schritte statt Heldentaten. Ein Training zur Förderung von Zivilcourage gegen Fremdenfeindlichkeit (Small steps instead of heroic deeds. A training program to foster moral courage against hate crimes). In Jonas, K. J., Boos, M., and Brandstätter, V. (eds.), *Zivilcourage trainieren! Theorie und Praxis* (Training moral courage: Theory and practice). Göttingen: Hogrefe.

Brandstätter, V., and Frank, E., 2002. Effects of deliberative and implemental mindsets on persistence in goal-directed behavior. *Personality and Social Psychology Bulletin* 28:1366–1378.

Deci, E. L., and Ryan, R. M., 2002. Self-determination research: Reflections and future directions. In Deci, E. L., and Ryan, R. M. (eds.), *Handbook of self-determination research*. Rochester, NY: University of Rochester Press.

Fischer, P.; Greitemeyer, T.; Schulz-Hardt, S.; Frey, D.; Jonas, E.; and Rudukha, T., 2004. Zivilcourage und Hilfeverhalten: Der Einfluss negativer sozialer Konsequenzen auf die Wahrnehmung prosozialen Verhaltens (Moral courage and helping behavior: the impact of negative social consequences on the perception of pro-social behavior). *Zeitschrift für Sozialpsychologie* 35:61–66.

Fitzsimmons, G. M., and Bargh, J. A., 2004. Automatic self-regulation. In Baumeister, R. F., and Vohs, K. D. (eds.), *Handbook of self-regulation: Research, theory and applications*. New York: Guilford.

Gilligan, C., 1982. *In a different voice: Psychological theory and women's development.* Cambridge, Mass.: Harvard University Press.

Gollwitzer, P. M., 1999. Implementation intentions: Strong effects of simple plans. *American Psychologist* 54:493–503.

Higgins, E. T., and Spiegel, S., 2004. Promotion and prevention strategies for self-regulation: A motivated cognition perspective. In Baumeister, R. F., and Vohs, K. D. (eds.), *Handbook of self-regulation: Research, theory and applications*. New York: Guilford.

Higgins, E. T.; Friedman, R. S.; Harlow, R. E.; Idson, L. C.; Ayduk, O. N.; and Taylor, A., 2001. Achievement orientations from subjective histories of success: Promotion pride versus prevention pride. *Journal of Experimental Social Psychology* 31:3–24.

Higgins, E. T., 1998. Promotion and prevention: Regulatory focus as a motivational principle. In Zanna, M. P. (ed.), *Advances in experimental social psychology* (vol. 30). San Diego, Calif.: Academic Press.

Higgins, E. T., 1997. Beyond pleasure and pain. *American Psychologist* 52:1280–1300.

Jonas, K. J., 2007a. *Automatic vigilance revisited: The impact of regulatory focus.* Manuscript submitted for publication.

Jonas, K. J., 2007b. *The impact of regulatory foci on courageous bystander interventions.* Manuscript submitted for publication.

Jonas, K. J.; Boos, M.; and Brandstätter, V., 2007a. Zivilcourage trainieren (Training moral courage). In Jonas, K. J.; Boos, M.; and Brandstätter, V. (eds.), *Zivilcourage trainieren! Theorie und Praxis* (Training moral courage: Theory and practice). Göttingen: Hogrefe.

Jonas, K. J.; Boos, M.; and Brandstätter, V. (eds.), 2007b. *Zivilcourage trainieren! Theorie und Praxis* (Training moral courage: Theory and practice). Göttingen: Hogrefe.

Jonas, K. J., and Brandstätter, V., 2004. *Zivilcourage*—Definitionen, Befunde, Maßnahmen (Moral courage—Definition, findings and intervention). *Zeitschrift für Sozialpsychologie* 35:185–200.

Jonas, K. J.; Boos, M.; Backes, S.; Büttner, N.; Ehrenthal, J.; and Prasse, A., 2002. Göttinger Zivilcourage training (Göttingen moral courage training). *Polizei und Wissenschaft* 1/2002:72–82.

Kruglanski, A. W.; Shah, J. Y., Fishbach, A.; Friedman, R.; Chun, W. Y.; and Sleeth-Keppler, D., 2002. A theory of goal systems. *Advances in Experimental Social Psychology* 34:331–378.

Kuhl, J., 1994. Motivation and Volition. In d'Ydewalle, G.; Eelen, P.; and Bertelson, P. (eds.), *International perspectives on psychological science*, Vol. 2: The state of the art. Hillsdale, N.J.: Lawrence Erlbaum.

Labuhn, A. S.; Wagner, U.; van Dick, R.; and Christ, O., 2004. Determinanten zivilcouragierten Verhaltens: Ergebnisse einer Fragebogenstudie (Determinants of moral courage behavior: Results from a questionnaire study). *Zeitschrift für Sozialpsychologie* 35:93–103.

Laner, M. R.; Benin, M. H.; and Ventrone, N. A., 2001. Bystander attitudes towards victims of violence: Who's worth helping? *Deviant Behavior* 22:23–42.

Latané, B., and Darley, J.M., 1970. *The unresponsive bystander: Why doesn't he help?* New York: Appleton-Century-Crofts.

Levine, M.; Prosser, A.; Evans, D.; and Reicher, S., 2005. Identity and emergency intervention: How social group membership and inclusiveness of group boundaries shape helping behavior. *Personality and Social Psychology Bulletin* 31:443–453.

Levine, M., and Thompson, K., 2004. Identity, place and bystander intervention: Social categories and helping after natural disasters. *The Journal of Social Psychology* 144:229–245.

Meyer, G., 2004. *Lebendige Demokratie: Zivilcourage und Mut im Alltag* (Democracy alive: Moral courage and courage in everyday life). Baden-Baden: Nomos.

Nunner-Winkler, G., 2007. Zum Begriff Zivilcourage (Regarding the concept of *Zivilcourage*). In Jonas, K. J.; Boos, M.; and Brandstätter, V. (eds.), *Zivilcourage trainieren! Theorie und Praxis* (Training moral courage: Theory and practice). Göttingen: Hogrefe.

Nunner-Winkler, G., 2002. Zivilcourage als Persönlichkeitsdisposition— Bedingungen der individuellen Entwicklung (Moral courage as a personality trait—individual development prerequisites). In Feil, E.; Homann, K.; and Wenz, G. (eds.). *Zivilcourage und Demokratische Kultur: 6. Dietrich Bonhoeffer-Vorlesung Juli, 2001 in München*. Münster: LIT.

Pratto, F., and John, O. P., 1991. Automatic vigilance: The attention-grabbing power of negative social information. *Journal of Personality and Social Psychology* 61:380–391.

Sassenberg, K.; Jonas, K. J.; Shah, J. Y.; and Brazy, P. C., 2007. Why some groups just feel better: The regulatory fit of group power. *Journal of Personality and Social Psychology* 92:249–267.

Sassenberg, K., and Hansen, N., 2006. The impact of regulatory focus on affective responses to social discrimination. *European Journal of Social Psychology* 36:1–24.

Scheele, B., and Kapp, F., 2002. Utopie Zivilcourage: zur Integration von Fürsorgemoral und öffentlichem Handeln (Moral courage as utopia: Towards the integration of care ethics and public behavior). *Kölner Psychologische Studien*, VII/2002.

Schwartz, S. H., and Howard, J. A., 1981. A normative decision-making model of altruism. In Rushton, J. P., and Sorrentino, R. M. (eds.), *Altruism and Helping Behavior*. Hillsdale, N.J.: Erlbaum.

Semin, G. R.; Higgins, E. T.; de Montes, L. G.; Estourget, Y.; Valencia, J. F., 2005. Linguistic signatures of regulatory focus: How abstraction fits promotion more than prevention. *Journal of Personality and Social Psychology* 89:36–45.

Staub, E., 1993. The psychology of bystanders, perpetrators and heroic helpers. *International Journal of Intercultural Relations* 17:315–341.

Staub, E., 2003. *The psychology of good and evil: Why children, adults and groups help and harm others*. New York: Cambridge University Press.

Staub, E., 2005. The roots of goodness: The fulfillment of basic human needs and the development of caring, helping and nonaggression, inclusive caring, moral courage, active bystandership, and altruism born of suffering, In: Carlo, G., and Edwards, C. (eds.), *Moral motivation through the life span*. Nebraska Symposium on Motivation, Lincoln: Nebraska.

Staub, E., 2006. *A brighter future: Raising caring, nonviolent, morally courageous children*. New York: Oxford University Press.

PART II

Care, Social Identification, and Altruism: Examples from the United States, Poland, and Finland

CHAPTER 6

The Psychology of Natural Law and Care

C. Fred Alford

What would happen, I wondered, if I asked young people some simple moral questions, such as the following: "The UN Declaration of Human Rights says that 'Everyone has a right to life, liberty and security of person' [Article 3]. Do you think this is true? How would you answer someone who said 'that's ridiculous'?" I didn't expect many of my informants (I use the anthropological term) to say no, but I expected many to have trouble defending their answer, especially when confronted with the specter of relativism that seems to haunt our age. It was, in any case, not their answers I was primarily interested in, but their reasoning. This is why my research took the form of hour-long (or longer) interviews with thirty young people between the ages of eighteen and twenty-eight, almost equally divided between men and women.

Hardly a random sample, they were nonetheless diverse, holding half a dozen different religious beliefs, with family connections all over the globe. Almost one-fourth were first-generation Americans—that is, the first generation of their family to be born and raised in America. More non-whites than would be found in a strictly random sample were interviewed. Though my sample size is too small to draw any conclusions, it is not my impression that race or religion made the slightest difference in how informants answered the questions. What did seem to make a difference for several informants was being raised by parents with strong continuing ties to traditional Asian, African, or South American cultures. Overall, however, it is the similarity in the beliefs of this demographically diverse group of young people that is most striking. Being born and bred in America is by far the most important variable of all.[1]

---

[1] Details of my research can be found in Alford, *Psychology of the natural law of reparation* (2006). Questions asked are in the Appendix to this essay. Further discussion of my results can be found there.

While being born and bred in America is the most important variable, I was asking informants to talk about the larger world, an increasingly confusing place for many who live in the United States, especially since the terrorist attacks of September 11, 2001. My research bridged these attacks (see research appendix). What I cannot say is that the attacks themselves made a difference in the answers I received. What matters is that the larger framework of my research changed, as the psychology of care in a globalized world suddenly became more complex. One might speculate that fear and distancing would each play a greater role.

This is not what I found, but my research did not draw on enough subjects, or cover a long enough time-span after the attacks to support any definitive conclusion. What I can say is that young people in the United States do not share the relativism that many of their elder critics attribute to them. On the contrary, my informants see themselves as part of a shared humanity. The bonds that tie most informants to billions of people all over the world, my research also reveals, are tenuous. There is no reason to think that domestic pressures, crises, and catastrophes, if sufficiently extended (or politically exploited) will not take their toll.

Contrary to my expectations, as well as those of several cultural critics, such as Alan Bloom (1988, 25), and Alasdair MacIntyre (2000), informants were neither drawn to relativism, nor intimidated by it. On the contrary, most held quite definite beliefs about right and wrong; moreover, they regarded these beliefs as binding on others as well as themselves. Only one informant said anything like Rita: "For me, abortion isn't just wrong. It's murder. But that's only my opinion." That is, only one informant made a universal moral claim in one breath, and in the next qualified it as pertaining only to herself, a mere opinion. Hers was a position as incoherent as that described by MacIntyre, where the language of universal principles is used to express what are in fact personal preferences. Or is it vice-versa? For Rita there was hardly any difference.

Informants' moral views were not always crystal clear. They were, however, almost always expressed in the form of a coherent narrative, a story about the conditions of a decent human life, albeit not an excellent one. To be sure, the story told by most informants had the quality of a radically simplified narrative, one in which most of the details are glossed over, so that it reads more like a plot outline that a story. But a plot outline is not incoherent, just something that needs to be filled in. How that might work is addressed in the conclusion to this chapter.

In one respect my approach was straightforward, in another not. The questions I asked were ones to which I really wanted to know the answers. What was not quite so straightforward was my focus on the moral reasoning involved.

- Why do you think that way?
- What has led you to that conclusion?
- What if I don't accept your assumption—is there any way you could persuade me?
- Not everyone thinks the way you do. How is it you came to this particular conclusion?
- What if I were to say that's a really strange opinion? How would you respond?

It is with follow-up questions like these that I tried to get at the reasoning involved, and ultimately to find the informant's stopping place, beyond which he or she could not go without falling into incoherence or silence. One way or another, I kept asking "why?" This meant that I pushed a little harder than I was comfortable with, harder than I have in other interviews for other research projects. Still, none of the informants seemed to get angry, or become agitated. Perhaps this is because we were talking about an issue, and using examples that were not terribly close to the heart of most informants.

I expected informants to stop either at God (that is, sacred scripture) or sociological relativism. When pressed by a series of "why" questions about morality, I expected them either to rest their argument on an ultimate authority, God, or the opposite, such as the informant who said "that's just how we do things in our culture." This informant was, however, not the norm. Indeed, my expectations were met neither about God nor about relativism, though one could argue that the "social contract," a common answer, is a version of sociological relativism.

This, though, is not how most informants talked about the social contract. For most of those who referred or alluded to the social contract (in one way or another, almost eighty percent did), the social contract is rooted in what I call "metaphysical biology." As one informant put it, "we are all born in the same way, we all came from the same place," so that makes everybody equal. Actually, Robert said "so that makes everybody the same." It is I who translated "the same" into "equal," and not without some difficulty.

Fred Alford: Do you mean everyone is identical?
Robert: No, of course not. I mean that because we all come from the same place we are all the same.
F.A.: Ah, you mean that we all have the same basic human rights?
R.:. Not exactly. That's the way you put it in the language professors use. I mean something simpler than that. I don't know how to put it into your words. I mean that about some things we really are the same. Not about baseball and grades, things like that, but about life.

Though I continued to ask Robert questions, I never got any closer to what he really meant. One possibility is that he could not articulate what he really meant. The other was that he could articulate what he really meant, and this was it. In the end I was never quite sure with Robert.

Robert was an exception, but he was not the lone exception. Jacques Maritain (2001, 34–35), the twentieth century's most influential exponent of Thomistic natural law, compares natural law to a "melody produced by the vibration of deep-rooted tendencies made present in the subject." If so, then imprecision is something we must accept. Natural law was never a law or precept to begin with; that comes much later, the product of schoolmen and lawyers. The problem is that melodies are open to interpretation, both by the interviewer, and by the subject. But there seems to be no alternative. I will try to state when I am doing more than the usual amount of filling in.

Robert's position was shared by most informants, even as they themselves were generally the ones to conclude "so that makes us equal" (or some similar phrase) without any prompting. I call this position *metaphysical biology* because biological facts, that we are all born in the same way and headed for the same end, are seen as the ground of an ethical claim. More precisely put, for most informants, biological fact is an ethical claim; there is no gulf between "is" and "ought" to be bridged. Metaphysical biology is natural law, albeit a radically simplified version.

Why not lie, cheat, or steal, I asked? (the burden of several questions). "Because if everybody did that, there would be no society left. Society is based on a contract. Without rules there would be nothing," is how Don put it. Sam put it a little differently.

> From kindergarten on, everyone learns the rules of life. Play fair, don't cheat, don't steal. Most people don't even think about it, but when you do, you see that it's like we all born into the same club. You get to join just by being a member of the human race, but you only get to stay a member if you play by the rules. Most people want to belong, and even if they don't, they're too scared not to.

Joyce explained the social contract this way.

> Joyce: No one ever says "sign this piece of paper and you can belong to society." But that's the way it works. With millions of people you have to have rules.
> Fred Alford: Do the rules make sense?
> J.: Usually they do, but it doesn't really matter. Having the rules is more important than agreeing with every little detail.
> F.A.: Why?
> J.: Because without rules no one would know what to expect. If you want to play, you have to have rules. Otherwise you get hurt or killed . . . . When my mom was a kid they used to have a game called "Life." She made me and my sisters play it with her when we

were kids, like it was a big treat. [Joyce rolls her eyes.] Well, that was just a game. What we are talking about now, that's the real rules of the game of life.

If one were going to characterize the view of the majority of informants, *positivistic natural law* would appear to come closest to the mark. The preeminent theorist of positivistic natural law is H. L. A. Hart (1994). Given certain facts of human nature, Hart argues that enforceable law is necessary if humans are to live decently among each other. The facts of human nature include the following:

- Human vulnerability: if humans had exoskeletons, natural law would look quite different.
- Relatively equality: the weakest can kill the strongest because even the strong must sleep.
- Limited altruism: people are not devils, but neither are they angels.
- Limited resources: people need food and shelter, and so some institution of property, though not necessarily private property, is needed.
- Limited understanding and strength of will: most can see the point of this minimal natural law (for that is what Hart calls it), but they frequently lack the foresight and strength of will to stick to these arrangements. (Hart 1994, 194–198)

Given these facts, says Hart, one can see that the laws of states and nations, what is called *positive law*, are rooted in natural necessity, which Hart readily characterizes with the term *natural law*. "These simple truisms we have discussed ... disclose the core of good sense in the doctrine of Natural Law" (1994).

Trouble is, the natural necessity Hart refers to is void of moral content. An unjust legal system would fulfill the needs of stability as well as a just legal system. A system of laws that preserved the security, stability, and property of its members would be valid, even if these laws condoned slavery and the persecution of minorities. One thinks here of National Socialism in Germany, a system of obsessive legality, under which the dispossession and persecution of the Jews was entirely legal.

Hart recognizes this problem. He simply does not think it is best solved under the guidance of the natural law. On the contrary, men and women must take the moral burden upon themselves to violate an iniquitous law, as Hart calls it (1994, 211–212). Hart holds this position because he believes that "the *minimum content* of Natural Law" is supported by the facts of human nature, whereas "a teleological conception of nature as containing in itself levels of excellence" is "too metaphysical for modern minds" (1994, 192–193, emphasis his).

Where Hart goes wrong, or at least provides insufficient guidance, especially in light of the experience of my informants, is in implying that in stepping outside the law one is stepping into a realm of moral nothingness, or at least into a realm in which nothing useful can be said. Hart does not state this explicitly, but because he says nothing else about this realm outside the law, that is the conclusion one must draw. The complement of Hart's positivistic natural law is moral decisionism (arbitrariness).

Freud said that neurotics, and many others besides, "take exception to the fact that *'inter urinas et faeces nascimur* [we are born between urine and faeces]'" (Freud 1930, 108). Informants are neither this graphic, nor quite this reductive. Yet, far from objecting to this fact, almost half of my informants referred in one way or another to the physical facts of birth or death as conveying moral as well as legal equality.

> *John: We all enter the world the same way, and we leave in the same way too.*
> *Fred Alford: What does that mean?*
> *J.: It means that we are all equal.*
> *F.A.: Do you mean physically the same?*
> *J.: I mean we all deserve to be treated equally [in a tone that suggested I just didn't get it].*

Not sociological relativism, and not God, but a version of natural-law thinking based on biological commonality grounds a basic set of human rights that almost all these informants share: they want these rights for themselves, and they recognize that others, so similar to themselves as far as the basics are concerned, possess these rights as well (though this last point gets a little complicated, as we shall see). Or as King Solomon put it,

> When I was born, I breathed the common air, and was laid on the earth that all men tread: and the first sound I uttered, as all do, was a cry.... There is no king that had any other beginning; for all come into life by a single path, and by a single path go out again. (Wisdom of Solomon, 7:3–6)

Morris expressed a similar idea, albeit less elegantly, when he said:

> *Morris: we're born, we live, we die, and along the way we try to be happy?*
> *Fred Alford: Does everyone have a right to be happy?*
> *M.: Yes, but that doesn't mean that everyone gets to be happy. That depends on luck and how hard you work. Mostly luck, like not being born in Iraq.*

Like Hart, informants hold to the minimum content of natural law. Unlike Hart, they make no distinction between what is contingently necessary to hold society together and what men and women ought to do. For informants, *is* and *ought* flow into each other as readily as the Tigris and Euphrates, but only about the practices that make civilization possible. Unlike Thomas Aquinas, as well as so many other theorists of the natural law, they do not go on to derive or (in what amounts to the same thing) tell a story about the development of this confluence in history, or contemporary experience. On the contrary, a number of informants who believe in the minimal natural law went on to say that they would cheat on a test, or even a government contract, if doing so meant the difference between passing and failing, keeping the job or getting fired. The minimal natural law is just that: minimal. It does not extend to or imply practices such as honesty, trustworthiness, commitment to community, love of justice, and so forth, at least not when issues of life and death are not involved.

IS METAPHYSICAL BIOLOGY A MINIMAL VERSION OF THE NATURAL LAW?

The history of the natural law, at least in the tradition of Aquinas, has been to derive this or that principle or practice from the founding principle of natural law, "good is to be done, and evil is to be avoided" (ST I–II, 94, 2). From this single assumption, Aquinas derives a wide range of obligations, from procreating and caring for children, to fostering community and not giving unnecessary offense to others. Much argument among believers in the traditional natural law concerns whether this or that is a true derivation.

For most informants, the natural law implies only itself. One should not lie, cheat, or steal if that is going to cost another person his life, liberty, or large amounts of his property. But if the result is that the liar gets better grades and a better job, so be it. Not every informant concluded in this way, but a surprising number did.

Why? Because metaphysical biology is quite literally superficial, concerning only the basics we share as embodied humans. Metaphysical biology lacks the teleological structure that has traditionally defined natural law, and almost totally lacks the complex narrative structure that has taken the place of teleology in the work of MacIntyre (1981) and others. Jacques Maritain (2001, 29), the most brilliant Thomist of the last century, exemplifies both traditions when he calls the natural law "the ideal formula of development of a given being." Natural law does not just characterize the stories we have in common. Natural law anticipates the stories we could have in common if we were to develop ourselves more perfectly and completely.

Metaphysical biology, while having a teleological structure—to be born is already to share equally and rightfully in the goods of life, liberty, and security, an assumption that presumes a lifetime—gets stuck at the beginning, evidently because it is so biological, so body-based. In this respect, metaphysical biology comes close to Hobbes's account of the fear of violent death that unites us all under the sovereign. Hobbes (1968) understands his account in *Leviathan* as being entirely in accord with the natural law, and others, such as Norberto Bobbio (1993), have interpreted Hobbes in this vein. But it is a vein that runs no deeper, and more important can run no deeper, than Hart's positivistic natural law. That is, no deeper than the metaphysical biology of most of my informants.

One apparent consequence of the way informants view the social contract—not as a rational agreement, but as a fact of life—is that not a single informant thought that the "defect strategy," as it is called in game theory, was worth arguing against, and not because they assumed it in advance. They just did not think that way. What would happen, I asked, if someone said, in effect, "Let everybody else obey the social contract; that just means more opportunity for me to lie, cheat, and steal"? (This question is implicit in several questions, and explicit in question 9.) This is the position of Plato's Thrasymachus (*Republic* 336b–354b), and it is why Hobbes thought a mighty sovereign was necessary.

Informants who saw the social contract as self-evident did not talk this way. Since most were more than willing to indulge their selfishness about other matters, I have no reason to think they were misleading me or themselves. In this regard, the informants fail to fulfill MacIntyre's (2000) assumption that the culture of advanced modernity is one of extreme individualism. For game theory (even so-called cooperative games, such as the famous "prisoner's dilemma") assumes that the individual always puts him or herself first. About the minimal content of natural law, as Hart calls it, most informants were willing to see themselves as equals.

> Joan: Most people are socialized to play by the rules, and those who aren't will one day pay the price.... And even if a few don't, most still play by the rules, and that's enough.
> Fred Alford: Do people like to play by the rules?
> J.: It's not a matter of like or dislike. It's the way people are brought up.
> F.A.: Do you think it's natural to want to play by the rules?
> J.: What's natural? It's whatever you want to do, that's what's natural, and most people either want to play by the rules or are too scared not to, and that's enough to keep society going.

Enough to keep society going, but not enough to make it a very pleasant place to live. Joan elaborated.

> I believe in the social contract, and I try to follow it. But if I were really under pressure for the grade or the job, I'd lie or cheat if I had to. I think most people would. The social contract is what keeps civilization from falling apart. It's not really about small things. It's about not killing, stuff like that.

Most informants were neither this bold nor this harsh, but they came close. None, by the way, seem particularly bothered by the minimal character of the contract. Nor are they bothered by the failure of the Enlightenment project, as Alasdair MacIntyre calls it—that is, the failure of reason to justify morality (MacIntyre 1981, 49–75). Not reason, but common humanity, minimal as it is, grounds the beliefs of most young people in the minimal social contract.

CARE AND IMAGINATION ARE MISSING

Missing among most informants is a concept of care and community, a view of society loosely based on the extended family. To be sure, contract has its place in the modern world, but not as the alpha and omega of the natural law. The extended family is the framework within which Aquinas viewed the natural law (ST I–II, 94, 4, 6). Which is why many, such as Reinhold Niebuhr (1988), argue that Thomistic natural law remains inextricably bound to a medieval worldview. Whether or not this is true of Thomas, it is certainly not true of many of his followers, such as Maritain, once considered socially radical, "The Red Christian," who argued until the end of his days that one most fully experiences the natural law by sharing in it with a community of others (Maritain 2001, 35).

Nothing of this way of thinking was present in more than several informants. Had the way of care and community been absent in all informants, I don't think I would have noticed, since its absence defines our society. Striking was the contrast between several informants who talked about care and community, and the rest for whom this way of thinking was absent. Consider Maya, who says she is shocked at the carelessness and callousness of many Americans. Morality, she says, "means to behave in a manner in which one is not ashamed." She continues,

> Maya: When I walk down the street [in Washington, D.C.] I'm shocked at all the homeless people. It makes me feel less moral.
> Fred Alford: Do you mean it makes you feel ashamed?
> M.: Yes, exactly. It makes me ashamed to be an American.

Maya says not one word about the social contract. Her context is care and shame. Then she goes on to say something truly shocking, for I had not heard its like before. "Most humans aren't good. Not just Americans. I mean most people." Taken aback, all I could think to ask was how this fit in with her morality. To Maya the answer was obvious.

M.: Because most people aren't good, they have to be taught to feel shame at the right things. People don't have to be good. They just have to be taught.
F.A.: Should people feel shame for not caring?
M.: Absolutely, that's number one.

A number of years ago now, Carol Gilligan (1982) wrote *In a Different Voice*, which argued that women think about morality in terms different from men: men think in terms of principles and cases, women in terms of details and caring. Whether or not one agrees with Gilligan, the care that several informants talked about (two were men) seems at first glance to fit Gilligan's model. The minimal social contract version of the natural law, held by almost eighty percent of informants, represents principled thinking, or at least that is the way most seem to talk about it. Care represents a concern for others, such as the homeless whom Maya sees almost every day.

With the term *care*, Gilligan refers to a way of experiencing the world that sees moral problems as marked by how we show concern for and responsibility toward particular others, rather than as a problem of rights and rules. "Thus, the logic underlying an ethic of care is a psychological logic of relationships, which contrasts with the formal logic of fairness that informs the justice approach" (Gilligan 1982, 73). From the perspective of care, I need to gather all the information I can, all the details that are generally absent from hypothetical situations, in order to minimize the chances of hurting anyone. Against the care perspective Gilligan sets what is often called universal morality, the morality of Immanuel Kant for example, which determines our obligations by figuring out which general rules apply to a particular situation.

In fact, Gilligan's concept of care does not fit my informants' use of the term. Though my sample is too small to be more than suggestive (Gilligan never discusses her sample size or characteristics), when the few informants who did talk about care they talked in universalistic and abstract terms. In other words, they talked about care in terms that were oxymoronic, as Gilligan formulates the concept.

What seems to be happening with Maya, as well as several other informants, is that the unstructured questions I asked turned them away from hypothetical scenarios such as "Should Heinz steal a drug he can't afford in order to save his wife's life?" (a standard "stages of moral development" test question employed by Gilligan, as well as her teacher and *bête noire*, Lawrence Kohlberg), and toward real-world ethical problems they faced as thoughtful young men and women almost every day of their lives. Above all, how to care for the suffering of those whom they barely know, or may never even see, except perhaps on television? In such circumstances, care itself becomes the problem. Not whether to care or to follow universal rules, but how to care in an anonymous, rationalized world in which human suffering seems endless, and often nameless and faceless as well. Or as Marc put it,

> *I know how to care for my friends and my family. Oh, I don't always get it right, but I have the basic idea. What I don't know how to do is care for the people who need it most, people who live in some country I've never heard of, people I'll never meet, never even see, except on television, and then I'll probably turn it off because I'm eating dinner. But I won't be able to turn it off in my head, if you know what I mean.*

Here is a dimension of the problem of caring that does not even arise in Gilligan's account. A few informants struggle with an even more difficult question: how to find a place for care in a political (indeed, global) world that has no place for such personal impulses, whose very size and anonymity seem to drive out the human connections upon which care is based. I do not know the answer to this question, but it seems to me that it is the more important and difficult question in our era.

Care in a Global World

Two essays in this collection represent complementary ways of thinking about care in a globalized world. Paul Nesbitt-Larking's "Terrible Beauty: Globalization, Consciousness, and Ethics" addresses the liberation that may take place in the spaces opened up by globalization. Identities imposed by others, by tradition, and by habit are every day being broken on the wheel of globalization. As an example, he refers to a study exploring the possibilities of "queer identities in Hong Kong," something that would not have been possible even a dozen years ago.

Yet it should not be overlooked that the postmodern critique of globalization, fruitful in many respects, particularly as it discovers the emancipatory potential of dialectic (that is, dialogue) and doubt, is not the same as care. Furthermore, care for others is not really part of the vocabulary of this approach. The postmodern critique of globalization identifies spaces in which care might emerge, but it lacks any vocabulary, or intellectual heritage, in which to talk about care. (In my book on Emmanuel Levinas [Alford 2002], I argue that this lack is why a surprising number of postmoderns have turned to a previously obscure Talmudic scholar, but that is another story.) In the end, space for care is not enough. The heart must be there too, an identification with the suffering of others. Sometimes one wonders if academics idealize otherness in order not to have to address—to feel—the terrible sameness of all human suffering.

Sarah Scuzzarello's "Multiculturalism and Caring Ethics" goes directly to the heart of the matter, asking how can we understand difference from the perspective of care. Her refreshing answer is to focus less on general critiques of globalization, and more on "concrete political activity guided by a moral and theoretical framework that sees responsibilities as the very basis of our existence as relational and human beings." And if this sounds a little abstract, she certainly is on the right track in redefining the individual in relational terms, while seeking to "restructure the democratic practices in a way which recognizes the giving and receiving of care as a central aspect of human existence."

Trouble is, even though Scuzzarello recognizes the importance of empirical research in finding instances of care, she sometimes writes as if to say that if we could only get our "non-liberal ontology" right, everything else would follow. What if it doesn't? Not because people are by nature as I have described them (or rather, as they have described themselves), but because the social forces that make Western men and women who they are will not give way lightly to the theorist's pen (or word processor). Sometimes social theorists, including myself, write as if our just saying it right will compel reality to follow. This is why it is so important, and humbling, to go out and ask people how they experience their moral world. The problem of caring for anonymous others will not be solved by "saying it right," or even "doing it right" on any scale now imaginable. Should social theorists still wish to talk about the political practice of care in today's massified, globalized, world, then the insight shared by Nesbitt-Larking and Scuzzarello—that this will best take place in small spaces, generally on the margins of society, or at least with those on the margins—seems correct. One longs only for a little more of Max Weber's dark insight; the iron cage of rationalization has not nearly enough small spaces for all its inmates.

Once an Ethic of Care was Created by a Pen . . . and a World War

Consider the preamble to the United Nations' Universal Declaration of Human Rights, which refers to "the equal and inalienable rights of all members of the human family" as "the foundation of freedom, justice, and peace in the world" (Glendon 2002, 310). The purpose of the preamble, according to its author, René Cassin, was to establish an intellectual or philosophical perspective from which to understand the rights enumerated by the Declaration. That perspective, it turns out, was remarkably similar to the care perspective. To be sure, diplomats generally do not use the language of the care perspective per se. My point is that the Declaration was conceived less as a liberal document, and more as an expression of

> the dignitarian rights tradition of continental Europe and Latin America. . . . Dignitarian rights instruments, with their emphasis on the family, and their greater attention to duties, are more compatible with Asian and African

tradition. In these documents, rights bearers tend to be envisioned within families and communities. (Glendon 2002, 227)

It is this dignitarian tradition that comes remarkably close to the care perspective. Not the care perspective of Gilligan, but that of several informants, who struggle with how to care for abstract and anonymous others.

One should perhaps not make too much of intellectual foundations of morality, particularly as far as the United Nations Declaration of Human Rights is concerned. Jacques Maritain, who played a leading role in the UNESCO philosophers' committee, which advised the Declaration drafting committee, liked to tell the story of how a visitor to one meeting was amazed that men of such vastly different cultures, beliefs, and ideologies could agree on a list of fundamental rights. Yes, the man was told, "we agree about the rights but on the condition no one asks us why" (Glendon 2002, 77).[2] The tougher question is whether the experience of care, whatever it is called, must become attenuated unto nothingness as it is extended to encompass a family too big to be a real family—the human family. Can a species ever become a family? Or perhaps I am being too literal. Perhaps the care we receive in families remains a useful moral metaphor or narrative for those with the imagination to adopt it.

In another chapter in this collection, Katarzyna Hamer and Jakub Gutowski write about "Social Identifications and Pro-Social Activity in Poland." They find that "people high in identification with all humanity" donated more to charity, as well as participating somewhat more in civic life, even if "identification with all humanity" is not a strikingly powerful explanatory variable. The first thing to notice is that any overlap between identification with humanity and the metaphysical social contract, which emphasizes "that we all come from the same place, and that we are all headed for the same end," is more apparent than real. By "identification with humanity," they mean a strong we-feeling "theoretically connected with Maslow's high level of self-actualization." But while there is little theoretical overlap between their study and my own, it is nevertheless the

---

[2] The UNESCO philosophers' advisory group advised the Declaration drafting committee, chaired by Eleanor Roosevelt, and later, Charles Malik. Maritain evidently did not regard the lack of agreement on foundations as fatal, understanding that the Declaration was a practical document, not a profession of faith (Glendon 2002, 77–78). The sadder part of the story is that the drafting committee apparently did not find the philosophers' work particularly helpful or relevant. Several felt UNESCO was treading on their turf, an old bureaucratic story (Glendon 2002, 83–84).

case that metaphysical biology certainly involves (indeed requires) a level of universal identification.

Yet, if my small study is valid, one can identify with others without this leading to a desire to care for them. Identification and care belong to different dimensions of experience. Identification stems from such a primordial level of experience that it does not even begin to enter the higher reaches of Maslow's, or Kohlberg's, hierarchies. That is at once its virtue and its limit. It is a virtue because it means that identification with all others will never be easily or completely obliterated, even by the most vicious regime or corrupt way of life. It is a limit because this identification does not readily translate into higher morality.

CONCLUSION

The moral relativist to whom so many refer, and against whom so many are rendered speechless, seems not to exist, at least not among those where one most expects to find him or her—the young.[3] Expressed more precisely, relativism is absent among the young whom I interviewed, most of whom hold to a minimal version of the natural law. Conversely, cultural critics such as MacIntyre and Bloom write as though the secular relativist dominates the culture. Not moral relativism, but moral minimalism, is the problem.

This may not seem like an important distinction, but I believe it is. Academics devote an enormous amount of time to grounding or founding moral claims, or (more commonly these days) showing why that is impossible, indeed undesirable: an act of intellectual imperialism. Jean-François Lyotard famously defines postmodernity as incredulity toward metanarratives (Lyotard 1984, xxiv). Yet it is upon a metanarrative that informants base

---

[3] Relativism is a subtle and complex teaching that should not be employed to hit opponents over the head, or intimidate students and educated laypersons. Consider "Protagorean relativism," as it is called. If one holds, as many scholars do, that the "man" in "man is the measure of all things" refers to humanity in general, not a particular individual, then we are talking about what best suits human beings, given their nature as humans. Seen from this perspective, Protagoras is doctor to humanity, saying simply that humanity is the measure of what works to cure humans of their failure to thrive. As with most illnesses, there may be more than one medicine that works, but there are even more that do not, and quite a few that are poisonous. Protagorean relativism, so interpreted, is not far distant from that Aristotelian strand in natural law that sees it as an expression of tutored human nature.

their morality—a minimalist metanarrative to be sure, but it is still a meta-narrative, not a mininarrative.

Theirs is not a mininarrative because while it lacks character, detail, and development, all the things we look for in a good story, Article 3 of the United Nations Declaration and its like are nonetheless about the most important things. There is nothing "mini-" about life, liberty, and security of persons. Nor is there anything "mini-" about the universality of the social contract. Thus, it is incorrect to state (as did a well-known and respected theorist of the natural law who responded to a version of this chapter when it was presented at a conference) that informants have abandoned the hierarchy of goods traditionally associated with the natural law. No, they have simply truncated the hierarchy, so that it stops short.

The difference between abandoning and truncating the hierarchy is important in determining if the minimal natural law provides more to work with than the liberalism that is supposedly everywhere triumphant. There is, after all, a difference between seeing human freedom as the highest value because it allows individuals to choose, and a viewpoint that sees the equality of all humans under the (admittedly truncated) natural law as the highest value. Under the former perspective, the choosing individual is rendered sacred; under the later, it is the metaphysical bond among individuals, what they share, that is, if not sacred, then at least the locus of value. Or as Henry Veatch (1978) puts it, do we believe in natural rights because people have rights merely by virtue of being individuals, or because we believe that it is right that all people observe the natural rights of others? Informants came a bit closer to the second sense of natural right than the first. That is actually a big difference, and a big deal. Enough so that I shall have to revise my statement that only several informants shared the care perspective. Only several informants articulated the care perspective; it is latent but implicit in the worldviews of several more.

Why do I say this? Because metaphysical biology is about what humans possess in common. For all that it lacks in teleological ambition, metaphysical biology possesses a keen sense of humans as common creatures, in the double sense of sharing much, as well as being at heart ordinary and unrefined. This perspective on humanity should be neither underestimated nor undervalued, particularly by those who aspire to the higher reaches of the natural law. Though no one put it as Freud did ("we are born between urine and faeces"), I don't believe it was an accident that this phrase kept recurring to me as I listened to informants describe what we have in common.

We all come from the same place, and we are headed for the same grave. There is nothing all that special about you, or about me. We are just naked biological beings in this world together for a little while, so we had better not put on airs, and not pretend that anyone is better than anyone else.

No informant put it quite this way, but this is the implication of metaphysical biology for most as far as the natural law is concerned.

Such a view, by the way, is quite compatible with considerable income inequality, as long as it does not threaten life, liberty, or security of persons. In economics, hard work and luck play leading roles, and Raymond's reasoning tends to prevail. People are enough alike that right now they are figuring out how to climb over me, so I had better get to work figuring out how to climb over them. Needed are basic rules, not the welfare state.

The result is hardly an image of man or woman *imago Dei*. Nor is the result one that aspires to hierarchies of virtue, development, or goodness. One would hope for something more elevated. And yet let us not overlook what is here to work with: an abstract (because it is based on an idea) but body-based and hence real, not ideal, sense of commonality (but not community) among all persons. What we have in common comes first. Here is the non-liberal, non-individualistic basis of the minimum natural law. At least this is the implication of metaphysical biology. The implication is not elevated, but it has little to do with the liberalism, or relativism, or most of the other "isms" that critics of the culture seem to find there.

And yet a puzzle remains. If informants hold a non-liberal justification of the natural law, it is hardly in the dignitarian tradition Glendon refers to, and not just because it does not sound very dignified. In responding to critics of the United Nations Declaration of Human Rights who argued that it reflected Western values, the Declarations' drafters, as well as the UNESCO philosophers who advised them, repeatedly invoked the similarity among all human beings. "Their starting point was the simple fact of the common humanity shared by every man, woman and child on the earth, a fact that, for them, put linguistic, racial, religious and other differences into their proper perspective." All, continues Glendon (2002, 232–233), would have agreed with a statement made by a representative of Human Rights Watch/ Asia in 1993: "Whatever else may separate them, human beings belong to a single biological species, the simplest and most fundamental commonality before which the significance of human differences quickly fades."

Put aside, dear reader, for just a moment your philosophies of *différence*, whether you spell the term in English or French. Put aside for a moment whether you think Glendon *et al.* are denying real human differences, and ask yourself the following question: why is it that the simple fact of shared humanity, including the recognition that we are a single species, leads the drafters of the UN Declaration to a complex and elaborate account of what we owe each other, whereas the simple fact of shared biological humanity leads my informants to a limited, truncated view of what we owe each other? This, I believe, is the puzzle we have only begun to solve. The answer, I believe, has to do with the biological reductionism of my informants. They mean something different by "shared humanity." Not entirely different, of course, but "shared humanity" means something more literal, less imaginative.

How to proceed in light of these considerations? Begin with the moral intuitions of most people (an approach famously practiced by Aristotle), which turns out to be, at least for the young people I spoke with, a minimalist version of natural law. Build on this basis, criticize it, all while taking the moral intuitions of citizens seriously. Academics could be helpful here, but only if they make an effort to learn and speak the moral language of everyday life. Ironically enough, that turns out to be a version of the natural law. One reason it is ironic is because many academics cannot get even this far, getting stuck at questions such as why we should not drop uranium on people from airplanes if it happens to make the sunset more radiant[4].

Academics did not create this world of moral abstraction. Credit belongs to the modern world itself, best summarized by what Max Weber called *rationalization*, in which it seems every aspect of one's life, including one's soul, comes to be managed by bureaucrats and experts (Weber 1948, 181). It is important that academics not further this process, rendering citizens even more defenseless when asked to explain their moral intuitions. Instead, academics should help clarify, develop, and expand these intuitions. The language of natural law, which joins intuition with tradition, community, and shared narrative, provides a moral *lingua franca* that comes closer to how average people think than many academics (including myself at the beginning of my research) recognize. But first we have to learn what moral intuitions people actually hold, and what there is to work with. That was the purpose of the research on which this essay is based.

APPENDIX

The following questions were asked of 22 informants. The remaining 8 answered a shorter questionnaire composed of questions 1, 2, 3, 6, 8, 10.

---

[4] I'm taking liberties with an example employed by T. M. Scanlon (1998, 168) in *What We Owe Each Other*. McGinn (1999) also takes a few liberties in a highly critical review in *The New Republic*.

I found that almost every response elicited by the longer questionnaire was elicited by the shorter, while providing a somewhat more relaxed atmosphere for discussion. More information can be found in Alford (2006).

1. The UN Declaration of Human Rights says that "Everyone has a right to life, liberty and security of person." [Article 3] Do you think this is true? How would you answer someone who said no?

2. You're in a tough chemistry class in which it seems that almost everyone cheats. The professor doesn't seem to care, leaving the classroom during exams for long periods of time. On the midterm you got a D. The people who cheated got all A's and B's. It's time to take the final. What do you do? Why?

3. You're on a committee developing the new moral education curriculum at Thomas Jefferson High School. What's the single most important thing you should teach? Why?

4. The UN Declaration of Human Rights says "All human beings are born free and equal in dignity and rights." [Article 1] Do you think it's true? What if someone says "No, I think some people are better than others and ought to have more rights." What do you say?

5. You are working on a government contract. Your company is in economic trouble, and your boss asks you to over-bill the government—that is, bill the government for hours that you didn't work. If you don't, the company might go under, and many would lose their jobs. What would you do? Why?

6. What's the most important thing in the world? Why?

7. Imagine that you are about fifty years old. As a young man/woman, you were very aggressive in getting to the top. Along the way you told some lies, and ruined some reputations. Some people were hurt. Now you regret that deeply. What do you do about it?

8. What is morality? Why be moral?

9. What if someone said to you "I lie, cheat, and steal any time I think I can get away with it? Sometimes I get caught, but it's worth it. I do it for the thrill, like playing the lottery." What do you say or do? What do you think?

10. What's the worst thing in the world? Why?

My research was approved by the Institutional Review Board of my university. About half of the informants were interviewed before September 11, 2001.

REFERENCES

References to Thomas Aquinas's *Summa of Theology*, abbreviated in the text as ST, are given in the text in the form that is usual in classical studies.

Alford, C. F., 2002. *Levinas, the Frankfurt School, and psychoanalysis.* Middletown, Conn., and London: Wesleyan University Press and Continuum Books.

Alford, C. F., 2006. *Psychology and the natural law of reparation.* Cambridge: Cambridge University Press.

Bloom, A., 1988. *Closing of the American mind.* New York: Touchstone Books.

Bobbio, N., 1993. *Thomas Hobbes and the natural law tradition,* translated by Daniela Gobetti. Chicago: University of Chicago Press.

Freud, S., 1930. "Civilization and its discontents," in *The standard edition of the complete psychological works of Sigmund Freud,* edited and translated by James Strachey et al. 24 vols. London: Hogarth Press, 1953–1974, vol. 21: 59–148.

Gilligan, C., 1982. In a different voice: Psychological theory and women's development. Cambridge: Harvard University Press.

Glendon, M. A., 2001. A world made new: Eleanor Roosevelt and the Universal Declaration of Human Rights. New York: Random House.

Hamer, K., and Gutowski, J. (2009). "Social identification and pro-social activity in Poland," in On behalf of others. New York: Oxford University Press.

Hart, H. L. A., 1994. *The concept of law,* 2nd ed. Oxford: Clarendon Press of Oxford University Press [with new postscript].

Hobbes, T., 1968. *Leviathan,* edited by C. B. Macpherson. Harmondsworth, England: Penguin Books.

Lyotard, J.F., 1984. *The postmodern condition: A report on knowledge,* translated by Geoff Bennington and Brian Massumi. Minneapolis: University of Minnesota Press.

Maritain, J., 2001. *Natural law: Reflections on theory and practice,* edited by William Sweet. South Bend, Ind.: St. Augustine's Press.

McGinn, C., 1999. "Reasons and Unreasons." In *The New Republic,* May 24 (pp. 34ff.) [review of Scanlon, *What We Owe Each Other*].

MacIntyre, A., 1981. *After virtue.* Notre Dame, Ind.: University of Notre Dame Press.

MacIntyre, A., 2000. "Theories of natural law in the culture of advanced modernity," in *Common truths: New perspectives on natural law,* edited by Edward McLean. Wilmington, Del.: ISI Books.

Nesbitt-Larking, P., 2009. "Terrible beauty: Globalization, consciousness, and ethics," in On behalf of others. New York: Oxford University Press (unpublished).

Niebuhr, R., 1988. "Christian Faith and Natural Law," in *Saint Thomas Aquinas on politics and ethics,* edited by Paul Sigmund (pp. 222–225). New York: W. W. Norton.

Scanlon, T. M., 1998. *What we owe each other*. Cambridge: The Belknap Press of Harvard University Press.

Scuzzarello, S. 2009. "Multiculturalism and Caring Ethics," in On behalf of others. New York: Oxford University Press.

Veatch, H. 1978. *"Natural law: Dead or alive?"* In Literature of liberty, vol. 1, no. 4: 7–31.

Weber, M., 1958. *The Protestant ethic and the spirit of capitalism*, translated by Talcott Parsons. New York: Charles Scribner's Sons.

CHAPTER 7

Empathy, Prejudice and Fostering Tolerance

Kristen Renwick Monroe and Maria Luisa Martinez

> If you just learn a single trick . . . you'll get along a lot better with all kinds of folks. You never really understand a person until you consider things from his point of view . . . Until you climb inside of his skin and walk around in it.
>
> *Harper Lee, To Kill a Mockingbird*

As globalization effectively makes the world smaller, bringing us into contact with people from a wider variety of backgrounds, it has highlighted the importance of differences. One major question thus becomes: What is the political significance of difference?[1] Why are ethnic, racial, or religious differences frequently politically significant, while differences in height, hair color, or weight are not? Why are linguistic differences sometimes relevant politically, and other times are not salient? What about age? Gender or sexual preferences? What fosters tolerance of differences judged ethically and politically salient? What encourages respect for these differences, leading some of us to reach out across divides that isolate others? These questions take on a poignant immediacy with reports of continuing prejudice, discrimination, ongoing ethnic, religious and sectarian violence— even genocidal activities and war—and increasing polarization over issues of race, religion, and ethnicity, at home and abroad. They are questions students need to consider as they go out into a world where they will meet new people, from diverse cultures, religions, and ethnicities. How can we best prepare them for this?

---

[1] We define politics to include normative concerns.

This chapter describes results from an experimental course program designed to use empathic involvement with "the other" to help students think deeply about their own attitudes toward people adjudged "different," whether these differences are associated with race, ethnicity, and religion, or with age, disability, sexual preference, etc. How can we understand these differences and address diversity among individuals and groups—which often arise as a consequence of globalization, immigration, and rapid social changes—as a normal condition of existence and not as a threat? We argue here that differences exist, but their ethical salience is socially constructed, shaped and perceived through a cognitive classification of oneself in relation to others. We further argue that empathy will help increase the understanding and tolerance of these differences. The course based on these assumptions was funded by the Ford Foundation Program on Difficult Dialogues and was taught at the University of California at Irvine, one of the most ethnically diverse campuses in the United States.[2] Subject to many of the same group tensions experienced at other American universities, it provided a particularly rich laboratory for our experiment.

The program followed traditional academic and literary readings on "difference" with a narrative interview project structured to heighten empathic involvement with at least one member of a group judged to be different and frequently discriminated against in contemporary American society. Students were asked to measure their own attitudes, using both quantitative and qualitative measures of prejudice, including a series of Implicit Association Tests (IAT, Greenwald, McGhee, and Schwartz, 1998) designed to measure sub-conscious attitudes toward prejudice. These tests were administered both before and after the intervention, and students were asked to choose a pseudonym and to track the shifts in attitudes of this pseudonymous person over the course of the term. A control group of analogous students, obtained via a respondent-driven nominee sample, participated in the same Implicit Association Tests (IAT), minus the course intervention.

This chapter describes results of the class experiment in three parts. Part 1 describes the underlying premises and how we structured our class experiment to focus on age as a wedge issue that would both tap into our philosophical/theoretical concerns and help detect more politically divisive instances of prejudice. Part 2 describes how we measured prejudice, pre- and post-intervention, using both extensive written work and Implicit

---

[2] In 2005, the 20,061 undergraduates at UCI identified themselves as Asian (49 percent), African American (2 percent), Chicano (12 percent), Caucasian (26 percent), other (8 percent), and foreign (2 percent). Other statistics are not available.

Association Tests. Part 3 presents the results from the experimental course that utilizes empathic involvement with "the other" to effect changes in attitudes toward members of groups frequently discriminated against in American society. A conclusion discusses the limitations in the experiment. While we note the need to expand and refine the program, overall, we found the experimental course offers a useful tool for scholars concerned with group identity, prejudice, and tolerance.

PHILOSOPHICAL, PEDAGOGICAL, AND THEORETICAL PSYCHOLOGICAL PREMISES

We adopted three underlying philosophical premises that distinguish this course experiment from the more traditional treatment of differences. (1) Differences exist. It is not the existence of a difference that is critical politically, but the ethical significance that is accorded the difference. (2) The ethical salience of a difference is socially constructed. There is no inherent reason why one difference—race or religion—should be politically significant when other differences—musical ability or weight—are not politically relevant. (3) The key to understanding the politics of difference is to think of cultural differences not as intrinsic and immutable but as the result of how differences are shaped and perceived—by oneself and by others—through a cognitive classification of oneself and of oneself in relation to others. Our treatment of others thus results, not from a rational calculus of interests that flows naturally from innately derived and immutable differences—such as race, gender or ethnicity—but rather from our perceptions of others as derived from the moral salience accorded these differences via a cognitive categorization and classification of others in relation to ourselves (Monroe, 1996; 2004, 2009).

Pedagogically, we assumed: (1) Students learn best not by listening to lectures but by being forced to examine their own preconceptions in the light of empirical evidence. (2) Emotions play an important part in permanent shifts in attitudes; hence, we emphasized narrative interviews designed to tap into emotional ties (McGaugh, 2003).

Theoretically, we adopted the assumptions underlying social identity theory (Tajfel, 1981; Turner, 1987) concerning psychological origins of inter-group *discrimination*. (1) People need to classify information and therefore frequently put themselves and others into categories. Labeling someone—Christian or Muslim, jock or nerd etc.—is a way of saying other things about these people and locating them in our own cognitive landscape. (2) Group identification arises from the human need to associate with certain *groups* (our in-groups) and relates to our own need to bolster our *self-esteem*. (3) Comparison between groups involves a process in which humans compare their groups with other groups and, in doing so, tend to exert favorable bias toward the groups with which they self-identify or to which they belong. (4) Finally, and perhaps most important, every individual has a wide repertoire of individual and group identities, and each identity helps inform the individual about who she or he is and what this identity entails; which aspect of this complex identity will become most salient for an individual at any time will vary depending on the social context. This context will be affected by diverse factors, one of which includes how the individual sees the person with whom she or he is interacting. This interaction will be highly dependent on the character traits of, and any personal relationship existing between, the individuals.

Empathic involvement with "the other" thus can enter the equation and influence ethical treatment of "the other" because of this psychological process. By emphasizing empathic involvement with "the other" as a critical part of ethics, we test a longstanding philosophical tradition locating empathy (Smith 1759) at the foundation of morality. We thus designed the course to encourage the empathic involvement that leads to seeing the world through the eyes of "the other," hoping this process would increase understanding and tolerance of differences.

Age as a Wedge Issue to Test Prejudice

We designed the experiment to combine readings about differences with a "hands-on" experience that combined cognitive analytical skill with the emotional impact psychologists now tell us influences cognition (McGaugh, 2003). We did so by examining a group often omitted in discussions of the politics of difference, a group into which none of us is born, that each of us frantically tries to avoid, that most of us—if we are very lucky—eventually move into and out of, depending on chance and situation, and a group that all of us—if we are fortunate—desperately hope to join eventually: the elderly.

Elders are treated differently by various cultures. Many UCI students were first-generation immigrants from Asia or the Middle East, living in extended families, and highly sensitive to the ways elders are treated by different cultures. Our study of these cultural differences attempted to help students disentangle what is "intrinsic" and immutable about becoming old (the loss of physical vigor, for example) from what is not (decline in financial resources, loss of a spouse), and to focus their attention on both the cultural differences and their own more individual views of the elderly. We designed the study specifically to help students see that, although some attributes exist independently of social construction, many are culturally imposed and hence are neither intrinsic nor immutable. A key goal in the course was helping students understand the normative political importance of categorization and the according of moral salience to other groups in our society.

Before beginning their interviews, students considered what part of the elderly identity relates to differences that are "real," such as the declines in health, deaths of a spouse or friends; and which differences exist primarily in the eyes of the beholder, such as those that occur when an otherwise sprightly older person is treated as infirm simply because of having white hair. We intended this exercise to encourage students to ask whether some of the differences other groups are said to have—often considered attributes that are "real" and that threaten our identity—are socially constructed. Do we have more in common with, and thus less to fear from, others than we realize?[3] Answering this key question helped students understand the importance of categorization and the according of moral salience to other groups in our society. The importance of approaching differences this way, of course, is normative as well as intellectual. To the extent that such differences are a function of cognitive construction, their ethical and political impact can be muted and reshaped through the kind of contact and understanding we hoped to foster in this course.

The class read traditional material on differences, such as social psychological work on prejudice, discrimination, and identity.[4] We gave special attention to social identity theory and self-categorization theory and also assigned novels (e.g., Tan's *The Joy Luck Club* and Ellison's *Invisible Man*) to supply the personal link psychologists now tell us provides the emotional clout to change opinions. One typical assignment linked philosophical work in ethics (Kant's categorical imperative), social psychological work on identity, and self-categorization theory to *Invisible Man* by asking students to describe a time when they were made to feel invisible and a time when they made someone else feel invisible. Students were encouraged—but not required—to share their essays with the class.

Students did extensive writing as part of the course and were trained in interviewing, editing, and writing narratives as a tool for understanding the psychology of another human being (Bar-On, 2006). After training in this

---

[3] This kind of contrast is evident in many areas, including immigration: For example, survey questions ask:" Will immigrants steal American jobs or enrich OUR economy?"

[4] Full details and course syllabus available upon request from KRMonroe@UCI.Edu

technique, each student focused closely on one elderly person to interview. Each student independently constructed a list of questions to pose to their elder. These questions were discussed in class, and all the questions were compiled and grouped into topical categories to form a master question-naire that all students could use as prompts. Students were encouraged to be flexible in their interview technique, to treat the interview as a dialogue or a conversation, and to follow the elder's lead, rather than enforcing a rigid interview schedule. In particular, students were told never to press an issue that seemed unsettling or difficult for the speaker to discuss, such as the death of a loved one. (See Monroe, 2004 on the interview technique.) Each student then chose an elder to interview; we encouraged interviews with someone in the speaker's family, both to strengthen and build on existing familial ties and to provide the student with a historical record of his or her own past. The professor conducted an in-class interview with her mother to illustrate and discuss the process and the challenges in doing such an interview. Students then conducted and transcribed the interviews with their elders, edited the transcriptions to try to capture the speakers' voice, and developed the interview into an analysis of the speakers' mindset, emotional terrain, values, beliefs, and worldview in contrast to the student's.

We began with age for several reasons. (1) Age is a relatively non-controversial difference associated with prejudice. (2) It is a "difference" that carries both "real" and socially constructed ethical significance. (3) Age is not a difference that is immutable; the elderly are not born old, and most students will themselves someday become old. (4) Age allowed us to inter-view someone with whom the student might already have existing ties of affection that could help bridge any gap associated with difference. (5) It avoided having students stuck into categories—being a Muslim or a Jew, a Hispanic or an Asian—they could not get out of during the rest of the term. We wanted to avoid the uni-dimensionality and rigidity that could occur if we began our discussions of prejudice and difference by identifying any class member as an X or a Y. For all these reasons, we hoped that age would act as a wedge to open broader discussions of prejudice that might be too tough to tackle in a group of students who initially would not know whether they could trust either the professor or their fellow students. The process worked well, and the general consensus was, as one student remarked, that "old people are just young people who've been around a long time." Perhaps more important, the exercise helped us have surpris-ingly frank discussions about the nature of prejudice, which consists—students decided—of denying others their individuality and rights as an individual.

MEASURING SHIFTS IN PREJUDICE

We used three measures of shifts in prejudice: (1) Implicit Association Tests, designed to tap into deep-seated, subconscious cultural prejudice, plus (2) written work and (3) class discussions to detect more conscious shifts in prejudice.

Design and Sample

The study is a quasi-experimental design with one experimental group and one control group. We used repeated measures in the experimental group, before and after the class, and one measure of the control group that we compared with the experimental group. Because the class was structured as a seminar, to maximize interaction, the total sample size was 28 subjects, distributed between both the experimental and control groups. The experimental group ($n = 15$) was composed of the students who participated in a class called The Politics of Difference. The experimental group was composed of 8 men and 7 women; 7 students were identified as Asian, 5 as Caucasian or White, 2 as Hispanic, and 1 as African-American.

Results for participants in the course were contrasted with comparable students whose names were secured through a respondent-driven nominee sample, a form of snowball sampling in which each student provided the names of friends not enrolled in the course but who corresponded with the student on critical background characteristics, such as age, ethnicity, religion, etc. Nominees took the same IAT tests but, of course, did not participate in the course. The control group was composed of 8 women and 5 men; 7 self-identified as Asian, 5 White, and 1 Hispanic.

Implicit Association Tests

To assess unconscious prejudices, we used the Implicit Association Tests (Greenwald, McGhee, and Schwartz, 1998). The IAT measures differential association of two target concepts with an attribute. The two concepts appear in a two-choice task (e.g., Young vs. Old), and the attribute in a second task (e.g., Pleasant vs. Unpleasant words for an evaluation attribute). When instructions oblige highly associated categories (e.g., Young + Pleasant) to share a response key, performance is traditionally faster than when less associated categories (e.g., Old + Pleasant) share a key. This performance difference implicitly measures differential association of the two concepts with the attribute. Widely utilized in psychology, the IATs have nonetheless been criticized as providing unreliable measures of prejudice (Cunningham, Preacher, and Banaji, 2001). These tests are available on several websites; we used tests at www://implicit.harvard.edu/implicit/demo/selectatest.html.

The IATs thus are computer-based tests in which the subject performs a classification task of different stimuli in different categories and the results are generated automatically by the program. There are seven possible results, which vary depending on what the specific test is assessing. The possible results—for all the IATs—were coded by the course assistant in a 7-point scale, in which 1 means strong preference toward one group and 7 means strong preference for the other group. For example, consider race. A 1 indicated preference for White in comparison to Black, 2 a moderate preference toward White in comparison to Black, 3 a slight preference toward White in comparison to Black, 4 meant little or no automatic preference toward any category, 5 indicated slight preference toward Black in comparison to White, 6 moderate preference toward Black in comparison to White, and 7 strong preference toward Black in comparison to White. All the IATs results used this same 7-point scale, with 4 the midpoint.

We chose six tests to assess unconscious attitudes concerning a potential prejudice that might affect our sample: race, age, Arab/Muslim, Asian, Judaism, gender-career. These tests were chosen because each one tapped into prejudice for one of the major four discriminators: race, gender, religion, and nationality or ethnicity. Since the logic behind each of these is rather straightforward, we note just one example, the scale for race, to suggest the logic and process for all the tests. Race has long been a divisive issue in the United States, and our working hypothesis thus was that many students would have had few contacts with but some negative stereotypes of, if not open prejudice toward, African-Americans. This IAT requires the ability to distinguish faces of European and African origin, and to associate these faces with pleasant and unpleasant words, thus generating results that we coded using the 7-point scale measuring implicit association of one race with favorable attitudes and the other with negative attitudes. Other tests followed an analogous logic.

To control for the effect of the order of administration of the tests over the performance, each of the students took the six tests following a different order. To control for external influences over the student's performance, all the tests were administered in the same place and computer and by the same person. The total time of administration of the six tests was approximately one-two hours, at both the beginning and end of the class term.

RESULTS: EXPERIMENTAL COURSE PROGRAM USING EMPATHIC INVOLVEMENT WITH OTHERS

Our results were interesting on several dimensions. (1) Students reported in their written work that they did not begin the course with prejudice. (2) They resented the findings of pre-intervention IATs, which suggested many students did exhibit implicit prejudice toward diverse groups. The IATs were criticized heavily for this. (3) Yet the students' own written reports of shifts in prejudice throughout the term indicated that the students *had* undergone changes in their attitudes toward certain groups. The fact that students indicated a seemingly impossible shift—from self-reports of "no prejudice" to self-reports of "less prejudice" as a result of the course—suggest both cognitive dissonance and a desire to please the professor by reporting on a change that students reported could not exist. (4) The post-intervention IATs did not indicate a significant shift in prejudice toward the elderly but did suggest statistically significant shifts in attitudes toward women in careers and the weaker but still statistically significant shift in attitudes toward Asians. We considered several possible explanations for the findings concerning Asians, but found none fully satisfactory. We explained shifts toward women in careers as a function of the gender of the professor and the teaching assistant, both of whom spent extensive time with the students, working closely with them on their written work and the testing and participating in emotionally charged class discussions that struck a deep personal chord for many students. Our overall conclusion, then, is that empathic involvement with "the other" can shift attitudes toward members of that group, but that the involvement needs to be more extensive than simply a one- or two-hour interview. Let us now elaborate on these findings.

Implicit Association Tests

To assess changes in the unconscious prejudices in the experimental group (the class members) after the class intervention, we carried out a paired t test for the equality of means. To our surprise, we obtained statistically significant differences in the gender-career IAT and in the Asian American IAT. The descriptive statistics for these tests are shown in Table 7–1.

Table 7.1 Descriptive statistics for associations between gender and family or career, and Asian and American or foreign, before and after the class on ethics in experimental group.

VARIABLE	M	SD	n
Association between gender and family or career			
Before the class on ethics	2.666*	.899	15
After the class on ethics	3.800*	1.014	15
Association between Asian and American or foreign			
Before the class on ethics	2.400*	1.404	15
After the class on ethics	3.400*	1.549	15

Note: Paired t tests for the equality of means were performed.
*Means in the same dependent variable differ at $p < .05$.

These data show a positive change in prejudices in the students. For the gender-career test, students shifted from a moderate-slight association of women with family and men with career, to a virtually neutral association between gender and family or career (t (14) $= -3.199, p = .008$). Regarding the Asian American IAT, we also found a shift from moderate-slight to a slight-neutral association of Asian American with foreign and White American with American (t (14) $= -2.562$, $p = .023$). No significant association was found between either gender or ethnicity of respondents with the changes reported, but N's are small.

To compare the means in these two tests between the experimental and control groups after the class, we performed an unpaired t test for the equality of means. We found statistically significant differences in the gender-career test (t (25) $= 3.298, p = .003$), showing that, whereas the control group showed a moderate-slight association between women with family and men with career, the experimental group showed a practically neutral association between gender and family or career after the class on ethics. (Descriptive statistics for this test are in Table 7–2.)

Written and Oral Discussions of Shifts in Prejudice

To further detect shifts in prejudice, we contrasted measurements from the IATs with written reports and class discussions of prejudice. This simple methodological contrast provided interesting results. In their written work and class discussions, few students initially identified themselves as having any prejudice. Yet their later assessments, using both class and written measurements, claimed the class had caused them to be more tolerant. This was evident in both comments from class discussion and in written assessments of the students' pseudonymous selves and their shifts in prejudice. Consider just a few of these quotes, using fictitious names, to capture these seemingly contradictory findings and the hostility toward the IAT scores. John: "After this class, I know I have a prejudice towards the Muslims on this campus. . . . I'm not sure how accurate my implicit prejudices were recorded.

Table 7.2 Descriptive statistics for associations between gender and family or career between experimental and control group after the class on ethics.

VARIABLE	M	SD	n
Association between gender and family or career after the class on *ethics*			
Experimental group	3.800*	1.014	15
Control group	2.416*	1.164	13

Note: Unpaired *t* test for the equality of means was performed.
* Means in the dependent variable differ at $p < .05$.

I mean, it (the IAT) was on a computer, the same pictures over and over, what's accurate about that?" Anna said that "the course affected my attitudes in a positive way.... The interview affected me in a way that initially I thought it would.... Regarding the IAT, well, I was upset at them."

Marta typified the other students in claiming not to have any initial prejudices: "I am already aware of how different we all are, but at the same time, we are vastly more similar. I didn't have many, if any, negative prejudicial views before I took this course. In all honesty, I hold most people in too much of a positive light. It was good to come to class and know that it is an open, honest, and safe environment." Marta's last comment touches on an important finding: the value of using age as a wedge issue. Although age is one of the top four discriminators, it is less controversial for students, and focusing on it provided students the time to trust a new professor and fellow students. In discussing their written work on the elderly, students said they "loved doing the interview.... My thoughts overall [toward the elderly] were not changed, but rather confirmed by this interview. I don't see other groups very differently now, but I know that everyone is discriminated against in some way. So if anything, what changed is my perspective." Marta's opinion about the IATs was typical of those of her classmates: "The IAT was an interesting test, but I don't believe that this particular one was accurate in judging/measuring prejudice.... Those results should be taken in the context of the setting and the person's fatigue (or other carry-over effects)."

Students claimed that talking with their classmates made them realize that "although different, we all have similar characteristics" (Kelly). One student claimed the readings and the interview affected the way she saw the elderly and made her appreciate them more. "When I began this course I thought I was a very tolerant and accepting person. I knew I had a few prejudices ... but I thought that I was working on these attitudes and that if I tried hard enough I could make myself a good person. I think this class helped with that. The way the course was structured (a small group of people) made it comfortable and easy to talk to classmates and because of that I learned that though we were all different, we had similar goals, dreams and fears. I also enjoyed the readings ... especially Pipher's *Another Country* because it gave me an inside look at the emotions and actions of the elderly. The interview of Bettye (the elderly person I interviewed) also added to this. It affected the way I saw the elderly, made me appreciate them a lot more. It also made me more patient and more interested in people different than me. Bettye was great and I loved her energy, her attitude, her personality and her stories and it taught me that if I give my time to people and show an interest, people will teach me great things and tell me wonderful stories. This is a lesson I'll apply with other groups as well." Concerning the IATs, Kelly said: "I want to say that the IAT didn't accurately capture my thoughts but that would be a lie. I think the IAT might have captured something about me that I either refused to see or didn't know about. I can only hope that the second time I take the test the results will be much more preferable." Kelly was unusual in this candid assessment of her prejudice.

We were concerned students who chose to take the course might give us a pre-selection of students who were concerned with ethical issues; however, we were fortunate that most students said they took the course because it fulfilled an upper-division writing requirement, not because of a pre-course concern with prejudice itself. Nonetheless, most students felt the class caused them to change their tolerance and appreciation for others: "This course changed my appreciation for other individuals" (Peter). Concerning the IATs, Peter said: "I felt the IAT test was too long where reverse biases were created. We all want to view ourselves as unprejudiced so we counter our true biases." Peter was in the minority however, with most students claiming to have been "profoundly affected" by the course and the interview process, which "expanded my intellectual capabilities, but it also helped me reflect on my attitudes and life in general. It shed light on feelings and assumptions that seem to be automatically granted as innate facts, when in reality they can be explained and have unique origins. This class is a reflection of self, environment, and life. It reveals how everything is connected in some way. This course expedites the constant growth and maturation process of humanity . . . . I really enjoyed conducting the interview with my grand-mother. We talked about topics that we hadn't touched on before. I was never prejudiced toward the elderly. I am extremely close with my parents and my aunt. I spend quite a bit of time associating with people who are much older than me. I've always enjoyed the profound perspec-tives prevalent amongst older people and the extreme elderly" (Lisa). Yet when referring to the IATs, Lisa said: "I don't advocate the IATs as valid evaluations of prejudice. My results were not accurate. They portrayed me as biased towards certain groups. I do not consider myself prejudiced in any way."

Another student claimed that "this course really made me rethink how I regard others who have had more—or just different—experiences than me. It made me realize that just because I may not have prejudices, I still cannot expect to know what everyone's life experiences have been like. The inter-view didn't change much of my perception of the elderly because I never really had any prejudices but that may be cause I didn't think much about the elderly at all. So I believe if anything has changed, it has been my belief that the elderly have very much to offer younger generations and should not be treated as if they are on their way out the door. The interview also helped me realize how much I have in common with those generations older than me" (Kathy). Others shared Kathy's view of the broadening experience of the interview, coupled with negative response to the IATs: "The IATs, they're a unique experiment that talks about prejudice but there are some flaws to it, such as the setup and making people think a certain way .... Overall, this class helped me see issues in a broader perspective, and allowed me to be somewhat more critical of relationships" (Griffin).

In general, then, students felt the class affected them in a positive way. The use of age as a wedge issue provided time to get to know and trust the professor and other students, and was closely related to the students' assessing the class as an open, safe, and diverse environment that fostered candid communication and difficult dialogues. As a consequence of this context and the work carried out, students felt they gained a larger understanding of the nature of prejudice and discrimination, a deeper appreciation for and interest in others and an awareness of the fact that although different, we all are human beings, with the same "goals, dreams and fears" (Shoshona), their opinion regarding the IATs was generally negative, however. Most students considered the IATs biased and therefore not an accurate measure of their own attitudes. But since the majority of the students also claimed to be free of any initial kind of prejudice, one conclusion may be that the students were—not surprisingly—simply uncomfortable being told they held implicit prejudice.

CONCLUSION

This paper presents results from a class that used a narrative interview technique to foster empathic involvement with "the other," in the hope that such involvement would foster more tolerant attitudes and compassionate treatment of others. Students in the class were tested for their attitudes toward diverse groups, both before and after the class intervention, using verbal and written assessments and Implicit Association Tests of tolerance toward these various groups. Results were compared with similar tests for a control group, obtained through a respondent-driven nominee sample. Since our intervention focused on the elderly, we expected a shift in attitudes toward old people. Here we found mixed results. Students' verbal and written assessment of their overall attitudes toward the elderly suggested a change, but the IAT results showed no statistically meaningful change in attitudes toward old people. This gap between the students' qualitative assessment of their overall attitudes toward the elderly and the quantitative measure (IAT) may be due to the effect of power dynamics in the classroom. In order to please the professor and teaching assistant, students may have expressed verbally a change in their attitudes toward the elderly. Nonetheless, the quantitative data, which reflect unconscious attitudes, show no change of these attitudes. This is an issue that may be resolved— or at least addressed—by controlling for social desirability in future studies and assuring the anonymity of the students when writing about their attitudes. (See note 5 on the social desirability index.)

The IAT measurements did, however, reveal a strong and significant shift in attitudes toward women with careers, a group with whom we had designed no intervention. But the fact that both the professor and the teaching assistant were female, in an intense and well-received seminar setting where students had extensive faculty involvement, might have inadvertently served as a way to foster empathic involvement with members of a group—in this case, career women—that was heretofore unknown to most students, many of whose mothers were immigrants who stayed at home or whose jobs were not viewed as careers but as secondary jobs with low status. If so, this would suggest that our initial hypothesis is correct; empathic involvement with a member of a group that is discriminated against can shift attitudes toward such group members. But the involvement required to shift attitudes needs to be more extensive than simply a short (1–3 hour) narrative interview.

The weaker but still statistically significant shift in attitudes toward Asians also may relate to the increased involvement with fellow students, half of whom were Asian. Another, more skeptical interpretation, might be that these changes in attitudes toward women with careers and toward Asians as foreigners may be also reflecting the effect of the power dynamics in the classroom. Since there was no power dimension in the shift in attitudes toward Asians—neither the professor nor the teaching assistant was Asian— and since the IATs are based on measuring minute shifts in response time, it would be likelier that any shift related to power in the classroom would surface in the written or oral measures of attitudinal changes, not in the IATs. This was not the case. We thus rejected this more cynical view of the shift in attitudes toward professional women in favor of an explanation that attributes the shift to empathic involvement.

Our main substantive finding, then, is that the class had a positive effect on student attitudes in general and reflected a genuine improvement of their understanding and appreciation of members of a group initially judged to be "different." Our study raises interesting questions. It deserves further work designed to use critical methodological improvements in the measurement of attitudes.[5] We plan on teaching the course again but expanding it in size, which will increase the statistical reliability of our findings, and having two sections, which may help us control for the effects of the teaching assistant's gender on students' responses. Even our tentative, initial results, however, shed light on the possible factors that may influence a positive change in attitudes toward the others and represent an

---

[5] In methodological terms, how do we interpret the negative student comments regarding the IAT tests? How reliable are they? It is possible that students may have rejected the IAT results because of their denial of being prejudiced people. Or perhaps the IATs actually failed to capture students' real attitudes. We found a few studies evaluating the reliability of some specific IAT tests, but no definitive evidence on the IATs' reliability (Cunningham, Preacher and Banaji, 2001). One way to address these considerations in future work is to include a test-retest of the IATs. Analysts also might include a social desirability scale to control the possible tendency of students to show themselves as not having any prejudice. Scales such as the Paulhus Deception Scales (Paulhus, 1998) measure both self deception and impression management. "Self-deception" represents an unconscious process to deny psychologically threatening thoughts and feelings reflective of psychoanalytic conflicts, and "other-deception" represents conscious distortion toward self-enhancement. Certain other methodological aspects of the study could be improved in future tests of our experiment. For example, to increase the statistical reliability of results and obtain more robust findings, future experimental courses could increase the number of students. While still keeping the seminar format necessary to facilitate class dialogue, the course could be expanded to 40 students. All students would meet once a week with the professor and TA for a lecture and discussion. The course could then be broken into two smaller groups, for more intense discussion among 20 students and the faculty. Each of these groups would then provide 20 nominees, producing an experimental group of 40 students with 40 nominees, which would form the control group. The following table suggests the structure and schedule of the sample proposed:

	Professor lecture 1 (1 hour 30 min. approx)	Professor lecture 2 (1 hour 30 min. approx)	Groups A + B form the experimental group (40 students) and the control group would be another 40 students nominee group.
A week class	Group A (20 students) Teaching assistant's sections 1 (1 hour) Group A (20 students)	Group B (20 students) Teaching assistant's sections 2 (1 hour) Group B (20 students)	

Also, this control group would be assessed before and after the course. Another critical part of our experiment is not reported upon here. This is a follow-up study to detect how long-lasting are the effects of the course intervention. This was planned for March 2008, via a mail survey.

important step in developing interventions in ethics in the academic environment.

Acknowledgments

Generous financial support was provided by the Biosophical Institute and the Ford Foundation, via their Difficult Dialogues Program. UCI's Vice Chancellor for Student Affairs Manuel Gomez, Nancy Minear, Gloria Mark, Mark Petracca, John Sommerhauser, and Dean Barbara Dosher assisted in administrative arrangements for the course. Special thanks go to Frank Lynch, Gertrude Monroe, Prem Chadha, Jerome Tobis, Bettye Vaughen, and the class grandparents who gave extensive interviews to the class members. We appreciate the participation of the nominee sample and the comments of the anonymous referees. An earlier version of this appeared in *PS: Politics, Science and Politics* (October, 2008). We are grateful to Rob Hauck and the editors for their permission to reprint this article, in modified form.

REFERENCES

Bar-On, 2006. *Tell me your story*. Budapest: Central European Press.

Cunningham, W. A., Preacher, K. J., and Banaji, M. R., 2001. Implicit attitudes measures: Consistency, stability and convergent validity. *Psychological Science* 12:163–170.

Devine, P.G., 1989. Stereotypes and prejudice: Their automatic and controlled components. *Journal of Personality and Social Psychology* 56:5–18.

Greenwald, A. G., McGhee, D. E., and Schwartz, J. L. K., 1998. Measuring individual differences in implicit cognition: The Implicit Association Test. *Journal of Personality and Social Psychology* 71:1464–1480.

McGaugh, J., 2003. *Memory and emotion*. New York: Columbia University Press.

Monroe, K. R., 1994. *The heart of altruism*. Princeton, N.J.: Princeton University Press.

Monroe, K. R., 2004. *The hand of compassion*. Princeton, N.J.: Princeton University Press.

Monroe, K.R. 2009. The Ethical Perspective: An Identity Theory of the Psychological Influences on Moral Choice: The 2008 Presidential Address. *Political Psychology*. 30(3): 419–444.

Paulhus, D.L., 1998. *The Paulhus deception scales: BIDR Version 7*. Toronto/Buffalo: Multi-Health Systems.

Pipher, M., 2000. *Another country: Navigating the emotional terrain of our elders*. New York: Penguin.

Tajfel, H., 1981. Human groups and social categories. *Studies in Social Psychology*. New York: Cambridge University Press.

Turner, J., 1987. *Rediscovering the social group*. Oxford: Basil Blackwell.

Wilson, T. D., Lindsey, S., and Schooler, T. Y., 2000. A model of dual attitudes. *Psychological Review* 107:101–126.

CHAPTER 8

Social Identifications and Pro-Social Activity in Poland

Katarzyna Hamer and Jakub Gutowski

In this chapter we focus on two issues: social identities in a global era and their possible connection with pro-social behaviors. We analyze spontaneous definitions of the "we" category and the different levels of group identifications among respondents. We also analyze the extent to which we can talk about the existence of parallel identities (two or more strong social identities at the same time). As to pro-social behaviors, we study whether the level of different social identities could be a predictor of helping behaviors.

Issues of social identities are difficult to conceptualize outside the context of globalization (Arnett, 2002; Hoshmand, 2003; Sampson, 1989; Marsella, 1998). In recent decades the degree and intensity of connections among different parts of the world, cultures, and countries have risen dramatically (see also Paul Nesbitt-Larking's chapter in this book). As Arnett (2002) emphasizes, globalization encompasses a wide range of issues and phenomena, but one needs to pay particular attention to its psychological meaning. Forces of globalization have important psychological influences on identity processes. According to Arnett (2002, 777), "most people in the world now develop a bicultural identity, in which part of their identity is rooted in their local culture while another part stems from an awareness of their relation to the global culture . . . a sense of belonging to a worldwide culture. . . ." Some sociologists argue (e.g., Appadurai, 1996), that the development of societies in a global world has changed from an actual division of "us" versus "them" (e.g., us—Poles, them—Russians) to a postmodern division of "me" versus "us" (e.g., me—individual, us—humans), although this process may have been slowed down by world terrorism (Marody and Giza-Poleszczuk, 2004). The concept of supranational identities, such as a European identity, is also common in the literature (Roland-Levy and Ferrari, 2005; Cappoza and Brown, 2000; Breakwell and Lyons, 1996; Sousa, 1996), as well as identification with all humanity (McFarland and Webb, 2003).

As Deaux writes, "social identification is a fundamental concept for understanding of the relationship between the person and the social system" (2000, 14). Of importance then is what we refer to when we talk about social identification. A human is a social creature to the extent that even his or her own identity is defined through references to other people. Comparisons with others lead to the formation of personal identity, while identification with a group (e.g., nation, race, sex), leads to the formation of a social identity. The first type of identity is connected to the concept of *self*, the self-perception of a unique individual, with his or her own goals and standards. Social identity, according to one of the well-known psychological theories in the area, Social Identity Theory (SIT) by H. Tajfel (1974a; 1974b; 1982), is defined as "that part of individuals' self-concept which derives from their knowledge of their membership of a social group (or groups) together with the value and emotional significance of that membership" (Tajfel, 1982, 24). As J. Turner (1987), the author of Social Categorization Theory (SCT) underlines, social identity results from the categorization of the social world into ingroups and outgroups ("us" versus "them"). This identification process includes two aspects: (1) knowledge of being a part of a group and labeling oneself as a member of the ingroup, (2) affect towards the group, which includes commitment, feeling of belonging, closeness to the group, and identifying with the group's goals and values. The concept of "identification" is evidently different from "belonging" (Chryssochoou, 1996)—we can formally, sociologically belong to a group (e.g., single income families in rural areas) but not identify with it. In this chapter we mainly focus on groups of identification in relation to forces of globalization. We use the concept of social identities as defined in accordance with SIT and SCT.

In the literature we find that one can have many social identities, be a member of many communities (e.g., Jarymowicz, 2002). But the strength of those identities can differ (Sousa, 1996; Deaux, 2000), as well as their kind (McManus-Czubińska, Miller, Markowski, and Wasilewski, 2002): a social identity can be closed to other social identities (e.g., exclusively national identity) or it can be open to such identities. In this case we can talk about so-called parallel identities (two or more strong social identities; e.g., parallel national and European identities). As Sousa's study showed (1996), it is possible to have more than one strong social identity; e.g., national. One can, for example, have a strong national identity and a strong European identity at the same time. In an era of globalization such multiple identifications will probably become increasingly common.

What constitutes important social identities today? Some scholars argue that "new global requirements for multiple group loyalties, multiple identities, multiple citizenships relating to groups, organizations, cities, regions, and ultimately the world no longer situate the nation as a defining determinant of culture or behavior" (Marsella, 1998, 1284). But national identity is certainly still one of the most important social identities, much stronger than, for example, a European identity is for citizens of United Europe (as showed by the Eurobarometer; see also Skarżyńska, 2005). The Eurobarometer from the years 1992–2004 posed the question: "In the near future do you see yourself as: [nationality] only, [nationality] and European, European and [nationality], European only." The results of these analyses show that the number of people defining their social identity in a parallel way (as national and European), but with nationality as more important, is stable (40–45 percent), and that there is a similar number of people defining their social identity as national only. Not many citizens of the European Union (EU) place European identity first (1–10 percent). A similar study in Poland (McManus et al., 2002) showed that 34 percent of the respondents declared to have only national identity, while 23 percent defined themselves as having both a national and a European identity, but where the national was stronger than the European. Equally strong national and European identity only occurred among 23 percent of participants. On the basis of these figures it is of interest to study the strength of national and European identity in Poland in, 2005; i.e., after one year of membership in the European Union.

Considering the intensity of social identities, we can expect respondents to be most strongly connected to the family (as shown in Inglehart's cross-country studies, for example: Inglehart, Basanez, Diez-Medrano, Halman, and Luijkx, 2004). Furthermore, value studies from 2004 made by CBOS (an institution conducting opinion polls in Poland) demonstrated that the family was the most important value for Poles (Falkowski, Lewandowska, Wciórka, and Wenzel, 2005). Why does the family play such an important role? Identification with the family is the most natural and satisfactory human basic psychosocial need (Szawiel, 1989). It has an important adaptive function because, according to socio-biology, strong family bonds help individuals and their genes survive (Hamilton, 1964). Many studies have showed that we help our relatives first (e.g., CBOS study for Poland, 1999), especially when we feel close to them (Korchmaros and Kenny, 2001). We can thus expect strong identification with the family among Polish people.

But it seems that for some people the "we" category is much wider and even extends to all mankind (McFarland et al., 2003). In a global world, with increasing connections between people, such broad identities could become more common. As Marsella writes; "never before in our world have our destinies been so tied to one another in such an intricate maze of changes, forces and institutions that are global in proportion and scope" (1998, 1289).

What does it mean to identify with people all over the world? According to SIT and SCT definitions of social identification, it would mean to view oneself as being a part of humanity, having a feeling of belonging and commitment to that group, caring about its members, etc. Does such a broad conception of social identity ever occur? Studies of Szawiel (1989), Monroe (1996), McFarland et al. (2003), Hamer and Hamer-Gutowska (2005), or Hamer-Gutowska (2006; 2007) confirm the existence of such identity. For example, common characteristics of individuals who rescued Jews during the Holocaust consisted of a shared perspective "of belonging to one human family" (Monroe, 1996, 205), effectively erasing all distinctions of race, religion, and nationality (McFarland et al., 2003). We can find this broad perspective also in the personality theories of Adler and Maslow. A central feature of Adler's (1927/1954) theory was *gemeinschaftsgefuhl*. This German word refers to a sense of "oneness with humanity" (Adler, 1954, 38), also translated as "social interest." A person with mature social interest acts "in the interests of mankind generally..., all mankind, present and future" (Adler, 1929/1964, 78). Therefore Adler viewed oneness with humanity as an innate potential in all humans, but one that must be nurtured to develop fully. According to his theory, less mature forms of social interest may focus on the welfare of one's family, community, and ingroup, but with maturity, social interest extends to the community of all people, even to unborn generations. Also Maslow's concept of "self-actualized individuals" refers to the identification with, and concern for, all humanity (Maslow, 1954). "Human kinship" is one of the fifteen qualities that Maslow's self-actualizing people were said to exhibit. Individuals with this quality "have a deep feeling of identification, sympathy, and affection for human beings in general... [a] feeling of identification with mankind" (1954, 138). They are psychologically "members at large of the human species" (1954, 145) rather than ethnocentrically identified with a nation or other ingroup (McFarland et al., 2003). Such broad social identity seems to have a psychological basis. As Hamer-Gutowska's (2008a) study revealed, empathy is a main predictor of such broad social identity. McFarland et al.'s (2003) studies showed that identification with all humanity correlates negatively with ethnocentrism, blind patriotism, authoritarianism, social-dominance orientation, and religious fundamentalism. It predicted commitment to universal human rights beyond the effects of those variables. Another study of Hamer and Hamer-Gutowska (2005), conducted on Polish students, revealed the existence of identification with all humanity among the subjects under study and showed it to be a good predictor of commitment to universal human rights.

Studying Poland in the context of social identities seems especially interesting. The system transformation in this country and the sudden opening-up to the world entailed exposure to global processes. A closed country with a communist past became a member of international organizations like NATO and the European Union. What changes in social identities could that cause? Measuring levels of different social identities in Poland is also interesting because of the strong religious perspective in this country. As opinion polls have shown for years, the Poles have a strong Catholic identity. In, 2004, 84 percent of the respondents perceived themselves as believers, and 11 percent as deep believers (Roguska and Wciórka, 2005). According to the Bible, all humans are equal before God (see, e.g., Acts 10:34), and followers of Christ should even care for persons of despised races (Luke 10:25–37). The Bible recommends loving all humans as brothers. Hence, in the same opinion poll, 77 percent of the respondents declared that they made efforts to live according to the teachings of Pope John Paul II, who was known as a supporter of these religious principles. On that basis we could expect a high level of identification with all humanity among the Poles. But at the same time we observe increasing support for the death penalty (not used in Poland for many years and abolished in 1997): in 2004 almost 80 percent of the Poles were in favor of reintroducing the death penalty (Strzeszewski, 2005), despite knowing that the Pope strongly opposed it. According to another opinion poll (by SMG/KRC from 2002), as many as 81 percent of the Poles believe that "every person should help those who need help." At the same time only 11 percent of the respondents declared that they participated in volunteering activity, while in the United States, for example, the figures are 56 percent; and 34 percent in Germany. Direct helping is more popular—29 percent of the Poles declare that they would help strangers in need, while 50 percent declared that they help charity organizations (Gazeta Wyborcza, 2002).

What is the reason for such low popularity of volunteering in Poland and also, as studies by Salamon, Sokolowski and List (2003) have shown, for the extremely low level of civil society participation in Poland (as in other Central and Eastern European countries)? It could be due to the fact that Poles rarely understand what *volunteering* is (this word did not exist in the Polish language before 1992, see Kalbarczyk and Maciula, 2002). There is still a vivid tradition of strong familial, clan, or village networks, and people do not refer to helping in such networks as "volunteering."

Another reason, however, can be the fact that Poland was a Soviet-style regime in the aftermath of World War II. This is likely to be a reflection of the social welfare policies of the Soviet-era governments, which relied on direct provision of the most important social services by the "workers' state" and discouraged reliance on private voluntary groups, including those affiliated with religious groups (Salamon et al., 2003). There was also a tradition of so-called social works, when the communist government would order people to work for others from time to time without payment. As such pro-social activity was conducted under compulsion, it did not have anything to do with volunteering. But a lot of people still remember these kinds of "social works," and their aversion to such (perceived) "communist" ideas may prevent them from engaging in similar activities now, especially for people they do not know.

This is quite different from the situation in other Western countries, especially if one compares the Polish experience to that of the United States. In the United States, traditional social policy has been characterized by a relatively small, "hands-off" role for the state. Instead it has, to a great extent, relied on private, charitable activity. Reflecting this tradition, non-profit organizations occupy a significant role in the United States (Salamon et al., 2003). Such differences in tradition can be viewed as one of the main reasons for dissimilarities in the popularity of pro-social behavior in Poland and other Western countries.

On one hand we have the high declared religiousness of Poles, while on the other hand, results of opinion polls show that real behaviors do not reflect such attitudes. The extent to which such high levels of declared religiousness of Poles means real internalization of Christian values to love and help all humanity can thus be doubted. It can further be questioned whether the identification with such broad social identities—the identification with mankind as an example of a mature social interest (according to Adler), for instance—is indeed very common. In Szawiel's study (1989) 13–19 percent of questioned Poles declared they were "connected to all humanity," but that finding cannot be generalized as the sample was not representative for Poland (respondents were from two big cities only). Moreover, since 1989 Poland has gone through economic and cultural transformations, it has become a member of the European Union, and it has started to experience the effects of globalization. What changes in social identities could that cause? How do people in Poland conceive of their social identities, especially young people? And if identities are broader than before this opening up to the world in 1989, does this mean that people are more willing to help others, because they are treated as members of an ingroup?

The present study, conducted on a representative sample for Poland, analyzed the level of identification with different groups in Poland and how social identities could influence pro-social behaviors (helping others). Over 1000 respondents from 15 to 75 years of age answered questions about the strength of their social identities and frequency of helping behaviors. Their answers were analyzed with reference to a few social variables like sex, age, level of education, income, and place of residence.

Why did we assume that social identities can influence pro-social behaviors? According to many researchers, social activity needs social capital (e.g., Putnam, 1995; Skarżyńska, 2005). This refers to facilitating interactions with others, social trust for example (Fukuyama, 1995; Inglehart and Baker, 2000). We assume that strong social identifications, especially broad ones, could be facilitators of interactions and thus of pro-social behaviors. Strong social identifications could therefore be part of a social capital similar to trust. One can find indirect proof for this in Szwed's study (2003), which shows that a broader "we" category is connected to a smaller distance to outgroups, and in Czapiewska's study (2006), which emphasizes a connection between strong identification with all humanity and a high level of openness (as a personality trait).

As McFarland underlines, "oneness with all humanity is more than an absence of ethnocentrism" (McFarland et al., 2003, 4), it is rather "a genuine desire to help the human race" (Maslow, 1954, 138). If this is true, we should expect behavioral consequences to stem from identification with all mankind, including helping other people. According to Social Identity Theory, ingroup identity instigates discrimination in favor of the ingroup (Tajfel, 1982; Noel, Wann, and Branscombe, 1995). For example, we are more willing to help members of our ingroup than those of an outgroup. If an individual strongly identifies with "people all over the world," she should be more willing to help others than somebody with a low level of such identification. One of McFarland's studies (McFarland, and Hamer-Gutowska, 2006) revealed that Amnesty International members had stronger identification with all humanity than members of a local Chamber of Commerce. Gruszczak (2006) found that volunteers (helping others as a nonprofit hobby) were more concerned with human rights and had a stronger identification with all mankind than had nurses (helping others as a job). These results seem to confirm the assumption that the strength of broad social identifications can be a predictor of pro-social behaviors.

METHOD

Participants: The study was conducted on a representative sample for Poland ($N = 1005$) in July 2005, by the SMG/KRC Corporation. The sample consisted of 491 men and 514 women aged 15–75 (mean age = 40).

Measures: The questionnaire started with an open question to analyze main social identities in Poland. It was as follows: "When you think 'we,' whom do you mean? Give us your first thoughts." The main element of a social identity is a subjective feeling of belonging, often connected with using the word "we." That is why one of the methods to measure social identities was to ask directly about the feeling of belonging, using the word "we" as a label (e.g., Jarymowicz, 2002).

The open question was followed by two questions from the Polish version of the Identification With All Humanity Scale by McFarland and Webb (2003), prepared by Hamer-Gutowska and Hamer. This scale tests the strength of social identities. In our study we used the following six identification groups: family, neighbors, citizens of the same town/city, the Poles, citizens of the European Union, and people all over the world. These two questions were:

- How close do you feel to each of the following groups?
- How often do you use the word "we" to refer to the following groups of people?

The answers ranked from 1 ("not at all") to 5 ("very close" or "very often"). On the basis of these two questions, the strength measure of each social identification consisted of a sum of points for that identification.

Then we asked about the frequency of helping behaviors (from 1— "never" to 5—"very often"), such as:

- giving donations to charity organizations (money, buying things for charity; e.g., candles, bricks),
- working as a volunteer,
- giving (money, bread, etc.) to people in need (face-to-face helping).

RESULTS

Social Identities

Open question: when you think "we," whom do you mean? Regardless of socio-demographic variables (sex, age, level of education, place of residence), most Poles spontaneously identified themselves mainly with their closest people (84 percent of indications—including: 69 percent—with family, 6 percent—boyfriend/girlfriend, 5 percent—friends, 2 percent—people from their surroundings, etc.). None of the rest of the spontaneously given identities exceeded 5 percent of indications (Fig. 8–1).

Some respondents (around 4 percent) identified themselves with Poles (national identity), and similarly, about 4 percent with all humanity. Lack of a European Community identity draws attention, especially remembering that Poland had been in the European Union for over a year when the study was conducted. This identity appeared only once in the answers, and it was the participant's second association with the word "we," while the first one was once again "family."

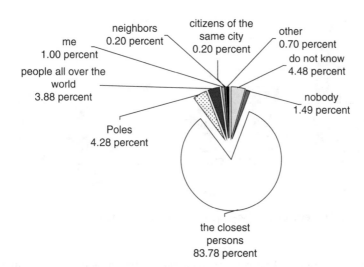

Figure 8.1 Social identities in Poland 2005 (answers to the open questions)

Among the answers there were also single identifications with other groups; e.g., anglers, youth, religious community (it is notable that "religious community" only received one indication although it was only a few months after Pope John Paul II's death), students, workers, etc. (category "other" on Fig. 8–1)

Identification with Six Indicated Groups. The next two questions checked the level of identification with each of the following groups: family, neighbors, citizens of the same town/city, the Poles, citizens of the whole European Union, and all humanity. These two questions were analyzed together.

We used an analysis of variance (ANOVA) with repeated measures. It showed the main effect of identity group: $F(5.4650) = 1141.15$; $p < 0.001$ (Fig. 8–2). As in the open question, the strongest identity was with the family. In second place, in regard to intensity, was national identity; in the third—identification with neighbors and citizens of the same town/city (no differences between them), while in fourth place was identification with all humanity. The European Community identity was the weakest one, weaker even than identification with a larger group—all humanity. Post=hoc tests (NIR) showed that the above differences were statistically significant.

The group obtaining most positive answers concerning "strong" or "very strong" affiliations was the family: 85 percent of the respondents felt such affiliations, leaving all other groups far behind. Strong affiliations with Poles were observed among 29 percent of the respondents; with

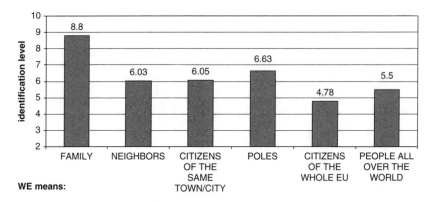

Figure 8.2 The level of identification with 6 indicated groups

neighbors—around 24 percent; with citizens of the same town/city—around 22 percent; with people all over the world—around 11 percent; and with citizens of the European Union—around 5 percent only.

In addition, the study showed the main effects of the age of the respondents: $F(3.928) = 7.94$; $p < 0.001$ (here we used multivariate analysis of variance, MANOVA). The older individuals (40 years of age and above) identified themselves significantly more strongly with all identity groups than did the younger ones (NIR post-hoc tests). Moreover, the youngest respondents (15–24 years of age) felt weaker bonds with their families than did all the older respondent groups (Fig. 8–3).

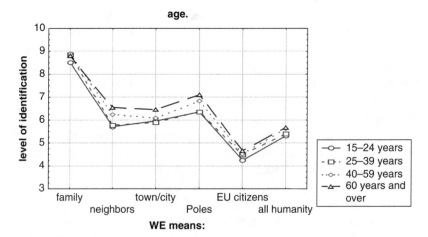

Figure 8.3 The level of identification with six indicated groups depended on respondents' age

Parallel Identities

The study showed high correlations between the broadest identification (with people all over the world) and identification with Poles as well as identification with citizens of the European Union (both correlations close to $r = 0.6$, $p < 0.001$). There were also high correlations between other broad identities (e.g., citizens of the same town/city and Poles). All correlations among social identities are shown in Table 8–1.

Further analyses of broad social identities showed that 70 percent of the respondents who declared strong national identity (6 or more points on a scale from 2 to 10) also declared strong identification with people all over the world (6 or more points). As to European identity, 38 percent of respondents who declared strong national identity also declared strong identification with the citizens of the whole European Union. As many as 74 percent of the respondents who declared strong identification with people all over the world also declared strong national identity. 42 percent of the respondents who declared strong identification with all mankind also declared strong EU identity.

These results, as well as the correlations mentioned above, show the existence of parallel identities (strong social identities with different groups coexisting) among the Poles. We will come back to this result in the discussion.

Helping Behaviors

The results show that over 70 percent of Poles declare that they help people in need whom they encounter, while more than 80 percent

Table 8.1 Correlations of all indicated social identifications in closed questions.

IDENTIFICATION WITH:	FAMILY	NEIGHBORS	CITIZENS OF THE SAME TOWN/CITY	POLES	CITIZENS OF EU
family	–	0.27[a]	0.24[a]	0.26[a]	0.07[b]
neighbors	0.27[a]	–	0.61[a]	0.34[a]	0.29[a]
citizens of the same town/city	0.24[a]	0.61[a]	–	0.51[a]	0.44[a]
Poles	0.26[a]	0.34[a]	0.51[a]	–	0.47[a]
citizens of EU	0.07[b]	0.29[a]	0.44[a]	0.47[a]	–
people all over the world	0.17[a]	0.33[a]	0.48[a]	0.58[a]	0.59[a]

Note: Superscripts a and b indicate significance levels for retention were $p < .001$ and $p < .05$, respectively.

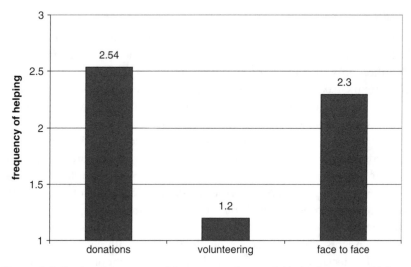

Figure 8.4 Declared frequency of three types of prosocial behaviors among Poles

declare that they help through donations for charity organizations. Volunteering is not popular—as many as 88 percent of the Poles declare that they do not do it at all.

But how often do the Poles help others? Figure 8–4 shows frequencies of different helping behaviors among respondents (possible answers were on the scale from 1—"never" to 5—"very often"). As we can see, Poles rather seldom give donations to charity organizations or help encountered people in need (Fig. 8–4). Volunteering is very rare.

Further analyses confirmed the assumption that broad social identities were connected to more frequent pro-social behavior (see tables 8–2 through 8–4). It draws attention to the fact that no influence of respondents' incomes was noticed for any tested pro-social behavior, although two of these kinds of behaviors could be found in giving donations.

As stepwise regression revealed, national identity was the best predictor of charity donations (Table 8–2). The others were education level, identification with family, neighbors, EU citizens, and sex of respondents. These results show that people who identify stronger with Poles, with family, with neighbors, or with the citizens of the European Union, as well as educated people, more often give money to charity organizations than people with weaker mentioned identities or with lower levels of education. It also turned out that women declare giving money for charity donations more frequently than men.

Table 8.2 Stepwise regression of social identities and other predictors upon charity donations.

VARIABLE	B	SE OF B	BETA
Identification with Poles	0.09	0.02	0.15[a]
Identification with family	0.07	0.02	0.09[b]
Education level (lower/higher)	0.20	0.06	0.10[b]
Identification with neighbors	0.04	0.02	0.09[c]
Place of residence	−0.09	0.03	−0.10[b]
Sex	0.14	0.06	0.07[c]
Identification with EU citizens	0.04	0.02	0.07[c]

$R2 = .05$. Income, age, and other social identities did not approach significance and were deleted.
Note: Superscripts a, b, and c indicate significance levels for retention were $p < .001$, $p < .01$ and $p < .05$, respectively.

Table 8.3 Stepwise regression of social identities and other predictors upon face-to-face helping.

VARIABLE	B	SE OF B	BETA
Identification with Poles	0.07	0.03	0.10[a]
Identification with EU citizens	0.06	0.02	0.10[a]
Age	0.06	0.03	0.06[b]

$R2 = .07$. Income, place of residence, sex, and other social identities did not approach significance and were deleted.
Note: Superscripts a and b indicate significance levels for retention were $p < .05$ and $p = .06$, respectively.

As for face-to-face helping, the best predictors were identification with Polish people and identification with EU citizens (see Table 8–3). Sex, place of residence, income, and other social identities did not approach significance, which means that these variables do not play any role in this kind of helping behavior. Age contributed only marginally to face-to face-helping. These results show that people who identify more strongly with Poles and with the citizens of the European Union more often help encountered people in need than people with weaker national and EU identities.

As the following stepwise regression revealed (Table 8–4), their level of education and identification with all humanity were the only predictors for volunteering. Other variables did not approach any significance. These results show that better-educated people and those who identify more strongly with people all over the world volunteer more often than people with lower education level and weaker mankind identity.

Table 8.4 Stepwise regression of the identification with all humanity and other predictors upon volunteering.

VARIABLE	B	SE OF B	BETA
Education level (lower/higher)	0.13	0.04	0.10 [a]
Identification with all humanity	0.03	0.013	0.07 [b]

$R2 = .02$. Sex, place of residence, income, age, and other social identities did not approach significance and were deleted.

Note: Superscripts a and b indicate significance levels for retention were $p < .01$ and $p = .04$, respectively.

As additional analyses showed, comparing frequency of pro-social behaviors between people of lower and higher levels of identification with every indicated group revealed that the effect of identities was unspecific. Stronger identification of almost every kind (except for identification with family); with neighbors, citizens of the same town/city, Poles, EU citizens and people all over the world, meant significantly more frequent donations (both for charity organizations and in face-to-face helping). There were no differences for volunteering. Strong identification with family turned out to have negative effect on volunteering frequency ($t(980) = 4.2$; $p < 0.001$) and had no effect on donations.

DISCUSSION

The collapse of the former Soviet Union, attempts to unify Europe, and the process of globalization have provided challenges to the social identities of Poles. A closed, communist, Catholic country suddenly opened up to the world. What then are the most important social identities of the Poles after more than fifteen years of system transformation and one year of membership in the European Union? It is not surprising that Poles, like other nationalities, identify themselves more with their families than with the nation (second place as regards intensity), neighbors and citizens of the same town/city (third place), or with all humanity (fourth place). After one year of membership in the European Union, the European Community identity was the weakest one (fifth place), weaker even than identification with a larger group—all humanity. This should come as a surprise considering how strongly the Poles wanted to become a part of the European Union (according to Roguska, 2005, 70 percent of them declared such a wish in 1993–1997). On the other hand, EU identity is rather weak also among the citizens of the "old European Union" (see the beginning of this chapter). According to the Eurobarometer in 2000, more than 40 percent of the entire EU population was afraid that belonging to the European Union meant a loss of national identity and culture. Fortunately, in 2001, that rate dropped to around 10 percent, leaving hope that this fear will be vanishing. As for the Poles, according to CBOS, they feel like third-class citizens of the European Union (Roguska, 2005), which may also be the reason for low European identification. But Poles' future in the European Union seemed attractive to the Poles questioned before 2004, as well as for their country (Boski, 2005). In addition, according to CBOS (2004), Polish people's images of themselves and the image of a European citizen had increasingly more in common during the years of 1992 to 2004. Because of facilitated flows of information and cultural values, easier traveling through the entire European Union, and increasing financial interactions, it seems that this trend will continue. Studies of Lickel, Hamilton, Uhles, Wieczorkowska, Lewis, and Sherman (2000) show that the more EU citizens see the European Union as a community of nations and societies similar and close to each other, the more they identify themselves with the European Union. Europe's single currency as a symbol of unity should help in perceiving this similarity and bounds. According to Cinnirella (1996), there are a few other facilitators forging a stronger European identity, such as the networking of national and European identities. In this sense they are increasingly being perceived as mutually compatible rather than conflicting, emphasizing that the European Union is not a threat to national cultures but a complement. Through education it should be possible to show cultural and historical ties between the European nations and how these can be advanced in the future. According to Roland-Levy et al. (2005), adapting to today's society requires a multifaceted identity, which is what the euro symbolizes: one side of a coin pictures the European Union, the other is specific to the country.

The same thing can be said about global identity, such as the identification with all humanity It seems that in a global era, national and global identity can complement each other—they could be two sides of the coin. High correlations between broad identities show that perceiving people all over the world as an "ingroup" exists next to perceiving the nation as an ingroup as well as perceiving Europeans as an ingroup. We especially observed how global and national identities coexist (parallel identities)— around 70 percent of the respondents who held one of those identities strongly also held the other one at a high level. Although identification with all humanity has not been very strong in Poland so far, the comparison between the results of Polish (conducted by Hamer-Gutowska) and American (conducted by McFarland) studies in this area shows no differences in the level of identification between citizens of those two countries. As a very broad identification, theoretically connected to Maslow's high level of self-actualization, it is probably not very common in either society. But one could certainly use similar facilitators for forging a stronger global identity like those described in the case of EU identity above. Hence in future studies it would be very interesting to observe the evolution of a global identity as well as other supranational identities in Poland and other countries. This is especially important in the context of national identities, where global and national identities may be or may not be in competition with each other. We can anticipate that parallel identities will become increasingly common with the progress of intensified processes of globalization.

Social identities are also predictors of pro-social behaviors. The study confirmed, as it was assumed, that people with stronger broad social identities (e.g., national identity) much more often helped other people by giving donations to charity organizations and also by helping people in need in face-to-face interactions. The broadest identification, with all mankind, was also a good predictor of volunteering while controlled for education level (people with a higher level of education more frequently volunteered than people with a lower level of education) and would probably also be a good predictor of donations to international charity organizations (such a study is currently being devised: in this study it was not specified what kind of charity organization the respondents referred to). But the effect of identity strength turned out to be unspecific: stronger identification with all other groups (excluding family) meant more help by donations and in face-to-face interactions. It turns out that strong identification with social groups broader than family and (probably) friends, could then be treated as a part of social capital, and seems to act as a facilitator of social activity (especially of pro-social behaviors, but also of other kinds of social activity—see Hamer-Gutowska, 2006; 2007).

Why does strong identification with the family prevent pro-social behavior (volunteering) or have no effect on such behavior (donations)? It seems that the activity of individuals with strong identification with their families might be benevolence-minded (Schwartz, Rubel, 2005). Probably for many Poles their strong identification with their families prevents them from helping others (not the closest ones), as it could interfere with family welfare (less resources for them). According to Inglehart; "prolonged periods of prosperity tend to encourage the spread of post-materialist values; economic decline tends to have the opposite effect" (2000, 221). It seems that Poland nowadays is in a materialist period, due to system transformation and a high level of unemployment. In such periods survival strategies are very common

(Inglehart, 2000). After some time and with the rise of personal security the Poles may be more able and more willing to help others, not only the closest ones, even while having strong identification with family.

Other results of the study showed that young people had the weakest social identities, no matter which group identification was considered: family, neighbors, citizens of the same town/city, Poles, citizens of the European Union, or all humanity. They are the least-rooted age group in Poland nowadays. There could be a few reasons for this. It is possible that young people are still searching for the social group they would like to belong to. As Arnett (2002) emphasizes, as local cultures change in response to globalization, some people, especially the young, experience identity confusion. They see themselves as being excluded from both local and global culture, truly belonging to neither, and they encounter problems in adapting to rapid changes due to globalization. "The images, values, and opportunities they perceive as being part of the global culture undermine their belief in the value of local cultural practices" (Arnett, 2002, 778). This may be reflected in an increased wave of suicides, depression, and substance abuse among young people as a result of the rapid move towards joining global society, noticed also in Poland (there are twice as may suicide attempts among adolescents today as there were in 1991: Wprost, 2003). According to Arnett (2002), we also observe another phenomenon in the wake of globalization: emerging adulthood—the timing of transition to adult roles, such as marriage, work, and parenthood is slower nowadays. But there is certainly one more possible reason for weak social identities among young people in Poland—system transformation. According to sociologists (e.g., Marody and Giza-Poleszczuk, 2004), massive uprooting of individuals from the communities they were once planted in is the most important feature of adapting to a new form of social organization. It is an attempt to cope with new conditions that facilitates solving new problems. For example, during ten years of system transformation in Poland, a 12 percent decline in the strength of national identity has been observed, as well as a decline in behavioral indicators of religiousness (Jasińska-Kania and Marody, 2002). Similar studies conducted by PGSS (Cichomski, Jerzyński, and Zieliński, 2006) showed a significant drop in the strength of national identity in year 2005 compared to year 1995 (Hamer-Gutowska, 2008b). Perhaps the weakening of parents' cultural traditions hinders the process of transferring identity to their children, whose identity seems less rooted in a time of transformation. These weak roots may perhaps make young Poles more adaptable to new conditions and could thus be a sign that a new society is approaching.

REFERENCES

Adler, A., 1964 [1929]. *Problems of neurosis*. New York: Harper Torchbooks.

Adler, A., 1954 [1927]. *Understanding human nature*. (Wolfe, W. B., trans.) Greenwich, Conn.: Fawcett Publications.

Appandurai, A., 1996. *Modernity at large. Cultural dimensions of globalization*. London: University of Minneapolis Press.

Arnett, J., 2002. The psychology of globalization. *American Psychologist*, 57(10).

Boski, P., 2005. Czy wyraża Pan/i zgodę . . . (Do you agree . . .) In: Jakubowska, U., Skarżyńska, K. (eds.), *Demokracja w Polsce. Doświadczanie zmian* (Democracy in Poland. Experiencing the changes). Warsaw: Academica .

Breakwell, G., Lyons, E. (ed.), 1996. *Changing European identities*. Oxford: Butterworth-Heinemann.

Capozza, D., Brown, R. (ed.), 2000. *Social identity processes*. Sage Publications.

CBOS, 1999. *Czy grozi nam samotność w tłumie?* (Are we threatened by loneliness in the crowd?). Study announcement.

CBOS., 2004. *Typowy Polak i Europejczyk—podobieństwa i różnice* (Typical Pole and European—similarities and differences). Study announcement.

Chryssochoou, X., 1996. How group membership is formed . . . . In Breakwell, G., Lyons, E. (eds.), *Changing European identities*. Oxford: Butterworth-Heinemann.

Cichomski, B., Jerzyński, T., Zieliński, M., 2006. *Polskie Generalne Sondaże Społeczne: skumulowany komputerowy zbiór danych, 1992–2005* (Polish General Social Surveys: machine-readable data file, 1992–2005). Institute for Social Studies, Warsaw: University of Warsaw.

Cinnirella, 1996. A social identity perspective on European integration. In: Breakwell, G., Lyons, E. (eds.). *Changing European identities*. Oxford: Butterworth-Heinemann.

Czapiewska, E., 2006. *Cechy osobowości młodzieży a identyfikacja z całą ludzkością* (Personality traits and identification with all humanity). Unpublished master's thesis, Warsaw School of Social Psychology.

Deaux, K., 2000. Models, meaning and motivations. In Capozza, D., Brown, R. (eds.), *Social identity processes*. London: Sage Publications .

Eurobarometer, http://europa.eu.int/comm/public_opinion/cf/waveoutput_en.cfm (accessed 22-2-2006).

Falkowski, M., Lewandowska, J., Wciórka, B., Wenzel, M., 2005. System wartości materialnych i niematerialnych (System of material and nonmaterial values). In: Zagórski, K., Strzeszewski, M. (eds.), *Polska-Europa-Świat*. (Poland-Europe-World). Warsaw: Scholar.

Fukuyama, F., 1995. *Trust: The social virtues and the creation of prosperity*. New York: Free Press.

Gazeta, Wyborcza. *Polak dla innych* (Poles for others). http://bazy.ngo.pl/search_old/gfrBrdWycinkiSHOW.asp?nr_wycinka_nowe=36300 (accessed 5-12-2002)

Gruszczak, J., 2006. „Oni" czy „My"— identyfikacja z całą ludzkością z perspektywy wolontariusza ("They" or "we"—identification with all humanity from volunteers' perspective). Unpublished master's thesis, Warsaw School of Social Psychology.

Hamer, H., Hamer-Gutowska, K., 2005. Tożsamość społeczna polskich studentów (Social identity of Polish students). Unpublished manuscript. Warsaw: Polish Academy of Science.

Hamer-Gutowska, K., 2006. Social identities and their influence on social activity. XXXI IAREP proceedings. Paris.

Hamer-Gutowska, K., 2007. Co to znaczy MY we współczesnej Polsce? (What does it mean WE in contemporary Poland). In: Skarżyńska, U. Jakubowska, J. Wasilewski (eds.), Konflikty międzygrupowe: przejawy, źródła i metody rozwiązywania (Intergroup conflicts: symptoms, origin and methods of resolving). Warsaw: Academica.

Hamer-Gutowska, K., 2008a. Predictors of wide social identities. Study report. Unpublished manuscript. Warsaw: Polish Academy of Science.

Hamer-Gutowska, K., 2008b. Social identities of Poles in globalisation and system transformation period. Unpublished manuscript. Warsaw: Polish Academy of Science.

Hamilton, W., D., 1964. The genetical evolution of social behavior. Journal of Theoretical Biology 7:1–52.

Hoshmand, L., 2003. Moral implications of globalization and identity. American Psychologist 58:814–815.

Inglehart, R., 2000. Globalization and postmodern values. The Washington Quarterly. Winter.

Inglehart, R., Baker, W. E., 2000. Modernization, cultural change and the persistence of traditional values. American Sociological Review 65:19–51.

Inglehart, R., Basanez, M., Diez-Medrano, J., Halman, L., Luijkx, R., 2004. Human beliefs and values: A cross-cultural sourcebook based on the 1999–2002 value surveys. Mexico City: Siglo XXI.

Jarymowicz, M., (ed.), 2002. Poza egocentryczną perspektywą widzenia siebie i świata (Beyond egocentric perspective of self and the world). Warsaw: Polish Academy of Science.

Jasińska-Kania, A., Marody, M., 2002. Integracja europejska a tożsamość narodowa Polaków (European integration and national identity of Poles). In: Jasińska-Kania, A., and Marody, M. (eds.), Polacy wśród Europejczyków. (Poles among Europeans). Warsaw: Scholar.

Kalbarczyk, M., Maciula M., 2002. Okiem badacza (In the eye of a researcher). In: Maciula, M. (ed.) Kolory wolontariatu (Colors of volunteering). Roczniak 7, Warsaw: Boris, SCW.

Korchmaros, J., Kenny, D., 2001. Emotional closeness as a mediator of the effect of genetic relatedness on altruism. Psychological Science, 12 (3): 262–265.

Lickel, B., Hamilton, D., Uhles, A., Wieczorkowska, G., Lewis, A., Sherman, S., 2000. Varieties of groups and the perception of group entitativity. Journal of Personality and Social Psychology, 78(2): 223–246.

Marody, M., Giza-Poleszczuk, A., 2004. *Przemiany więzi społecznych* (Changes in social bounds). Warsaw: Scholar.

Marsella, A., 1998. Toward a "global-community psychology": Meeting the needs of a changing world. *American Psychologist* 53:1282–1291.

Maslow, A. H., 1954. *Motivation and personality*. New York: Harper and Row.

McFarland, S., Hamer-Gutowska, K., 2006. *All humanity is my ingroup: A measure and studies of "identification with all humanity."* Unpublished manuscript.

McFarland, S., Webb, M., 2003. *Measuring Gemeinschaftsgefuhl: Identification with all humanity*. Paper presented at the International Society of Political Psychology Annual Convention, Lund, Sweden.

McManus-Czubińska, C., Miller, W., Markowski, R., Wasilewski J., 2002. Podwójna tożsamość Polaków (Double identity of Poles). In Markowski, R., (ed.). *System partyjny i zachowania wyborcze* (Party system and voting behaviors). Warsaw: PAS, F. Ebert Fund.

Monroe, K., 1996. *The heart of altruism: Perceptions of a common humanity*. Princeton, N.J.: Princeton University Press.

Noel, J., Wann, D., Branscombe, N., 1995. Peripheral ingroup membership status and public negativity toward outgroups. *Journal of Personality and Social Psychology*, 68(1): 127–137.

Putnam, R., 1995. Bowling alone: America's declining social capital. *Journal of Democracy*, 6(1): 65–78.

Roguska, B., Wciórka, B., 2005. Religijność i stosunek do Kościoła katolickiego (Religiousness and attitudes toward the Catholic church). In: Zagórski, K., and Strzeszewski, M. (eds.), *Polska-Europa-Świat* (Poland-Europe-World). Warsaw: Scholar.

Roguska, B., 2005. Polska droga do Unii Europejskiej. (Polish way to European Union). In: Zagórski, K., and Strzeszewski, M. (eds.), *Polska-Europa-Świat* (Poland-Europe-World). Warsaw: Scholar.

Roland-Levy, C., Ferrari, J., 2005. *The euro and European identity*. XXX IAREP proceedings, VSFS, Prague.

Salamon, L. M., Sokolowski, S. W., List, R., 2003. *Global Civil Society: An Overview*. Baltimore: Johns Hopkins Center for Civil Society Studies.

Sampson, E., 1989. The challenge of social change for psychology. Globalization and Psychology Theory of the Person. *American Psychologist* 44 (6): 914–921.

Schwartz, S., Rubel, T., 2005. Sex differences in value priorities: Cross-cultural and multimethod studies. *Journal of Personality and Social Psychology*, 89(6): 1010–1028.

Skarżyńska, K., 2005. *Człowiek a polityka. Zarys psychologii polityczne.* (Human and the politics). Warsaw: Scholar.

Sousa, E., 1996. Components of Social Identity or the Achilles Heel. In Breakwell, G., and Lyons, E. (eds.). *Changing European identities*. Oxford: Butterworth-Heinemann.

Strzeszewski, M., 2005. Poczucie bezpieczeństwa i stosunek do kary śmierci (Sense of security and attitudes toward the death penalty). In: Zagórski, K., and Strzeszewski, M. (eds.), *Polska-Europa-Świat* (Poland-Europe-World). Warsaw: Scholar.

Szawiel, T., 1989. Grupy społecznej identyfikacji (Groups of social identification). In Nowak, S. (ed.), *Ciągłość i zmiana tradycji kulturowej* (Continuity and change of cultural tradition). Warsaw: PWN.

Szwed, R., 2003. *Tożsamość a obcość kulturowa* (Identity and cultural foreignness). Lublin, Poland: KUL.

Tajfel, H., 1974a. Social identity and intergroup behaviour. *Social Science Information* 13:65–93.

Tajfel, H., 1974b. The exit of social mobility and the voice of social change. *Social Science Information*, 14 (2): 101–118.

Tajfel, H., 1981. *Human groups and social categories.* Cambridge: Cambridge University Press.

Tajfel, H., 1982. Social psychology and intergroup relations. *Annual Review of Psychology* 33:1–39.

Turner, J., 1987. A self-categorization theory. In Turner, J., Hogg, M., Oakes, P., Reicher, S., Wetherell, M. (eds.), *Rediscovering the social group: A self-categorization theory.* Oxford: Basil Blackwell.

Wprost http://www.zom.cor.pl/Grzesiuk/kondycja.html (accessed 22–6–2003).

CHAPTER 9

Spirit of Altruism? On the Role of the Finnish Church as a Promoter of Altruism of Individuals and of Society

Anne Birgitta Pessi

It is widely argued that increased globalization leads to a increased indivi-dualization and a move away from altruistic solidarity. In a world where previous securities are questioned, and where solidarity is increasingly based upon the attribution of similarity among people who share a common identity perceived as harmed or threatened either by geopolitical ruptures or by societal and cultural changes, altruism has become a timely issue of great importance and interest. The rise in communal values, main-tained in the early 1990s during the severe economic depression in many European countries, ceased in the latter part of the decade. Since then values have taken a more individualized direction. Demands for social justice and high social morality, however, as well as political frustration, also increased in the late 1990s (Salonen et al., 2001; Helander, 1999), and altruism is still one of the strongest European values (Puohiniemi, 2002). Looking at the Nordic countries, and especially Finland, attitude surveys have indicated that peo-ple's trust in social and economic help offered by communal welfare services has decreased in recent years (2000–2003) (Monitor, 2003 reported in *Kirkko muutosten keskellä*, 2004). A need for various agents of altruism is evident.

This chapter sets out to analyze the place of the Church in promoting altruism in Finland, and it questions those who claim that individualism is the core of late-modern societies. While this may be accurate in some cases, I shall argue that contemporary societies are characterized by increased interdepen-dence between people, countries, and groups; phenomena that may foster altruism (see also Nesbitt-Larking's chapter in this volume). Various institu-tions, among others churches, are still places of different interactions and net-works, including networks of altruism. In the Nordic context, usually thought of as a blueprint for secularism, the societal and individual-level influence of the churches is a complex question that needs to be the subject of further scrutiny. In Finland, religion and religiosity clearly endure, but in privatized forms. Considering the welfare cuts following the economic recession of the 1990s, the unique Finnish system of congregational church social work is interesting as its public role has become increasingly visible in the last decades. In the following sections I shall analyze if the Finnish church can be conceived of as an agent of altruism, or if it has other missions, and how Finnish people perceive the role of the church in their society.

ALTRUISM AND ITS AGENTS

Altruism is a form of social action in which the actor aims to increase the resources of another person at the expense of her or his own, and in which the primary factor motivating this action is not her or his own subjective advantage but an interpretation of right and wrong based on a comparison of welfare differences. Each one of these concepts is relative by nature.

Individuals—and perhaps also societies—seem to differ in altruism. Elsewhere in this book, Gerd Meyer analyzes the fascinating question of why some people show social courage, whereas others do not. Considering altruism raises the fundamental question of whether it is acquired or innate. Many scholars have debunked the myth of everyone's being born self-centered and egocentric (e.g., in a literature review by Piliavin and Carng, 1990). Children are able to share at a very early stage, and people (most individuals anyway) have an innate capacity for both empathy (capacity to feel with others) and sympathy (capacity to feel for others).

Various scholars, however (Allport, Kohlberg, Rushton, etc.) have also provided evidence supporting the theory that altruism is learnt and can be further developed by teaching and learning (see, e.g., Hoffman, 1981; Grusec, 1981). Hunt (1990) has summed up three elements that characterize altruists, particularly altruistic children, as (1) happy, well-adjusted, and socially popular, as well as (2) sensitive and emotionally expressive, and (3) having high self-esteem. In their illuminating works, Krebs and Van Hesteren (1992) have argued that everyone shares altruism to a greater or lesser degree, and that the capacity for it grows with both social and cognitive development. Their developmental-interactional model of the stages of altruism consists of seven structures: (0) undifferentiated responsiveness, (1) egocentric accommodation, (2) instrumental cooperation, as well as (3) mutual, (4) conscientious, (5) autonomous, (6) integrated, and (7) universal love.[1] Altogether, what

---

[1] The model has been developed further in Van Hesteren (1992), in a direction not entirely approved of by Krebs (see Krebs & Smolenska, 1992).

distinguishes individuals at different stages of altruism, according to Krebs and Van Hesteren, is as follows:

- First, their more direct focus on enhancing the welfare of other individuals as an end in itself.
- Second, their capacity to respond more adequately to others.
- Third, their capacity to perform a broader range of more altruistic acts.

This seven-stage model has also been criticized (see Blumenthal, 1992, especially on the stage viewpoint). The model, however, actually departs from highly constructivist stage theories by assuming, for instance, that individuals always retain previous stages (and may act accordingly), and that altruism is a product of interaction between the various stage structures that an individual has obtained. Furthermore, individuals may acquire different stages in different domains of the development of altruism.

All in all, altruism development research offers us the hopeful notion that altruism can be developed by teaching, learning, and socializing all throughout an individual's life. Families, peers, and schools play a fundamental role here. Other institutional agents such as churches may also play a surprisingly strong and multifunctional role, however. This is the focus of this chapter.

The role of institutions is not an entirely novel one in altruism literature. One central dilemma of altruism relates to the fact that since the recipient does not have the right to require altruistic treatment, true altruism must be based on free will. This point is crystallized in the social policy classic *The Gift Relationship* by Richard Titmuss (1971). The point of departure of this study is that altruism manifested in blood donation reflects the basics of social policy more generally. Titmuss's research problem is how individuals learn to give help to anonymous strangers irrespective of the strangers' race, color or religion. He directs special attention to the significance of the instruments of public policy in promoting (or preventing) altruistic behavior, concluding that social policy is the social manifestation or societal embodiment of altruism located in some "social area." It is crucial that person B cannot require resources of A by appealing to A on the basis of B's rights. In Titmuss's writings, this challenge was resolved partly by the third party; the state, which defines the needs and resources to be used. In other words, the institutional structure of a society should be organized so as to enable altruistic action.

The role of societal institutions has changed immensely during recent decades. Contemporary associational life, to take an example, is characterized by its activeness as well as individualization and diversity of interest, narrow commitment, and grass-roots initiatives with modest structures serving the needs of small circles of members (Siisiäinen, 2003). It has been claimed that people in advanced industrial societies have experienced a shift away from tradition, respect for authority, and material values and towards self-fulfillment and emancipation (Fukuyama, 1999, 59–60). Social institutions, including the churches, are becoming increasingly porous and their boundaries less rigid (Wuthnow, 1998, 5, 30). Present-day institutional religiosity, for instance, is characterized as vicarious rather than personal; individualism and choice being at the heart of late-modern religiosity. At the same time, however, there is increasing uncertainty, risk, and ambiguity as well as difference, marginalization, and exclusion (Davie, 1994, 194). Many of these notions relate to very large societal processes, such as globalization; Nesbitt-Larking, elsewhere in this volume, hence links analyses of globalization with discussions of ethics.

Despite the emphasis on increasingly independent individuals, social networks continue to be fundamental to most people's contentment, happiness, and self-esteem. Individuals continue to be members of networks, even of "tribes" (Maffesoli, 1996). Even if present social ties exist in a challenging context, people's interest in social and altruistic interaction endures and may take surprising forms (Yeung, 2004c). In fact, to consider individualism as the core of the post-traditional social order may be a mistake, since a global society is re-centered in terms of dilemmas and opportunities and is focused upon new forms of interdependence. Various institutions, such as the churches, are still places of various interactions and networks, as well as networks of altruism.

THE NEED FOR ALTRUISM RESEARCH ON INSTITUTIONS

A marked paradigm shift in social psychology, sociology, economics, and political science away from the position that behavior must reveal egoistic motivation has recently taken place. New theory and data are more compatible with the view that "true altruism" does exist (e.g., Pilivian and Charng, 1990; Monroe, 1996; Monroe, 2004; Saari et al., 2005).

Furthermore, some prominent recent social scientific theory discourses concern altruism (e.g., civil society and social capital discourses), but they do not explain this link or relate it in any detail to faith and religion. Black-and-white juxtapositions such as communality versus individuality, as well as communal religion versus individualized religiosity/spirituality, egoism versus altruism, or self-centeredness versus compassion still characterize the social sciences. Such simplistic dichotomies inform empirical research as well: for instance, we often label the forms of communality that are subtle and more difficult to identify with traditional theories, concepts, and measurements as "passivity" and "lack of interest." We need a scholarly *excursus* away from such dichotomies.

Recent research on the interrelations between religiosity and voluntarism (e.g., Yeung, 2004c) suggest that individualized forms of religiosity do not necessarily promote less religious, or even in some sense less ecclesiastical religiosity. Private, publicly passive religiosity does not imply distrust of the church institution and its activities. Quite the contrary; the church and its societal engagement may remain one reference point for values even if people enact their values and religiosity through volunteering without attending services. Furthermore, volunteering *per se*, even outside the church context, may represent a mode of practicing religion. Furthermore, the religiosity–altruism link takes several forms in individual experience. Concepts such as "faith-based volunteer work" seem too blinkered. Matters such as religiosity, spirituality, the context of volunteering, and one's personal set of values should be considered together, specifically as they concern church volunteering. My preliminary conceptualizations (Yeung, 2004c, 102) of "religious altruism" (with its core in activities and helping, faith as its additional aspect) and "altruistic religiosity" (basically faith, with helping as its manifestation) might serve as elements for coming inquiries.

Our understanding of altruism—as well as the links between altruism and religion—will remain limited, however, if we focus simply on individuals, without understanding how social groups and institutions contribute to the construction of well-being and maintenance of altruistic values. Even though public institutions (e.g., the public sector and the Lutheran church in Finland) do not assist individuals primarily because they experience altruistic urges, but base their actions on statutory, value-based regulations, we should explore individual expectations of and trust in institutional support and the role individuals see institutions as having in promoting societal values and faith in compassion and altruism.

New information on the social engagement of churches and individuals is vital to understanding individual-level experiences of well-being and shared altruism, and the maintenance of the societal heritage of altruism.

This chapter focuses particularly on the role of institutions in promoting altruism (i.e., "teaching" the ethics and morality related to altruism and caring). It is a rather interesting angle that has not received much attention. One could even question the entire role of larger institutions (where individuals do not necessarily participate much at all)—and this makes the theme rather provocative. The empirical focus of this chapter will be on the role of the Lutheran church of Finland. *The aim of the chapter is to analyze the role the Finnish church as an altruism promoter?— its role in the "spirit of altruism" of individuals and of Finnish society.* The analysis includes both the institutional perspective of the church and the viewpoints of Finnish citizens. The latter part of the chapter aims to take us one step further: to sketch a novel model of (possible) common ground between the altruism of the church *and* of citizens. But before that, the next two sections will present the context (both European and Finnish) where the church operates.

WELFARE AND RELIGION IN EUROPE

The future of welfare systems is high on the agenda in Europe, as it is in many countries around the world. The responsibilities of various agents in the welfare field are being debated. Since we live in the age of the welfare mix, simple models cannot be used to describe present-day European welfare pluralism.

The division of roles among various welfare-providing agents has changed over time as well as in different parts of Europe (Jeppsson Grassman, 2004). Family and relatives have historically taken the main responsibility for providing assistance for individuals in need. During the industrial expansion period in the nineteenth century, voluntary organizations based on altruistic social support grew up in many new settlements. These organizations were often linked with churches in some way. The idea of a state with a dominant public sector in northern Europe relieving the family of many of its traditional responsibilities and taking over many former voluntary social activities grew in the twentieth century (Yeung et al., 2005).

Europe has traditionally been depicted as a classic example of secularization. It has lately become increasingly obvious, however, in sociological research into religion that European religiosity has not vanished—nor will it in the perceivable future. Although contemporary European religious landscape is privatized, individual interest in spirituality may actually be increasing. Moreover, the European churches have taken on novel public roles in many countries during the 1990s and more recently; for instance, in defending the rights of marginalized individuals (Davie, 2000; Yeung et al., 2005).

The dominant religious institutions, which in Europe are the historical majority churches, have had an impact on the construction of the present organization of welfare in different ways (Yeung, 2004c; Bäckström (ed.), 2005). Depending on how responsibility is divided between agents, the European welfare systems can be divided into different ideal types of "welfare regime[s]" (e.g., Esping-Andersen, 1990). Four types can be sketched: a Nordic social-democratic model, a Continental corporate model, a British liberal model and a Southern European conservative corporate model. In addition, we can separate five major church traditions in Europe, as indicated by the following Table 9–1:

Table 9.1 European models of welfare and the church tradition (Yeung et al., 2005).

	LIBERAL SOCIAL STATE	NORDIC SOCIAL-DEMOCRATIC	CONTINENTAL (CORPORATIVE)	SOUTHERN EUROPEAN (CONSERVATIVE)
Lutheran/ Protestant (80% in Sweden, Norway, Finland)		Sweden Norway Finland		
Evangelical Lutheran Reformed (40% in Germany)			Germany	
Roman Catholic (90% in Italy, 70% in France, 40% in Germany)			Germany France	Italy
Anglican (55% in England)	England			
Greek Orthodox (90% in Greece)				Greece

A number of questions can be raised when reflecting upon the interplay between majority religions and welfare systems. How do contemporary churches, through their actions and roles in public debates, influence welfare at a normative level? What welfare expectations come from the citizens? These questions will be pondered in the following sections.

THE CHURCH IN FINLAND—AGENT OF ALTRUISM?

The Nordic nations (Finland, Sweden, Norway, and Denmark) form a quite distinct group. They share values concerning politics, work and family, morality, and the roles of church and religion. These countries also have a common welfare ideology, strong—and positively viewed—welfare states covering citizens from cradle to grave having been established in the latter half of the twentieth century. The Lutheran churches have played a vital role in shaping Nordic society, and the churches have supported the teachings of caring for one's neighbors and serving the community. The churches have a strong foothold among the Nordic cultural tradition and citizens. High membership rates and the popularity of church ceremonies offer the churches multiple contact points with the majority of the people—despite a clear majority of citizens being passive churchgoers. The role of the church as a welfare provider in each Nordic country has taken a slightly different form. At present, the trend seems to be towards an increasingly parish-based diaconal ministry (Bäckström, 2004; Helander, 2005; Gustafsson and Pettersson, 2001; *Över gränser*, 1999)

What makes Finland a relevant European case for study? The Finnish religious environment is interestingly homogenous, 83 percent of Finns being members of the Evangelical Lutheran church. Finland has relatively high levels of private religiosity (e.g., private prayer and belief in God), yet only a small minority (8 percent) are monthly church-goers—lower than in most European countries (Niemelä, 2002; Salonen et al., 2001). Religion and religiosity clearly endure in Finland, but in a private form. From an international perspective, the Finnish system of congregational church social work is an interesting subject owing to its uniqueness. Social work in the church involves a large group of paid workers and has a central position in canon law and the church organization as a whole (to take an example, every parish must by law have at least one social-work post). In 2000, the number of priests in the Finnish Lutheran church was 2,162, and the number of church social workers as high as 1,462—almost 70 percent of the number of priests. The forms of activity in Finnish church social work now range from food banks to counseling, from home visits to various camps, from financial assistance to support groups, etc. Today, the church social workers themselves want more resources for family work and preventive help. They see work with the elderly and children as particular future challenges (*Kirkko muutosten keskellä*, 2004.)

Macroeconomic decline meant the Nordic countries (excluding Denmark) were hit by a severe economic depression in the early 1990s. The Finnish welfare state was particularly challenged; the country facing a more severe recession since the Second World War than any other country with a developed market economy (Kiander and Vartia, 1998,112–114). Although the height of the economic depression was fairly short, its aftermath is still present in Finland. Ever since the depression, the social and voluntary work carried out by the church has been an increasingly important component of the Finnish and Nordic social welfare system, as can been seen in the following section.

Both during and since the economic recession of the early 1990s, there has been powerful resistance in all Nordic countries to changes in the welfare model. There are, however, some indications of a shift from a welfare state model to a welfare society (Helander, 2005; Kautto et al., 2001).

Municipalities in all Nordic countries seek collaborators from various agents, including the churches. The Nordic churches have responded quite positively to these recent economic and societal welfare demands.

Although the welfare budgets of the church of Finland are only a fraction of those of the Finnish state and municipalities, the visibility of the church's welfare actions is indeed important. This was particularly apparent during the recession of the early 1990s. The recession caused difficulty and criticism over public-sector social policy. Budget cuts were abruptly initiated. The nonprofit sector, voluntary work and Christian social work, became very timely issues. They were recognized on a larger scale as a chance to plug the gaps in services created by the budget cuts in the public sector (Helander and Laaksonen, 1999, 83). The church reacted quickly, setting up funds to help the over-indebted, providing meals, and organizing meeting places and activities for the unemployed. Its employees helped mental-health patients who had been moved to outpatient care. The cooperation between the municipalities, congregations and associations also increased (Heino et al.,1997, 81; 154). Altogether, the church invested significant resources in social work (50 million euros in 1994). The recession also caused a significant change in the nature of church social work, the emphasis shifting from the elderly and handicapped to those of working age and those experiencing economic or psychological problems.

With its increasing social services during the recession, the church attained a very visible, public role in Finnish society in the 1990s. The rise in church social services was widely reported by the media.[2] At the individual level, this activity by church representatives resulted in a more positive public image for the church (Heino et al.1997, 25; 59–60). The church social workers have remained active participants in public debate on a variety of social, environmental, and human rights issues in the early twenty-first century.[3] The need for the church social responsibility continued even in the late 1990s and early 2000s.

---

[2] This resembles the new forms of political engagement by church leaders that Taylor (2003) has reported from England. Herbert (2003) also illustrates how religions from Britain to Egypt adapt by functioning within an instrumental system of modernity; e.g., through social welfare and the private voluntary sector. Increasing social work activities of the church in Finland were not viewed entirely positively by the church staff; there have been similar developments in the church in Sweden (Bäckström 1994, 229).

[3] In 1997, for instance, there was considerable public debate about Sunday trading. Representatives of the church took a prominent role in the debate and questioned the promotion of the culture of consumption. Following the public debate, the Finnish parliament modified the original proposals for a law on trading hours (Salonen et al., 2001)

All in all, even though the Nordic countries are often presented in the sociology of religion as a textbook example of the secularization thesis, it may well be argued that the question of the societal and individual-level influence of the churches—e.g., on the values of solidarity and the actions of altruism—is a far more intricate question, and that the role played by their social engagement is of particular interest.

As Europe undergoes significant economic and social change, the role of the church and its social work is an urgent question of altruism, the church confronting the provision of welfare, and the maintenance of solidarity and cohesion. Can we really talk about "an agent of altruism" in discussing the Finnish church, however? The next section will illuminate the views of the church employees further.

CHURCH EMPLOYEES AND THE IDEAL OF THE CHURCH

Finnish church employee polls indicate that the majority consider parishes and church associations crucial to various societal tasks now and in the future. Yet the need for financial assistance and support of the unemployed is seen as declining in the current situation of the 2009 and global recession that seems a far hope—or rather, it is hoped that it will, since the public sector is expected to do this better than the church representatives (Salonen et al., 2001). A majority of the church staff, according to the surveys, thus seems to favor church social engagement.

Posing the same questions to the interview data, however, reveals the complexity of these issues. Two matters in particular on which the views of the church representatives vary have appeared in recently compiled Finnish interview data.[4] First, what really is the mission of the church institution? Is it primarily or even entirely preaching dogma and evangelizing, or is it rather concentrated with putting the dogma into action, the holy words into flesh? Second, what is the ideal concerning the church's societal visibility? To be in the middle of the social action—acting and commenting loudly and clearly or behaving as a silent, reliable background agent?

---

[4] For the international WREP (Welfare and Religion, 2003) research project, I have recently conducted a small survey ($N = 100$), consisting of 29 interviews with church representatives (four elected officials and 25 employees, mostly priests and church workers), ten interviews with municipal authorities, and six group interviews with the local citizens in Lahti, a middle-sized town in Southern Finland. My aim has been to document how representatives of the local church see the organization and development of welfare and the role of the churches in it.

Based on these questions, two intersecting dimensions can be sketched to describe the interviewees' ideals of the church: *spirituality* versus *social work*, and a *loud* versus *mild, muted* societal voice. Four different idealized orientations concerning the societal role of the church institution can be outlined as in Figure 9–1:

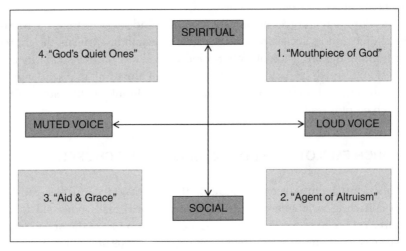

Figure 9.1 The ideal of the church: four orientations (Yeung 2005; Yeung 2006)

The two orientations "the mouthpiece of God" and "God's quiet ones" describe some of the church representatives of the data well, mostly priests and vicars. Some social workers, however, also emphasized the spiritual rather than the social aspects of their work. One social worker noted, for example, that "the main thing and the core must be in spiritual work. If my work and time and energy start to go more into these practical matters, like getting walkers for the elderly, I have to sort of sit down and start to think whether am I in the right position and place."

The two orientations mostly focused on helping and social assistance, "agent of altruism" and "aid and grace" were most typical perspectives among the church social workers, as well as among a few priests. These views are apparent, for instance, in the following quotes: "The church must first give food, before evangelizing. If one does not give food and offer help, it is really hard to start preaching. And trite if one does." One priest said that "the helping activity of the church reminds us of the human values of justice and hope and equality. This is true counseling for everyday life!" Social workers often also emphasized the flexibility of the church institution and its altruism: "What would be bad about the entire church emphasizing the social work dimension? I think it would be good. Our work and our helping should always be changing. Overall, the responsibilities of our social work could be greater. Diaconal social work is at the heart of church activities. We must remember that the church is not simply an expert in spiritual matters."

The dimensions do not exclude each other in all four orientations but illustrate differences in primary emphasis. All in all, social work is apparently a divisive issue within the church. The acts of altruism divide viewpoints. Altruism of the church institution cannot be taken for granted.

REFLECTIONS ON THE CITIZENS' PERSPECTIVE

Finnish people trust the church. Although trust in many central institutions plummeted during the economic recession of the early 1990s, trust in the church increased. When a national poll was taken in 1990, only one-third (32 percent) acknowledged their trust in the church, but when a similar poll was conducted in 2000, the level of confidence had almost doubled (57 percent). Furthermore, the proportion of people believing in God "as the church teaches" rose in the latter half of the 1990s (Niemelä, 2003). The positive image of the church among Finns has even increased into the twenty-first century, since 77 percent of Finns currently view the church positively (8 percent higher than in 1999) (*Gallup Ecclesiastica, 2003*).

But why do Finns trust the church? The role of church social work is an essential factor, since more than 90 percent of people consider the work of the church with the elderly, the disabled, and the young as either important or very important. Furthermore, most Finnish church members (82 percent) consider church social work with the elderly and the handicapped an important reason for their church membership (Salonen et al., 2001; *Gallup Ecclesiastica*, 2003). Interestingly, the very latest figures also indicate that Finns are most dissatisfied with church activities with the unemployed, which seems to indicate their desire for further church action.[5] Similar

---

[5] Those dissatisfied represent 23 percent, and almost as many (18 percent) are displeased with the church's public ethical statements (*Gallup Ecclestiastica* 2003). The latter reaction is more difficult to interpret as it is probably divided between those who wish the church were louder and those who wished it were quieter in public, even political debates. Furthermore, one in three Finns currently trusts the church to provide valid answers to moral dilemmas and everyday-life family problems, and one in four to provide answers to social problems (EVS 2000, Finnish data). Related to the church's role in maintaining societal values of giving, a recent study (Yeung 2003b) has also illustrated that, even though religious elements are not very important in Finns' perceptions of volunteer work, the Lutheran church is explicit in these perceptions.

attitudes toward the church can also be seen in the Finnish political discourse. Before the latest municipal elections (late autumn, 2004), all political parties from left to right wing acknowledged the importance of the church as a service provider (e.g., *Pääpuolueet yksimielisiä*, 2004).

Furthermore, according to very recent survey material[6] a clear majority (81 percent) of Finns agree with the statement that the "Church should strongly participate in public discussions on, e.g., fairness" and with (90 percent) agreeing that the "Church should both do spiritual work and help the needy, and sometimes helping is even more important." If we apply the model in Figure 9–1 above to the national data on citizens, together with the viewpoints of politicians and political parties, the picture is clearly that they mostly seem to stress the orientations of "aid and grace" and specifically "agent of altruism" in their considerations of the church institutions and their social involvement.

But what about personal viewpoints? According to recent survey material the majority (67 percent) regard helping personally as important or very important, while only a third agree with the claim that "all the people should care primarily for themselves." More than half also identify with the claim that people should care for others more than they do at present. Similarly, over half believe that other people are helpful, generally speaking. Also in relation to the question "have you helped the following groups during the last two years?" Finns seem rather altruistic (of course, if people have helped only once during this time, it is not very much at all): a clear majority have helped their relatives (total 84.8 percent, women 87.5 percent, men 79.7 percent), friends (91.1 percent, w 93.7 percent, m 86.1 percent), as well as someone/some individuals unknown to themselves (85.7 percent, w 88.5 percent, m 80.6 percent). All these new figures seem very high. The question arises of whether these views might reflect the model of altruistic actions by the church and the solidarity and altruistic values it promotes, at least to some extent.

Do these positive views and high expectations take the form of practical citizen action? Looking at the Finnish sample of the European Values Study data (EVS), Finns actively participate in volunteer work by international standards (38 percent volunteers), and church volunteering is also higher than in many other European countries (7.1 percent) (Yeung, 2004a). However, since the latter number is not very high, it seems that while the citizens do value the social engagement of the church institutions highly, they do not seem motivated or feel obliged to participate themselves.

---

[6] Random sample survey of Finns, N = 1040, collected in 2006; only statistically significant results reported here.

Different congregational structures promote communal spirit and church volunteering differently; the smaller Finnish religious institutions support closer social ties than do large and scattered Lutheran congregations. Smaller faith communities may also promote a more holistic relationship between beliefs, values, altruism, and putting them into practice. Previous studies (e.g., Yeung, 2004a) have also indicated the particular power of faith as a basis for togetherness. The membership of the large Lutheran state church does not provide a successful basis for a sense of communality manifested in church voluntary work.

Furthermore, Messer (1998,10) has noted that by appointing individuals as permanent staff members, the potential for social capital formation within the church is diffused, diminished, or perhaps never even formed. Although this view is rather extreme, it may in part apply to the Finnish church as there might not appear to be a great need for volunteers. Furthermore, as the Finnish volunteers are characterized in general by highly altruistic wishes,[7] the members of the Lutheran congregations might think that their help is needed more elsewhere.

Related to these—and even more interestingly—religiosity (specifically, churchgoing and the importance of God) has positive correlation not only with church volunteering but also with non-church volunteering (Yeung, 2003b). Church as an institution may support citizens´ altruistic motivation even though these altruistic acts are not always directed to the church activities.

Interestingly, church fund-raising seems to produce the most money in those parishes where the church social work budgets are the highest (Saari et al., 2005.) This may well in part reflect value maintenance and support for overall altruism through the social engagement of the church.

CONTRIBUTING TO THE SPIRIT OF ALTRUISM?

But how might these two different viewpoints—the social engagement of the church and citizens' viewpoints—really relate to each other? Let us look for tools from altruism literature. What kind of links might there be? The following Figure 9–2 summarizes four possible perspectives that might serve to link our two perspectives.

All in all, the concluding hypothesis here is that these four elements—(1) to (4) in the figure above—are basically about the role of *the social engagement*

---

[7] 41 percent of Finnish volunteers choose altruism as their main motive; Yeung 2004b.

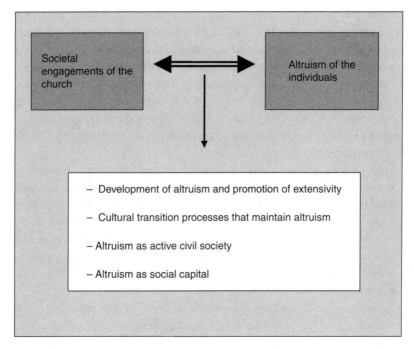

Figure 9.2 Possible common ground between the altruism of the church and of individuals

and teachings of the church in maintaining the value of altruism in our society and in socializing individuals into (further) altruism. Similarly, the *altruism of individuals supports and further maintains the societal structures of altruism* (including that of the church, as argued here).

Let us next look at the literature on which the figure and its four possible elements are based. The elements form a continuum: the first one (on development) concerns the level closest to the individual, and the last one (on social capital) includes the most general societal perspective.

Development and Motivation to Altruism

Research on *altruism development* (e.g., Allport, Kohlberg, Rushton, etc.) offers us the hopeful notion—as noted in the introduction—that altruism can be developed by teaching, learning, and socializing. The development of altruism is a lifelong process. In their research on individuals who had rescued Jews during the Nazi era, the Oliners (Oliner and Oliner, 1988) indicated that the rescuers were marked by "extensivity"; being more attached and committed to people in their social relationships and having empathy as well as an inclusive sense of obligation toward various groups. The Oliners (1992) have since written on eight social processes that may encourage such extensive orientation. Four of the processes relate primarily to *forming attachments* to others:

- *Bonding;* forming enduring emotional attachment to both groups and individuals
- Emphasizing caring norms
- Learning caring norms
- Participating in caring behaviors

Four other processes concern developing a sense of obligation:

- *Diversifying;* enlarging the group of people with whom an individual ordinarily interacts, diminishing divisions into "us" and "them"
- *Networking;* forging linkages with the broader society.
- *Reasoning;* developing shared problem-solving strategies; rational solutions to problems based upon empirical evidence and logic, as such solutions have a role to play in bringing about a more caring society
- *Forming global connections;* linking the local context and "here-and-now" to the global perspective

These eight processes can certainly be inculcated by parents, peers, and schools. Yet the teachings and actions of religious institutions—even the churches—may play a significant role in many of these processes—perhaps in all of them. For instance, the public statements of the Finnish bishops concerning poverty emphasize learning caring norms, diversifying, and forming global connections.

But—to put it in black-and white—what really separates altruists and non-altruists? Kohn (1990, 67–82), utilizing an extensive literature, has answered the broader pro-social behavior question of "who helps and when?" as follows:

- *Environmental factors.* Individuals are more likely to help in smaller communities and/or if s/he believes there is no one else to help; i.e., the bystander theory. Social norms, too, play a definite role here.
- *Interactive elements.* The less ambiguous one's misery is, the more others are likely to help. Similarity between individuals also increases the probability of helping.
- *The individual's state of mind.* To put it simply, happier people and individuals in a good mood are more likely to help others. But people

who feel sympathetic guilt or sadness are also more likely to offer their help. Furthermore, self-awareness enhances helping behavior.

- *Individual traits.* Several factors play a role here:

  1. First, self-esteem; the healthier the level of self-esteem, the more likely an individual is to be caring and helpful.

  2. Second, interpersonal skills and assertiveness; i.e., caring for one's own needs and another's needs often go hand-in-hand.

  3. Third, politics and religiosity; especially egalitarian political views and internalized religiosity, according to some studies; but these, like others, are very complex issues. Similarly, some have indicated that religion affects giving to organizations that help the poor (e.g., Regnerus et al., 1998; Donahue, 1994).

  4. Fourth, gender roles; again, a complex issue, but in Western cultures women are often socialized into more altruistic and caring norms.

All in all, these four elements play both individual- and situation-related roles in pro-social behavior and altruism. The church—its model, encouragement, value-promotion, teachings, etc.—may play (at least a potential) role in all of these.

Furthermore, looking at the literature on the motivation of altruistic behavior in various fields (e.g., Seidler, 1992, in philosophy; Monroe, 1996, in political science; Cohen, 1992a, in evolutionary studies and anthropology; Jarymowicz, 1992, in psychology), particular elements can be identified as critical to altruism and its motivation:

- First, the *conception of self* (i.e., sense of self, self-awareness).
- Second, *perspective on the other* and inclusive identity (seeing past all the social categorizations dividing people, or even the absence of differentiation between self and other as Jarymowicz, 1992, has stated).
- Third, empathy.
- Fourth (but this is not underscored in as many studies) *higher moral principles.*

The motivation elements of altruism are interconnected in various ways. For instance, looking at the list of elements in pro-social motivation provided by Kohn (1990) above, we can see that the individual's state of mind relates to the conception of self, and environmental factors relate to such matters as socialization and education, which in turn relate to all four elements above. To sum up, as Kohn (1990, 100) has put it, an altruistic attitude concerns experiencing both *otherness* and *sharedness*: both appreciating otherness,[8] including perspective-taking (spatial, cognitive, and affective)[9] and empathy, and appreciating shared humanness.

Civil Society and Transition Procesesses of Altruism

Two factors are crucial in the maintenance of altruism: the maintenance of strong altruism-promoting transitions and strong cooperative culture. Both prevent the spread of selfish behavior in populations and support altruistic cultures. Recent altruism research has indicated that pro-social action can move from one person to another through three different transitional displacement and transition processes (Gintis, 2003):

- First, in *vertical* transition, values and attitudes are transferred to children from adults.

- Second, in *horizontal* transition, values are transformed with the help of peer learning.

- Third, in *socializing* transition, social—or antisocial—operation/action becomes common through various rituals, education systems or media (cf. Rushton 1982).

Here again: the statements, teachings, and activities of the church can certainly promote both horizontal and specifically socializing transitions; for instance, in organizing self-help groups and voluntarism activities (horizontal) and spreading the values and norms of altruism (socializing transitions, e.g., through teaching in church services and confirmation schools, and particularly—as it was argued above—via the example of church social services).

The role of *altruism in civil society* may also mediate our two perspectives. The anthropologist Cohen has analyzed the positive elements of altruism and civil society in some interesting ways. Cohen defines civil society to include both *civil life* (nongovernmental social life) and *civility* (actions on behalf of other individuals that take also the other's welfare and well-being into account). Cohen further argues that civil society is evolving through the dual inheritance process (both genetic and sociocultural) in which altruism is incorporated into cultural beliefs, values, norms, and regulations. The defining features of a civil society for Cohen are: (1) the freedom to assess regulations and rules critically, (2) an

---

[8] Kohn (1990, 106–114) has further specified what is meant by "other": *everyone* (collective other), *someone* (the hypothetical other), and *you* (the actual other).

[9] Flavell (1968, 208–211) has identified five more components of perspective-taking: (1) recognition that other people's viewpoints exist, (2) realization that it can be useful to make those inferences, (3) making inferences, (4) continuing to summon the other individual's viewpoint(s), and (5) applying it to onés own behavior.

expansion of the boundaries of the moral universe, including those outside one's own group, and (3) an increase in the value of altruism, empathy, and sympathy (Cohen, 1992a, 104; 119–123; see also Cohen, 1992b). The third one especially—the promotion of altruistic values—relates to the role of larger institutions (citizen associations, churches, etc.) in promotion of altruistic values and behavior.

Churches, Social Capital, Altruism

What about the discussion of *social capital and the bonds of our society*? The fact found in various studies that smaller groups and churches promote societal activities and cohesion better is not very surprising. More challenging to understand is the potential of the established majority church (such as the Finnish church) and the role of its social involvement.

Social capital in its most general sense includes not only horizontal and vertical social relationships, but formal institutions as well (Loranca-Garcia, 2000, 7). In fact, institutions are crucial in establishing the social and political atmosphere of a society. The church institution may promote societal social capital in three ways (which all relate to the three elements noted above):

- First, by providing psychological as well as actual frames of reference that sustain norms.
- Second, by offering venues for communal activities and networks. This notion is crucial because studies have indicated a strong link between churchgoing, spending leisure time with one's congregation members, and volunteering for one's church (Yeung, 2004a).
- Third, by being a highly trusted reference point, thus acting as a maintainer of trust.

The question arises of what this threefold role means in practice, and how it is maintained in the pluralistic late-modern world; how does the church maintain the voice and visibility of its value-basis? I argue that church social work plays a particularly important role in all three. For instance, visible and active social work may vitally influence the maintenance of the cultural tradition of altruism (quite strong in Finland), sustaining this societal norm of altruism even in the pluralist and somewhat secularized present-day context.

But why do I emphasize social work—why not dogma? Social engagement and social work activities, both actions and public statements, are where the teachings of the church are given flesh and blood and made a lived reality. They are the ways in which the teaching of altruism may become more familiar, even to those who do not participate in church activities, either through services or through church volunteering. This proposition is underscored by the late-modernity context of the privatization of religion.

Such considerations illustrate the cultural continuity of the national rhetoric, atmosphere, and spirit of altruism in late modernity. The background for this is that in the Nordic context, the Finnish church has had a particularly democratic history, and the established Finnish church oriented itself rapidly and relatively early towards civil society. Could it even be that the atmosphere of altruism in Finnish volunteering and the more general values partly reflect the religious tradition of the Lutheran church as a vital, national arena for values and altruism?

The church thus seemingly continues to play a role in both symbolic and actual maintenance of social bonds. The Finnish church sustains the societal norm of altruism even in the present-day pluralist and somewhat secularized context; paradoxically, perhaps particularly so.

CONCLUSION

All in all, the Finnish church continues to shape values and behavior intentionally by planning and coordinating its activities and expenditure. It seems that the church may still offer a possible reference point for some cohesion and bonding in Finnish society—not so much in the religious sense but in the sense of values and norms, altruism and caring. It can be argued that it may indeed play a role in promoting social responsibility and the development of individual moral courage. Thus, the church may indeed contribute to the overall societal spirit of altruism.

This may not concern the church institution alone, however. On the level of individuals, emphasized individualism and pluralism of values may support peoples' respect—and even search for—value-oriented institutions, institutions of authenticity where words and deeds meet. On the level of society, communal life needs its glue; for instance, solidarity- and altruism-promoting institutions. Such 'institutions of authenticity,' or 'societal glue,' may be found—to a certain extent—in churches but also in human rights movements and other altruism/solidarity-promoting agents.

But do churches play a specific role in such institutional altruism-promotion? On one hand we must take a critical look; not all religious institutions promote altruism, at least not to the same extent. Also the Finnish church is an independent agent in its decision-making and planning of its budget and activities.[10] Furthermore, churches may also promote altruism *only* within their own members (i.e., promote bonding social capital instead of bridging social

---

[10] This concerns at least its legal status as a societal institution. One may of course also take a more theological viewpoint and ask whether altruism is self-evident in Christian dogma—dogma that binds Christian churches.

capital)—and in such cases they might even decrease the overall societal solidarity and altruism. On the other hand, churches of large world religions are institutions shared by large majorities. In Finland for instance, no other institution is as shared by citizens in terms of belonging, familiarity, media visibility, cultural connections, etc. Thus, we can conclude that the role of the church—at least in the case of this chapter, the church of Finland—can play a specific, and positive, role in overall altruism of the Finnish society.

Religion in late modernity faces difficulties, but perhaps some new opportunities as well. This leads us to ask whether it might be that, as institutions become increasingly fragmented, fluid and porous, the weight of the social and welfare activities of the church may actually increase.

REFERENCES

Data

SAAT 2006 (*Suomalaisten Altruismin Asenteet ja Teot*) [The Attitudes and Actions of Altruism by Finns] 2006 data, Anne Birgitta Yeung, Collegium for Advanced Study, University of Helsinki. (*N* = 1040)

Gallup Ecclesiastica data on Finns. 2003. Tampere: KTK (*N* = 1009)

EVS (European Value Study), Finnish data. 2000 (*N* = 1038)

WREP (Welfare and Religion in European Perspective), 2004. Finnish case study with the following data:

CATEGORY OF DATA	N
background interviews	7
survey data of church employees	100
person-to-person interviews	41
group interviews	6
observation of group discussion event	3
going through local church documents and year books	(2000–2005)
going through the newspaper archives of the parish union	(1985–2005)

Literature

Blumenthal, D, R., 1992. Review Essay [on "Embracing the other. Philosophical, psychological, and historical perspectives on altruism. Ed. by P. M. Oliner, et al., New York: New York University Press"]—*Pastoral Psychology*, 46(2): 131–134.

Bäckström, A., 2004. The church in a new century. In Gunnar, O. (ed.), *Contemporary religion and church. A Nordic perspective* (pp. 81–99). Trondheim, Norway:Tapir.

Bäckström, A., 1994. *För att tjäna (To serve)*. Svenska kyrkans utredningar 1994, vol.1. Uppsala, Sweden: Svenska Kyrka.

Bäckström, A., (ed.)., 2005. *Welfare and religion*. Uppsala, Sweden: Uppsala Institute for Diaconal Studies.

Cohen, R., 1992a. Altruism and the evolution of civil society. In Oliner, Pearl M., et al. (eds.), *Embracing the other. Philosophical, psychological, and historical perspectives on altruism* (pp. 104–129). New York: New York University Press.

Cohen, R., 1992b. Endless teas: An introduction. In Cohen, R., Hyden, G., and Nagan, W. (eds.), *Human rights and governance in Africa*. Gainesville: University of Florida Press.

Davie, G., 2000. *Religion in modern Europe. A memory mutates*. Oxford: Oxford University Press.

Davie, G., 1994. Religion in modern Britain: Believing without belonging: Oxford: Blackwell.

Donahue, M. J., 1994. Correlates of religious giving in six Protestant denominations. In *Review of Religious Research*, 36(2): 149–157.

Esping-Andersen, G., 1990. *The three worlds of welfare capitalism*. Cambridge: Polity Press.

Flavell, J. H., 1968. The development of role-taking and communication skills in children. New York: John Wiley.

Fukuyama, F., 1999. The great disruption. Human nature and the reconstitution of social order. London: Profile Books.

Gintis, H. Solving the puzzle of prosociality. In *Rationality and Society* 15(2003): 2, 155–187.

Grusec, J. E., 1981. Socialization processes and the development of altruism. In Rushton, J., Philippe, J., and Sorrentino, R. M., *Altruism and helping behavior: Social, personality and developmental perspectives*. Hillsdale, N.J.: Lawrence Erlbaum.

Gustafsson, G., and Thorleif, P., 2001. National churches and religious pluralism— The Nordic religious model. In Ståhlberg, K. (ed.), *The Nordic countries and Europe I* (pp. 19–36). Copenhagen: Nordic Council of Ministers.

Heino, H., et al., 1997. Suomen evankelis-luterilainen kirkko vuosina 1992–1995 (The Evangelical Lutheran church of Finland in 1992–1995). Tampere, Finland: Kirkon Tutkimuskeskus.

Helander, E., 2005. Churches and Nordic identity—Churches as welfare providers. In Bäckström, A. (ed.), *Welfare and religion*. Uppsala, Sweden: Uppsala Institute for Diaconal Studies.

Helander, E., 1999. Uskonto ja arvojen murros (Religion and transition of values). In Heikkilä, M. (ed.), *Uskonto ja nykyaika* (pp. 54–89). Sitran julkaisusarja no. 217. Jyväskylä, Finland: Atena.

Helander, V., and Laaksonen H., 1999. *Suomalainen kolmas sektori (The Finnish third sector)*. Helsinki, Finland: Sosiaali- ja terveysturvan keskusliitto.

Herbert, D., 2003. Religion and civil society. Rethinking public religion in the contemporary world. Aldershot, U.K.: Ashgate.

Hoffman, M. L., 1981. The development of empathy. Altruism and helping behavior: social, personality and developmental perspectives. In Rushton, J. P., and Sorrentino, R. M. (eds.). *Altruism and Helping Behavior: Social, Personality and Developmental Perspectives.* Hillsdale, N.J.: Lawrence Erlbaum.

Hunt, M., 1990. The compassionate beast. What science is discovering about the humane side of humankind. New York: William Morrow.

Jarymowicz, M., 1992. Self, we, and other(s): Schemata, distinctiveness, and altruism—embracing the other. In Oliner, P. M., et al. (eds.), *Philosophical, psychological, and historical perspectives on altruism.* New York: New York University Press. 194–212.

Jeppsson Grassman, E., 2004. Welfare in Europe: New trend and old regimes. In Bäckman, N. E. (ed.) *Welfare, church and gender in eight European countries.* Working Paper 1 from the project WREP. Uppsala, Sweden: DVI.

Kautto, M., et al., 2001. Nordic welfare states: Distinct or extinct? In Ståhlberg, K. (ed.), *The Nordic Countries and Europe I.* Copenhagen, Denmark: Nordic Council of Ministers.

Kiander, J., and Vartija P., 1998. *Suuri lama (The great recession).* Helsinki, Finland. ETLA.

Kirkko muutosten keskellä. Suomen evankelisluterilainen kirkko vuosina 2000–2003. 2004. Tampere, Norway: Kirkon tutkimuskeskus.

Kohn, A., 1990. The brighter side of human nature. Altruism and empathy. In *Everyday life.* New York: Basic Books.

Krebs, D. L., and Smolenska, Z. M., 1992. Introduction. In Oliner, P. M., et al. (eds.), *Embracing the other. Philosophical, psychological, and historical perspectives on altruism.* New York: New York University Press.

Krebs, D. L., and Van Hesteren, F., 1992. The development of altruistic personality. In Oliner, P. M. et al. (eds.), *Embracing the other. Philosophical, psychological, and historical perspectives on altruism.* New York: New York University Press. 142–169.

Loranca-Garcia, S., 2000. Paikallisen sosiaalisen pääoman rakentaminen Euroopan unionissa (The construction of local social capital in the European Union). In Kajanoja, K., and Simpura, J. (eds.), *Sosiaalinen pääoma: Globaaleja ja paikallisia näkökulmia.* Helsinki, Finland: Stakes and Government Institute for Economic Research.

Maffesoli, M., 1996. *The time of the tribes.* Trans. by D. Smith. London: Sage.

Messer, J., 1998. Agency, communion, and the formation of social capital. *Nonprofit and Voluntary Sector Quarterly* 27:5–12.

Monroe, K. R., 1996. *The heart of altruism.* Princeton, N.J.: Princeton University Press.

Monroe, K. R., 2004. *The hand of compassion.* Princeton, N.J.: Princeton University Press.

Niemelä, K., 2003. Usko Jumalaan ja kirkon oppiin (Belief in God and church teachings). In Kääriäinen, K., et al. (eds.), *Moderni Kirkkokansa.* Tampere, Norway: Kirkon Tutkimuskeskus.

Niemelä, K., 2002. Suomalaisten uskonnollisuus uuden vuosituhannen alussa (The religiosity of Finns at the beginning of a new millennium). In Helander, E. (ed.). *Muutoksen tulkkina*. Helsinki, Finland: Kirjapaja.

Oliner, S. P., and Oliner, P. M., 1988. *The altruistic personality: Rescuers of Jews in Nazi Europe*. New York: Free Press.

Oliner, P. M., and Oliner, S. P., 1992. Promoting extensive altruistic bonds: A conceptual elaboration and some pragmatic implications. In Oliner, P. M., et al. (eds.), *Embracing the other. Philosophical, psychological, and historical perspectives on altruism*. New York: New York University Press.

Piliavin, J. A., and Charng, H., 1990. Altruism: A review of recent theory and research. *Annual Review of Sociology* 16:27–65.

Puohiniemi, M., 2002. Arvot, asenteet, ajankuva (Values, attitudes, period piece). Espoo, Finland: Limor.

Pääpuolueet yksimielisiä (All major parties in unisono). *Kotimaa* 29–10–2004.

Regnerus et al., 1998. Who gives to the poor? The influence of religious tradition and political location on the personal generosity of Americans toward the poor. *Journal for the Scientific Study of Religion* 37(3): 481–493.

Rushton, J. P., 1982. Altruism and society—A social learning perspective. *Ethics* 92:425–446.

Saari, J.; Kainulainen, S; and Yeung, A. B., 2005. Altruismi. Teoreettiset perusteet ja tutkimus antamisen lahjasta Suomen evankelis-luterilaisessa kirkossa (Altruism). Helsinki, Finland: Yliopistopaino.

Salonen, K.; Kääriäinen K.; and Niemelä, K., 2001. *The Church at the turn of the millennium*. Tampere, Norway: The Research Institute of the Evangelical Lutheran Church of Finland.

Seidler, V. J., 1992. Rescue, righteousness, and morality. In Oliner, P. M., et al. (eds.), *Embracing the other. Philosophical, psychological, and historical perspectives on altruism*. New York: New York University Press.

Siisiäinen, M., 2003. Vuoden 1997 yhdistykset (The associations of the year 1997). In Hänninen, S., Kangas, A., and Siisiäinen, M. (eds.), *Mitä yhdistykset välittävät* (What do associations care?). Jyväskylä, Finland: Atena.

Taylor, J., 2003. After secularism: British government and the inner cities. In Woodhead, L.; Heelas, P.; and Davie, G., *Predicting religion. Christian, secular and alternative futures*. Aldershot, U.K.: Ashgate.

Titmuss, R., 1971. *The gift relationship—From human blood to social policy*. London: Allen and Unwin.

Van Hesteren, F., 1992. The self in moral agency: Toward a theoretical model of the ideal altruistic personality. In Oliner, P. M., et al. (eds.), *Embracing the other: Philosophical, psychological, and historical perspectives on altruism*. New York: New York University Press. 170–193.

Welfare and religion in a european perspective, 2003. Project description. Edited by A Bäckström. Uppsala, Sweden: DVI.

Wuthnow, R., 1998. Loose connections. Joining together in America's fragmented communities. Cambridge, Mass.: Harvard University Press.

Yeung, A. B., 2006. A trusted institution of altruism. The social engagement of the Nordic churches. In Harito, R., and Inaba, K. (eds.), *The practice of altruism: Caring and religion in global perspective*. Cambridge, U.K.: Cambridge Scholars Press.

Yeung. A. B., 2005. The Finnish Lutheran church as a welfare agent—the case of Lahti. In Yeung, A. B. (ed.), *Majority churches in Europe as agents of welfare—eight case studies*. Working Paper 2 from the project WREP. Manuscript. Uppsala, Sweden: DVI

Yeung, A. B., 2004a. An intricate triangle: Religiosity, volunteering, social capital. European perspective—the case of Finland. *Nonprofit and Voluntary Sector Quarterly* 33(3): 401–423.

Yeung, A. B., 2004b. The octagon model of volunteer motivation: Results of a phenomenological analysis. *Voluntas. International Journal of Voluntary and Nonprofit Organizations* 15(2): 21–47.

Yeung, A. B., 2004c. Individually together. Volunteering in late modernity: social work in the Finnish church. Helsinki, Finland: The Finnish Federation for Social Welfare and Health.

Yeung, A. B., 2003b. Civil society, social capital and volunteering in Finland. Contemporary trends in finnish volunteering. *Tidskrift for kirke, religion, samfunn*, 3/2003, 63–80.

Yeung A. B., Bäckman, N. E, and Pettersson, P., 2005. Introduction. In A. B.Yeung (ed.), *Majority churches in Europe as agents of welfare—eight case studies*. Working Paper 2 from the project WREP. Manuscript. Uppsala, Sweden: DVI

Över gränser, 1999. Diakonalt arbete I nordiska kyrkor (Over the borders). Stockholm: Verbum.

PART III

Challenges and Obstacles to Tolerance, Care, and Altruism: Israel and Northern Ireland

CHAPTER 10

Moral Aspects of Prolonged Occupation: Implications for an Occupying Society

Nimrod Rosler, Daniel Bar-Tal, Keren Sharvit, Eran Halperin, and Amiram Raviv

> *The subjection of peoples to alien subjugation, domination and*
> *exploitation constitutes a denial of fundamental human rights.*
> *—UN's declaration on the granting of independence*
> *to colonial countries and peoples*
> *The violation of right in one place of the earth is felt in all places.*
> *—Immanuel Kant*

During the twentieth century, the long process of human moral development advanced a few additional steps, as international conventions concerning individual and collective basic moral rights became globally accepted. One of the phenomena influencing this moral development is the process of globalization, addressed in the present volume, which has facilitated the proliferation of liberal-democratic moral principles through different global channels. In line with this process one could expect the phenomenon of prolonged occupation of nations to disappear. But a closer look at the international arena reveals, not only examples of terrible atrocities against moral principles, but also quite a few examples of long lasting occupations, such as the Chinese 59-year-old occupation of Tibet, the occupation of north Cyprus since, 1974 by Turkey, the Israeli occupation of the West Bank and the Golan Heights seized during the, 1967 war, the prolonged Russian occupation of Chechnya, and the recently commenced American occupation of Iraq. In all these cases we can probably find various acts done by the occupier that violate different moral codes, such as, for instance, the sporadic or systematic cases of killing civilians, deportation of parts of the occupied population, populating the occupied territory with the occupying population, collective punishment of the occupied population, demolition of houses, and the damaging of other private property in the occupied territory.

We would like to argue that beyond the obvious harsh effects of prolonged occupation on the occupied society, the occupation also creates a moral dilemma and dissonance, poses psychological challenges, and carries severe moral and social consequences for the occupying society. Therefore, the present chapter examines moral and socio-psychological implications of the occupation for the perceptions and the belief system of the occupying society, as well as on its moral stature, in a period of global processes of social change affecting individual and societal moral conceptions and behavior. This analysis is done through the presentation of the Israeli case of the occupation of the West Bank and Gaza Strip territories in the 1967 war[1], and by extensively referring to it as a prototypical example of prolonged occupations.

In order to comprehend why these effects result from prolonged occupations, we must first define what *prolonged occupation* is, and differentiate it from similar concepts.

PROLONGED OCCUPATION: LEGAL AND SOCIO-PSYCHOLOGICAL APPROACHES

A review of the literature reveals that most current definitions of the term *occupation* are found in the field of international law (for elaboration see Benvenisty, 1993; Cohen, 1981; Negbi, 1981; Playfair, 1989; 1992; Roberts, 1985; 1990). A currently common definition is "effective control of a certain power (be it one or several states or an international organization), over a territory which is not under the formal sovereignty of that entity, without the volition of the actual sovereigns of that territory" (Benvenisty, 1993, 4). According to the Hague Convention three conditions must be present for the regulations of humanitarian law to take effect in an occupied territory: (1) an armed international altercation has taken place; (2) a military force of Party A has invaded a territory known to belong to Party B; and (3) this force exercises some manner of control over the population residing in that territory.

Roberts (1990), who distinguishes between 17 types of military occupation, argues that "prolonged occupation" must be regarded as a category that is entirely distinct from temporary military occupation. Prolonged occupation is defined as lasting more than five years and continuing even when military hostilities subside or cease. We would like to suggest in addition that an occupation that lasts for an extended period of time not only has particular legal, political, and economic implications, but also has moral and socio-psychological

---

[1] In the present chapter we will focus on the most obstinate part of the territorial consequences of the 1967 war, in which Israel seized Syrian, Egyptian, and Palestinian territories: the occupation of the West Bank and Gaza Strip.

ramifications. This is mainly due to the fact that the definition of any given state depends on individuals' perception of reality, which is a function of their moral values, ideologies, and motives—an aspect that is not exhausted in the legal sphere. These ramifications are integral parts of an occupation because they almost inherently involve violations of basic moral principles that have bearing on the prohibition of such negative behaviors as exploitation, discrimination, aggression, or oppression (Roberts, 1985; Lustick, 1993; Howe, 2002).

In keeping with this position, it may be suggested that from a socio-psychological perspective, the term *occupation* carries negative connotations to many peoples: it implies a negative, subjugating act; an inherent conflict of interest between occupier and occupied, immanent wrongdoing, injustice, and immorality; and finally, it involves a large degree of empathy toward the occupied and a negative attitude towards the occupier. This view of occupation, with its associated meanings that underlie the thinking of many individuals, collectives, and organizations, confronts the occupants with difficulties relating to their self-image as moral individuals, their collective self-view as a just society, and their relationship with the international community.

We think that under these circumstances, for an occupation to persist, the occupying society must be driven by intense and significant motives. Furthermore, in order to cope with the above mentioned moral and socio-psychological difficulties, occupying societies will most likely refuse to accept the definition of their reality as a state of occupation. As a socio-psychosocial mechanism of coping with this difficulty, they may attempt to offer alternative definitions of the situation (see Halperin, Bar-Tal, Sharvit, Rosler, and Raviv, 2007).

Having clarified the nature of occupation, both from a legal and a socio-psychological perspective, we shall now explore the Israeli occupation of the territories of the West Bank and Gaza Strip. The Israeli occupation, as subsequently elaborated, may serve as a test case that may clearly exemplify the different aspects and implications of prolonged occupation.

THE ISRAELI OCCUPATION

While many countries in the world moved towards the termination of periods of occupation, colonialism, and imperialism, Israel, paradoxically, moved in the opposite direction.[2] Although by now Israel has withdrawn

---

[2]It should be noted that the controversy regarding the very definition of Zionism in general, and the Israeli rule of the West Bank and Gaza Strip in particular, as colonialist projects, has greatly intensified in recent years (see, for example, Greenberg, 2005; Hass, 2004; Kimmerling, 1992; Lustick, 1993; Shenhav, 2003).But a thorough discussion of the distinction between the terms *occupation* and *colonialism* is beyond the scope of the current chapter.

from the Gaza Strip, it continues to occupy the territories of the West Bank and Golan Heights. A prevalent assumption among most analysts of Israeli politics following the 1967 war, when the territories were seized, is that the prolonged occupation, rather than being the result of a well-considered decision-making process, is the product of an inability to decide or a "decision not to decide" (Gazit, 2003; Horowitz, 1987; Morris, 2001). An alternative approach to this claim is proposed by Pedatzur (1996) and others, who maintain that the prolonged occupation of the territories of the West Bank and the Gaza Strip is a precise reflection of Israel's aims and interests, as seen by the country's leaders at the time, as well as by some present-day leaders (Eldar and Zertal, 2004; Gorenberg, 2006; Playfair1989; Segev, 2005).

In keeping with its interests and due to the legal and socio-psychological ramifications we explained above, Israel has invested immense efforts over the years in rejecting the definition of its control of the territories as occupation. As a rule, ever since June 1967, the Israeli government has maintained in all international forums that the territories do not constitute "occupied territories.." This argument was based on the supposition that the territories had never been under either Jordanian (in the West Bank) or Egyptian (in Gaza) sovereignty. Thus, the Israel Defense Force cannot be seen as an occupier that has taken the territories from their legal owners (Negbi, 1981; Playfair, 1989; Roberts, 1985). In accordance with this view, Israel preferred to regard the territories as being "under dispute," assuming that this definition extends the room for maneuver in future negotiations. Nonetheless, shortly after the occupation began, the Israeli legal authorities declared that Israel will comply with some of the laws pertaining to an occupying force (Playfair, 1992; Roberts, 1990). As years went by, however, the influence of this legal view on Israel's conduct in the territories weakened, many self-imposed restrictions became loosened, and Jewish settlement there prospered in contradiction to international laws (Horowitz, 1987; Morris, 2001; Eldar and Zertal, 2004).

The ambivalence in Israel's legal practices regarding the West Bank and the Gaza Strip indicates a strong relationship between the formal-legal and the socio-psychological aspects of occupation. From a socio-psychological point of view, defining the territories as "occupied" would imply to Israel's citizens and the rest of the world that Israel's presence in the occupied territory was temporary; that Israel accepted the historic right of the Palestinians to the territories, at least to some degree, and that Israel recognized that its very presence in the territories violated the fundamental rights of their inhabitants. The internal and external debate that Israel confronts over the definition of the state in the West Bank and the Golan Heights as occupation reflects the moral burden embodied in such a state. We will now examine the basic moral principles that an occupying society violates.

PROLONGED OCCUPATION AND THE VIOLATION OF BASIC MORAL PRINCIPLES

The prevalent current moral codes were constructed with international agreements and conventions that regulate the relations between states and peoples. In a globalizing world states' laws, rules and social norms have changed (see, for example, Fernández's discussion in this volume of the changing nature of tolerance). Whether they are considered as part of a natural moral order (Trigg, 2005) or created by social contract (Grice, 1967; Rawls, 1971), we suggest that there is set of fundamental moral principles that have become widespread among states and peoples as a result of the openness that characterized recent decades. These principles have been accepted as social norms, while some of them have been codified into laws. Prolonged occupation inherently contains violations of these shared basic moral principles on three levels: the international level, the societal level, and the individual level. These moral violations and their consequences are one of the main sources for the formation of the moral-psychological challenges, which occupying societies have to cope with, and which will be elaborated later in this chapter. We will first delineate the occupier's actions that cause these violations, and then discuss the contravened moral principles and the processes that have disseminated these principles globally.

During the occupation, the occupying power is conceivably taking different actions that serve its ideological, political, economic, military, and social self interests. Many of these actions cause significant offense to the occupied population as a collective and as individuals. We can note some of these direct actions such as confiscation of land, placement of civilian settlers from the occupying state in the occupied territory, utilization of natural and economic resources of the occupied land, economic exploitation of the occupied population, and the list can go on. In addition, the occupying force might also strive to maintain its superiority and domination by exercising control and surveillance over the local population. In order to accomplish such domination, the occupant may control the occupied population's education and health systems, and movement and migration, as well as preventing their economic and cultural development.

Looking at the history, we can assert that in most cases of prolonged occupations, the occupied societies resist the occupation. The resistance can be manifested in political action, civilian disobedience, or other forms of peaceful protest. But in many cases it may also turn to violent actions, such as attacks against the occupying military forces, as well as against the occupying civilian population[3].

The occupier always attempts to prevent the resistance and punish its initiators. Prevention measures may take the form of restrictions and prevention of free movement by using roadblocks and checkpoints, as well as extensive arrests and torture. The preventive measures might also reflect the will to punish the resisting occupied groups, which may lead to other retributive measures, such as imprisonment without trial, collective punishment, deportation of individuals and/or mass forcible transfer, demolishing houses, and the use of excessive force against civilian population that can come to mass killing and even genocide. Many of the retributive measures, as well as the preventive ones, include prominent breaches of basic moral codes. Perhaps such actions were considered acceptable in the distant past, but in the light of normative and moral developments over the years, presently—in the twenty-first century—these actions are morally intolerable on three levels: the international level, the societal level, and the individual level.

On the international level, prolonged occupation firstly violates the self-determination principle, as it replaces former indigenous political institutions with military rule or an imposed puppet government. Self-determination as a basic moral right was elaborated by John Stuart Mill (2005, 153–178), and is mentioned by Walzer (1977) alongside two other closely connected collective rights that are denied during prolonged occupation: the right to independent sovereign rule, and the right to territorial integrity. In regards to sovereignty, prolonged occupation negates the possibility that the occupied nation or ethnic group can express its collective right to independent sovereign rule, which represents the maximal expression of the self-determination principle. A state of prolonged occupation substantially and durably violates self-determination and political independence of people in a territory that was previously self-governing, as well as the rights of previously non–self-governing territories. As to the respect of the integrity of national territory, Walzer (1977) compares the social moral right of a collective to protect their territorial integrity to the individual moral right to protect his or her life and freedom. During prolonged occupation, the basic principle of territorial integrity is constantly contravened, together with repeated violations of moral code that take place in the form of partial or full

---

[3]Violent resistance to occupation, especially when turning to atrocities against civilians, might also violate basic moral principles; the important discussion of these violations is beyond the scope of the current chapter, which deals with the actions of the occupying society.

annexation of the occupied territory, land confiscations, establishment of settlements for occupants-civilians, and so on. The establishment of settlements and the transfer of parts of the occupant's civilian population into the territory it occupies are not only moral malpractice, but also considered to be a transgression of international law[4].

The principles of self-determination, political independence, and territorial integrity all gained worldwide acceptance as basic moral principles of states and collectives, reflected in their articulation and formulation in several international declarations and conventions. The right to self-determination was declared as one of the main principles of the United Nations in the first article of its Founding Charter[5]: "To develop friendly relations among nations based on respect for the principle of equal rights and self-determination of peoples." This principle gained prominence in the United Nations' Declaration on the Granting of Independence to Colonial Countries and Peoples[6]: "All peoples have the right to self-determination."

The international recognition of the self-determination principle does not refer only to previously self-governing communities. The United Nations charter places moral and legal responsibility on the ruling force of previously non–self-governing territories "to develop self-government, to take due account of the political aspirations of the peoples, and to assist them in the progressive development of their free political institutions" (Article 73). The United Nations' support for political independence for previously non–self-governing territories gained further endorsement in the Declaration on the Granting of Independence to Colonial Countries and Peoples[7], claiming that "all armed action or repressive measures of all kinds directed against dependent peoples shall cease in order to enable them to exercise peacefully and freely their right to complete independence, and the integrity of their national territory shall be respected."[8]

---

[4] According to Article 8 of Rome Statute of the International Criminal Court, grave breaches of the Geneva Conventions of 1949 (including unlawful transfer of civilians) are considered war crimes.

[5] http://www.un.org/aboutun/charter [Accessed on February 13, 2007]

[6] http://www.ohchr.org/english/law/independence.htm [Accessed on February 13, 2007]

[7] The UN resolution refers in its title to colonial countries and people; but as reflected in the body of the declaration, it applies to "all dependent peoples" and to "Non–Self-Governing Territories"—expressions that pertain to people under prolonged occupation as well.

[8] See also Article 1 in *International Covenant on Economic, Social and Cultural Rights*, http://www.ohchr.org/english/law/cescr.htm [Accessed on February 13, 2007]

In addition, prolonged occupation and the occupier's previously noted actions may violate various moral principles that are the bases of universal human rights, on the societal and individual levels. The most important of these principles that is violated is dignity of human life with special regard to life of noncombatants during occupation. This principle, viewed by many as a superior value, is also considered as a basic principle in the ethics of war (Walzer, 1977). A second breached principle is the right of individual and collective freedom and independence that is considered by Rawls (1999) as the first principle in *the law of peoples*. The law of peoples is offered by Rawls as a moral code, which can be common to all "well-ordered peoples"; that is, both liberal-democratic societies and decent hierarchical societies (for further discussion of these terms, see Rawls, 1999, 54–70). The eight proposed principles, which include collective freedom, independence, human rights, and restrictions in the conduct of wars, serve as bases of international laws (Brierly, 1963; Nardin, 1983).

We can trace several processes contributing to the global assimilation of societal and individual basic moral principles. In the international arena, moral principles have been formalized in several international declarations during the twentieth century, the most important of them being the Universal Declaration of Human Rights[9] adopted and proclaimed by the General Assembly of the United Nations on December 10, 1948. Other major declarations regarding basic moral principles are the International Covenant on Economic, Social and Cultural Rights[10] and the International Covenant on Civil and Political Rights[11], both adopted by the United Nations on December 16, 1966. The former was signed by 155 countries and the later by 160 countries.[12]

These moral foundations further gained codification in a few international conventions that became part and parcel of the common international law. The first important convention concerning moral codes in occupied territory was the Hague Convention of 1907. Later, the Geneva Conventions of 1949, which lately has achieved universal acceptance,[13] and its additional protocols deepened the codification of moral principles regarding occupation. Another cornerstone for assimilating basic moral

---

[9]http://www.un.org/Overview/rights.html [Accessed on February 13, 2007]

[10]http://www.ohchr.org/english/law/cescr.htm [Accessed on February 13, 2007]

[11]http://www.ohchr.org/english/law/ccpr.htm [Accessed on February 13, 2007]

[12]See http://www.ohchr.org/english/countries/ratification/index.htm [Accessed on February 13, 2007]

[13]See http://www.icrc.org/Web/eng/siteeng0.nsf/html/geneva-conventions-news–210806 [Accessed on February 13, 2007]

principles regarding war and occupation is the Rome Statute of the International Criminal Court[14] that was adopted by the United Nations Diplomatic Conference in 1998, and was joined by 104 countries as of the beginning of 2007.[15] According to the Rome Statute, grave breaches of the Geneva Conventions of 1949 by persons are considered war crimes, and can be judged and punished by the International Criminal Court. Besides the significance of the United Nations' resolutions and conventions, we can find another globalization process affecting moral reasoning and behavior: the growing influence of additional international governmental organizations (IGOs) that is considered as supportive of democratic transitions and of social and individual moral codes (Mueller, 2002).

Another element contributing to global acceptance of social and individual basic moral principles are the writings of scholars regarding ethics in times of war. In fact the moral principles of desired conduct are usually first formulated by thinkers and only later appear in the international political discourse. Since the early works of Aquinas (1948) and Grotius (1901), through the more recent writings of Hanna Arendt (1969), philosophers have always referred to the moral aspects of war as one of the pivotal issues in human thinking (for a review, see Orend, 2006). Michael Walzer's "just war" theory regarding ethics in wartime (Walzer, 1977), for example, has gained worldwide acceptance and deeply influenced political decision makers. In his propositions, Walzer (1977) asserts that individual rights for life and liberty are palpable features of our moral world generally, and basic elements in moral judgments regarding war specifically.

Following the gradual global assimilation of fundamental moral principles, most nations nowadays are interested in acting in accordance with these norms in order to be part of the international community. The international formulation and codification of these norms has made them an "entrance ticket" to the club of decent states, while their violators may be rejected. In some cases in the past, the international community took considerable actions against such violators: South Africa was internationally isolated during the apartheid era, sanctions were drawn on Iraq after its invasion of Kuwait in 1990, and international criminal tribunals were established after the war in former Yugoslavia and the genocide in Rwanda that took place during the 1990s.

On the societal and state level we can notice global changes that affect moral perceptions and behavior through the growing influences of

---

[14] http://www.ohchr.org/english/law/criminalcourt.htm [Accessed on February 13, 2007]

[15] See http://www.icc-cpi.int/statesparties.html [Accessed on February 13, 2007]

liberal-democratic ideas and practices, which stress human rights and therefore point to the immoral aspects of prolonged occupation. The multifaceted globalization process has facilitated the dissemination of liberal-democratic moral principles to states and peoples through global trade, open communication, and activities of civil societies (Fisher, 1998; Diamond, 1999; Pratt, 2004). Cultural globalization processes have also enabled liberal-democratic moral values to permeate local traditions (Boli and Thomas, 1999), without encountering contestant global power and economic-political doctrine following the collapse of the Communist bloc (Latouche, 1992; Strang and Meyer, 1993; Della Porta, 2005).

The frequent rhetorical and actual use of moral liberal-democratic principles by both democratic and nondemocratic modern regimes can be seen as part of their efforts to establish popular domestic legitimization. Since these moral standards are considered in the global community as just, progressive, and enlightened, governments and states often use them in order to justify their existence, and to construct their epistemic basis for various lines of action.

On the individual level, some psychological-developmental theories perceive moral principles as resulting from human development and socialization processes (see, for example: Hoffman, 1979; Gilligan, 1982[16]). From another perspective, Kohlberg (1984) maintains that most humans are morally developed up to the conventional level in which they accept the moral principles and rules that are part of their social system. Therefore, the integration of basic moral principles into the social normative system, whether through social or individual developmental processes, may result in their internalization by most society members. When these moral principles are contravened, such as in the case of prolonged occupation, they are likely to inflict psychological hardship on their violators. In sum, the assimilation process is completing a circle and becomes interactive: liberal-democratic moral values become basic common norms and laws among "decent peoples" (Rawls, 1999), which disseminate them among their society members, who in turn adopt them and reinforce them by putting individual and group pressure on their violators.

The above analysis suggests that global assimilation processes of moral codes pose great difficulty for occupying societies, which almost inevitably will contravene fundamental moral principles. These societies have to psychologically and socially cope with their contravention of these norms and can result in efforts to bring multilevel pressure to bear on them. For example, the international pressure can be political, economic, or even

---

[16]Gilligan's theory deals with the psychology of women's development.

armed, and domestic pressure can be public, political, and judicial. These pressures may undermine social order, economic stability, and the legitimization of the government that carries out the occupation. While we recognize the importance of the above noted external challenges, as well as internal political and judicial ones, we will focus the present chapter on the intra–socio-psychological difficulties members of the occupying society must cope with as individuals and as a collective. We begin by presenting the challenges and then proceed to analyze the socio-psychological mechanisms that assist the occupants in coping with them.

SOCIO-PSYCHOLOGICAL CHALLENGES AND COPING MECHANISMS OF AN OCCUPYING SOCIETY

The global internalization of basic moral principles poses great challenges to the occupying societies regarding how to cope with the situation. These societies tend to avoid using the term *occupation* as a reference to their own acts, because of its moral and psychologically negative meaning. The central socio-psychological challenge that an occupying group faces is resolution of the discrepancy between the positive manner in which the group members perceive themselves, on various levels, and their role as occupier with all its negative implications (for a detailed discussion, see Halperin et al., 2007). This discrepancy may induce a psychological state of *cognitive dissonance* (Festinger, 1957), which creates discomfort and subsequently a drive to reduce the inconsistency between the group members' behaviors and their perceptions of themselves. An emotional experience of *guilt* is yet another possible result of the self-discrepancies between the "actual self"—occupying group members' perceptions of their behaviour; and the "ought self"—their perception of their responsibilities and obligations according to moral values (Higgins, 1987). A recent study (Binberg, 2006) exposed the deep feelings of guilt that Israeli soldiers felt after serving in the territories during the second *intifada*, committing and witnessing various harsh immoral acts. Although only some members of the occupying group are directly involved in actions that violate moral standards, all group members may experience collective or "group-based" guilt (Branscombe, Doosje, and McGarty, 2002; Doosje, Branscombe, Spears, and Manstead, 1998; Powell, Branscombe, and Schmitt, 2005). Thus, one of the challenges that an occupying society faces is coping with the guilt that may be evoked by the state of occupation and attempting to reduce it.

In order to cope with the challenges, individuals and societies may develop and use a set of psychodynamic and socio-psychological mechanisms that will now be briefly presented (for a detailed discussion, see Halperin et al., 2007). From a psychodynamic perspective, Freud (1915/1961) and his successors identified specific defense mechanisms that help individuals cope with the anxiety aroused by situations including, but not limited to, the challenges we described. Hence, mechanisms of *repression, denial* and *avoidance* (A. Freud, 1966) are likely to underlie the psychological coping with the challenges of occupation. These mechanisms are normal, universal, and functional, but unconscious. While *repression* is a mechanism that suppresses threatening information, *denial* creates an inclination to deny the information's existence, and *avoidance* causes people to distance themselves from the threatening situation. In the context of prolonged occupation, studies that were carried out among Jewish Israelis, found that many Israelis refrain from exposing themselves to media reports that describe the situation in the occupied territories and especially the suffering of the Palestinians (Herzog and Lahad, 2006; Levy, 2006). An additional mechanism, *projection*, appears when individuals find it difficult to accept their own negative qualities, and particularly their aggressive tendencies, and therefore attribute these qualities or tendencies to others. As will be mentioned below, in situations of occupation, projection at the social level is manifested in the delegitimization and dehumanization of the occupied population (Moses, 2002). The defense mechanisms of *intellectualization* and *rationalization* may also contribute to the justification of immoral acts of the occupier by providing complex and sophisticated reasons and explanations to account for the violent behaviors of the occupier.

In addition to the psychodynamic coping mechanisms, members of an occupying society develop a system of societal beliefs,[17] which constitute a socio-psychological infrastructure that enables coping with the occupation reality that is widely considered illegal and immoral (Bar-On, 1992; Halperin et al., 2007). We suggest that this socio-psychological infrastructure is based on three themes. The first theme concerns beliefs that provide *justification* and explanation for the goals and the means of conducting the occupation, initially in order to present it as legitimate and moral to society members, and later also as a source of social motivation. In the Israeli case, the occupation of the Sinai Peninsula, the West Bank, the Gaza Strip, and the Golan Heights in the 1967 war was justified as an act of liberation and redemption of territories

---

[17]Societal beliefs are ideas that members of a given society share, which address issues that are of particular concern to the society, and which contribute to its members' sense of uniqueness (Bar-Tal, 2000). The contents of societal beliefs include characteristics, structures, and processes that exist in various areas of the society's life. In addition, some societal beliefs form the collective narrative of the society.

that were ostensibly intended to be parts of the Jewish state according to the borders delineated in the Bible (for details, see Gorenberg, 2006; Schwartz, 1997). The second theme focuses on *delegitimization of the occupied nation*, which denies the humanity of the occupied society (Bar-Tal, 1990). This is done by ascribing dehumanizing labels to this group (for example, *savages* or *primitives*), or labels that imply highly negative features or social deviation (for example, *they are violent, murderers* or *terrorists*), and thus also justifying the occupation. In the Israeli-Palestinian context, it is worth noting that the delegitimization of the Palestinians began already in the early years of the conflict, and continued along the years. Palestinians were labeled as "Arabs," hence denying their existence as a Palestinian nation, and were negatively stereotyped as primitives, murderers, cowards, terrorists, and evil (Bar-Tal and Teichman, 2005). A third theme of societal beliefs constructs a *positive collective self-image of the occupying group* and suppresses information that may damage this positive image. As part of the effort to create a positive self-image in the Israeli case, the term *purity of arms* was frequently used to indicate that Israeli soldiers use force and weapons only in moral and humane ways, and the Israeli army was presented as the most moral in the world (Bar-Tal, 2007). Interestingly, the stronger the Palestinian resistance to the occupation and the more forceful the response of the occupying Israeli military, the more frequently avowals of the military's morality appear in the Israeli media (for further examples, see Halperin et al., 2007).

It seems that the coping mechanisms to some extent enable the occupying society to meet the challenges that it faces following its violations of basic moral principles. But they do not save the occupying society from paying a price for the occupation. In the last section we would like to describe the moral and social costs that the occupying societies often pay for the violations of the moral code of human behavior.

MORAL-SOCIAL COSTS OF PROLONGED OCCUPATION FOR THE OCCUPYING SOCIETY

In a prolonged occupation, the direct victim of the recurrent violation of the basic moral principles by the occupier is undoubtedly the occupied society. Its basic rights for individual and collective liberty and independence, as well as for self determination, territorial integrity, and economic prosperity are greatly deprived. However, paradoxical as it may seem, the consequences and costs of these violations, in spite of and because of the major use of the psychological and social coping mechanisms we noted, do not spare the occupying society. We believe that an examination of the prices of occupation from the occupant's moral and social point of view may have significant implications for understanding situations of occupation as well as processes that may lead to their termination. Alongside general propositions regarding costs of prolonged occupation to the occupying society, we will provide examples from the Israeli case that can serve as a prototypical test case.

We propose the following two propositions that illuminate the costs of the occupation for the occupying society:

Proposition 1: During the occupation, the occupying group becomes accustomed to mistreating the occupied population; because of the inevitable generalization mechanism, it is impossible for the occupying society to keep a clear boundary between the two normative codes of behavior, one meant for the occupied and the other for the occupier, and breaches of moral principles infiltrate other domains of the occupying society's life.

Proposition 2: The prolonged and recurrent usage of socio-psychological coping mechanisms diminishes the sensitivity to breaches of moral values, and desensitizes the moral constraints of the occupying society.

We will now elaborate on these two propositions, basing the analysis on the examples from the Israeli occupation.

Proposition 1. As stated in the first proposition, the state of prolonged occupation brings about a moral downward slope, especially in the treatment of the occupied society by the occupier, but also inside the occupying society. One of the most salient harsh phenomena caused by this state is the devaluation of the rule of law and the justice system. During the 40 years of the Israeli occupation, a deep-rooted system of dual sets of legal norms developed in the West Bank: one for the Jewish settlers and one for the Palestinian population (Horowitz and Lissak, 1989; Eldar and Zertal, 2004; Kretzmer, 2002; Negbi, 2004). These dual sets enabled the establishment of a system of segregation and discrimination on ethnic grounds in the occupied territories with two different legal systems: military courts for Palestinians versus civilian courts for Jewish settlers (Horowitz and Lissak, 1989). Furthermore, authorities have practiced leniency and understanding toward Israeli violations of the law in the occupied territories. Soldiers brutally beating to death Palestinian detainees during the first years of the *intifada* were sentenced to a few months in jail, while many of their high commanders, who issued the orders, were exempted from punishment (Negbi, 2004). Jewish settlers who damaged Palestinian property, blocked roads, and shot and killed Palestinians were brought to trial under reduced counts (such as manslaughter instead of murder), and were usually sentenced to decreased punishments (Eldar and Zertal, 2004; Negbi, 2004).

The devaluation of the rule of law is also reflected in the hesitant reaction of the Israeli government and legal system towards illegal practices of the

Jewish settlers, backed by messianic-political ideology, establishing the first settlements in the West Bank after the 1967 war (Shprinzak, 1987; Eldar and Zertal, 2004; Negbi, 2004). Over the years, these illegal practices of plundering or confiscating Palestinian lands and establishing unlawful settlements that gained *post-factum* legalization have become the norm (Peace Now, 2006). In fact, the Israeli formal authorities often collaborated in advance with these immoral and illegal violations (Eldar and Zertal, 2004; Sasson, 2005). Another aspect of the illegal and immoral practices exercised in the occupied territories is the corruption that spread in several domains of the Israeli Military Government (Gazit, 2003). Examples can especially be found in the area of issuing permits for movement inside and outside the territories, as well as working permits in Israel for Palestinians (see, for example, B'Tselem, 1994; Regular, October 24, 2003). This civilian and governmental conduct poses a genuine threat to the rule of law in Israel, and is likely to infiltrate other domains of conduct by individuals, groups and leaders in Israel (Negbi, 2004). In this context, we concur with Moshe Negbi's approach, who—already, in 1981—wrote:

> A great deal has been said and written about incidents of corruption frequently observed in Israeli society as a result of our extended domination over a foreign and hostile nation. Indeed, it appears that the famous epigram by Lord Acton—regarding absolute power that corrupts absolutely—is true sevenfold when it comes to military domination over a foreign population. (Negbi, 1981, 164)

It would probably not be an overstatement to propose that the illegal activities conducted as part of the occupation throughout the years have undermined the perception of the rule of law as a central norm in Israel (Horowitz, 1987; Hofnung, 1996). Furthermore, as a result of the generalization mechanism, it is more than plausible that soldiers coming back from compulsory or reserve service in the occupied territories will bring home with them the same norms and behaviors common under the occupation rule (Negbi, 2004). The same goes for settlers who brought to the Israeli public sphere the option, which gained legitimacy, of breaking legal and moral norms under ideological cover.

Proposition 2. As we suggested in the second proposition, one of the natural outcomes of prolonged occupation and extensive usage of socio-psychological coping mechanisms is diminishing sensitivity to breaking social norms and rules. Occupying societies who execute or allow such breaches selectively against the occupied population may become blind to violations of norms and ethics in their own courtyard. The justifications given for violent and exclusionary behaviors in the service of reducing cognitive dissonance and guilt, as well as repression and denial of those aggressive behaviors, will be likely to permeate other domains of life in the occupying society, even if involuntarily. As a result, the moral constraints are easily broken, and a culture that justifies the use of force in order to achieve personal and collective goals, or the "banality of brutalization," may develop (Lissak, 1990; Zerubavel, 2006).

Referring to the Israeli occupation, Landau (1998) asserts that the frequent exposure to violence carried out by soldiers and settlers in the occupied territories alongside the increasing indifference of the Israeli society towards it has contributed to the brutalization of interpersonal relations in Israel. Furthermore a culture of domination and delegitimization of the occupied is likely to lead to a general decline in the value of human life and consequently to an increased tolerance of exploitation, discrimination, and interpersonal violence in the occupying society itself. Such diminution of the value of human life, combined with the expansion of social processes of repression and denial, may lead to disregard and negligence of weakened groups within the occupying society, such as ethnic and religious minorities or illegal immigrants, thus contrasting the concept of tolerance both in its liberal and multicultural meanings (see Fernández, this volume). It may also lead to projection of the guilt resulting from the occupation into these weak groups.

Another possible consequence of the breach of the moral constraints, when reflected in the diminution of the value of human life in the occupying society and combined with the increasing polarization regarding the continuation of the occupation is outbursts of political violence (Horowitz, 1987; Horowitz and Lissak, 1989; Landau, 1998). A prominent example in the Israeli case for such violence occurred in 1983, when a peace activist, Emil Gruenzweig, was assassinated during a "Peace Now" demonstration, and in 1995, when the Israeli Prime minister, Yitzhak Rabin, was assassinated by a right-wing religious student who objected the peace process that Rabin led (Landau, 1998; Negbi, 2004). On more general level, a number of social scientists suggested that the violence that plagues the Israeli society (for example, in schools or in the streets) is a result of the violent norms that penetrated the society because of its violent patterns of actions that characterize the Israeli handling of the Israeli–Arab conflict and especially of the occupied Palestinians (Landau, 1990; 1998; Lissak, 1990; Zalmanson-Levy, 2005).

As noted, the massive use of psychological and social coping mechanisms may lead to similar results. Justification of occupation and stressing the positive image of the occupier, especially when external and internal criticisms appear, may lead to internal pressure for conformity even with immoral acts in the name of patriotic mobilization (Bar-Tal, 1997). In addition, it can lead to delegitmization and exclusion of social groups opposing the consensus, repressive measures towards them, and justification of violence. A third possible result of prolonged usage of these mechanisms is disregard, repression or silencing of criticisms regarding the immoral behavior in the context of occupation in order to erase the sense of guilt and prevent the appearance of unpleasant information (Bar-Tal, 2007).

We can conclude by saying that the violation of basic moral principles and the major usage of coping mechanisms are destabilizing the social and moral order and acting as a two-edged sword. It seems to be impossible to keep the moral and social boundaries of the occupying society intact while grave breaches of moral values are carried out by its representatives and justified by the majority of its members.

DISCUSSION

In this chapter we suggested a thesis that examines prolonged occupation from a moral and socio-psychological perspective. It appears that the prolonged occupation bears harsh moral, social, and psychological consequences, not only for the occupied population, but to the occupying society as well. Prolonged occupation does not refer only to a statutory or geographical situation, but inherently carries with it moral and socio-psychological meanings. Occupying societies and their members are inevitably committing grave and different violations of basic moral principles, and have to cope with the dilemmas and dissonance that their acts are creating. These dilemmas are further intensified by global processes of international codification of moral basics, as well as growing acceptance (reluctantly or willingly) of liberal-democratic moral values by governments and their permeation into local traditions. The usage of psychodynamic coping mechanisms, as well as the development of a system of societal beliefs that justify the occupation, allow the occupying society to continue its misdeeds, but do not enable it to escape significant costs. These immoral acts and their justifications severely impair the social and moral fabric of the occupying society.

We hope that our thesis opens up a new path for researching the difficult phenomenon of prolonged occupation. In this preliminary step we have taken, it is obvious that we have not exhausted the moral, psychological, and social aspects of occupation. The absence of an academic discussion from the occupier's point of view invites further inquiry into the various social and ethical implications of prolonged occupation.

In this last part, we would like to offer a few implications from our analysis regarding the long process of terminating prolonged occupations.

Other than political and military interventions, any movement toward termination of an occupation must involve considerable erosion of the socio-psychological mechanisms that members of the occupying collective use, and awareness of the moral and social costs they pay. Recognition of the situation *as* occupation, undermining psycho-dynamic defense mechanisms and social constructions, and illuminating the moral misdeeds and their social prices, may weaken the confidence in the central societal beliefs that support the occupation, and therefore may facilitate its termination.

The Israeli arena, which ever since the Oslo agreement is characterized by the execution of the disengagement plan and the possibilities of further withdrawals, is gradually moving toward termination of the occupation. This constitutes an appropriate example that may demonstrate the important contribution of the moral and socio-psychological factors to the continuation of the occupation. The sincere long-standing beliefs, held by the majority of the Israeli public, that the domination of the territories of the West Bank, Gaza, and Golan Heights is an act of self-defense based on historical justifications, and the rooted perception of its own morality (see Arian, 1995; Bar-Tal, 2007; Oren, 2005), has provided the Israeli public with means of coping with the challenges of occupation for many years. But through the years the Israeli society has paid severe social prices for the continuation of the occupation, such as undermining the rule of law and high levels of individual and social violence in different manifestations. An analysis of the changes that the Israeli society is experiencing in recent years, alongside the fixation of other processes in this respect, can provide researchers with a vivid but painful example of a society moving back and forth in the process of terminating prolonged occupation.

REFERENCES

Aquinas, T., 1948. *Introduction to Saint Thomas Aquinas.* With an introduction by Anton C. Pegis. New York: Modern Library.

Arendt, H., 1969. *On violence.* New York: Harcourt Brace Jovanovich.

Arian, A., 1995. *Security threatened: Surveying Israeli opinion on peace and war.* Cambridge, U.K.: Cambridge University Press.

Bar-On, D., 1992. A testimony on the moment before the (possible) occurrence of a massacre: On a possible contradiction between the ability to adjust which means mental health and the maintaining of human moral values. *Journal of Traumatic Stress* 5:289–301.

Bar-Tal, D., 1990. Causes and consequences of delegitimization: Models of conflict and ethnocentrism. *Journal of Social Issues* 46:(1), 65–81.

Bar-Tal, D., 1997. The monopolization of patriotism. In Bar-Tal, D., and Staub, E. (eds.), *Patriotism in the life of individuals and nations* (pp. 246–270). Chicago: Nelson Hall.

Bar-Tal, D., 2000. *Shared beliefs in a society: Social psychological analysis.* Thousand Oaks, Calif.: Sage.

Bar-Tal, D., 2007. *Living with the conflict: Socio-psychological analysis of the Israeli-Jewish society.* Jerusalem: Carmel. (in Hebrew)

Bar-Tal, D., and Teichman, Y., 2005. *Stereotypes and prejudice in conflict: Representations of Arabs in Israeli Jewish society.* Cambridge, U.K.: Cambridge University Press.

Benvenisty, E., 1993. *The international law of occupation.* Princeton, N.J.: Princeton University Press.

Binberg, A., 2006. The "guilt question" in stories of Israeli soldiers that served in the second intifada. Thesis dissertation submitted to Haifa University (in Hebrew).

Boli, J., and Thomas, G. M., 1999. *Constructing the world culture: International nongovernmental organizations since 1875.* Stanford, Calif.: Stanford University Press.

Branscombe, N. R., Doosje, B., and McGarty, C., 2002. Antecedents and consequences of collective guilt. In Mackie, D. M., and Smith, E. R. (eds.), *From prejudice to intergroup emotions: Differentiated reactions to social groups* (pp. 49–66). Philadelphia: Psychology Press.

Brierly, J. L., 1963. *The law of nations: An introduction to the law of peace.* Oxford: Clarendon Press.

B'Tselem, 1994. *Collaborators in the occupied territories: Human rights abuses and violations.* Jerusalem: B'Tselem.

Cohen, E. R., 1981. The Fourth Geneva Convention and human rights in the Israel occupied territories, 1967–1977. Unpublished doctoral dissertation, the Hebrew University of Jerusalem.

Della Porta, D., 2005. Globalizations and democracy. *Democratization* 12(5): 668–685.

Diamond, L., 1999. *Developing democracy: Toward consolidation.* Baltimore: Johns Hopkins University Press.

Doosje, B., Branscombe, N. R., Spears, R., and Manstead, A. S. R., 1998. Guilty by association: When one's group has a negative history. *Journal of Personality and Social Psychology* 75:872–886.

Festinger, L., 1957. *A theory of cognitive dissonance.* Evanston, Ill.: Row Peterson.

Fisher, J., 1998. *Nongovernments: NGOs and the political development of the Third World.* West Hartford, Conn.: Kumarian Press.

Freud, A., 1966. *The ego and the mechanisms of defense.* New York: International Universities Press.

Freud, S. [1915]1961. *The standard edition of the complete works of Sigmund Freud* (J. Strachey ed. and trans., Vol. 14). London: Hogarth Press.

Gazit, S., 2003. *Trapped fools: Thirty years of Israeli policy in the territories.* London: Frank Cass.

Gilligan, C., 1982. *In a different voice: Psychological theory and women's development.* Cambridge: Harvard University Press.

Gorenberg, G., 2006. *The accidental empire: Israel and the birth of the settlements, 1967–1977*. New York: Times Books.

Grice, G. R., 1967. *The grounds of moral judgment*. Cambridge: Cambridge University Press.

Grotius, H., 1901. *Rights of war and peace: Including the law of nature and of nations*. Trans. by A. C. Campbell. New York and London: M. Walter Dunne.

Halperin, E., Bar-Tal, D., Sharvit, K., Rosler, N. and Raviv, A., 2007. Prolonged occupation: The psychosocial aspects of an occupying society. Manuscript submitted for publication.

Hass, A., 2004. Colonialism under the guise of a peace process. *Theory and Criticism* 24:191-, 202 (in Hebrew).

Herzog, H., and Lahad, K., 2006. *Knowledge and silence: On mechanisms of denial and repression in Israeli society*. Tel-Aviv: Hakibbutz Hameuchad (in Hebrew).

Higgins, E. T., 1987. Self-discrepancy: A theory relating self and affect. *Psychological Review* 94:319–340.

Hoffman, M. L., 1979. Development of moral thought, feeling, and behavior. *American Psychologist* 34(10): 958–966.

Hofnung, M., 1996. *Democracy, law and national security in Israel*. Aldershot, U.K.: Dartmouth.

Horowitz, D., 1987. Israel and the occupation. *The Jerusalem Quarterly* 43:21–36.

Horowitz, D., and Lissak, M., 1989. *Trouble in Utopia: The overburdened polity of Israel*. Albany: State University of New York Press.

Howe, S., 2002. *Empire: A very short introduction*. Oxford: Oxford University Press.

Kimmerling, B., 1992. Sociology, ideology, and nation building: The Palestinians and their meaning in Israeli sociology. *American Sociological Review* 57:446–460.

Kohlberg, L., 1984. *The psychology of moral development: The nature and validity of moral stages*. San Francisco: Harper and Row.

Kretzmer, D., 2002. The occupation of justice: The supreme court of Israel and the occupied territories. Albany, N.Y.: State University of New York Press.

Landau, S. P., 1990. Possible effects of the intifada on criminal behavior among Israeli citizens. In: Gal, R. (ed.), *The seventh war: The effects of the intifada on the Israeli society*. Tel Aviv: Hakibutz Hameuchad (in Hebrew).

Landau, S. F., 1998. Security-related stress and the quality of life. In Bar-Tal, D., Jacobson, D., and Klieman, A. (eds.), *Security concerns: Insights from the Israeli experience*. Stamford, Conn.: JAI Press.

Latouche, S., 1992. *L'occidentalizzazione del mondo: Saggio sul significato: La portata e I limiti dell'uniformazione planetaria*. Turin: Bollati Boringhieri.

Levi, G., 2006. On the day that Israeli society will really know. In Herzog, H., and Lahad, K. (eds.), *Knowledge and silence: On mechanisms of denial and repression in Israeli society*. Tel Aviv: Hakibutz Hameuchad (in Hebrew).

Lissak, M., 1990. The intifada and the Israeli society: A historical and sociological perspective. In R. Gal (ed.), *The effects of the intifada on Israeli society: Data, evaluations, predictions*. Zichron Yaakov: The Israeli Institute for Military Studies.

Lustick, I. S., 1982. *Arabs in the Jewish state.* Austin: University of Texas Press.

Lustick, I. S., 1988. *For the land and the Lord: Jewish fundamentalism in Israel.* New York: Council on Foreign Relations.

Lustick, I. S., 1993. *Unsettled states, disputed lands.* Ithaca and London: Cornell University Press.

Mill, J. S., 2005. *Dissertations and discussions: Political, philosophical and historical* (Vol. III). London: Adamant Media.

Morris, B., 2001. *Righteous victims: A history of the Zionist-Arab conflict, 1881–2001.* New York: Vintage Books.

Moses, R., 2002. Unconscious defense mechanisms and social mechanisms used in national and political conflicts. In Bunzl, J., and Beit-Hallahmi, B. (eds.), *Psychoanalysis, identity, and ideology: Critical essays on the Israel\Palestine case.* Norwell, Mass.: Kluwer Academic Publishers.

Mueller, K., 2002. *Globalisierung.* Frankfurt am Main: Campus Verlag.

Nardin, T., 1983. *Law, morality, and the relations of states.* Princeton, N.J.: Princeton University Press.

Negbi, M., 1981. *Justice under occupation: The Israeli Supreme Court versus the Military Administration in the occupied territories.* Jerusalem: Cana (in Hebrew).

Negbi, M., 2004. *Coming apart: The unraveling of democracy in Israel.* Jerusalem: Keter (in Hebrew).

Oren, N., 2005. The impact of major events in the Arab-Israeli conflict on the ethos of conflict of the Israeli Jewish society (1967–2000). Doctoral dissertation submitted to Tel Aviv University (in Hebrew).

Orend, B., 2006. *The morality of war.* Canada: Broadview Press.

Pappe, I., 1997. Zionism as colonialism—A comparative view on the mixed colonialism in Asia and Africa. In Weitz, Y. (ed.), *From vision to revision: A hundred years of historiography of Zionism.* Jerusalem: The Zalman Shazar Center (in Hebrew).

Peace Now, 2006. *Breaking the law in the West Bank: One violation leads to another: Israeli settlement building on private Palestinian property.* Jerusalem: Peace Now.

Pedatzur, R., 1996. *The triumph of embarrassment: Israel and the territories after the Six-Day War.* Tel Aviv: Yad-Tabenkin-Galili Research Institute and Bitan Publishers (in Hebrew).

Playfair, E., 1989. Legal aspects of Israel's occupation of the West Bank and Gaza: Theory and practice. In Aruri, N. H. (ed.), *Occupation: Israel over Palestine* (2nd ed.). Belmont, Mass.: Association of Arab-American University Graduates.

Playfair, E. (Ed), 1992. *International law and the administration of occupied territories.* Oxford: Clarendon Press.

Powell, A. A., Branscombe, N. R., and Schmitt, M. T., 2005. Inequality as ingroup privilege or outgroup disadvantage: The impact of group focus on collective guilt and interracial attitudes. *Personality and Social Psychology Bulletin* 31:508–521.

Pratt, N., 2004. Bringing politics back in: Examining the link between globalization and democratization. *Review of International Political Economy* 11(2):311–336.

Rawls, J., 1971. *A theory of justice.* Cambridge: Harvard University Press.

Rawls, J., 1999. *The law of peoples.* Cambridge: Harvard University Press.

Regular, A., October 24, 2003. Suspicion: Two officers distributed passage permits in exchange for bribe. *Haaretz* (in Hebrew).

Roberts, A., 1985. What is a military occupation? *British Yearbook of International Law*, 1984, 55:249–305.

Roberts, A., 1990. Prolonged military occupation: The Israeli-occupied territories since 1967. *The American Journal of International Law* 84:44–103.

Sasson, T., 2005. Summary of the opinion concerning unauthorized outposts. Jerusalem: Prime Minister's Office Communications Department (in Hebrew).

Schwartz, D., 1997. *The land of Israel in religious Zionist thought*. Tel Aviv: Am-Oved (in Hebrew).

Segev, T., 2005. *Israel in 1967*. Jerusalem: Keter (in Hebrew).

Shenhav, Y., 2003. *The Arab-Jews: Nationalism, religion and ethnicity*. Tel Aviv: Am-Oved (in Hebrew).

Shprinzak, E., 1987. *Every man whatsoever is right in his own eyes: Illegalism in Israeli society*. Tel Aviv: Sifriat Poalim (in Hebrew).

Strang, D., and Meyer, J. W., 1993. Institutional conditions for diffusion. *Theory and Society* 22/4:487–511.

Trigg, R., 2005. *Morality matters*. Malden: Blackwell.

Walzer, M., 1977. *Just and unjust wars: A moral argument with historical illustrations*. New York: Basic Books.

Zalmanson-Levy, G., 2005. The instruction of the book of Joshua and the occupation or homage to George Tamarin. In Gor, H. (ed.), *The militarization of education*. Tel Aviv: Babel (in Hebrew).

Zertal, I., and Eldar, A., 2004. *Lords of the land*. Tel Aviv: Kinneret, Zmora-Bitan and Dvir Publishers (in Hebrew).

Zerubavel, E., 2006. *The elephant in the room: Silence and denial in everyday life*. New York: Oxford University Press.

CHAPTER 11

Political Conflict and Moral Reasoning in Northern Ireland

Neil Ferguson

As Kinnvall, Renwick Monroe and Scuzzarello (this volume) remind us in the introduction, more and more of the world's political conflicts are intranational or proxy wars sponsored by outside influences. Northern Ireland features aspects of both these types of conflicts, and, as Northern Ireland is also the most researched conflict on the planet (Whyte, 1990; MacGinty, Muldoon, and Ferguson, 2007) it offers a portentous test bed for research exploring how conflict and conflict transformation impact on human morality at the beginning of the twenty-first century. Indeed, this chapter will use Northern Ireland's unique position to expand upon previous research exploring the impact that living with ethno-political conflict has on individual moral reasoning, while drawing comparisons with findings from the wider literature examining the impact of political violence and conflict escalation on moral thought and cognition.

Northern Ireland has witnessed periods of sectarian and politically moti-vated violence since its inception in 1921. Until the signing of the Good Friday Agreement in 1998, the last period of sustained political violence lasted almost 30 years and left over 3,600 dead and 40,000 injured (Fay, Morrissey, and Smyth, 1999). "The Troubles" in Northern Ireland are widely perceived as a primordial ethnic or religious conflict between Protestants and Catholics; however, these religious labels are used as badges of convenience in what is effectively a political struggle between those who wish to see Northern Ireland remain within the United Kingdom and those who desire a reunification of the island of Ireland (Darby, 1983). The majority of unionists who wish to remain within the United Kingdom. are also Protestants, while the majority of nation-alists who desire to reunify Ireland are Catholic, so the religious labels reflect these political aspirations, but are by no means exclusive, with up to 28 percent of Catholics holding pro-union attitudes (see Darby, 1997; Leach and Williams, 1999; Lowe, Muldoon and Schmid, this volume).

Northern Ireland's long history of interethnic violence has led to the Troubles' being viewed as a "double minority conflict" (Jackson, 1971). This double minority situation means that both Catholic and Protestant communities feel threatened, fear marginalization and a destruction of their identity through being the persecuted minority either on the island of Ireland (for Protestants) or within Northern Ireland (for Catholics). Richmond (1999) suggests these double minority conflicts are subject to more significant internal tensions when, as is the case with Northern Ireland, they have neighboring allies (Britain or the Republic of Ireland) acting as partisan sponsors. The impact of having this partisan external support has led some researchers (Cairns, 1982; Douglas and Boal, 1982; Darby, 1983) to view the Northern Irish conflict as a "double majority conflict" rather than a double minority conflict, as both ethno-political groups are confident and feel themselves to be the legitimate majority. This confidence then encourages violence through a sense of perceived strength and moral right to dominate the "other" that it fosters.

Rosler, Bar-Tal, Sharvit, Halperin, and Raviv (this volume) explore the potential impact this need to dominate the other has on morality of the external oppressor, and although many politicians and political commentators view Northern Ireland as an occupied state, it differs from the West Bank and Gaza in that the majority of the population living in Northern Ireland desire the British presence and unity with Great Britain, while Northern Ireland is under the formal sovereignty of the United Kingdom. The conflict in Northern Ireland, however, has involved checkpoints, surveillance, riots, assassinations, bomb attacks, the deployment of military and paramilitary forces, etc., as part of the wider political conflict, so many of Rosler et al.'s concerns are shared by Northern Ireland's research community, churches, politicians, and the media. Indeed there are over 30 years of research exploring the implications that living with this political conflict has had on community and individual moral reasoning. One of the major concerns this research shares with Rosler et al. is whether there will be a loosening of moral constraints across society due to the permeation of violence into other domains of life (for a review, see Ferguson and Cairns, 1996). These fears that the ugliness and brutality of political violence will result in the immorality inherent in war becoming the norm also gain theoretical support from cognitive-developmental approaches to moral reasoning and development (Rest, Narvaez, Bebeau, and Thoma, 1999).

Indeed, Haste (1996) suggested that "morality can not be understood unless we take full account of the social, cultural and historical context," while Kohlberg proposed that the "moral atmosphere" of a community has a "profound influence on the moral decision making of individuals"

(Kohlberg, Levine and Hewer, 1983, 53). Cross-cultural studies have evidenced support for these theoretical ideas, demonstrating that the moral atmosphere found in different types of communities may influence the moral development of individuals (for example, Snarney, Reimer, and Kohlberg, 1984).

More closely related to the idea of political activity determining moral atmosphere are the ideas of Charlesworth (1991) and Garbarino and Bronfenbrenner (1976). Garbarino and Bronfenbrenner suggested that different types of societies encourage the development of different types of morality. Thus in an anomic setting only the lowest (self-oriented) level of moral development is likely to be reached—Level I in terms of Kohlberg's stages (see Table 11–1 for a description of reasoning

Table 11.1 Summary of Kohlberg's Stages of Moral Development

Level I: Preconventional Morality

- *Stage 1: Punishment and Obedience Orientation.* The individual decides what is right or wrong on the basis of what is punished. Avoidance of punishment and complete deference to the superior power of authorities are valued in their own right, without respect to the underlying morality supported by the authority and the punishment.

- *Stage 2: Individualism and Exchange.* Behaviour which the child considers to be right consists of that which instrumentally satisfies his or her own needs and occasionally the needs of others when it is self interest. Right is what is fair, an equal exchange, a deal or an agreement.

Level II: Conventional Morality

- *Stage 3: Good Boy, Nice Girl Orientation.* Behaviour that is morally right is that which is expected from people close to the individual or what people generally expect of people in their role as friend, sibling, spouse etc. "Being good" is important; it means conformity to stereotypes, having good motives, and showing concern about others.

- *Stage 4: Law and Order Orientation.* There is a strong orientation towards authority, fixed rules and the maintenance of the correct social order. Right behaviour consists of fulfilling the duties you have agreed to and contributing to society. The laws of society are to be upheld for their own sake and to avoid the breakdown of the social system, except in extreme cases.

Level III: Post-conventional Morality

- *Stage 5: Social Contract and Individual Rights.* Actions must achieve the greatest good for the greatest number. Laws are seen as changeable, although they should be upheld in order to preserve social justice.

- *Stage 6: Universal Principles.* What is considered right is defined by a personal decision of conscience following self chosen ethical principles. These principles are universal principles of justice, such as the reciprocity and equality of human rights and the utter respect for the dignity of human beings as individual persons. When societal values come into conflict or violate these universal principles, the individual will act in accordance with his/her principles at Kohlberg's six stages), while in societies organized around a single set of goals, a pattern of morality develops where allegiance to group goals is most likely to dominate. Therefore only in pluralistic settings "in which social agents and entities represent somewhat different expectations, sanctions, and rewards for members of society" (Garbarino and Bronfebrenner, 1976, 75) are people given the "opportunity, security, and social support for the development of abstract thinking and speculation as a consequence of partially competing and overlapping social allegiances" (1976, 75).

Charlesworth's (1991) model also postulated that real-life circumstances, such as conditions created through warfare and political violence, create external ceilings that can constrain moral reasoning. Rest, Narvaez, Bebeau, and Thomas (1999) support these ideas and suggest a "system of cooperation at a society-wide level calls for impartiality, generalizable norms and a level playing field among diverse ethnic, religious, and racial groups" (1999, 15), while "favoritism to kin, or friends, tribalism, and ethnic particularism are enemies of a system of cooperation" (1999, 5) and thus reduce the ability to reason at the optimum level.

This cognitive-developmental approach to moral reasoning may provide a useful way to consider moral development in Northern Ireland and other countries suffering the evils of intra-state conflict. Northern Ireland is a society that can be thought of as tribal rather than pluralistic or impartial. In fact it could be argued that the society is built around the two respective national identities, both of which command a high degree of loyalty and with which most people in Northern Ireland identify, creating two distinct bipolar communities, rather that one integrated society (Cairns, 1982). This lack of pluralism and impartial co-operation between the two conflicting groups would then restrict moral reasoning to that of "vendetta and vigilantism" (Fields, 1989, 205) and constrain moral reasoning.

Impact of the "Troubles" in Northern Ireland on Moral Reasoning

Throughout the Troubles researchers have suspected that the political conflict in Northern Ireland may be impacting moral development (Fields, 1973; Punamaki, 1987). In particular it was suggested that this conflict was leading to the moral "retardation" of Northern Irish children and adolescents (Fields, 1973, 1976; Fraser, 1974), and further, that this moral retardation would outlast the conflict (Lyons, 1973) or generalize violent and antisocial behavior from actions against the security forces to other figures of authority (Lorenc and Branthwaite, 1986).

To explore these predictions, research in Northern Ireland has examined the moral attitudes, moral behavior, and moral reasoning of young people (see Cairns, 1987; Cairns, 1996; Ferguson and Cairns, 1996 for reviews). These studies suggested that there was no evidence for changes in moral attitudes or moral behavior (measured, for example, in terms of crime rates) among Northern Irish young people. There have been some claims, however, that there is evidence that the political conflict has had an impact on moral reasoning. In particular, the early research (Fields, 1973; 1976) portrayed Northern Irish children and adolescents as developmentally delayed in their moral reasoning. The research in this area has, however, been methodologically weak and has been contradicted by later research (Breslin, 1982; Cairns and Conlon, 1985).

Virtually all of this work has focused on young people in Northern Ireland, and in general, has suggested that the political conflict in Northern Ireland has pervaded the whole moral atmosphere of the society. Not all of Northern Ireland, however, has been equally exposed to political violence (Cairns and Darby, 1999). A study by Ferguson and Cairns (1996) used this knowledge to compare children and adolescents from two areas of high political violence and two areas of low political violence. The results indicated that young people from areas characterized by high levels of political violence presented significantly lower levels of moral maturity.

As Kohlberg predicted, the moral atmosphere created through social division, threat, avoidance, and fear in the high-violence areas (Fields, 1976; O'Donnell, 1977; Darby, 1986; 1991) was causing these developmental delays in moral reasoning among children and adolescents living in these areas. This truncating atmosphere then acts as a moral developmental "ceiling" (Kohlberg, 1984), which restricts upward progression and encourages individuals from the high-violence communities to seek solutions to moral problems based on ingroup loyalty and partisan social perspectives.

A later cross-national study of moral reasoning among adolescents in Northern Ireland, Scotland, and the Republic of Ireland by Ferguson and Cairns (2002) suggested that despite the violent atmosphere over the last thirty years, the moral reasoning of Northern Irish adolescents was not developmentally delayed, when compared to their counterparts across the border or across the Irish Sea, as had been previously feared (Fraser, 1972; Fields, 1973; 1976; Lyons, 1973). At first glance this result seems to contradict

Ferguson and Cairns's (1996) earlier findings. When the findings of the two studies are integrated, however, the results complement each other. The 1996 study had high internal validity, was highly controlled, and explicitly compared towns with low levels of political violence with towns of a similar demography, but with high levels of political violence; thus this study explored the impact of political violence at a local level. The 2002 study explored the impact of the conflict across Northern Ireland, rather than the impact of violence on adolescent moral reasoning linked to specific locations. Therefore, at a societal level the Northern Irish adolescents demonstrate comparable levels of moral reasoning to their Southern Irish and Scottish counterparts, but those Northern Irish children and adolescents living with intense levels of political violence are being delayed in their moral development.

Conflict Intensification, Moral Reasoning, and Cognitive Function

These findings are congruent with other research exploring the impact of political violence intensity on moral reasoning (Elbedour, Baker, and Charlesworth, 1997; Ferguson, Willis, and Tilley, 2001), a wider literature exploring the relationship between conflict escalation and cognitive regression (Fisher and Keashly, 1991; Spillmann and Spillmann, 1991) and conflict-induced stress and resorting to magical thinking (Keinan, 1994).

Ferguson, Willis, and Tilley (2001) compared the moral reasoning of Northern Irish children with a comparison group of Nigerian children. Their findings suggested that the greater level of conflict intensity in Nigeria, coupled with an unquestioning obedience to religious and external authority, contributed to lower levels of moral reasoning among Nigerian children, especially in relation to concepts of law and legal justice, in comparison to their Northern Irish peers. Elbedour, Baker, and Charlesworth's (1997) research in Israel/Palestine with children living under varying war conditions also illustrated that political violence has a negative influence on moral reasoning among children who were exposed to greater levels of conflict intensity. Indeed, they suggested that an increased intensity or escalation of conflict may cause a regression of perspective-taking to that of egocentric levels, as do Fisher and Keashly (1991) and Spillmann and Spillmann (1991).

Fisher and Keashly (1991) argue that conflict escalation negatively impacts communication, interaction, perceptions, issue identification, and the management of the conflict. Fisher and Keashly's model charts conflict-escalation over four stages, labeled *discussion, polarization, segregation,* and *destruction,* and each incremental increase in escalation brings about a degradation of cognitive ability and a narrowing of perception. At the discussion stage, group perceptions are accurate, and the groups are open to using negotiation to construct a stable and mutually beneficial solution to the conflict. At the polarized stage, perceptions become distorted and based on stereotypes, while the conflict destroys intergroup trust and respect. At the segregated stage, intergroup hostility and a cycle of threat and counter-threat predominate. At the final stage of conflict escalation, the destructive stage, the warring parties attempt to destroy each other against a background of nonexistent communication, violent confrontation, and perceptions of the outgroup as inhuman, while a peaceful resolution of the conflict is viewed as a hopeless dream. Thus as conflict intensifies and escalates, the use of "enemy" images increase, thinking becomes degraded and moral reasoning becomes truncated.

Spillmann and Spillmann (1991) propose a similar model to Fisher and Keashly's, again viewing each increase in conflict escalation as a deterioration in cognitive ability and a regression in development. Spillmann and Spillmann argue that individuals develop empathy as they progress through life, yet an escalation in conflict seems to reverse this process, and they begin seeing life in terms of "black" and "white," "right," "wrong," "them" and "us." This regression in cognitive reasoning has a devastating impact on or moral development, until the only way to "solve" the conflict is to destroy the enemy before they destroy us.

Keinan (1994) provided a novel approach to examining the impact that stress caused by political conflict has on cognitive functioning. Keinan explored the impact of stress on "primitive" patterns of reasoning, by exploring how Israeli citizens faced with the risks and associated stress of Scud missile attacks during the Gulf War in 1991 engaged in "magical thinking." Magical thinking is "a belief that (a) transfer of energy or information between physical systems may take place solely because of their similarity or contiguity in time and space, or (b) that one's thoughts, words, or actions can achieve specific physical effects in a manner not governed by the principles of ordinary transmission of energy or information" (Zusne and Jones, 1980, 13). As conditions of stress and uncertainty are believed to promote a reliance on magical thinking and increase dependence on superstitious rituals (Zusne and Jones, 1989), Kenian expected Israelis who faced the daily worry of potential Scud attacks to engage in these behaviors and thoughts more often than Israelis from cities outside the range of these weapons. Kenian's findings supported the possibility that the stress placed on the respondents in range of Scud attacks did increase the frequency of magical thinking. Kenian postulated that this increase was due to their attempts to regain control over a stressful situation through a reliance on superstitious beliefs or employing magical rituals in an attempt to control the source of threat. Thus Kenian's findings also indicate that conflict escalation and intensity can regress or truncate cognitive functioning among "normal" populations.

Bandura's social-cognitive model of moral disengagement (Bandura, 1991; Bandura, Barbaranelli, Caprara, and Pastorelli, 1996) and Janis's (1982) model of Groupthink offer some further suggestions as to why warfare and political conflict can lead people to break with moral standards and engage in inhumane conduct. Bandura argues that dehumanizing and aggressive behaviors towards the outgroup are initiated by a process of moral justification, in that the direct impact of conflict and violence on the victim is disregarded or distorted, while the reasons for the conflict are justified in the name of group goals, group honor, etc. Therefore the promoted advantages of the action outweigh the disregarded disadvantages, thus inhumane behavior and dehumanization become acceptable and approved moral conduct in times of political crises.

Although Janis (1982) conceptualized Groupthink as occurring within small groups of policymakers and causing defective decision-making and risky behavior, the theoretical framework could be expanded to deal with the problems that instigate and propagate intergroup conflict. Janis defines *Groupthink* as "the deterioration of mental efficiency, reality testing, and moral judgment that results from ingroup pressures" (Janis, 1982, 5). Indeed, Janis proposes that, when people are under stress and facing external threats, it is easier to accept partisan group decisions that violate societal standards than search for more suitable alternatives. The conditions created in societies actively engaged in political conflict provide a moral ceiling similar to that proposed by Kohlberg (1984) under which "loyalty to the group is the highest form of morality" (Janis, 1982, 11), resulting in the creation of dehumanized enemy images, calls on a higher morality to justify the risky and aggressive ingroup actions, and pressure to conform and fly the flag.

These theorists and researchers, although approaching this topic from different perspectives, do agree that political conflict or intergroup warfare can create the conditions under which child moral and cognitive functioning may be developmentally delayed, while adult cognitive and moral reasoning may actually go through a regression that is inversely linked to the escalation and intensity of the ongoing conflict.

Lind's Dual Aspect Theory of Moral Behavior and the Impact of Political Conflict

The Moral Judgment Test (MJT; Lind and Wakenhut, 1985) was constructed to measure moral judgment competence, which, in the words of Kohlberg (1964, 425; taken from Lind, 2000, 1) is "the capacity to make decisions and judgments which are moral (i.e., based on internal principles) and to act in accordance with such judgments." The MJT is a behavioral test of an individual's ability to judge controversial moral dilemmas on the basis of moral principles rather than on the basis of their opinion or whether the actions taking place in the dilemma are perceived as right or wrong.

Lind's (2000) method of measuring moral reasoning examines both the affective and cognitive aspects, viewing them as inseparable parts of human behavior. Lind's (2004) MJT employs two dilemmas: the first dilemma, *the worker's dilemma*, is based on a trade union dispute between workers and management; while the second dilemma, the *doctor's dilemma*, is based on euthanasia. Handziska (2005, July) rewrote the MJT to create the Re-drafted Moral Judgment Test (RMJT) in order to explore the impact of political conflict on socio-moral and socio-political reasoning. Handziska investigated how capacity for moral reasoning was affected when Macedonian students reasoned about situations of aggression towards state symbols of the Republic of Macedonia, in contrast to their level of reasoning on neutral moral tasks, during a period of civil upheaval. Her findings indicated that Macedonian adolescents had significantly lower levels of moral competence on the RMJT moral tasks than on the regular MJT moral dilemmas. These results suggested that reasoning about socio-political issues at a time of political crisis had a negative impact on moral competence. The adolescents also reported feeling unsafe and that the State of Macedonia, which they felt attached to, had no future.

Handziska's sample comprised ethnic Macedonians and in both dilemmas the participants were challenged with transgressions against Macedonian State symbols. Research employing the MJT (Schillinger, 2006) in Brazil has also indicated that participants can score differently on the dilemmas due to religious and cultural beliefs; in the case of Brazilian participants there was a tendency to evince lower levels of moral competence on the euthanasia dilemma due to the Catholic Church's taking a strong stance on this topic. Elbedour, Baker, and Charlesworth's (1997) research in Israel/Palestine also found differences in levels of reasoning on abstract dilemmas and dilemmas related to the political situation in the Middle East, with the children more likely to resort to reasoning based on ingroup loyalty in the political dilemmas. Lind (2003) refers to this process as moral segmentation. Moral segmentation means that some individuals apply a different level of moral judgment competence when deciding on different moral issues depending on their cultural background and beliefs.

Rationale for Current Study

This study will build on the previous research in Northern Ireland and primarily further the work of Ferguson and Cairns (1996; 2002) by taking their 2002 recommendations into consideration: (a) to take account of ingroup loyalty or how strongly the people identify with their communities and (b) to establish whether the partisan macro-moral solutions associated with moral obligations to the group are still apparent among adult residents of Northern Ireland to a greater degree than their cross-national counterparts. In addition this study will build on the work of Handziska (2005, July) and involve the development of dilemmas that have an ethno-political focus to explore how Northern Irish adults' reasoned on ethnic conflict–focused dilemmas in relation to the traditional MJT dilemmas.

In the current study the Northern Irish adult participants will compose both the main ethno-political communities. As years of education and discipline studied have a significant impact on moral competence (Schillinger, 2006), the sample will be drawn from a population of second-year psychology students. To control for a possible area effect, the sample will be drawn from two Northern Irish universities. A sample of second-year psychology students from a university in the northwest of England will be sampled to provide a cross-national comparison.

In addition to completing the MJT, the participants completed a redrafted MJT. The redrafted dilemmas dealing with ethnic conflict are based on Handziska's "transgressions against Macedonian State symbols" dilemmas, as the use of flags and emblems in Northern Ireland also has a contentious history. The Northern Irish dilemmas (see Appendix) deal with transgressions focused on the flying of ethno-nationalist flags. In the first dilemma there is a transgression against the majority community, and in the second there is a transgression against the minority community. Although the dilemmas do not explicitly deal with Northern Ireland, instead dealing with an unnamed European country, it may be possible for Catholics and Protestants to identify with the protagonists in the dilemmas in terms of being members of the majority (Protestant/ British) or minority community (Catholic/Irish); thus this study will also test for the possibility of moral segmentation among the Northern Irish sample.

METHOD

Participants

A total of 133 undergraduate psychology students (17 males and 116 females)[1] participated in the study. Ninety-two students were from two Northern Irish universities, and 41 were from an English university. The students were aged between 18 and 48 years ($M = 21.39$, $SD = 5.49$). A list-wise deletion of missing data reduced the total effective sample size to 132.

Materials and Procedure

The participants completed the Moral Judgment Test (MJT; Lind and Wakenhunt, 1985; Lind, 2004) which was designed to simultaneously measure moral judgment competence and moral attitudes. The MJT is an $N = 1$ multivariate behavioral experiment with a $6 \times 2 \times 2$ dependent, orthogonal design; thus the measurement of moral judgment competence is based on the assessment of an individual's pattern of behavior, rather than on the sample pattern. The cognitive aspect is measured through the C-index, and the affective aspect is assessed through the individual's attitudes towards the six stages of moral development as devised by Kohlberg (1984).

To assess these affective and cognitive elements, the MJT employs two moral dilemmas (one is based on euthanasia while the other deals with a conflict between workers and management). The participants are required to judge six arguments in favor and six arguments against the dilemma's protagonist's decision. The C-index is the participant's ability to judge arguments according to their moral quality rather than whether or not the participant simply agrees with them. The C-index ranges from 1 to 100. Based on Cohen's proposals (1988) a score of 1–9 is considered low, 10–29 medium, 30–49 high, and above 50 very high.

The Political Judgment Test (PJT) has been created for this research study and replicates the structure of the MJT. The dilemmas and the six arguments for and against the protagonists have been altered, however. The two dilemmas in the PJT relate to the flying and desecration of ethno-nationalist flags (see Appendix) and have been adapted and developed from

---

[1] There has been considerable debate about gender bias in the capacity for moral reasoning (Gilligan, 1982). Yet most research fails to find sex differences in the types of moral judgments individuals make generally (see Cohen, 1991; Kohlberg, Gibbs, and Lieberman, 1983) or specifically within a British or Irish socio-moral environment (see Ferguson, McLernon, and Cairns, 1994; Ferguson and Cairns, 1996, 2002). Thus, although the sample is predominantly female, this should not impact the reliability of the results.

Handziska (2005, July). Thus the PJT is also an $N = 1$ multivariate behavioral experiment with a $6 \times 2 \times 2$ dependent, orthogonal design and measures both affective and cognitive aspects. The PJT also creates a P-index, which measures participant's ability to judge arguments according to their quality in the same manner as the MJT.

Strength of identity withone's community was measured by three items, which were adapted from Brown, Condor, Mathews, Wade, and Williams (1986); namely, "I identify with my religious community"; "Being a member of my community is an important part of how I see myself"; "My religious community is an important group to me." The response format was a 7-point Likert-type scale ranging from *strongly disagree* (1) to *strongly agree* (7). Following previous research practices in Northern Ireland (see Cairns, Kenworthy, Campbell, and Hewstone, 2006; also Tausch, Hewstone, Kenworthy, Cairns, and Christ, 2007) the items were averaged to form an index of ingroup identification and then subjected to a median split to distinguish *high* identifiers from *low* identifiers.

The participants completed the questionnaire in their classrooms during scheduled sessions using the standard procedure for MJT presentation (Lind, 2004).

RESULTS

Study 1: Reliability and Validity

Both the MJT and the PJT were developed to simultaneously measure affective aspects independent from cognitive aspects of socio-moral or sociopolitical behavior. The affective aspect is reflected in the preference towards the six Kohlbergian (1984) stages, while the cognitive aspect is reflected in the C- or P-index score. Thus, to test that the measures are valid and reliable, Lind (2000) suggests that they must demonstrate (a) a hierarchical preference order, (b) a quasi-simplex structure, and (c) cognitive-affective parallelism.

Hierarchical preference order. In Lind's (2000) theory, the hierarchical preference for moral stages is the indicator for the affective aspect of moral reasoning. Therefore higher stages of moral reasoning should be preferred to lower ones. Analysis of this concept evinces the hierarchical preference order for the Kohlbergian stages and also confirms Lind's (2000) assumptions for both the MJT and PJT, as an analysis of the preference order demonstrated that the higher stages (5 and 6) are the most preferred, while stage 1 and 2 are the least.

Quasi-simplex structure. The stage preference in each level is required to correlate most highly with its neighbors, while the correlation decreases as the levels are increasingly distant. To assess the quasi-simplex structure, the components of the MJT and PJT were subjected to principal components analysis. Prior to performing the principal components analysis, the suitability of the data for factor analysis was assessed. The Kaiser-Meyer-Oklin value was .70 and .78 for the MJT and PJT, respectively, while the Barlett's Test of Sphericity reached statistical significance for both the MJT and PJT.

The principal components analysis for the MJT revealed two components with eigenvalues greater than 1 explaining 66.6 percent of the variance for the MJT. A varimax rotation was performed on the two factor solutions for the MJT and indicated a simple structure with all variables loading substantially on only one component. These results are consistent with previous research on the MJT, and they illustrate the quasi-simplex structure of the MJT (e.g., Schillinger, 2006).

The principal components analysis of the PJT revealed two components with eigenvalues exceeding 1, explaining 44 percent and 17 percent of the variance, respectively. An inspection of the scree plot, however, revealed a clear break after the first component, so it was decided to accept a one-factor solution. This was further supported by the results of a Parallel Analysis, which demonstrated that only one component showed eigenvalues exceeding the corresponding values for a randomly generated data matrix of the same size. These results are consistent with previous MJT research.

Cognitive-affective parallelism. Lind (2000) assumes that there is a positive correlation between the cognitive and affective aspects of moral reasoning. Therefore the C-index and P-index scores should correlate with the participant's attitudes towards each of Kohlberg's stages. As expected, both the MJT and PJT C-index and P-index scores correlate with the participants' attitudes towards the six stages of moral orientation. Socio-moral and socio-political judgment competence correlate highly negatively towards the lower stages and highly positively with the higher stages.

After an analysis of these three tests for reliability, both the MJT and the PJT provided satisfactory reliability and validity (for a full discussion of the measures reliability in a British and Irish setting, see Ferguson, 2007, July).

Study 2: Socio-Moral and Socio-Political Reasoning in Northern Ireland

The C-index and P-index scores were analyzed using a two-way ANOVA (Religion x Identity Strength) for both scores. The choice of employing two two-way ANOVA's rather than a one-way between-groups MANOVA was taken due to limitations in the sample size that would have violated MANOVA assumptions of normality. There was a significant main effect for identity strength with low identifiers scoring significantly higher on the C-index than high identifiers $F(1, 79) = 5.26$, $p = .025$, partial $\eta^2 = .066$. This result still meets significance after a Bronferroni adjustment, which reduced the level of significance from $p = .05$ to $p = .025$, while the partial η^2 indicates a moderate effect strength. Thus the mean score for the low identifiers was ($M = 21.85$, $SD = 13.77$) and was significantly higher than the high identifiers ($M = 15.04$, $SD = 12.98$), while there was no significant difference $F(1, 79) = .14$, $p = .71$ between Protestants ($M = 19.02$, $SD = 12.33$) and Catholics ($M = 17.13$, $SD = 14.38$) and no significant interaction effect $F(1, 79) = .669$, $p = .41$).

The results for the 2 x 2 ANOVA for the P-index produced no significant main effects for identity strength $F(1, 80) = .153$, $p = .70$ or religion $F(1, 80) = .002$, $p = .97$, therefore there were no significant differences between Protestants ($M = 13.85$, $SD = 13.58$) and Catholics ($M = 13.54$, $SD = 11.92$) or low ($M = 14.38$, $SD = 11.71$) and high ($M = 13.13$, $SD = 13.04$) identifiers. There was no significant interaction effect $F(1, 80) = .004$, $p = .95$.

Study 3: Cross-National Comparisons

A one-way between-groups MANOVA was performed to investigate cross-national differences on socio-political and socio-moral reasoning. The dependent variables of C-index and P-index scores were used; the independent variable was nationality. There was no significant difference between English and Northern Irish students on the combined dependent variables $F(2, 132) = .98$, $p = .38$, partial $\eta^2 = .015$. Therefore there were no significant differences between the English ($M = 15.84$, $SD = 12.85$) or Northern Irish students ($M = 18.58$, $SD = 14.43$) on the C-index or between English ($M = 11.20$, $SD = 9.41$) or Northern Irish students ($M = 13.68$, $SD = 12.09$) on the P-index.

Study 4: Socio-Political Segmentation

A related t-test was performed to explore whether there were differences in reasoning between the participants' performance on the MJT and PJT. There was a significant difference between MJT and PJT performance ($t(131) = 3.54$; $p < 0.001$) with participants demonstrating higher levels of competence on the MJT ($M = 17.73$, $SD = 13.97$) than on the PJT ($M = 12.87$, $SD = 11.32$).

As each of the PJT dilemmas deals with the actions of members of one community against the other (see Appendix), it is possible that the nature of the dilemma interferes with socio-political competence depending on the role of the group in the dilemma (see Table 11–2).

The descriptive results indicate that there is greater socio-political segmentation among the Northern Irish Catholic group than for the either of the other two groups. Lind (2000a; 2003) suggests that a variation of approximately 15 points is indicative of moral segmentation. The Northern Irish Catholic sample has a difference of 13.03 on the local council and individual

Table 11.2 Moral competence scores on the local council dilemma and the individual dilemma

GROUP	N	P INDEX	SD
Catholic:			
Local Council Dilemma	52	35.45	21.11
Individual Dilemma	52	22.42	19.11
Protestant:			
Local Council Dilemma	28	31.46	24.90
Individual Dilemma	28	27.38	24.71
English:			
Local Council Dilemma	41	25.36	19.24
Individual Dilemma	41	24.90	22.67

dilemma scores for the PJT and would seem to indicate an element of segmentation.

DISCUSSION

From the results obtained in the first study, the clear conclusion is that the MJT and PJT evince suitable reliability and validity with this sample of British and Irish undergraduates. The measures demonstrate a hierarchical preference order, a quasi-simplex structure and cognitive parallelism in line with Lind's (2000, 2004) assumptions.

The results from Study Two do not indicate any significant differences in socio-moral or socio-political competence between Catholics and Protestants, but they do demonstrate a significant and moderately strong effect for identity strength, with high identifiers scoring significantly lower levels of moral competence than low identifiers. These results add to the growing body of literature from Northern Ireland that indicates identity strength can effect emotions, cognitions, and behaviors such as influencing ingroup bias (Cairns, Kenworthy, Campbell, and Hewstone, 2006) and the impact of intergroup contact on cross-community relations (Tausch, Hewstone, Kenworthy, Cairns, and Christ, 2007). This contemporary research (Cairns et al., 2007; Tausch et al., 2006) indicates that Protestants and Catholics who show a strong identification to their group differ from low identifiers by showing greater ingroup bias, regardless of their ethno-religious background. The findings from this study coupled with the conclusions drawn by Cairns et al. (2007) and Taush et al. (2007) proffer support for Ferguson and Cairns' (2002) conclusions that the major factor that impacts moral reasoning is not the obvious conflict between Irish Catholics and British Protestants, but the conflict between those who embrace the conflict and show group loyalty, and those who seek a culture of coexistence and resist the call to "fly the flag" or engage in outgroup denigration, etc. Thus, those who identify most strongly with their community are more likely to offer greater support for what Darby (1997, 116) calls the "culture of violence"; thus demonstrating a greater reliance on solutions that focus on Stage Three reasoning, which emphasizes moral obligations to the ingroup when dealing with macro-moral problems.

In Study Three there were no significant differences in levels of moral competence between English and Northern Irish undergraduate psychology students: these results mirror Ferguson and Cairns' (2002) findings with a cross-national comparison of Northern Irish, Scottish, and Southern Irish adolescents, and indicates that generally Northern Irish adults are reasoning and developing normally in comparison with their peers across the Irish Sea. It could be argued that due to the developing peace process, these findings are less surprising now that they were five years ago, as they reveal how people's involvement in and experiences of the conflict are lessening. This conclusion is further enhanced by the findings from the pilot study. During the pilot study[2] for this research, I measured the respondents' ($n = 54$) direct experience of the violence, and only 6.3 percent of the relatively young sample ($M = 22.81$, $SD = 7.34$) had direct experiences such as being intimidated from their home, having their home damaged in an attack, or being injured in a sectarian attack. In contrast, in an earlier survey conducted by Cairns, Mallet, Lewis, and Wilson (2003) in 2001, 15.4 percent reported having direct experiences of the conflict. Thus there seems to be a considerable drop in the proportion of the population who suffered direct exposure to the conflict over the last five to six years. One reason for this drop in the frequency of experiences of the conflict is the fact that Northern Ireland is developing into a post-conflict society (MacGinty et al., 2007) and the physical and psychological impact of the conflict may be beginning to fade.

Study Four explored whether there was evidence of moral segmentation, and an exploration of the means for socio-political competence provided some indication of moral segmentation among the Catholic undergraduates. Lind (2000a; 2003) has found that different samples from different cultures can reason about the dilemmas in different ways. Lind also proposed that moral segmentation was due to internalized societal or community rules'

---

[2] Due to the small number of respondents with experiences of the conflict and the desire to reduce the cognitive load of the questionnaire, these items were removed for the main study.

constraining autonomous moral reasoning. As the Irish Catholic sample demonstrated less competence when dealing with the dilemma they disagreed with (the individual desecrating the flag), it would seem to indicate that their desire to disagree with the individual's actions overwhelmed their ability to reason about the quality of the arguments provided for his or her actions. If this were the case, we would have also expected a similar result for the local-council dilemma with the Protestant sample, but perhaps the small sample size of this group affected this insignificant result. This area of study is new, however, and Lind is only beginning to develop the parameters of what the differences on competence levels across the dilemmas indicate and whether moral segmentation is present, so this conclusion has yet to be fully verified.

Interestingly, both the English and the Northern Irish samples demonstrated significantly greater moral competency on the MJT than on the PJT. Therefore the differences in competency scores on these two measures are unlikely to be due to the conflict in Northern Ireland. This finding poses a question for the conclusions of Handziska (2005, July), as she suggested that the differences in reasoning on the hypothetical dilemmas and the dilemmas related to the conflict were a result of the respondents' experiences of violence. Perhaps the differences could be due to the ability of the flag-based dilemmas to stimulate moral reasoning to the same extent as the standard dilemmas in the MJT.

Overall, this study builds on previous research in Northern Ireland (see Ferguson and Cairns, 1996, 2002, for a detailed discussion) exploring the impact that living in a divided society has on individual moral reasoning. The results indicate the suitability of the MJT or a redrafted MJT for use with Northern Irish populations. The findings further suggest that the conflict has not had the detrimental impact on reasoning predicted by Fields (1973, 1976), Fraser (1974), and Lyons (1973); nor does it indicate that this impact would outlast the conflict. Comparison with the findings from countries with greater intensities of political violence than those currently witnessed in Northern Ireland (Ferguson, Willis, and Tilley, 2001; Handziska, 2005) also suggest that the peace process seems to have reduced the pressures on the general population to consider solutions to socio-moral dilemmas that are bound to community discourse. This suggestion would offer support to McLernon, Ferguson, and Cairns' (1997) conclusion that the peace process is allowing Northern Ireland to move towards a situation when hostility to the outgroup is openly discouraged within societal discourse.

But the evidence of differences in reasoning between high and low ingroup identifiers and the limited evidence of moral segmentation among the Irish Catholic sample does indicate that, for some, the legacy of the conflict could be coloring their ability to reason at their optimum level.

These studies are ongoing, and further data will be collected in England
and Northern Ireland to improve the sample and hopefully explore these
issues again in more depth.

ACKNOWLEDGEMENTS

I would like to thank Ed Cairns, Georg Lind, and Orla Muldoon for all their
help and assistance in the completion of these studies.

APPENDIX

Flag Dilemma I

One local council in a European country failed to fly the state flag on the
occasion of a public holiday as directed by law. Instead of flying the state flag
as directed, the local council decided to break the law and fly the flag of the
ethnic minority, which constituted the majority of the population in that
particular council borough.

Flags Dilemma II

A political organization that represents the political and cultural concerns of
the minority population of a European country commemorates a historic
military victory over the country's majority community with a series of
parades and speeches at locations across the country each spring. Although
these occasions cause offence to many members of the majority community,
they are enjoyed by members of the minority community and are deemed
legal by the State. While television stations were broadcasting one of the
speeches and parades live, a member of the majority community rushed on
to the stage, grabbed one of the minority community's flags and started to
trample on it.

REFERENCES

Bandura, A., 1991. Social cognitive theory of moral thought and action. In Kurtines,
    W. M., and Gertwirtz, J. L., (eds.), *Handbook of Moral Behaviour and Development:
    Theory, Research and Applications*, vol. 1. Cambridge, England: Cambridge
    University Press.
Bandura, A., Barbarabelli, C., Caprara, G. V., and Pastorelli, C., 1996. Mechanisms
    of moral disengagement in the exercise of moral agency. *Journal of Personality
    and Social Psychology* 71(2): 364–374.

Brown, R. J., Condor, S., Mathews, A., Wade, G., and Williams, J. A., 1986. Explaining intergroup differentiation in an industrial organization. *Journal of Occupational Psychology* 59:273–86.

Breslin, A., 1982. Tolerance and moral reasoning among adolescents in Ireland. *Journal of Moral Education* 11(2):112–127.

Cairns, E., 1982. Intergroup conflict in Northern Ireland. In H. Tajfel (ed.), *Social identity and intergroup relations*. Cambridge, England: Cambridge University Press.

Cairns, E., 1987. *Caught in crossfire: Children and the Northern Ireland conflict*. Belfast, Northern Ireland: Appletree Press, and Syracuse, N.Y.: Syracuse University Press.

Cairns, E., 1996. *Children and political violence*. Cambridge, England: Blackwell.

Cairns, E., and Conlon, L., 1985. Children's moral reasoning and the Northern Irish violence, unpublished paper.

Cairns, E., and Darby, J., 1998. The conflict in Northern Ireland—Causes, consequences, and controls. *American Psychologist* 53(7):754–760.

Cairns, E., Kenworthy, J., Campbell, A., and Hewstone, M., 2006. The role of in-group identification, religious group membership, and intergroup conflict in moderating in-group and out-group affect. *British Journal of Social Psychology* 45:701–716.

Charlesworth, W. R., 1991. The development of sense of justice: Moral development, resources, and emotions. *American Behavioral Scientist* 34:350–370.

Cohen, J., 1988. Statistical power analysis for the behavioral sciences. Hillsdale, N.J.: LEA.

Darby, J., 1983. Northern Ireland: Background to the conflict. Belfast, Northern Ireland: Appletree Press.

Darby, J., 1986. Intimidation and the control of conflict in Northern Ireland. Dublin, Ireland: Gill and Macmillan.

Darby, J., 1991. *What's wrong with conflict?* Occasional Paper Number Three, Centre for the Study of Conflict. Ulster, Northern Ireland: University of Ulster.

Darby, J., 1997. Scorpions in a bottle: Conflicting cultures in Northern Ireland. London: Minority Rights Publications.

Douglas, J. N. H., and Boal, F. W., 1982. The Northern Ireland problem. In Boal, F. W., and Douglas, J. N. H. (eds.), *Integration and division: Geographical perspectives on the Northern Ireland problem*. London: Academic Press.

Elbedour, S., Baker, A. M., and Charlesworth, W. R., 1997. The impact of political violence on moral reasoning. *Child Abuse and Neglect* 21(11):1053–1066.

Fay, M. T., Morrissey, M., and Smyth, M., 1999. *Northern Ireland's Troubles: The human costs*. London: Pluto Press.

Ferguson, N., 2007, July. *The impact of political conflict on socio-moral reasoning in Northern Ireland*. Paper presented at the International Society of Political Psychology, 30th Annual Scientific Meeting, Portland, Oregon, USA.

Ferguson, N., and Cairns, E., 1996. Political violence and moral maturity in Northern Ireland. *Political Psychology* 17 (4):713–727.

Ferguson, N., Willis, C. S., and Tilley, A., 2001. Moral reasoning among Nigerian and Northern Irish children: A cross-cultural comparison using the socio-moral reflection measure—short form. *I. F. E.—Psychologia: An International Journal* 9(2):1–6.

Ferguson, N., and Cairns, E., 2002. The impact of political conflict on moral maturity: A cross-national perspective. *Journal of Adolescence* 24(5):441–451.

Fields, R. N., 1973. *A society on the run: A psychology of Northern Ireland.* Harmondsworth, Middlesex, U.K.: Penguin.

Fields, R. N., 1976. *Northern Ireland: Society under siege.* New Brunswick and London:Transaction Books.

Fields, R. N., 1989. Terrorized into terrorist: "Pete the Para" strikes again. In O'Day, A., and Alexander, Y. (eds.), *Ireland's Terrorist Trauma: Interdisciplinary Perspectives.* London:Harvester Wheatsheaf.

Fisher, R. J., and Keashly, L., 1991. A contingency approach to third party intervention. In R. J. Fisher (ed.), *The social psychology of intergroup and international conflict resolution.* New York: Springer-Verlag.

Fraser, M., 1972. At school during a guerrilla war. *Special Education* 61:6–8.

Fraser, M., 1974. *Children in conflict.* Harmondsworth, Middlesex, U.K.: Penguin.

Garbarino, J., and Bronfenbrenner, U., 1976. The socialization of moral judgment and behaviour in cross-cultural perspective. In T. Lickona (ed.), *Moral development and behaviour: Theory, research and social issues.* New York: Holt, Rinehart and Winston.

Handziska, M., 2005, July. The moral judgement competence of adolescents in the Republic of Macedonia in the case of transgression towards state symbols. Paper presented at the MOSAIC Annual Conference, Konstanz, Germany.

Haste, H., 1996. Communitarianism and the social construction of morality. *Journal of Moral Education* 25(1):47–55.

Keinan, G., 1994. Effects of stress and tolerance of ambiguity on magical thinking. *Journal of Personality and Social Psychology* 67(1):48–55.

Kinvall, C., Monroe, K. R., and Scuzzarello, S. (this volume). Introduction.

Kohlberg, L., 1984. *Essays in moral development: Vol. II. The psychology of moral development: Moral stages, their nature and validity.* San Francisco: Harper and Row.

Kohlberg, L., Hickey, J., and Scharf, P., 1972. The justice structure of the prison: A theory and intervention. *Prison Journal* 51:3–14.

Kohlberg, L., Levine, C., and Hewer, A., 1983. *Moral stages: A current formulation and a response to critics.* Basel, Switzerland: Karger.

Jackson, H., 1971. *The two Irelands: A dual study of intergroup tensions.* London: Minority Rights Group Report No 2.

Janis, I. L., 1982. *Groupthink.* Boston, Mass.: Houghton Mifflin.

Leach, C. W., and Williams, W., 1999.Group identity and conflicting expectations of the future in Northern Ireland. *Political Psychology* 20(4):875–897.

Lind, G., 2000. *Review and appraisal of the Moral Judgment Test (MJT).* Available at www.uni-konstanz.de/ag-moral (document retrieved 19 June 2007).

Lind, G., 2000a. Off limits: A cross-cultural study on possible causes of segmentation of moral judgment competence. Available at www.uni-konstanz.de/ag-moral (document retrieved 19 June 2007).

Lind, G., 2003. *Does religion foster or hamper morality and democracy?* Available at www.uni-konstanz.de/ag-moral (document retrieved 19 June 2007).

Lind, G.,2004 *The Moral Judgement Test (MJT).* Available at www.uni-konstanz.de/ag-moral (document retrieved 19 June 2007).

Lind, G., and Wakenhunt, R., 1985. Testing for moral judgement competence. In Lind, G., Hartmann, H. A., and Wakenhunt, R. (eds.), *Moral development and the social environment. Studies in the philosophy and psychology of moral judgement and education.* Chicago: Precedent.

Lorenc, L., and Branthwaite, A., 1986. Evaluations of political violence by English and Northern Irish schoolchildren. *British Journal of Social Psychology* 25:349–352.

Lowe, R. D., Muldoon, O., and Schmid, K. (this volume). Expected and unexpected identity combinations in Northern Ireland: consequences of identification, threat, and attitudes.

Lyons, H. A., 1973. The psychological effects of the civil disturbances on children. *The Northern Teacher,* Winter, 19–30.

MacGinty, R., Muldoon, O. Ferguson, N., 2007. No war, no peace: Northern Ireland after the Agreement. *Political Psychology* 28(1):1–12.

McLernon, F., Ferguson, N., and Cairns, E., 1997.Comparison of Northern Irish children's attitudes to war and peace before and after the paramilitary ceasefires. *International Journal of Behavioural Development* 20(4):715–730.

O'Donnell, E. E., 1977. *Northern Irish stereotypes.* Dublin:Research Branch, College of Industrial Relations.

Power, C., Reimer, J., 1978. Moral atmosphere: An educational bridge between moral judgment and action. In W. Damon (ed.), *New directions for child development.* San Francisco: Jossey-Bass

Punamaki, R-L., 1987. Childhood under conflict: The attitudes and emotional life of Israeli and Palestinian children.Tampere, Norway: Tampere Peace Research Institute, Research Reports.

Rest, J., Narvaez, D., Bebeau, M. J., and Thoma, S. J., 1999. *Postconventional moral thinking: A Neo-Kohlbergian approach.* Mahwah, NJ: LEA.

Richmond, O. P., 1999.Ethno-nationalism, sovereignty and negotiating positions in the Cyprus conflict: Obstacles to a settlement. *Middle Eastern Studies* 35(3):42–63.

Rosler, N., Bar-Tal, D., Sharvit, K., Halperin, E., and Raviv, A. (this volume). Moral aspects of prolonged occupation: Implications for an occupying society.

Snarney, J., Reimer, J., and Kohlberg, L., 1984.The development of socio-moral reasoning among Kibbutz adolescents: A longitudinal cross-cultural study. *Developmental Psychology* 21:3–17.

Schillinger, M. M., 2006. Learning environment and moral development: How university education fosters moral judgment competence in Brazil and two German-speaking countries. Unpublished doctoral thesis, University of Konstanz, Germany.

Spillmann, K. R., and Spillmann, K., 1991. On enemy images and conflict escalation. *International Social Science Journal* 43(1):57–76.

Tausch, N., Hewstone, M., Kenworthy, J., Cairns, E., and Christ, O.,2007. Cross-community contact, perceived status differences, and intergroup attitudes in Northern Ireland: The mediating roles of individual-level versus group-level threats and the moderating role of social identification. *Political Psychology* 28(1):53–68.

Whyte, J., 1991. *Interpreting Northern Ireland*. Oxford: Clarendon Press.

Zusne, L., and Jones, W. H., 1989. *Anomalistic psychology: A study of magical thinking*. Hillsdale, N.J.: LEA.

CHAPTER 12

Expected and Unexpected Identity Combinations in Northern Ireland: Consequences for Identification, Threat, and Attitudes[1]

Robert D. Lowe, Orla Muldoon, and Katharina Schmid

The social identity approach in social psychology has been of demonstrable value in terms of explaining many intergroup phenomena such as prejudice, discrimination, and violent conflict. The social identity approach differs fundamentally from many existing psychological approaches in that its fundamental supposition is that these phenomena are the outcome of collective or group processes. Traditional psychological approaches have tended to explore such social and psychological pathologies by focusing on the individual, a consequence of which is the location of responsibility for such negative phenomena at individual level.

Our starting point is different. We believe that many social phenomena, and particularly those that threaten our contemporary world, are the products of a reciprocal relationship between structures and systems that serve to create and maintain social divisions, collectives, and groups; and people's adoption, everyday understandings, and use of these group memberships. In the same way that we argue that groups and collectives can be used to entrench existing divisions, we also argue that alteration of social and political structures can further support alternative ways of seeing oneself and one's place in the world. Invocation of alternate or conflicting group memberships can be used to undermine extant divisions. This position therefore suggests that there is much that social identity theory can offer to our understanding of pro-social, tolerant, and ethical behavior in the contemporary world.

A second important contention we posit is that social or group identities represent an important individual and collective resource for individuals

---

[1] This research was funded by the Cross-Border Consortium under the European Union Peace II Program and part-financed by the U.K. and Irish governments.

making their way in an ambiguous world. National, religious, political, racial, and gendered identities can provide an interpretative lens for understanding life experience, as well as provide group resources to deal with events and a framework that facilitates appropriate responses to events. Importantly, then, social or group identities can be viewed as highly adaptive in terms of individual and collective social functioning.

BACKGROUND TO THE CURRENT CHAPTER

There is considerable support for the supposition that in situations of intractable political conflicts, such as the Israeli-Palestinian conflict, the conflict in the Basque region, and that in Northern Ireland, that social categorization and social identification are of pivotal importance (Kelman, 1999). Identities that underlie conflict are perceived as both oppositional (e.g., Catholic and Protestant or Arab and Jew) and negatively interdependent (Kelman, 1999). Even in situations of violent intergroup conflict, however, these oppositional identities are but one dimension of the conflict. Other identities and categories coexist even with highly pervasive social divisions. Indeed, the theoretical literature has been criticized for overemphasizing unitary social categorizations. Practically, academics and commentators alike have been criticized for their emphasis on singular category differences, particularly in conflict situations where such emphases serve to reify and embed these group distinctions.

The current chapter therefore aims to embrace greater complexity in the analysis of the categorization processes that underlie intergroup conflict, and to consider the consequences that patterns of dual identification may have. The pervasive tendency to categorize others is viewed as a central prerequisite to prejudice and intergroup discrimination. For many social psychologists, the theoretical basis for conflicts is indeed this process of social categorization (see McGarty, 1999, for a review). As theoretical and empirical work into the categorization process has developed, however, it has become evident that multiplicity of identification and its potential consequences as both a positive and a negative force should be considered. For instance, in Northern Ireland, where this study was conducted, it has been evident that "identity" is much more complex than a simple but highly popularized Catholic–Protestant dichotomy (Gallagher, 1989). An array of social identities is meaningful in adolescence (Cassidy and Trew, 1998), and a blurring of national and religious categorizations appears to be prevalent in adults (Muldoon, Trew, Todd, Rougier, and McLaughlin, 2007).

In the literature there is also an acknowledgement of the importance of multiple dimensions of social categorization. For instance, Crisp, Hewstone, and Cairns, 2001) used a cross-categorization paradigm to explore the combined effects of religion and gender. *Crossed categorization* refers to the crossing of two dichotomized and orthogonal identity categories specifying a clear ingroup–outgroup dimension to form a set of four new composite identity dimensions (Deschamps and Doise, 1978; Crisp, Hewstone, and Rubin, 2001). For example, when employing the dichotomized identity category *gender* (male-female) and *religion* (Protestant-Catholic), these can be crossed to form four new identity categories: male-Protestant, male-Catholic, female-Protestant, and female-Catholic (Crisp et al., 2001). As such, these new composite identity categories can be organized into four specific groups, namely a double ingroup membership group (both criteria for membership in ingroup fulfilled), two crossed groups (one ingroup-outgroup and one outgroup-ingroup dimension whereby only one criterion for ingroup membership is fulfilled), and a double-outgroup membership group (no criterion for ingroup membership is fulfilled) (Hewstone, Islam, and Judd, 1993). Experimental research employing this crossed-categorization paradigm to investigate specific ingroup-outgroup phenomena indicates that information can be processed to accommodate these crossed dimensions (Crisp and Hewstone, 1999; Crisp, Hewstone, and Cairns, 2001), and this processing subsequently affects outgroup evaluations (Deschamps and Doise, 1978; Migdal, Hewstone, and Mullen, 1998; Vanbeselaere, 1987; 1991). As Eurich-Fulcher and Schofield (1995) point out, however, many social categories such as race, ethnicity, and nationality are highly correlated. Clearly this may affect the cross-categorization, as the crossed category groups are no longer orthogonal. As such, the exploration of the effects of real correlated categorizations in such contexts has been highlighted as a gap in the current literature (Crisp et al., 2001).

Given that in-intergroup conflicts often arise where factors such as religion, nationality, race, and ethnicity overlap to a high degree, this latter point has particular resonance. For instance, it is common to hear reference to Israeli-Jews, Palestinian-Arabs, Irish Catholics, and British-Protestants, despite the fact, for example, that not all Irish are Catholics or all Israelis, Jewish. Whilst there is a high degree of overlap between religious and national identification in Northern Ireland, research has shown that a minority of people cross-categorize, endorsing an unexpected combination of national and religious identities such as Catholic-British or Protestant-Irish identity (Fahey, Hayes, and Sinnott, 2005; Muldoon et al., 2007).

The national identities traditionally perceived as both oppositional and negatively interdependent in Northern Ireland have more recently been joined by a third national group, namely the "Northern Irish" group, which is preferred by some Catholics *and* Protestants (Muldoon et al., 2007). This national identity is arguably a common identity that transcends the extant ethno-religious social divisions, and we argue it is no surprise that it has arisen subsequent to the Belfast Good Friday Agreement, which provided a degree of structural support to this fledgling identity. On the other hand, others argue that the Belfast Good Friday Agreement served to formalize religious-political divisions in Northern Ireland by requiring elected representatives to identify as unionist or nationalist in the Assembly. Irrespective of this, what is clear is that current political structures in Northern Ireland allow for a degree of flexibility in the selection of national identities that may have been absent previously.

OBJECTIVES OF THIS CHAPTER

Given the existing literature, a number of predictions can therefore be developed. First, those with an expected and mutually reinforcing combination of national and religious identities are likely to have stronger group identification. Second, those with expected religious and national identity combinations will demonstrate more negative attitudes to the outgroup and more intolerant social attitudes. On the other hand, those with an unexpected combination of identities are likely to show weaker group identification due to the non–mutually reinforcing nature of their national and religious identities. Effectively this may facilitate more ambiguity around traditional patterns of identification, and therefore be related to more positive outgroup attitudes. Finally, those who identify as having a Northern Irish national identity are showing a preference for a new or alternate national identity, and it is interesting to consider whether this identity is indeed a common group identity attracting subscribers from both religious backgrounds. If this is indeed the case, this group may show lower levels of identification due to the non-reinforcing nature of the identities as well as evidence of more positive outgroup attitudes.

METHOD

The Sample

A random sample of household telephone numbers was drawn from an electronic copy of British Telecom's domestic listing for Northern Ireland and the Border Counties of the Republic of Ireland, matched with available postal address files. Following selection, a letter was sent to selected house-holds, explaining the nature and purpose of the study. Subsequently, each household in the sample was contacted by telephone. Where more than one adult resided in a household, the last-birthday technique was used to rando-mize the selection of respondents included in the sample.

A quota control mechanism was programmed into the Computer Assisted Telephone Interviewing (CATI) software used to conduct the inter-views, to control the number of interviews within each county. This facili-tated sampling proportionate to population across the six counties of Northern Ireland and the Republic based on the adult population statistics from the latest Census results (2001). The final achieved sample was 3,000 participants (1,307 males, 1,693 females; age range: 18–92 years). The overall response rate was 49 percent.

Procedure

The final questionnaire was programmed into the CATI application, and rigorous tests were carried out on the program to ensure that it exactly matched the logic and structure of the paper-based questionnaire. The pro-gram was piloted on a sample of 60 participants and amendments made to the program file.

In relation to quality-assurance procedures, all interviews were conducted at a professional Telephone Research Centre based in Northern Ireland, which incorporated Siemens telephony hardware, and "SurveyCraft" Computer Assisted Telephone Interviewing (CAPI) software (part of the SPSS group). A team of social research interviewers, specifically trained by the second author, was used to conduct the survey. Interviewer performance was monitored on a day-to-day basis through the CATI pro-gram, as well as through back-checking a 30 percent sample of each inter-viewer's allocation via the system's "listening in" facility. The data were recorded during interview using SurveyCraft software and subsequently exported into SPSS.

MEASURES

1. Self-categorization

Respondents were asked to subjectively self-categorize their national and religious identity. National self-categorization was obtained using a free response format; namely, "What do you consider your nationality to be?" Religious self-categorization was obtained by using a measure from the

Northern Ireland Life and Times Survey (2003): "How would you describe your religious tradition?"

2. Collective Identification

Multiple dimensions of collective identification were then examined in relation to national identification, and all scaled measures employed a Likert-type response format ranging from 1 (strongly disagree) to 5 (strongly agree), with higher scores indicating higher levels of the underlying construct being measured. Only national identification was assessed. The level of repetition that would have been required to assess strength of religious identification as well as national identification was considered problematic. Strength of national identification was favored over religious identification to prevent any potential confusion between religiosity and cultural/social definitions of religion.

A. *Prototypicality*: Two items were used to measure prototypical group membership. This scale was adapted from a measure employed by Hogg and Hardie (1991). Depending on the previous self-categorization, items were "To what extent are you typically (self-categorized nationality)," and "Would you think it was accurate if you were described as being typically (self-categorized nationality)?" The Cronbach's alpha for this scale was .78.

B. *Collective regard*: Private and public evaluation were measured by using two of the subscales of Luhtanen and Crocker's (1992) Collective Self-Esteem (CSE) scale. The Private CSE subscale consists of four items and assesses the degree to which an individual evaluates a collective identity in positive or negative terms for him- or herself. Depending on their previous choice of national identity, respondents were automatically routed into a set of items indicative of their national group membership; e.g., "In general, you are glad to be British." The Cronbach's alpha for this subscale was .70. The Public CSE subscale also consists of four items, and assesses the extent to which an individual believes other people to evaluate his or her collective identity in either positive or negative terms (e.g., "In general, others respect the Irish"). The alpha coefficient for this subscale in the present sample was .62. For both subscales, higher scores are indicative of more positive evaluations of the national identity under examination. The CSE scale has been widely employed in social psychological research and has shown to be a valid and reliable measure of the underlying constructs.

C. *Importance*: The degree to which respondents perceived their national identity as important to their self-concept was measured through Luhtanen and Crocker's (1992) Importance to Identity CSE subscales (e.g., "In general, being Northern Irish is an important part of your self-image"). This consisted of four items and yielded an acceptable alpha coefficient of .60.

3. Out-group and Political Attitudes

Multiple measures of outgroup attitudes were then undertaken. These included:

A. *Outgroup Liking*: A single item, which has been used in previous studies in Northern Ireland (Hewstone et al., 2002), assessed the degree to which respondents like those from their religious outgroup.

B. *Religious integration*: A second measure assessed opinions regarding religious integration and segregation in Northern Ireland. Taken from the ideology subscale of the Multidimensional Inventory of Black Identity (MIBI) (Sellers et al., 1997), five items were adapted to compute a score related to attitudes to religious integration and division in Northern Ireland.

C. *Political attitudes*: Two specific questions that resulted in categorical variables regarding the constitutional position/sovereignty of Northern Ireland (Table 12–2) and attitudes to the Good Friday Agreement (Table 12–3) assessed political attitudes. Both questions were taken from the Northern Ireland Life and Times survey.

4. Perceived Threat

Eight items were initially employed to measure perceived identity threat, which were subsequently reduced to five items due to unacceptable reliability scores. The five-item scale yielded a Cronbach's alpha of .65, which was deemed acceptable for the present study. Items were chosen that assessed respondents' perceptions of threat arising due to their identified religious group membership. More specifically, the aim was to measure the extent to which respondents feel directly threatened due to their identity, as well as the extent to which the source of threat stems from the expression of the outgroup's identity. In order to capture a clear ingroup-outgroup dimension of threat, the religious identities were employed. Depending on their choice of religious categorization, respondents were automatically routed into one of two alternative items, whereby either *Protestant* or *Catholic* was employed as the comparative category. Exemplar items on the scale included "I feel threatened when Protestants/Catholics express their identity and celebrate their cultural traditions," and "In certain areas I would be afraid of being identified as a Catholic/Protestant."

RESULTS

Patterns of Expected and Unexpected Identification

Overall, 90 percent of respondents self-categorized on the basis of nationality. The majority of respondents categorized their national identity as

"British" ($N = 1015$, 50.8 percent); over one third of respondents ($N = 685$; 36 percent) categorized themselves as "Irish"; and 9.5 percent describing their national identity as "Northern Irish" ($N = 190$). A further 3.1 percent of the sample fell into the category "Other." 10.6 percent of respondents failed or refused to categorize their nationality. These latter two groups were excluded from subsequent analyses. Overall 80 percent of respondents self-categorized on the basis of religion. With regard to respondents' religious identification, 919 respondents categorized as Protestant (46 percent), and 685 chose to describe their religious identity as Catholic (34.3 percent).

Moreover, the vast majority of respondents categorizing their national identity as "British" or "Irish" further identified as "Protestant" or "Catholic" respectively, hence endorsing what can be deemed an expected pattern of religious and national identification (see Table 12–1). A significant minority of Catholics, however, described their national identity as "British" (17.8 percent), while a somewhat smaller minority of Protestant respondents chose to describe their national identity as "Irish" (4.1 percent), thus endorsing unexpected patterns of identification. Exceptions to this pattern of expected–unexpected categorizations were respondents who categorized their national identity as Northern Irish. This national category was endorsed by almost equal numbers of Catholic and Protestant respondents, although the percentage of respondents for the Catholic group endorsing the Northern Irish identity was found to be slightly higher (13.2 percent).

1. How does Expected or Unexpected National and Religious Identification Affect Levels of National Group Identification?

The collective identity dimensions (prototypicality, private and public self-evaluation, and identity importance) were subjected to a 2 (religion: Protestant and Catholic) x 3 (nationality: British, Irish, and Northern Irish) MANOVA.

Table 12.1 Numbers and percentages for Protestant and Catholic respondents and the self-categorized nationality categories.

	PROTESTANT	CATHOLIC
British	*747 (86.7%)*	**116 (17.8%)**
Irish	**35 (4.1%)**	*451 (69.1%)*
Northern Irish	80 (9.2%)	86 (13.1%)
Total	862 (100%)	653 (100%)

Numbers and percentages in *italics* refer to *correlated* identity patterns, and in **bold** refer to **unexpected** identity combinations.

The overall multivariate test revealed a significant interaction between religious and national identity (with $\Lambda = .974$, F (8, 2699) = 5.008, $p = .000$, $\eta^2 = .013$). Univariate follow-ups indicated three significant interaction effects for prototypicality ($F(2.1486) = 16.285$, $p = .000$, $\eta^2 = .021$), private self-evaluation ($F(2.1486) = 7.129$, $p = .001$, $\eta^2 = .010$) and identity importance ($F(2.1486) = 7.356$, $p = 001$, $\eta^2 = .010$). Public evaluation did not yield an interaction effect. Multivariate effects also revealed a main effect for nationality ($\Lambda = .900$, F (8. 2966) = 20.140, $p = .000$, $\eta^2 = .052$). Follow-up univariate analyses supported this main effect across all four dimensions (prototypicality: $F(2.1486) = 10.387$, $p = .000$, $\eta^2 = .014$; Private self-evaluation: $F(2.1486) = 41.585$, $p = .000$, $\eta^2 = .053$; Public self-evaluation: $F(2.1486) = 32.826$, $p = .000$, $\eta^2 = .042$; Importance: $F(2.1486) = 38.759$, $p = .000$, $\eta^2 = .050$) although clearly any main effect of nationality is superseded by its interaction with religion. No main effects in relation to religion were observed.

Relevant means indicate that perceived prototypicality was higher for respondents who described themselves as Protestant and British (expected categorization) ($M = 3.80$, $SD = .97$) than those who viewed themselves as Catholic and British (unexpected categorization) ($M = 3.28$, $SD = 1.00$). Similarly, Irish Catholic identifiers (expected categorization) ($M = 3.95$, $SD = .95$) had higher levels of prototypicality than those who categorized as Irish Protestants (unexpected categorization) ($M = 3.51$, $SD = .95$). Respondents self-categorizing as Northern Irish and Catholic ($M = 4.05$, $SD = .91$) showed higher levels of prototypicality than Northern Irish Protestants ($M = 3.83$, $SD = .90$). Interestingly, respondents self-categorizing as Northern Irish generally showed the highest levels of prototypicality across both religious groups (see Fig. 12–1).

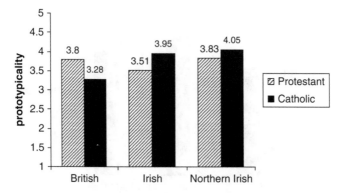

Figure 12.1 Perceived national prototypicality in relation to national and religious identity

Respondents indicating their nationality to be Northern Irish showed the highest levels of prototypicality ($M = 3.94$, $SD = .92$), followed by the "Irish" identifiers ($M = 3.90$, $SD = .96$), while respondents describing their national identity as "British" ($M = 3.71$, $SD = 1.02$) showed the lowest levels of prototypicality in the present sample. Differences reaching statistical significance lie between the British and Irish identifiers ($p = .002$), and between the British and Northern Irish identifiers ($p = .020$).

With regard to private evaluation, respondents who categorized as both Protestant and British (expected categorization) ($M = 4.00$, $SD = .64$) showed more positive evaluation of their identity than did Catholics who also categorized as British (unexpected categorization) ($M = 3.68$, $SD = .76$). Similarly, respondents who self-categorized as both Catholic and Irish (expected categorization) ($M = 4.46$, $SD = .52$) showed more positive levels of private self-evaluation than did Protestants also categorizing as Irish (unexpected categorization) ($M = 4.35$, $SD = .53$). For Northern Irish identifiers, Catholics ($M = 4.12$, $SD = .60$) showed slightly more positive private evaluation of their identity than did Protestants ($M = 4.06$, $SD = .62$) (see Fig. 12–2). The main effect obtained indicates that overall private self-evaluation was highest among respondents self-categorizing as Irish ($M = 4.44$, $SD = .54$), followed by Northern Irish respondents ($M = 4.10$, $SD = .63$), and British evaluating their identity as least positive ($M = 3.95$, $SD = .67$); although this effect is best interpreted in the context of the interaction outlined above. Statistical significance was reached for differences between all three national identity groups (British and Irish: $p = .000$, British and Northern Irish: $p = .027$, Irish and Northern Irish: $p = .000$).

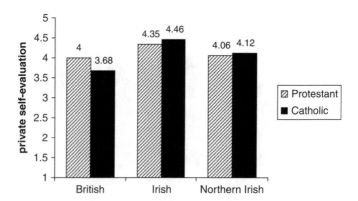

Figure 12.2 Private self-evaluation in relation to self-categorized national and religious identification

No interaction effects were observed in relation to public evaluation. A main effect for nationality was however apparent. Public evaluation was highest for Northern Irish respondents ($M = 4.10$, $SD = .63$), followed by Irish respondents ($M = 3.94$, $SD = .66$), and lastly British respondents ($M = 3.43$, $SD = .68$). Differences were statistically significant between British and Irish respondents ($p = .000$) and Irish and Northern Irish respondents ($p = .000$), but not between British and Northern Irish categorizers.

British identifiers who categorized their religious identity as Protestant (expected categorization) ($M = 2.79$, $SD = .83$) rated their identity as more important than did self-categorized British Catholics (unexpected categorization) ($M = 2.42$, $SD = .81$). Protestant Irish identifiers (expected categorization) ($M = 3.18$, $SD = .72$) rated their identity as less important than did Irish Catholics (unexpected categorization) ($M = 3.30$, $SD = .81$). Differences between Northern Irish Protestants ($M = 3.06$, $SD = .71$) and Northern Irish Catholics ($M = 3.11$, $SD = .64$) were not as pronounced, with the latter rating their identity as marginally more important (see Fig. 12–3). Finally, the main effect revealed that importance was rated highest among Irish identifiers ($M = 3.28$, $SD = .82$), while Northern Irish respondents ($M = 3.07$, $SD = .72$) rated their identity as more important than British respondents did ($M = 2.72$, $SD = .82$). Statistical significance was reached between all comparison groups (British and Irish: $p = .000$, British and Northern Irish: $p = .000$, Irish and Northern Irish: $p = .004$).

2. How did Expected and Unexpected National and Religious Identification Affect Social and Political Attitudes?

Analysis of variance examined the relationship between nationality, religion, and favorability ratings of the other main religious group. Generally, scores

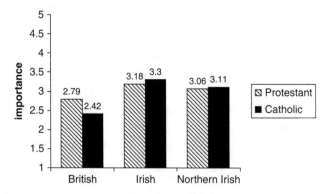

Figure 12.3 Importance of identity in relation to self-categorized national and religious identity

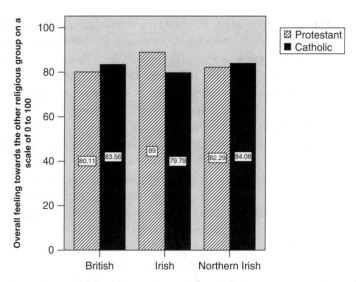

Figure 12.4 Favorability ratings of the religious outgroup by national and religious identity

on this scale indicated those from the other religious group were viewed favorably. A combination of nationality and religion related to perceived favorability towards the other main religious group [F(2, 1503) = 6.29, p < .01]. Figure 12–4 below illustrates this effect; overall, Protestants who identified as Irish and Catholics who identified as British had more favorable views of the opposing religious tradition. Conversely, it can be said that those with expected patterns of identification, Irish Catholics and British Protestants, had the least favorable views of the other main religious tradition in Northern Ireland.

Five items were used to tap attitudes towards religious integration and segregation. The mean score on the scale for the entire sample was 4.41. Analysis of variance (ANOVA) was again conducted to examine the effects of religion and nationality. Nationality and religion combined affected value scores (F (2, 2299) = 5.193, p < .01; see Fig. 12–5). Protestants who viewed themselves as British (expected combination), and to a lesser extent Protestants who self-categorized as Irish (unexpected combination), had less favorable attitudes than British and Irish Catholics. Catholics who identified as British (unexpected combination) had particularly favorable attitudes to integration.

Multilayered chi-square was used to examine the combined effects of nationality and religion on the ordinal level data relating to political attitudes. Again religion and nationality in combination were related to support

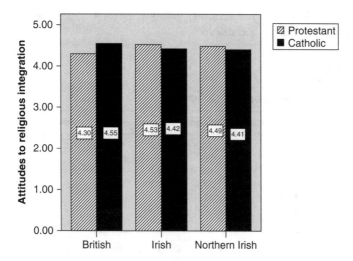

Figure 12.5 Attitudes towards integration by national and religious identity

for the Belfast Agreement ($\chi^2 = 88.9$; p < .01) and preferred solutions for the political future of Northern Ireland ($\chi^2 = 24.5$; p < .01). Reflective of the waning support for the agreement in the Protestant community, overall support for the agreement was higher amongst Catholics (85 percent) than Protestants (45 percent). Importantly, however, Catholic-Irish (87 percent) identifiers showed the greatest support and Protestant-British (42 percent) identifiers the least support for the agreement. Differences in levels of support for the agreement between the unexpected identifiers were less; Protestant Irish (76 percent) and Catholic British (82 percent) identifiers largely supported the agreement (see Table 12–2).

Similarly, in terms of preferred options for the future of Northern Ireland, traditional political aspirations were most common in the expected identifiers (see Table 12–3). For instance, 70 percent of British Protestant (expected) identifiers expressed a preference to remain part of the United Kingdom, the traditional unionist position. Only 27 percent of Irish Protestant (unexpected) identifiers, however, expressed a preference for the traditional unionist position. Similarly, 86 percent of Catholic Irish (expected) identifiers would prefer to see Northern Ireland become part of the Republic, where as only 6 percent of unexpected British Catholic identifiers endorsed this preference.

Expected and Unexpected Identity Combinations and Perceived Threat

Results of a 2 (religion: Protestant and Catholic) x 3 (nationality: British, Irish, and Northern Irish) ANOVA indicated that religious and national

Table 12.2 Percentage support for the Belfast Agreement by self-categorized nationality and religion.

WITH REGARD TO THE GOOD FRIDAY AGREEMENT, DO YOU...?	BRITISH		IRISH		NORTHERN IRISH		TOTAL	
	Protestant	Catholic	Protestant	Catholic	Protestant	Catholic	Protestant	Catholic
Strongly support it?	**10**	42.2	26.5	**47.3**	18.2	45.3	11.5	46.2
Support it?	**33.3**	41.3	50	**39.2**	32.5	38.4	33.9	39.5
Neither?	**28.3**	13.8	17.6	**10.2**	31.2	11.6	28.1	11
Oppose it?	**14.3**	1.8	2.9	**16**	6.5	0	13.1	1.4
Strongly oppose it?	**14.1**	.9	2.9	**1.6**	8.1	4.7	13.4	1.9

Percentages in *italics* refer to *correlated* identity patterns, and in **bold** refer to **unexpected** identity patterns.

identification interacted to affect levels of perceived identity threat ($F(2, 1501) = 22.232$, $p = .000$, $\eta^2 = .029$). This effect is illustrated in Figure 12–6. Respondents who categorized as British and Protestant (expected combination) ($M = 2.92$, $SD = .78$) showed higher levels of identity threat than did British Catholics (unexpected combination) ($M = 2.78$, $SD = .72$). Similarly, Catholic Irish identifiers ($M = 3.2$, $SD = .83$) showed very high levels of threat compared to Protestant Irish (unexpected combination) ($M = 2.3$, $SD = .69$). Finally, Northern Irish identifiers who

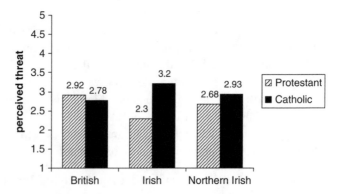

Figure 12.6 Perceived identity threat in relation to self-categorized national and religious identification

identified as Catholic ($M = 2.93$, $SD = .66$) showed higher levels of perceived threat than did Northern Irish identifiers who identified as Protestant ($M = 2.68$, $SD = .67$). A main effect for religious identity was also observed ($F (1, 1501) = 28.357$, $p = .000$, $\eta^2 = .019$). Respondents categorizing as Catholic ($M = 3.08$, $SD = .82$) showed higher levels of perceived threat than did Protestant identifiers ($M = 2.85$, $SD = .79$).

In order to examine whether collective identity differentially affected perceptions of threat, identity importance, prototypicality, and private and public identity regard were regressed on perceived threat for expected and unexpected identity combinations separately. For expected combinations, two of the identity components were found to be significant predictors of perceived threat (private evaluation ($\beta = .080$, $p = .027$) and importance of identity ($\beta = .238$, $p = .000$) explaining 7.7 percent of the variance in threat scores ($R^2 = .077$, $F (4, 1177) = 24.680$, $p = .000$). The more positive private evaluations and importance attached to national identity, the higher the level of perceived threat for British Protestant and the Irish Catholic identifiers; that is, those with expected national and religious identities. Prototypicality ($\beta = .020$, $p > .05$) and public regard ($\beta = -.038$, $p > .05$) did not contribute significantly to the amount of variance in perceived threat.

Table 12.3 Percentage support for the Belfast Agreement by self-categorized nationality and religion.

WOULD YOU PREFER	BRITISH		IRISH		NORTHERN IRISH		Total	
	Prot	Cath	Prot	Cath	Prot	Cath	Prot	Cath
Northern Ireland to remain part of the U.K.	**69.6**	*27.6*	*28.6*	**7.1**	15	7	66.4	10.7
Northern Ireland to become part of the Republic of Ireland	**2.4**	*11.2*	*11.4*	**41.7**	5	19.8	3	33.4
A Northern Ireland state independent of the U.K. and the Republic of Ireland	**9.1**	*12.1*	*20*	**13.3**	13.8	31.4	10	15.5
Joint control of Northern Ireland by Great Britain and the Republic of Ireland	**15.1**	*44.0*	*34.3*	**31.9**	28.8	36	17	34.6

Percentages in *italics* refer to *correlated* identity patterns, and in **bold** refer to **unexpected** identity patterns.

Table 12.4 Simultaneous regression analyses predicting perceived threat in expected and **unexpected** identifiers.

Regression predicting perceived identity threat with expected pattern of identification

	B	S.E.	B
Prototypicality	.016	.025	.020
Private CSE	.100	.045	.080*
Public CSE	−.044	.037	−.038
Importance CSE	.225	.030	.238**

Note: $N=1182$, $R^2=.077$, $F(4, 1177)=24.680$, $p=.000$: $*p<.05$ $**p<.001$

Regression predicting perceived identity threat with unexpected pattern of identification

	B	S.E.	B
Prototypicality	−.052	.055	−.073
Private CSE	−.361	.088	−.376**
Public CSE	−.188	.094	−.164*
Importance CSE	−.057	.076	−.063

Note: $N=149$, $R^2=.295$, $F(4, 144)=15.077$, $p=.000$: $*p<.05$ $**p<.001$

For unexpected identity combinations, 29.5 percent of the variance in perceived threat was accounted for by private regard ($\beta = -.361$, $p = .000$) and public regard ($\beta = -.164$, $p = .047$). In both instances, more positive private and public evaluations of national identity were associated with *lower* perceptions of threat in expected identifiers (British Catholic and Irish Protestant). Prototypicality ($\beta = -.073$, $p > .05$) and identity importance ($\beta = -.063$, $p > .05$) did not show a significant effect on perceived threat.

DISCUSSION

In line with previous research (Trew, 1996), a high degree of overlap between religious and national identities was evident. This pattern is indicative of the many non-orthogonal identities that exist in real-world situations (Eurich-Fulcher and Schofeld, 1995). In many contemporary societies that have experienced political violence (e.g., Assam [India], Abkhazia [Georgia], Cyprus, Ivory Coast, Kashmir, Moldova, Sri Lanka, Mindanao [Philippines] and Northern Ireland) (MacGinty, Muldoon, and Ferguson, 2007), the conflict is often characterized as a clash between two opposing ethnic, religious, or racial groups. The pervasive distinction between Catholics (the relative minority at 38 percent) and Protestants (the relative majority at 50 percent; Cairns and Darby, 1998) in Northern Ireland has led to its being regarded as the key cultural marker and social identity. Whilst clearly this categorization process is central to the dynamics of intergroup relations, the focus on a single dimension of difference is unrealistic and oversimplified. No doubt in the long term this has arisen from and is reflective of social divisions: it is also likely to perpetuate and re-create these divisions.

Indeed, the current study suggests that such uni-dimensional explanations of difference will mask both the complexity and the social reality of these situations. In Northern Ireland, for instance, political, economic, and ethnic differences all interact to create both differences and similarities within and between the two main protagonist groups in the conflict. A substantial minority of respondents endorsed an unexpected pattern of identification, with 17.8 percent of respondents categorizing as both Catholic and British and 4.1 percent of respondents categorizing as both Protestant and Irish. The presence of this unexpected identification pattern highlights the limitations of research employing a single identity category in fully capturing a clear representation of group identification even in situations where, *prima facie*, identity may appear to be highly polarized.

An interesting pattern of ingroup perceptions and evaluations and outgroup attitudes emerges for both expected and unexpected identity configurations, which holds across five of the six identity domains measured. Expected identifiers; i.e., respondents who categorized as British and Protestant or Irish and Catholic, generally saw themselves as more prototypical of their identity group, evaluated their identities as more positive, regarded their identities as more important to their self-concept, and had less favorable attitudes to the religious outgroup than those with unexpected patterns of identification. The expected identities appear to be additive in nature, to the extent that the respective expected identity choices clearly show higher levels of ingroup perceptions and evaluation and less tolerant social attitudes. Unexpected combinations generally show less perceived similarity with other group members, as well as less positive evaluations and lower levels of identity importance and more positive outgroup attitudes. This finding is important for two reasons. Theoretically, it corroborates the position that increasing levels of social identity complexity are related to more positive and inclusive attitudes to others (Roccas and Brewer, 2002). Practically, it emphasizes the limited value of multiple categorization interventions as a tool for increasing mutual understanding in situations where social identities are highly correlated. These interventions are only likely to improve intergroup relations where the identities employed are uncorrelated (Bremner, 2001). Unfortunately, identities uncorrelated to the major social divisions within a society (for example, gender in this instance) are likely to have limited resonance.

Interrelationships between the variables considered in those with expected and unexpected identity combinations also differed. In the case of highly overlapping, correlated identity configurations, higher levels of importance and private evaluation were related to higher threat perceptions. On the other hand, higher levels of private and public evaluation were related to lower perceptions of threat where identity combinations were unexpected. It can be said that the dimensions of identification relating to threat differ between these groups, as well as the nature of relationship between identification and threat. This finding is consistent with the expanding line of research that suggests that identity strength is an important determinant of perceived identity threat (Doojse, Spears, and Ellemers, 2002), particularly where identity threat is high (Branscombe and Wann, 1994), as it was amongst those with expected identity combinations identifiers in this study. Amongst the unexpected combinations, however, increased identity threat was related to lower collective identity scores. This finding clearly exemplifies the added value of considering multiple identities when testing such relationships. Amongst those with unexpected identity combinations, public and private regard for national identity appeared to reduce the felt threat related to religious identity. This finding may be of particular relevance in understanding conflict dynamics, and in turn resolving them, where perceptions of threat are often an inherent component of conflict.

This study is not without limitations. It is limited in terms of its conceptualization of identity threat as well as the constraints imposed by the real-world nature of the identities measured. Identity threat has been variously conceptualized as realistic or symbolic threat (Stephan and Stephan, 1996; 2000; Stephan and Renfro, 2003) and as a group level threat to values or beliefs, threats to an individual's position in a group, or a more personal threat emanating from the outgroup as experienced by the individual group member (Branscombe, Ellemers, Spears, and Doosje, 1999). Future research examining the role of these specific conceptualizations of threat across multiple identities would be useful. A second measurement issue arises from the necessity to assess national identification, but outgroup attitudes and identity threat in relation to religious affiliation. As stated previously, the major cultural division in Northern Ireland is marked by religion, and hence meaningful measurement of identity threat and outgroup attitudes can only be achieved using religious labels. Measurement of religious identification is highly problematic, however, because of the conflation of cultural and spiritual religion (Mitchell, 2005). Clearly our assessment of national identity overcame these problems.

In sum, the inclusion of multiple identities has shown itself to be a most revealing and fruitful approach to understanding collective identification. The findings contribute significantly to existing research on multiple categorizations and social complexity research, in particular by demonstrating, not only the complexities of identification in the real world, but also how those complexities describe discernible patterns. Demonstrable differences were found in own group evaluations for respondents choosing expected and unexpected identification patterns. Furthermore, differing relationships between the various dimensions of collective identity and identity threat have served to highlight the nature of the interaction between multiple identities and the multiple components of identity. Future research could usefully explore the effects of such expected and unexpected identities on intergroup evaluations, as well as general intergroup phenomena. This may be of particular relevance when examining conflict phenomena in real-world scenarios, where expected identifiers may contribute substantially to the dynamics of conflict, and in turn, where prospects for conflict resolution may be enhanced through a heightened understanding of identities in conflict.

More generally, the findings of the current study demonstrate the value of considering the role of psychological identification with groups in determining social and political attitudes. Not only that we have demonstrated that, though social identities may be deeply divisive, a focus on single dimensions of identity may exaggerate these divisions. Even in a society as divided as Northern Ireland, a significant minority of individuals categorize across traditional religious-national boundaries. A second important conclusion is that though identification is a significant psychological resource, the manner in which it is used and engaged is related to the choice and meaning of the identity. In our group of expected or overlapping identifiers where religion and nationality acted as mutually reinforcing fashion, identification could be considered a resource to deal with the more highly threatening environment these respondents considered their social reality to be. In our group of unexpected identifiers, however, identification with national group was related to lower levels of perceived threat and facilitated more positive social attitudes. This is consistent with the notion that holding non-orthogonal identities can serve to reduce prejudice. Respondents who chose to identify as Northern Irish, a common national group, had more positive attitudes to the other religious group and more integrationist social attitudes than those with expected identity combinations, but less positive attitudes than those with unexpected identity combinations. Certainly these data would seem to be consistent with many of the key contentions argued in Roccas and Brewer's model of social identity complexity (2002). Practically, these findings serve to signify the importance of patterns of identification as an interpretative lens in conflict environments.

Finally, these findings point to the importance of structural influences on preferred patterns of identification. In our sample, expected patterns of identification predominate, representing the extant political structures. Further support for this conclusion is evidenced in the higher number of British Catholics than Irish Protestants in the "unexpected identifiers" group. Available structural supports and political realities underpinning Irish national identification in Northern Ireland are very limited in comparison to those that may be invoked and available to those who may wish to identify as British. The higher proportion of British Catholics than Protestant Irish can be said to represent the scaffolding of civil society in Northern Ireland by the British State, whereas an Irish state presence has been historically absent north of the border. The appearance of the Northern Irish identity in significant proportions is representative of a relatively recent phenomenon. This identity may be seen as potential identity architecture for a religiously inclusive post-Agreement Northern Ireland. Given the importance, however, of reciprocal determinism in the development and maintenance of identities, political, social, and structural supports need to be developed to support this fledgling common group identity.

REFERENCES

Branscombe, N. R., and Wann, D. L., 1994. Collective self esteem consequences of outgroup derogation when a valued social identity is on trial. *European Journal of Social Psychology* 24:641–657.

Branscombe, N. R., Ellemers, N., Spears, R., and Doosje, B., 1999. The context and content of social identity threat. In Ellemers, N., Spears, R., and Doosje, B. (eds.), *Social identity. Context, commitment, content.* Oxford, U.K.: Blackwell Publishers Ltd.

Bremner, D., 2002. South African experiences with identity and community conflicts. *Journal of Peace Research* 38(3): 393–405.

Cairns, E., and Darby, J., 1998. The conflict in Northern Ireland: Causes, consequences, and controls. *American Psychologist* 53:754–760.

Cassidy, C., and Trew, K., 1998. Identities in Northern Ireland: A multidimensional approach. *Journal of Social Issues* 54(4): 725–740.

Crisp, R. J., and Hewstone, M., 1999. Differential evaluation of cross category groups: Patterns, processes, and reducing intergroup bias. *Group Process and Intergroup Relations* 2(4): 1–27.

Crisp, R. J., Hewstone, M., and Rubin, M.,2001. Does multiple categorization reduce intergroup bias? *Personality and Social Psychology Bulletin* 27(1): 76–89.

Crisp, R. J., Hewstone, M., and Cairns, E., 2001. Multiple identities in Northern Ireland: Hierarchical ordering in the representation of group membership. *British Journal of Social Psychology* 40:501–514.

Deschamps, J.-C., and Doise, W., 1978. Crossed category memberships in intergroup relations. In H. Tajfel (ed.), *Differentiation between social groups: Studies in the social psychology of intergroup relations*. London: Academic Press.

Dion, K. L., 1975. Women's reactions to discrimination from members of the same or opposite sex. *Journal of Research in Personality* 9:294–306.

Doosje, B., and Ellemers, N., 1997. Stereotyping under threat: The role of group identification. In Spears, R., Oakes, P. J., Ellemers, N., and Haslam, S. A. (eds.), *The social psychology of stereotyping and group life*. Oxford: Blackwell.

Doojse, B., Spears, R, and Ellemers, N., 2002. Social identity as both cause and effect: the development of group identification in response to anticipated and actual changes in the the intergroup status hierarchy. *British Journal of Social Psychology* 41:57–76.

Ethier, K. A., and Deaux, K., 1994. Negotiating social identity when contexts change: Maintaining identification and responding to threat. *Journal of Personality and Social Psychology* 67(2): 242–251.

Eurich-Fulcher, R., and Schofield, J.W., 1995. Correlated versus uncorrelated social categorizations: the effect on intergroup bias. *Personality and Social Psychology Bulletin* 21:149–159.

Fahey, T., Hayes, B. C., and Sinnott, R., 2005. *Conflict and Consensus. A study of values and attitudes in the Republic of Ireland and Northern Ireland*. Dublin, Ireland: Institute of Public Administration.

Gallagher, A. M., 1989. Social identity and the Northern Ireland conflict. *Human Relations* 42:917–935.

Hewstone, M., Islam, M. R., and Judd, C. M., 1993. Models of crossed categorization and intergroup relations. *Journal of Personality and Social Psychology* 64(5): 770–793.

Hogg, M. A., and Hardie, E. A., 1991. Social attraction, personal attraction, and self-categorization: A field study. *Personality and Social Psychology Bulletin* 17:175–180.

Jetten, J., Spears, R. and Manstead, A. S. R., 1997. Distinctiveness threat and prototypicality: Combined effects on intergroup discrimination and collective self-esteem. *European Journal of Social Psychology* 27:635–657.

Kelman, H., 1999. The interdependence of Israeli and Palestinian national identities: The role of the other in existential conflicts. *Journal of Social Issues* 55(3): 581–600.

Luhtanen, R., and Crocker, J., 1992. A collective self-esteem scale: Self-evaluation of one's social identity. *Personality and Social Psychology Bulletin* 18:302–318.

McGarty, C., 1999. *Categorization in social psychology*. Beverly Hills, Calif.: Sage.

MacGinty, R., Muldoon, O.T., and Ferguson, N., 2007. Neither war nor peace: Northern Ireland after the Agreement. *Political Psychology* 28(1): 1–11.

Migdal, M. J., Hewstone, M., and Mullen, B., 1998. The effects of crossed categorization on intergroup evaluations: A meta-analysis. *British Journal of Social Psychology* 37:303–324.

Muldoon, O. T., Trew, K. Todd, J., Rougier, N. and Mclaughlin, K., 2007. Religious and national identity after the Belfast Good Friday Agreement. *Political Psychology* 28(1): 89–103.

Northern Ireland Life and Times Survey, 2003. Retrieved July 2004, from http://www.arc.ac.uk/nilt/

Roccas, S., and Brewer, M., 2002. Social identity complexity. *Personality and Social Psychology Review* 6(2): 88–106.

Sellers, R. M., Rowley, S. A. J., Chavous, T. M., Shelton, J. N., and Smith, M. A., 1997. Multidimensional inventory of Black identity: A preliminary investigation of reliability and construct validity. *Journal of Personality and Social Psychology* 73:805–815.

Spears, R., Doosje, B., and Ellemers, N., 1997. Self-stereotyping in the face of threats to group status and distinctiveness: The role of group identification. *Personality and Social Psychology Bulletin* 23(5): 538–553.

Stephan, W. G., and Stephan, C. W., 1996. Predicting prejudice. *International Journal of Intercultural Relations* 20:409–426.

Stephan, W. G., and Stephan, C. W., 2000. An integrated threat theory of prejudice. In S. Oskamp (ed.), *Reducing prejudice and discrimination* (pp. 23–46). Hillsdale, N.J.: Erlbaum.

Stephan, W. G., and Renfro, C. L., 2003. The role of threat in intergroup relations. In Mackie, D. M., and Smith, E. R. (eds.), *From prejudice to intergroup emotions: Differentiated reactions to social groups* (pp. 191–207). New York: Psychology Press.

Trew, K., 1996. Complementary or conflicting identities? *The Psychologist* 9(10): 460–463.

Vanbeselaere, N., 1987. The effect of dichotomous and crossed social categorizations upon intergroup discrimination. *European Journal of Social Psychology* 17:143–156.

Vanbeselaere, N., 1991. The different effects of simple and crossed categorizations: A result of the category differentiation process or of differential category salience? *European Review of Social Psychology* 2:247–278.

PART IV

Conclusion

CHAPTER 13

Care and the Transformative Potential of Ethics

Catarina Kinnvall, Kristen Renwick Monroe, and Sarah Scuzzarello

In conclusion, let us revisit some of the major themes in this volume to raise further issues and discuss alternative possibilities for comprehending the increasingly complex and interrelated global world in which we live. In doing so, we suggest several critical questions future work might focus on, and speak in favor of a relational—i.e., non-individualistic—and transformative approach to ethics and morality in a global context. We end with a call for more collaborative work between scholars and practitioners concerned with the more humane treatment of others in a world in which we can no longer retreat to the safety of our own national, religious, racial, or ethnic group.

One of our intentions in assembling this volume was to address critical emotional, cognitive, political, and ethical challenges of living in the West in the late-modern era. With increasing globalization of the economy, politics, communication, and culture, new psychological challenges have arisen as people search for ways to make sense of their everyday lives. All the contributors to this volume have attempted to unravel the potentially uneasy relationship between globalization, ethical commitment, and behavior. How can we conceive of an ethic that promotes hope, inclusion, and action, given the potentially shattering aspects of globalization? The political psychology of real or perceived violence in a global world calls for new approaches for understanding the collective experience of diversity, violence, and ethics and the shaping of subjectivity. In this concluding chapter, we ask how these new approaches can be brought together and further analyzed and understood.

Consider the relationship between globalization and ethics. Nesbitt-Larking argues that we should interpret the insecurities of globalization in terms of doubt and accept the partiality of knowledge. Is this possible? Can people deal with such ambiguity and complexity in their responses to global change, or is this wishful thinking on the part of scholars? Fernandez argues for a public culture devoid of ethnic and religious traits and—in this sense—neutral and liberal, while Scuzzarello discusses the need for an ethics of care where difference is seen as neither threatening nor abnormal but rather as a normal condition of being. How can these pictures be reconciled? Can we be liberal, neutral, and caring at the same time?

Meyer advocates a stronger public promotion of courageous interventions since such acts can create a responsible and truly democratic social environment. One way of achieving this, according to Jonas, is to promote moral courage training programs. How are such interventions and programs to be encouraged and designed, considering how intergroup conflict is often pre-defined in a world characterized by limited social and economic resources? This discussion brings to light the complexity of social identity. Alford argues that it was a sense of common humanity that grounded his informants' reasoning about morality rather than any abstract notions of universal morality. Monroe and Martinez find that classroom-based intervention in a university setting can provide empathetic involvement. Both of these chapters are concerned with a broader understanding of ethics and morality in order to explicate a fuller comprehension of the context in which different narratives of moral behavior are created and intersect. Their findings—that empathetic involvement with "another" does have an impact on one's treatment of others—nonetheless leave several critical questions unanswered. Is it proper for professors to encourage behavior, even behavior that is commonly judged moral, such as fostering tolerance? What is the proper role of educational institutions in terms of moral education? Who decides that fostering greater tolerance for difference is a good thing, when another person, group, or society might argue that certain differences should be condemned and eradicated? To act on the basis of a common humanity is not, in other words, as straightforward as it may seem at first but may well be contextually dependent.

Such contextualization is noted by Hamer-Gutowska and Gutowski, who find that people generally tend to identify more strongly with those who are close to them, but that this may coexist with broader identifications in an increasingly globalized world. This involvement of social identity is further explicated in Pessi's discussion of the role of the Lutheran church in promoting altruistic behavior in Finland. Pessi presents an important challenge to the sometimes unquestioned individualistic orientation, and the political and moral secularism that permeate many discussions on how to teach and foster pro-social, altruistic behavior. Pessi's focus is on moral courage, pro-social behavior, and altruism in some form. The underlying question is: how important is such behavior in politics, especially in the newly-emerging global world? Is it harder to foster such behavior in a world where one's neighbors are farther away, faceless and remote? What role should this kind of moral courage and altruism play in our models and theories of political life? These are not idle questions. Instead they touch on yet another issue that lies at the foundation of normative political thought, psychology and social psychology: How is our behavior influenced by others and how does our treatment of them, in turn, feed back into who we are?

Violence and the creation and re-creation of subjectivity tend to be mutually interconnected and inform political action and reaction. This relationship lies at the heart of the chapters in the third part of this volume, as they grapple with the socio-psychological uneasiness of protracted identity-based conflicts. Rosler et al. are concerned with how occupying societies come to terms with the fact that they violate universal basic moral principles. If we are seriously interested in terminating prolonged occupations, we need to understand and erode the socio-psychological mechanisms that have developed within the institutional structure of the occupying society. This point is further reiterated by Ferguson, who provides evidence of how social and political violence carry moral and socio-psychological meanings. Similarly, Lowe, Muldoon and Schmid demonstrate how disregarding the complexity of social identity and the existence of unexpected patterns of identification run the risk of reinforcing negative intergroup relations.

ACKNOWLEDGING RELATEDNESS

These final chapters explicate the risks associated with closure and antagonism. As people think about their lives in a changing world, they need narratives that describe the foundations of their group's collective identity. This search leads to the establishment and reification of cognitive, semantic, and material boundaries that are likely to solidify closures between groups. This is regardless of whether the boundaries between groups are determined by gender, age, nationality, religion, culture, or ethnicity. In order to preserve the security of one's social space, the otherness of the other is reified, and inward-looking monologues are carried out among those who are considered part of the group. Such closure prevents social processes that could foster social courage (Meyer; Jonas), care (Scuzzarello; Alford), and altruistic behavior (Monroe and Martinez; Pessi). We argue here for the need for moving away from such an antagonistic way of relating to other groups or individuals. In developing this argument, we stress the analytical and political importance of drawing on a relational ontology.

An ethics that draws on relational ontology understands the political actor as constructed through connections, and life as dependent on these connections and "based on a bond of attachment rather than a contract of agreement" (Robinson, 1999, 39). This means that the self and its relationship to others are understood in relational terms. The self is not a self-contained, rational, and disembodied entity that enters into social interactions with other people. Rather, self and identity acquire meaning through constant interactions with others and contexts. Such a relational understanding must take agency and choice seriously. What makes one choose to act on behalf of others? What can be done to foster the kind of behavior called for in this volume?

If we accept the hypothesis that the human attempts to find meaning in our lives is an ever-changing process, a process that takes place in relationship with others, then our social-psychological questions in theoretical and empirical research will be posed differently than those asked in non-relational approaches. These questions should not conceive of individuals and groups as separate entities. Instead, our discussions should involve varieties of self–other relations, which cannot be anything but communicative. Thus, when investigating minorities, for example, one should view them as mutually interdependent with majorities. The interdependence of self and other thus constitutes a point of departure in social inquiry.

RELATIONAL ONTOLOGY AND SOCIAL IDENTITY THEORIES

Fostering courage, care, altruism, and tolerance in homes, universities, and the public sphere more generally becomes a way to insert a relational component into interpersonal cognition. A focus on the relational character of meaning-production also illustrates the complexity of social identity and how violence is as much a psychological as a structural condition—as explicated in the chapters by Rosler et al., Ferguson, and Lowe, Muldoon and Schmid. This raises the question of what this approach can add to existing theories of social identity. It does seem, at least at a first glance, that social identity theory (SIT) and its derivative, self-categorization theory (SCT), would be particularly useful devices for understanding the construction of self and others in a global context. Both social identity theory and self categorization theory have made some important observations concerning the tendency among individuals to positively regard themselves and their group in relation to other groups. Of importance also is the way these theories are able to account for the psychological processes by which the self is redefined in terms of group norms and the associated stereotypes of particular social categories (Monroe et al., 1999). Their strength can further be found in the attempts made to explain the behavior of large-scale collectives rather than just the small groups of laboratory research (Reicher and Hopkins, 2001). There are, however, a number of reasons why a relational approach to self and others may prove more useful for understanding how ethics and morality interact in a global world.

One has to do with the limited treatment of ideology, culture, and discourse by social identity and self-categorization theory, a treatment that makes it difficult to fully understand why some individuals of the group are prepared to make sacrifices for the group while others stay marginally involved in group activities. "Self-categorization theory," as argued by Reicher and Hopkins (2001, 39), "tends to treat context as if it were a given and categories as if they are largely read off from this context." Another reason can be found in these theories' often essentialist treatment of identity as something more ascribed than acquired. As noted by Huddy (2001), the minimal intergroup situation does not allow for identity choice and thus remains a deeply deterministic view of identity development. To this could be added the difference between belonging to a group and internalizing its meaning. This refers to the distinction between belonging to a common category by sharing certain characteristics obvious to the outsider, and group membership that is meaningful for the actual definition of oneself and one's identity (Jenkins, 1996, 23; c.f. Huddy, 2001). With its strong focus on categorization as a constant cognitive aim, self-categorization theory may find it difficult to explain subjective interpretations of what different group memberships mean for the individual. This, in turn, is likely to have an impact on its explanatory power for understanding how previously harmless others may suddenly become reconstructed into the stranger-enemy.

One significant difference between social identity theory and theories focused on relational ontology is the assertion in social identity theory that group membership creates self-categorization in ways that favor the ingroup at the expense of the outgroup; in contrast, relationality opens up for a different understanding of meaning and category productions than straightforward ingroup preference. As Lowe, Muldoon and Schmid argue in their chapter, there is a need to understand cross-categorization if we are to avoid negative intergroup evaluations. To adopt a relational ontology means that we depart from an understanding of in- and outgroup categories as rigid entities, but rather grasp their formation in terms of processes, where meaning changes in relationship to the context in which these categories are deployed.

This brings us closer to certain psychoanalytical accounts of intergroup conflict and antagonistic behavior. Psychoanalytical accounts of identity and identity conflict, such as Bion's (1961), Craib's (1989, 1994), Kristeva's (1983, 1991), and Volkan's (1988, 1997) put an emphasis on understanding present actions in the light of both the past and the future, at the same time that they provide explicit accounts of the emotional aspects of these processes. In their focus on the inner dimension of identity construction, they are predominantly concerned with the acquisition of identity in the process of socialization, rather than with roles and status positions, as has been the case with many sociological theories of symbolic interactionism. What psychoanalysis is able to do is to emphasize the inner life of human beings by seeing individuals as linked, not only structurally, but also through an emotional inter-subjectivity in which individuals continually receive and give emotional messages that often exist at an unconscious level (Kinnvall, 2004). This implies that emotions cannot be reduced to current social relations in society, as that would neglect the deeply rooted need for safety and stability in one's life circumstances, strongly emphasized by object relation theorists (e.g.,Winnicott, 1965, 1975).

Such emotions, however, are never purely biological. People are motivated to construct narratives centered on themes that help them deal with fundamental life issues while sharing these narratives with others (McAdams, 2006, Salvatore et al., 2004). Narratives are created through dialogue and relations and supply frameworks in which people are differently positioned. Here we find Peter Raggat's discussion of positioning useful. "Positioning" can be "understood as the discursive construction of personal stories that make a person's actions intelligible . . . as social acts, and within which the members of a conversation have specific locations" (Harré and van Langenhove, 1991, 395; quoted in Raggat, 2007, 359). Positioning, according to Harré and van Langenhove, takes place within a moral order, as people are positioned in various ways; dominant or submissive, dependent or independent, masculine or feminine, and so on. Such dichotomies reflect current power relationships and have consequences for how ethics and morality are conceived. Raggat (2007) finds Harré's and Langenhove's definition of positioning problematic, as it prioritizes the discursive aspects of positioning at the cost of the personal. Instead, he suggests a classification of forms of positioning based on three distinctions: (1) indicating *medium* or *mode of expression* of positioning (narrative/discursive, performative/expressive, and embodied), (2) *personal positioning* identifying conflict within a person, and (3) *social positioning involving social and cultural constructions* (conversational/discursive, institutional roles/rituals, political/hierarchical). The advantage of Raggat's classification is that it acknowledges both self and culture: it examines both personal and social constructions of self, and it forces us to think of self and identity in terms of both change and continuity. In this sense, it recognizes that the self is embodied and biological as well as social and cultural and demands that we examine the phenomenon at this depth to make sense of it.

NEW ENCOUNTERS AND THE INNOVATION OF THE SELF: TOWARDS A TRANSFORMATIVE ETHICS

The late-modern era brings with it an empowering and transformative potential. Indeed, globalization "incorporates aspects of accommodation and resistance in a range of domains" (Nesbitt-Larking, this volume). The oppressed have the possibility of organizing themselves against different kinds of oppressions. The multitude of encounters provides several opportunities for challenging one's mores and traditions, and for questioning those taken-for-granted narratives about a society, its members and their "proper" behavior. A direct consequence of our ethical approach is that it opens up a pathway for a potential innovation of the self. This does not mean that the self is constantly deranged; individuals need to seek a sense of continuity of their identity. Indeed, Hermans and Dimaggio (2007) contend that people, because of biological and social reasons, are apparently in need of an environment stable enough to feel at home and to experience a feeling of security and safety in a rapidly changing world. Increasing interconnections between cultural groups put pressure on the self to integrate an increasing number of voices. As a result, negative feelings of uncertainty caused by growing complexity, ambiguity, deficient knowledge, and unpredictability are released and evoke defensive strategies. On the global-local interface, Hermans and Dimaggio (2007, 43) see two risks. One is the domination by only one voice, leading to phenomena such as nationalism, fundamentalism, sexism, or terrorism. Another is the potential risk of identity confusion, lack of a meaningful direction in life, or rootlessness.

To avoid both scenarios, we need to distinguish between being *with* the other and being *for* the other; i.e., taking responsibility for him or her (Levinas, 1981). A relational ontology emphasizes the need to understand that we are not autonomous, independent individuals (as often presumed in liberal accounts), but are rather ontologically related to one another. Such a conceptualization carries important consequences for how we understand relations with those whom we identify as others, be they migrants (Nesbitt-Larking; Fernandez; Scuzzarello), strangers (Meyer; Jonas; Alford; Monroe and Martinez), or enemies (Hamer-Gutowska and Gutowski; Rosler et al; Ferguson; Lowe, Muldoon and Schmid). Accepting doubt and impartial knowledge, as Nesbitt-Larking suggests, means recognizing the liberating effects of uncertainty, thus bidding farewell to the dogmas and ideologies of institutions that restrict and confine the self and lead to inward-looking closure. But how is this to be achieved in real life? We argue that the concept of "transformative dialogue" as developed by Gergen et al. (2001) can be particularly useful in responding to this question.

The aim of "transformative dialogue" (Gergen et al., 2001) is to develop dialogues with members of allegedly antagonistic groups, such as between pro-life activists with supporters of abortion rights, or between members of the majority society with members of certain minority communities. This will enable people to problematize blame, hate, and stereotypes of the other. This does not mean that we should try to imagine ourselves in the position of the other. We agree with Young (1997, 38—57) that this is likely to obscure differences in power positions. Furthermore, attempting to put oneself in the situation of others often involves projections and fantasies about the other that are likely to counter a process of dialogue and empathy. As Scuzzarello (2008) has noted in the case of Sweden, for example, the wish to help immigrants integrate into the Swedish society is related to conceptions of what is held to be morally right and normal to do. Hence, despite good intentions, the normative boundaries of the majority are reproduced and strengthened in relation to representations of the other as socially less efficient. The immigrant thus needs to undergo a process of socialization in order to learn "the way we do things" in Sweden. Hence, instead of trying to imagine ourselves in the position of the other, we should retain an understanding of reciprocity that is asymmetrical; that is, one that recognizes power disparity, where each individual or group's unique life history and psychological constitution are taken into account.

While we find the ideas about "transformative dialogue" appealing, we find troublesome the assumption that everyone is able to access the arenas where dialogue takes place. Women, the disabled, national and migrant minorities (among others) have all at different times and in different ways been excluded from active political participation, mostly because of the fact that they have been depicted as less able (or less interested) to act as citizens. Feminist theory (e.g., Flax, 1990; Harding, 1991; Sevenhuijsen, 1998) alerts us to the fact that an analysis of the self must conceptualize historical, social, and material conditions as fundamental aspects of identities.

Hence, the approach to ethics and morality that we call for must address both the psychological underpinnings of closure and antagonistic relations as well as their structural causes. It also means that we need to recognize the political need to empower people in the actual conditions of their lives. Historically vulnerable group members must acquire the tools, knowledge, and resources needed to exercise greater leverage within the group as well as within the greater community. Only if equal access to resources and power is provided to the group members can they be expected to become less preoccupied with the search for security through closure and antagonism. Empowerment can here be employed to account for how marginalized group members must gain access to the resources and capacities needed to initiate change from within their communities (see Shakhar, 2001). In real terms it means recognizing the lived experiences of many community members.

But it also means finding ways in which we can become increasingly open to an ambiguous "other" and to an uncertain future. Hermans and Dimaggio (2007) envision two ways this could happen. The first refers to communication with real others; the second focuses on the contact and ability to relate to an imaginary other. In the first case, Hermans and Dimaggio show how experimental studies of adapting somebody else's narrative confirm that different positions produce different narratives. Hence, engagement with other people's narratives supplies a means for overcoming the fears and uncertainties of the late-modern West and provides the foundation for a critical and deep multiculturalism, as discussed in the chapter by Nesbitt-Larking. As shown by Rosler et al. in the case of Israel, however, this is as much an internal as an external process. Instead of narratives being formed through confrontation with real others, people's fears are often dominated by rumors, media images, and meta-narratives that divide worlds into neat categorizations (often in terms of civilizations). How can these images and narratives be countered through the use of an imaginary other?

Hermans and Dimaggio (2007) argue that experimental research in which participants communicate on the basis of a variety of instructed positions may be relevant for self-innovation. In the context of globalization, people who are in contact with an increasing diversity of significant others, groups, communities, or cultures may become positioned in direct or indirect ways. Experiments could be run with participants instructed to believe that they communicate with people from groups of diverse cultural origins. Such experiments could determine under which conditions participants—positioned as members of a particular cultural group—would learn from interlocutors positioned as members of another cultural group. An especially relevant question would be whether participants are able or willing to modify their selves, taking the otherness of the interlocutor into account.

Such experiments have a number of overlapping points with experiments made in the field of deliberative democracy and can also be related to work done on reconciliation in protracted conflicts. There are several problems with this approach, however. This method may be relevant for clinical work, but one should be aware that most of the positions that a person will identify with are suggested by the researchers, not the informants (Raggat, 2007). Furthermore, Hermans and Dimaggio's approach has significant problems in addressing real structural inequalities. Being able to envision yourself using alternative narratives, real or imagined, is only a temporary solution to structural discrimination. At the end of the day people will return to their actual material reality and structural inclusion or exclusion. If their lives run parallel to that of the majority of society, it matters little how much they understand others' life worlds since their life chances are still inhibited compared to those who share the majority narrative.

Some of the practices suggested in this volume may be more fruitful for addressing these problems. Meyer, for instance, argues that if a society truly wants to promote social courage, it has to appreciate and publicly support courageous intervention in favor of others. It has to create an atmosphere fostering "top-down" and "bottom-up" social courage at home, in school, and at the workplace, as well as in public administration and in national and international politics. Jonas's moral courage training programs can take us one step closer towards such courageous interventions. In line with Meyer's argument, Alford calls for a stronger, albeit critical, attentiveness to the "moral intuitions of most people." Finally, Monroe and Martinez have worked on an academic program that questions prejudice and fosters toler-ance among university students. These are all examples of practices of a transformative ethics that takes seriously the concept of identity as a contin-uous process of becoming and puts the relationships between individuals and groups at the center of the analysis.

CONCLUSION

Alleviating negative images of "the other" means changing the moral order in which these images are formed. To do this, we need to address the construction of this moral order at all three levels of analysis suggested by Raggatt (2007): mode of expression, personal positioning, and social posi-tioning. At the first level it involves changing the narratives that shape our performance as social and embodied actors. As Staub and Bar-Tal (2003) have argued, instead of promoting scapegoating and divisive ideologies, leaders can generate a vision of and plans for the future that include all groups, in shared efforts to improve life. Changing narratives affect personal positioning. We embody these value positions in myriad forms, according to our personal histories, the social context, and our repertoire of personal constructs. As Taylor (1989, 28, in Raggat, 2007, 364) observes: "To know who you are is to be oriented in moral space, a space in which questions arise about what is good or bad, what is worth doing and what not, what has meaning and importance for you, and what is trivial and secondary." Reorienting moral space in the direction of dialogue and inclusion is thus a fundamental task for practitioners involved in changing hostile attitudes and images between individuals and groups.

But we also need to address structural positioning. Initiating structural change, such as changes in the economic situation of a particular group, is crucial for creating narrative change in moral conceptions of self and others. As the chapters by Ferguson and Lowe, Muldoon and Schmid show in the case of Northern Ireland, greater economic opportunities and the greater material well-being of the Catholic minority have contributed to the possibilities of peace. Improving the life of less-privileged groups in society, as well as reducing inequalities, is thus a critical aspect of reducing conflict. Changes in structural positioning, however, must occur at all three dimensions outlined by Raggat: (1) the conversational/discursive form, which involves the micro-encounters of daily life, whether at work, in the home, or in the street; (2) the positioning in terms of institutional roles involving prevailing stereotypes, such as gender roles, parental roles, age roles, class behavior, etc.; and (3) the positioning arising from the effects of power in various social and political hierarchies. Political programs need to be designed that address all these dimensions. Here education is crucial. Writing about intractable conflicts, Staub and Bar-Tal (2003) point to the important role of peace education in schools; but they also argue that education can involve fostering among adults an understanding of the roots of violence. Such fostering aims to affect knowledge, perceptions, feelings, attitudes, and motives and must involve both instruction and experiential learning. It requires participation of all involved (perpetrator, victim, and bystanders) in order to promote positive attitudes toward people in general and towards other groups in society (migrants, strangers, enemies). It also includes promoting feelings of responsibility for taking action on behalf of others; i.e., caring for people beyond one's own group, including formerly devalued groups. As Staub and Bar-Tal (2003, 731) have argued, without addressing structural change, psychological change may not be possible to bring about or maintain.

The aim of this volume has been to illustrate the many different ways in which constructions of self and identity are challenged in an increasingly global world. In doing this, we have discussed a number of possible solutions to uncertainty, identity confusion, and the creation of stereotypes, prejudices, and "othering." In arguing in favor of a relational and transformative approach to ethics, we hope to provide critically necessary analytical tools to advance knowledge and further our understanding of group closure and conflict. But we also believe that the approach we have presented here can be an important instrument if we are to seriously grasp the promotion of social courage, pro-social behavior, tolerance, care, and altruism in a global world. Ultimately, such an analytical tool constitutes both a challenge and a contribution to much normative democratic theory and social and political psychology.

REFERENCES

Bion, W. R., 1961. *Experience in groups*. London: Tavistock.

Craib, I., 1989. *Psychoanalysis and social theory: The limits of sociology*. London: Routledge.

Craib, I., 1994. *The importance of disappointment*. London: Routledge.

Flax, J., 1990. *Thinking Fragments: Psychoanalysis, Feminism and Postmodernism in the Contemporary West*. Berkeley and Los Angeles: University of California Press.

Gergen, K, McNamee, S., and Barrett, F., 2001. Toward a vocabulary of transformative dialogue. *International Journal of Public Administration* 24:697–707.

Harding, S., 1991. *Whose science? Whose knowledge? Thinking from women's lives*. Ithaca, N.Y.: Cornell University Press.

Hermans , H., and Dimaggio, G., 2007. Self, identity, and globalization in times of uncertainty: A dialogical analysis. *Review of General Psychology* 11(1): 31–61.

Huddy, L., 2001. From social to political identity: A critical examination of social identity theory. *Political Psychology* 22:127–156.

Jenkins, R., 1996. *Social identity*. London: Routledge.

Kinnvall, C., 2004. Globalization and religious nationalism: Self, identity and the search for ontological security. *Political Psychology* 25(4), October 2004.

Kristeva, J., 1983. *Powers of horror: An essay of abjection*. New York: Columbia University Press.

Kristeva, J., 1991. *Strangers in ourselves*. New York: Columbia University Press.

Levinas, E., 1981. *Otherwise than being, or beyond essence*. The Hague: Martinus Nijhoff.

McAdams, D. P., 2006. The problem of narrative coherence. *Journal of Constructivist Psychology* 19:109–126.

Monroe, K., Hankins, J., and Van Vechten, R., 1999. The psychological foundations of identity politics: A review of the literature. *Annual Review of Political Science* 3:419–447.

Raggatt, P., 2007. Forms of positioning in the dialogical self. A system of classification and the strange case of Dame Edna Everage. *Theory and Psychology* 17(3): 355–382.

Reicher, S., and Hopkins, N., 2001. *Self and nation*. London: Sage.

Robinson, F., 1999. *Globalizing care. Ethics, feminist theory and international relations*. Oxford: Westview Press.

Salvatore, G., Dimaggio, G., and Semerari, A., 2004. A model of narrative development: Implications for understanding psychopathology and guiding therapy. *Psychology and Psychotherapy* 77:231–254.

Scuzzarello, S., 2008. National security versus moral responsibility: an analysis of integration programs in Malmö, Sweden. *Social Politics. International Studies in Gender, State & Society*, 15(1): 1–15.

Sevenhuijsen, S., 1998. *Citizenship and the ethics of care. Feminist considerations on justice, morality and politics*. London and New York: Routledge.

Shachar, A., 2001. *Multicultural jurisdictions. Cultural differences and women's rights*. Cambridge, England: Cambridge University Press.

Staub, E., and Bar-Tal, D., 2003. Genocide, mass killing and intractable conflict: Roots, evolution, prevention, and reconciliation. In Sears, D., Huddy, L., and Jervis, R. (eds.), *Oxford Handbook of Political Psychology*. Oxford, England: Oxford University Press.

Volkan, V., 1988. *The need to have enemies and allies: From clinical practice to international relationships*. Northvale, N.J.: Aronson.

Volkan, V., 1997. *Bloodlines: From ethnic pride to ethnic terrorism*. Boulder (Colorado): Westview Press.

Winnicott, D.W., 1965. *The Maturational process and the facilitating environment*. New York, International Universities Press.

Winnicott, D.W., 1975. *Through pediatrics to psychoanalysis*. New York: Basic Books.

Young, I., 1997. *Intersecting voices. Dilemmas of gender, political philosophy and policy*. Princeton: Princeton University Press.

Index

Note: In this index, tables are indicated by "t", figures by "f" and notes by "n".